ANALYSIS OF
URBAN HEALTH PROBLEMS

Health Systems Management
Edited by Samuel Levey, Ph.D. and Alan Sheldon, M.D.

ANALYSIS OF URBAN HEALTH PROBLEMS

Irving Leveson
Hudson Institute
Croton-on-Hudson, N.Y.

and

Jeffrey H. Weiss
Downstate Medical Center, SUNY
Brooklyn, N.Y.

S P Books Division of
SPECTRUM PUBLICATIONS, INC.
New York

Distributed by Halsted Press
A Division of John Wiley & Sons

New York   Toronto   London   Sydney

Copyright © 1976 by Spectrum Publications, Inc.

Spectrum Publications, Inc.
86-19 Sancho Street, Holliswood, N.Y. 11423

Distributed solely by the Halsted Press Division of John Wiley & Sons, Inc.
New York.

Library of Congress Cataloging in Publication Data

New York (City). Health Services Administration.
    Analysis of urban health problems.

    (Health systems management ; v. 6)
    Includes index.
    1. Public health administration--New York (City)--
Case studies. 2. Health services administration--New
York (City)--Case studies. 3. New York (City). Health
Services Administration. I. Leveson, Irving.
II. Weiss, Jeffrey H. III. Title. [DNLM: 1. Commu-
nity health services--New York City--Case studies.
2. Public Health Administration--New York--Case studies
3. Urban population--New York City--Case studies. W1
HE588f v. 6 / WA546 AN7 L6a]

RA448.N5N43   1975   362.1'09747   75-43979
ISBN 0-470-14983-3

FOREWORD

In the last two decades, there has been an accelerated rise in the application of analytic skills to problems of public policy. At the same time, with the rapid growth of resources used for the delivery of health services and an increasing public role, the health field has become an important subject for analysis. At first, attention was focused largely at the Federal level. The Department of Health, Education and Welfare prepared an extensive set of progam analyses in the mid-1960's as part of its efforts to introduce analysis into the budgeting process. Substantial policy-oriented efforts have been maintained in the Social Security Administration and in the Office of the Secretary of HEW.

In the last decade, we have witnessed the development of one new health program after another—Medicare and Medicaid, neighborhood health centers, drug abuse and alcoholism, prison health, paramedical training and many more. As the Federal Government has moved to define the basic parameters of financing and cost control, it has been looking increasingly to the states and cities to develop effective means of guiding and developing institutions and programs. Trends in health care, social changes, and Federal initiatives have worked together to produce a great broadening of activities and responsibilities of state and local health agencies. Great changes have taken place in the numbers, sizes, and roles of planning, regulatory, and training institutions.

Confronted with a wide range of new and complex problems, state and local agencies have made important beginnings toward the development of analytic capabilities consistent with their responsibilities. A particularly large and important effort occurred in the nation's largest city with the consolidation of diverse responsibilities into an overall Health Services Administration. An analytic unit with more than two dozen professionals worked directly with the agency head for almost four years.

The experience of the New York City Health Services Administration's Office of Program Analysis, Planning and Budgeting provides interesting lessons about the climate in which decision-making occurs. From it we can obtain important insights into the way decisions are made as to which studies to conduct and the factors which determine which studies will be used, whether they will have an impact, and where, how, and what kinds of changes they will produce. Leveson and Weiss give us a careful look at the background factors which bear on these questions. Twenty-five staff papers are presented and discussed. The authors provide a rare look into the way in which analysis relates to the processes of decision and implementation. While the pure researcher may react negatively to the lack of precision in some of these studies or the method by which areas were selected to be studied, as one who has worked in an environment similar to that of the Health Services Administration, I can only marvel at how well these studies were done.

The book should be of interest to officials of state and local health departments, Comprehensive Health Planning Agencies, Hospital Review and Planning Councils, City Planning Departments, Budget Bureaus, City Administrator's and to practitioners in program design, development, and administration. It provides an interesting source of material for courses in Public Policy, Public Administration, Public Health, Hospital Administration, and Health Planning and applied courses in the Social Sciences.

STUART ALTMAN
Deputy Assistant Secretary
U.S. Department of Health,
Education and Welfare

Acknowledgments

A book of this kind represents the efforts of many individuals whose untiring and dedicated service to the public continues with or without recognition. We are indebted to the authors of the selections presented here without whom this volume would not have been possible. We would also like to express our appreciation to the many unnamed analysts and administrators who contributed to the thinking and made contributions in numerous ways, helping forge a climate in which thoughtful work could take place.

We would like to express a special thanks to Gordon Chase, Robert Harris, Arnold Meltzner, and James Posner for their comments and suggestions. With their help, some of our recollections and interpretations were significantly improved. We would also like to express our appreciation for the comments of Anita Altman, Charles Atkins, and Robert Grosse.

Sam Levey provided encouragement and advice in his role as general editor, and we are grateful for his and Alan Sheldon's efforts and interest. Maurice Ancharoff, President of Spectrum Publications, was inspiring in his understanding and sympathy with our goals and was a pleasure to work with. We are grateful for the conscientious editorial assistance of Nancy Inglis and Rochelle Roth and for the typing of Barbara Leveson and Gloria Brown. We, of course, accept responsibilities for any errors which remain.

IRVING LEVESON
JEFFREY H. WEISS

CONTENTS

I

Introduction

ORIGINS

The material for this book is drawn from some of the many studies, reports, policy statements, and memoranda developed by the analysis staff of the Health Services Administration of the City of New York (HSA) during the period from May 1970 to January 1974.

The initial impetus for undertaking the task of editing these materials grew out of our belief that a substantial portion of the work produced by the analysis staff of HSA would be of interest to a broad and varied group of scholars, practitioners, and students concerned with health services, urban problems, and policy analysis per se. [1]

While the studies themselves were of substantive or methodological interest in many instances, their primary usefulness appeared to lie in the fact that they represented a rather unique effort to commit sizable resources to analyze a large city's problems in a particular policy area (i.e., health services). Efforts to understand the role, usefulness, and limitations of policy analysis are a recent development, and very few cities, counties, or states can afford or wish to make a commitment to policy analysis in a single field on a scale approaching the effort in New York City during Mayor John Lindsay's second term. [2] At the same time there has been rapid growth in federal initiatives to develop local capabilities in health planning and analysis.

The experience of HSA's analysis staff provides an opportunity for those interested in policy analysis, urban problems, and health services to gain a deeper understanding of such matters as why particular topics are selected for analysis, the conditions and considerations which determine meth-

odology, and the factors which influence the likelihood of
analyses having an impact. So that these issues may be understood in proper context we have attempted to outline the political, bureaucratic, institutional, personality, and substantive
factors of the climate in which the analyses took place. The
resulting discussion provides a rare look inside a government
agency concerned with developing and carrying out policy.

ANALYSIS AND ITS USES

The Nature of Analysis

     The role of analysis will be made clear in succeeding dis-
cussions in the course of considering in some detail the background of the subjects which were examined and the climate
in which the analyses were done. Before doing that, however,
it is useful to consider some of the general characteristics
of analysis which apply to a great range of situations and are
reflected in the specific situations described. The nature of
the analytic function derives at first from its goals but ultimately depends on the host of forces that determine the ability
to effect change.
     Analysis is part of a process for making choices. As
such, it depends upon the objectives of the policy-makers, and
analysis can be conducted more effectively when those objectives have been stated explicitly at the outset. The most critical phase of analysis is the problem-definition stage. The view
of the problem strongly influences the response, and it is often
necessary to redefine a problem until a definition which is
amenable to a solution is reached.[3] Defining a problem as
poor health may lead to a preventive solution that would not be
considered if the problem were defined as poor medical treatment. Concern with the development of poor children could
lead to proposals for income maintenance or food stamps, but
it could also lead to nutrition counseling or to vitamin supple-
mentation of staple foods rather than medical care. Through
redefinition the analysis can be targeted to the opportunities
to effect change in a particular time and place and not only to
a broader societal approach.
     Too restrictive a definition can of course lead to inappro-
priate responses when the special objectives and opportunities
of individual organizations are controlling. The alternative of
unrestricted choice of problem definition has its dangers too--
that it will lead to commitments of resources where there are
no effective solutions or commitments to solutions which cannot
be implemented. The discussion of the Kennedy Plan by Weiss
and Brodsky (see Chapter V) illustrates the conflict of multiple objectives in such a case.

If the problem is viewed as one of poor health, a range of solutions may be considered which include reducing poverty, improving the environment, sanitation, increasing education, or changing life styles. Defining the problem as inadequate medical care generally leads to efforts to change the quantity, quality, and availability of medical services. Such a strategy for dealing with unusually poor health conditions is often adopted whether or not the conditions are rooted in adverse social and environmental conditions or unequal medical care. The evolution of long-term care programs reflects this tendency (see Chapter VI). Such a response is generally a consequence of the policy tools one has available in a climate where little is known about how to effectively change social conditions so as to improve health. In fact, interest in lead-paint poisoning grew out of efforts to gain support for improved housing before the medical aspects began to be more exclusively emphasized.

It is often of great value to define a problem in quantitative terms. This provides a basis for estimating the size of the program or policy changes required to deal with it and yields measures with which to monitor the success of the actions against current conditions or expectations. Decision rules can be developed which use measures of problem magnitudes in highly specific ways. For example, if inadequate prenatal care is thought to contribute to infant mortality, a program objective of assuring that all expectant mothers see a doctor during the first three months of pregnancy can be adopted. The ability to get this specific depends on the program being considered, but it is often possible to go quite far in the development of quantitative decision rules.

When the problem-definition phase is complete, the objectives should have been stated in sufficient detail to permit careful examination of alternative methods of achieving them. This stage requires the introduction of a wide range of considerations--availability of funds, organizational capability, community acceptance, etc., in order to consider the feasibility of carrying out decisions as well as abstract advantages and disadvantages. This is reflected in a great many of the selections in this book.

In deciding among alternative courses of action it is most important to have knowledge of the effectiveness of programs and policies in producing end results such as improved health. But there are few areas where effectiveness is documented, and it often becomes necessary to rely on rules of thumb. The often debated guidelines or standards for physician/population or bed-to-population ratios can be viewed as statements of consensus by some experts or program proponents as to resource levels in lieu of information on effectiveness of services. In cost-benefit analysis of public health programs at HSA the required knowledge of effectiveness was often missing, but it was possible to do a great deal analytically where prevailing opinion could be accepted. Input/population ratios were more valid where the distribution of resources among communities was the focus of the analysis.

Case studies and partial analysis are often essential first steps in determining which factors are important for policy or amenable to further analysis. The system monitoring and description efforts in Chapter II and the productivity study in Chapter IV reflect this situation. When more complete information is available, it is often convenient to summarize payoffs in a cost-effectiveness calculation. This approach can be useful even with very incomplete data in examining the way payoffs to different programs change as assumptions vary. This is exemplified in the cost-benefit analysis of New York City's heroin programs in Chapter III.

When the target of the policies is a large sector such as the New York City municipal hospital system, consideration of the likely impact of alternatives often goes beyond assuming that actions will have a direct impact, as is the case with administrative change. Instead, it requires knowledge of the effects of those actions on the incentives which are provided and knowledge of the probable responses to changing incentives of affected persons and institutions.

When we move from consideration of a single problem or program to the examination of broad systems, there are a number of significant changes in the way in which analysis is carried out. In addition to direct effects of program and policy changes, there are often important interactions between programs that have to be taken into account. Building a hospital may change where doctors locate. A preadmission screening program may reduce admissions and length of stay and change the number of personnel to be trained. The diagrammatic structure of a system is a shell which becomes useful when the impact of possible changes can be examined through a scientific core. The value of a policy analysis is not only in providing a descriptive model of the system components but also in specifying a core set of interrelationships through which these effects can be traced and measured. Here analysis which examines cause and effect relationships plays a central role. This is reflected in analyses of the social experiment for national health insurance and the analysis of hospital utilization research in Chapter IV.

Analysis and Decision-Making

The analytic process is highly interpretive, operating as a means of structuring and evaluating information prior to its

change or by persons who wish to avoid making decisions. The exchange between HSA and HHC analysis staffs following the release of the physician staffing study (Chapter II) was encouraged by HHC management to avoid politically difficult actions.

The experienced analyst can take advantage of the repetitious nature of the administrative processes and routines to gain substantial lead time in dealing with issues. Often the timing of future demand for analytic studies and recommendations can be clearly anticipated, related to key points in an annual budget cycle or logical steps in the development of programs and policies. The ability to go beyond the short-term pressures and mount an effective program of in-depth analysis depends critically on skills in anticipating future decision points and structuring a long-term program to deal with them. For example, in the case of the alcoholism study (Chapter VI), the analysis was planned with the intent of influencing decisions at the appropriate point in New York City's budget cycle, the employee health benefits work (Chapter V) was timed to contract negotiations, and the home care paper (Chapter VI) was targeted to express the interests of an incoming administration in problems of the aged.

The ability to mount a program of in-depth analysis and to anticipate future decision points depends in part on the agency having a large enough analytic staff so that short-term pressures can be met effectively, since short-term demands will always have first claim on analysts' time. If the analytic effort is fed into the administrative processes of the agency, then others will find themselves responding to the recommendations of the analysts. Discussions will increasingly take place within the frameworks established by the analyses and relying on the information they provide. This is what happened in the case of gonorrhea control programs discussed in Chapter VI. Those who will find themselves trying to respond to the initiatives of the analysts will have less time to generate a large number of proposals which are not well thought out and which force the analysts to continuously provide short-term responses. This pattern was established in the capital planning area.[5]

As the experience in HSA illustrates, the demand for analysis will also depend upon the skills of the agency's management. A certain level of ability is required in order to make use of the products of the analytic team. However, when the management is particularly skilled, the knowledge which might be derived from analyses often will be part of the experience of senior officials. When this is the case, it is often more appropriate for analytic thinking to be part of numerous administrative processes which at the same time provide the follow-through to effect change. Under these circumstances a smaller analytic support and a larger information systems support are appropriate responses.

The use of analysis depends in part on a willingness of

a public body to tackle major problems and make decision-making visible. Ideally, good analysis is in the interest of the public at large because it can make objectives and criteria of decisions explicit and because it points out when problems are being ignored. However, analysis can also lead to social conflict, which may or may not be productive. The neighborhood family care center analysis (Chapter VI) was never released because of the climate of conflict between neighborhoods which it would have intensified when hard choices had to be made as to which neighborhoods would not get long-committed health centers.

When the climate is characterized by bureaucratic or political constraints, as was sometimes the case in HSA, the value of analysis falls sharply. Under these conditions analysts will be relegated to a secondary planning or implementation support function.

The value of analysis is greatest when there are substantial problems which have not been effectively analyzed or dealt with in the past. This has clearly been the case in much of the area of urban health services. There are few experts with the range and depth of experience to cope with the number and complexity of issues with which persons in positions of responsibility are faced. The pressures of work load and time diminish the ability of administrators to effectively utilize the experience that exists and to think through the consequences of alternative courses of action.

The Development of Analytic Abilities

The academic world has been slow to provide the inputs that the administrator in the health field needs to handle a broad range of problems. Many problems do not receive adequate attention because their importance is not understood or because they do not have sufficient theoretical interest, and research and training programs take a long time to develop even after issues are dramatized. Frequently training is too specialized and does not meet the tests of applicability to current priorities. Under these circumstances, the agency wishing to develop a strong analytic capability must invest heavily in training people with diverse backgrounds in order to create a cadre of experienced professionals for the future. After the need for persons with the new types of training is demonstrated, academic programs are more likely to follow suit. The development in the early 1970's of policy analysis programs in some schools of public health, public administration, and public policy in this country is an example of this type of response.

If the areas in which analytic efforts are expected to be

most useful are those where the state of the art is least well developed, then the large public agency must be concerned with the state of the art itself. If practitioners are not prepared with the knowledge that a body of analyses would have provided them with while they were being trained, then it is necessary to seek out or develop the knowledge base that fits the programmatic context in which the practitioners operate.[6]

The analyst first must be capable of using the analytic base which already exists. This means a high enough level of technical skills in <u>some</u> of the staff to understand the wide range of available professional literature. But when opportunities for change move in new directions, the published literature contains few and often unimaginative applications of appropriate skills to areas of policy concerns. New problems are not readily susceptible to a response in which a standard tool is applied in a reflex manner. The unfamiliarity of the terrain and the diversity of approaches which new problems often require result in a need for a sorting process to determine which models and techniques fit each situation. These may have to be borrowed or adapted from entirely different applications in order to meet the needs of a new problem. Furthermore, public policy problems that become the focus of new initiatives are often associated with a lack of relevant data for analysis. This was clearly the case with the alcoholism area (Chapter VI) and during the early stages of the addiction effort (Chapter III). Under these conditions sophisticated models and techniques may not be applicable and the greatest assets of the analyst will be his imagination, creativity, and perceptiveness.

Skills Required for Analysis

A broad-based analytic effort designed to provide systematic support for the decision-making processes of a large organization requires the development of a substantial nucleus of effort. A multidisciplinary team is necessary to deal with the number and complexity of issues which arise and to provide continuity from one phase of the work to another. The mix of skills which is useful depends on the organizational level at which analysis takes place and the kinds of change which are possible. Economics has been most useful where potential reallocations of substantial resources are being considered and when knowledge of behavioral responses of large organizations or systems to resource availability and financial incentives are required.[7] Operations research has been most useful in dealing with operating efficiency at the facility level. Urban planning backgrounds contribute to systematic exploration of a variety of issues and to analysis of physical planning questions. Public administration, business administration, sociology, political science, and law all are useful when the many details of successfully implementing or changing programs are to be addressed. Persons with all of these backgrounds were represented on HSA's analysis staff. There is generally a greater shortage of good implementors of change than of competent analysts or administrators of existing programs. Thus analysts and planners find themselves constantly under pressure not only to consider implementation factors in the analysis but to get involved in the details of implementation.[8] Knowledge of urban government and organizational and interpersonal skills take on great importance here.

THE NEW YORK SITUATION

Health Services in New York City

In order to enhance the reader's understanding of the materials contained in this book, we have sketched out some of the more relevant features of health services in New York City. The picture presented is intended to provide a feeling for the nature of the environment. It was not possible to describe all of the aspects which observers familiar with the situation will consider important.

As might be anticipated, important features of New York City's health system during the period under consideration were its size and the scope of its services and financing. There were substantially more physicians per capita available in New York City than in the country as a whole. In 1971 the New York City physician/population ratio was 294 per 100,000, as compared to 174 per 100,000 for the United States. It is estimated that about one-third of the nation's psychiatrists reside in the New York Metropolitan area. However, there are tremendous disparities in the distribution of health resources and indicators among poverty and nonpoverty health districts. Outpatient clinics and emergency rooms provided regular ambulatory health services for one-quarter of the city's population of eight million.

New York City had the most extensively utilized (and one of the most generous) Medicaid systems in the country. About one-fifth of the nation's total Medicaid expenditures during this period were generated in New York City. Since medically indigent persons were eligible for virtually unlimited nursing home services, if they were available, the city had substantially more nursing home patients than would be anticipated on the basis of the size of its population. In addition to its share of Medicaid, the state financed a major portion of a very sizable city public mental health budget ($140 million in 1974), which was used to contract for services with diverse

public and voluntary agencies. The city provided subsidies
for about 40 percent of the municipal hospital operating budget
of about $900 million in 1974.

The city also provided subsidies for a public health
department operating budget of about $90 million in 1974. The
New York City Health Department financed an unequaled variety
of public health activities, a network of twenty-three district
health centers providing a wide range of services without charge,
and programs firmly grounded in biomedical research. The
Health Department was in the forefront of national activities
to set standards for medical care and perform public health
inspections.

In addition to substantial public sources of financing,
there was strong private-sector financing based in part on
extensive and generous private health insurance available
through the efforts of private and public employers facing a
generally highly unionized labor force. These provided the
basis for an urban community which was relatively well off in
terms of any traditional measures of the supply and use of
health services by all segments of its population. This was
reflected in a tendency for the poor to use more health services
than middle-income groups.

The availability of a relatively resource-rich health
services system providing at its best superior medical treatment in a large number of first-class hospitals did not lead to
any noticeable reduction in any of the city's health status
indicators when compared to the country as a whole. The
city did, however, experience a reduction in its infant mortality
rate during this period, and it was widely believed that this
was due to the implementation in 1970 of the New York State
abortion law and also to the factors underlying the generally
declining national birth rate.

In 1970, and to a lesser extent by 1974, the health services system of New York was not generally prepared to cope
with extensive and rising rates of "social diseases" linked in
this country with conditions of urban living and poverty. In
1970 the number of estimated heroin addicts in New York City
ranged from 100,000 to 250,000. Cirrhosis of the liver was
the third leading cause of death among males ages twenty-five
to sixty-four. The known incidence of VD was rising rapidly,
and the incidence of such problems as lead-paint poisoning
was high in poverty areas. The incidence of these various
"social diseases" was thought to be comparable to other large
urban areas on a per capita basis although precise statistics
were not available.

A variety of different types of city, state, and private
health services and financing institutions helped to shape the
environment in which the New York City Health Services
Administration (HSA) functioned during this period.

The State Department of Health was the most important

CITY HEALTH AGENCIES

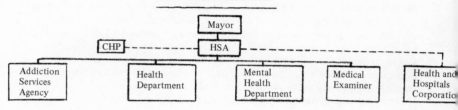

HEALTH SERVICES ADMINISTRATION

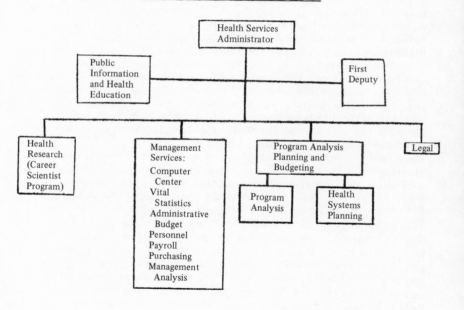

of those state institutions which had an impact on the rules
governing such matters as hospital rate setting, health facility
construction, and program financing. Although the State
Department of Social Services (i.e., Medicaid), the Narcotics
Addiction Commission, the Health and Mental Hygiene Facilities
Improvement Corporation (hospital construction) and the Housing
Finance Agency (hospital financing) all played important roles,
the state's Health Department was noteworthy because it exer-
cised two important powers which most states did not have in
the 1960's: (1) The New York State Cost Control Law gave the
commissioner of health the authority to establish hospital
reimbursement rates consistent with "the efficient production
of health services"; and (2) The State Health Department controlled approval of all new construction and major renovation
of health facilities through its longstanding certificate of need
powers.

In actual practice, the state did not vigorously enforce
its cost-control legislation until its authority was superseded
by Phase I of the National Wage-Price Control effort in August
1971. The State Health Department did not have either the
resources or the political will to actively regulate hospital
rates in line with "efficient production." The state certificate
of need powers in New York City were largely delegated to the
Health and Hospitals Planning Council of Southern New York
(HHPC), a nonprofit institution which was a creature of the
state. The board and committees of the Health and Hospital
Planning Council were dominated by the large voluntary hospitals and reflected the desires of both voluntary and municipal
hospitals to expand. By 1970 the HHPC had approved a substantial number of new hospital beds for both the private and
public sector, and the basis for a potential aggregate surplus
of hospital beds in New York City was created.[9] Six new
municipal hospitals were in various phases of construction
during this period.

Since the State Health Department did not stringently
enforce its major regulatory powers, there was little real
conflict between local and state health authorities over regularity
matters during the period 1970-74. Instead, most city-state
discussions concerned fiscal matters, with the city typically
seeking more funding or more generous Medicaid rates from
the state, and with the state typically striving to disallow for
state funding certain selected municipal health activities.

The New York City Comprehensive Health Planning Agency
(CHP) was established during the second Lindsay administration.[10] This institution devoted most of its energies during the
period to organizing local community planning bodies, and to
efforts to maintain the viability of the overall organization.
The New York City CHP, after some disputes about potential
infringements on its independence, was placed administratively

under the Health Services Administration, and the HSA administrator was made chairman of its board and executive committee.
As a practical matter, the administrative location of the CHP
was of not real consequence since its organizational structure
and other factors prevented it from engaging in effective planning or lobbying during the period under consideration.[11]   The
only real impact of CHP under HSA was through the diversion
of the HSA administrator's time in an effort to make CHP a
viable activity.

The Role of the City

With the main source of legal responsibility and authority for
overseeing the provision of health services in the state government, and the major system of health care characterized by a
network of physician's private offices, voluntary hospitals, and
medical schools, it was only natural that the New York City
government would define for itself a residual responsibility.
That responsibility had traditionally included the provision of
a wide range of public health services and public health regulatory functions, the central responsibility for emergency
medical services, and above all a commitment to assure the
provision of care for the medically indigent.

The major vehicle for the assurance of care for the
indigent was the evolution of a municipal system of sixteen
general care hospitals and three long-term-care facilities with
15,000 beds. The other major thrust had been an early commitment to funding care for the disadvantaged in voluntary hospitals.
A system of lump-sum payments had evolved under what was
known as the Charitable Institutions Budget. This approach
was superseded by the Medicaid program, which had broader
applicability and more explicit definitions of eligibility and
financial liability.

The period since HSA's creation in 1966 saw a rapid
growth of new programs to deal with the emergence and recognition of social conditions. The Health Department had just
become responsible for the review of professional standards
in the largest Medicaid program in the country. In succeeding
years under the leadership of Gordon Chase it entered into
performance contracts with voluntary hospitals as a condition
for subsidies to outpatient departments under the Ghetto Medicine program, developed a large alcoholism program, operated
a city-initiated methadone program, took over responsibility
for the prison health program, contracted for the training of
paraprofessionals, and implemented many categorical public
health programs such as hypertension and lead-poisoning
screening programs. The Comprehensive Health Planning
Agency was established within the Health Services Administra-

tion (1971) and the Addiction Services Agency was transferred to HSA from the Human Resources Administration (1972). The Health and Hospitals Corporation (HHC) was given responsibility for operating the first two of a network of seven neighborhood family care centers. The NFCC Program was a city-developed and funded program of large neighborhood health centers (up to 350,000 annual patient-visits per center), and HSA inaugurated contracts for the training of paraprofessionals to work in the centers.

HSA, HHC, and the city government also had important relationships with a number of voluntary health care institutions. The HHC relied upon large voluntary medical centers and most of the city's seven medical schools for the provision of physician services to its municipal hospitals under "affiliation agreements" amounting to $160 million in 1972. The Health Department under HSA administered a state program of subsidies for voluntary hospital outpatient departments running deficits because of services provided to the medically indigent. HSA increasingly relied upon voluntary hospitals to provide medical services on a contractual basis for many different types of health care programs (e.g., methadone maintenance, prison health services, alcoholism treatment programs). The Department of Mental Health, under HSA administratively, contracted with over a hundred voluntary agencies for the provision of mental health services. Furthermore, the city's department of personnel purchased private health insurance for the nearly one out of seven New Yorkers who were employees or dependents of employees of the city government. The city's purchase of private health insurance from the Health Insurance Plan of New York (HIP), from Group Health, Inc. (GHI), and from Blue Shield and Blue Cross gave it substantial potential leverage over these private insurance companies, which could have been utilized to encourage more progressive and efficient insurance practices for the benefit of New Yorkers generally. But the city historically has attempted to focus its relationships with these insurance carriers on the narrow issues of holding down direct costs to the city.[12] The HHC also had some dealings with Blue Shield and Blue Cross, since a small portion of their total income came from these sources.

The New York City Health and Hospitals Corporation

The New York City Health and Hospitals Corporation (HHC) was the most important city health institution relating to the Health Services Administration. The Health and Hospitals Corporation was established in July 1970 by state legislation initiated by Mayor Lindsay. The HHC was composed of eighteen (now nineteen) municipal hospitals which

previously were administratively part of the New York City
Department of Hospitals under the Health Services Administration. With a budget of $560 million in 1970 and nearly 40,000
employees, it constituted the largest nonfederal inpatient acute
care system; about half of the city's outpatient and emergency
medical care services were provided by the HHC.

The central purposes in establishing the HHC as a nonprofit operating corporation were: (1) to enable the municipal
hospitals to take advantage of modern management systems
and methods; (2) to free the municipal hospital system from
incredibly archaic, restrictive, and inefficient city government rules and practices governing such matters as purchasing,
accounting (or lack of it!), billing third-party payees, management salaries and job structures, personnel hiring policies,
budgeting, public works construction, and information systems;[13]
(3) to take advantage of possible economies of scale due to central management, purchasing, planning, computer operations,
etc. Thus it was hoped that establishing the HHC would ultimately result in operating efficiencies which would generate
funds to upgrade the quality of care in municipal hospitals.

The HHC, however, was faced with several very difficult obstacles to the tasks of upgrading its services and improving the efficiency of its operations. It inherited very strong
unions and professional associations and rigid civil service
job and salary structures. There existed a general lack of
middle management throughout the system and the top-level
hospital administrators were underpaid as compared to their
private sector counterparts. Much of the physical plant was
obsolete, although a massive new construction and renovation
program already underway would ultimately remedy the most
glaring deficiencies in this area. The inherited top management of the Department of Hospitals lacked certain capabilities
(e.g., no planning staff and no real fiscal capabilities). There
was a startling lack of the most basic financial information
and operating data. In short, in July 1970 the new HHC management inherited a system which was completely out of control
by top management.

To make matters worse, the HHC president, Dr. Joseph
English, and his key aides did not have time prior to assuming
their positions to become knowledgeable about HHC's problems.
One result of these difficult operating conditions was that HHC
management was faced in its first year with a substantial budget deficit due to uncontrolled spending by individual hospitals,
and to poor collections of third-party payments primarily
because of the movement of many collection personnel from
the HHC to line city agencies during the transition of HHC to
a public nonprofit corporation and because the Department of
Hospitals had not been doing a good job on collections. One
cause of the loss of control over spending was an explicit

decision by HHC management to decentralize some management functions to the hospitals prior to creating information
systems that would allow HHC central management to know
what the hospitals were spending. Fiscal difficulties would
continue to plague the HHC throughout the period under consideration.

The new HHC management also faced the difficulty of
responding to the increased expectations of politically strong
community groups and also of the general public. The old
Department of Hospitals had been very secretive. The creation
of a public benefit corporation made information freely available and raised expectations of accountability, unleashing
forces that had long sought to influence central office activities.

There were several important formal and financial
relationships between HSA, the city, and the HHC. The HSA
administrator was chairman of the board of directors of the
HHC. Four other city officials, including two reporting to the
administrator of HSA, sat ex officio on the board of HHC, and
the mayor appointed five other members of its sixteen-member
board. Five members of the board were appointed by the City
Council. These fifteen members in turn appointed the president of the HHC who served as the sixteenth member of the
board. During the initial period of its operation the HHC board
structure itself presented an obstacle to effective management
of the Health and Hospitals Corporation since different factions
often had conflicting objectives and goals. In particular, some
members of the board were extremely sensitive about the issue
of the degree of independence of the HHC from the city government.

Since the city provided the HHC with substantial direct
operating subsidies, and since the city also provided the mar-
gin of financing which enabled the HHC to avoid serious reductions in service as a consequence of its budget problems, there
is little doubt that the mayor effectively held the power to
influence top HCC management if he so desired. The capital
budget of the HHC was formally submitted through HSA to city
overhead agencies (i.e., the City Planning Commission and
the Budget Bureau). Finally, the city legislation establishing
HSA gave that agency the responsibility for coordinating and
evaluating health programs of the City of New York, including
those of the HHC.

The Political and Bureaucratic Context

Political and bureaucratic factors were extremely important in explaining the role and performance of the analytic
functions within the Health Services Administration. We consider these in an introductory way that is not expected to aid

the reader already familiar with the situation. The reader
who seeks extensive discussion of the issues and climate should
consult Sayre and Kaufman. [14]

One crucial feature of the New York City political
scene is the importance of the mayor. New York City has a
system of government which encourages a strong dominant
mayor and a weak legislative function. For example, the
mayor can initiate new programs almost at will at any point
after the city's budget has been adopted without the concurrence
of the City Council or Board of Estimate. [15] These legislative
bodies generally had nonexistent or weak staffs, and their
members usually did not have the time to clearly understand
most issues. They typically had a week or so to understand
and pass on a large operating budget ($11 billion in 1974) which
was presented in a format purposely designed to be unintelli-
gible to all but those who wrote it (i.e., the city's Budget
Bureau). As a consequence, the city's legislators tended to
focus on those few pet projects they could most easily comprehend (usually construction projects), and the mayor set policy
for the city government and established its priorities and new
programs.

One difficulty with this system of government is that when
programs do not function properly or policies are in the process of failing, the city's legislative bodies do not have the
capability to really comprehend what is happening until cor-
rective actions are no longer possible. Often the city's
legislators find out something is remiss when they read about
it in the newspapers.

The administrator's freedom to act was of course constrained by the normal budgetary stringencies. Furthermore,
the city's Budget Bureau, thought it often acted as a powerful
agent of the mayor, could serve as an independent bureaucratic obstacle and delay programmatic changes which it felt
were too costly--even if this sometimes meant frustrating the
mayor's own policies. The city's Department of Personnel
was another important constraint on action, since it sometimes
took months to approve the establishment of important new
jobs, and the city's comptroller's office often facilitated delays
by paying personnel several months after they started on the
job. This overcentralization of petty controls by the so-called
overhead agencies were (and still are) a major obstacle to
routine administration, let alone innovation. They conditioned
the environment in which city administrators acted and severely
hampered their ability to manage their agencies and solve city
problems. In an environment where senior Budget Bureau
examiners actually personally counted the buzzers on executives' telephones while ignoring million-dollar policy issues,
it was very difficult for an administrator to operate effectively.

The importance of the city bureaucracy is well stated in

a widely circulated memorandum from Rich Feeley, an HSA
analyst who had previously worked in the City Budget Bureau,
to Gordon Chase in August 1970.

> The hostile environment for change created
> by our sluggish executive procedures will soon
> claim its first victim--the Superagency. The cri-
> tics of Superagencies are right--another layer of
> bureaucracy is being imposed between operational
> problems and their solution. The answer is not
> the abolition of the Superagencies. The answer is
> a massive retrenchment of the routine powers of
> the central executive agencies--the Bureau of the
> Budget, the Departments of Personnel and Purchase,
> the Comptroller's Office, the Department of Public
> Works. What is good for the Hospital Corporation,
> should be good for government in general. The
> Mayor's opponents will not recommend this solu-
> tion. Only the administrators of the major agencies
> can perceive the useless obstacles to routine admini-
> stration, let alone innovation imposed by this
> archaic system of checks and counter balances.
> Unless the administrators of major agencies can
> remove some of the ossified structures which
> control their every action, they will never be able
> to establish an ability to manage their agencies and
> solve City problems. But if the Superagency cannot
> prove its viability, these organizations will be dis-
> membered by the next government, and the City
> will be plunged once again into a feudal chaos of
> warring bureaucracies.

In addition to the overhead agencies, there were a number of other important constraints on any New York City's
administrator's capabilities to effectuate change. First, and
perhaps most important, the varied and powerful New York
news media regularly informed the city's citizens about most
major and minor city government mistakes and problems. In
an administration which was probably more concerned than
most about its local and national press image, [16] the pervasive
but frequently unperceptive news coverage (on local government matters) by the news media gave administrators a strong
incentive to avoid or hide situations which might turn up in the
press as problems. It provided a very powerful incentive to
avoid correcting mistakes, because the process of correcting
a mistake was likely to be the trigger for a news story about
the problem rather than the correction.

Another constraint on any New York City administrator's
freedom of action was unusually well-organized, articulate, and
sometimes politically important community groups that lobbied
for programs to improve the welfare of their communities,

and that provided pressures for community control or a community voice in the governance of municipal programs and facilities. For example, although there were a sizable number of redundant, obsolete, and financially troubled hospitals among New York City's more than one hundred facilities, outright hospital closings were virtually unheard of in New York City, and numerous ways were found to keep open bankrupt facilities of marginal quality and usefulness.

Municipal unions were another important force that city administrators had to consider before making any changes that affected manning levels and job content. New York City municipal unions have been in the forefront of the labor movement's efforts to organize public employees, and they have in recent years been successful in obtaining generally better wages, fringe benefits, and conditions of employment for their membership than were obtainable at comparable jobs in the private sector. The effects of the unions were evident in a wide range of city-wide rules and processes. An important example was the difficulties in contracting out for services which the unions thought would reduce city jobs. Additional constraints included federal and state regulations and the complex process of contract and budget approvals involving the controller, the Board of Estimate, the City Council and the mayor.

All of these constraints ultimately affected HSA's relationships with the HHC and its own constituent agencies (the Departments of Health and Mental Health, and later the Addiction Services Agency), and they therefore influenced the type, nature, and consequences of the analytic work performed by HSA's analysis staff. For instance, the HHC was quite ineffective and under constant private and public criticism during the period which culminated in the resignation of the HHC president, Dr. English, at the insistence of members of HHC's Board of Directors in September 1974.

The Health Services administrator was constrained in his actions toward the HHC. Foremost was the fact that he was not a line administrator over the HHC.[17] Furthermore, the mayor's prestige was clearly on the line, since he was strongly associated with the establishment of HHC and with hiring its president. If the press ran stories about the failures of the HHC, this would reflect adversely on the mayor. Thus, for example, the HSA administrator could not effectively "push" HHC to act vigorously on the findings of an HSA study which showed that physicians were possibly seriously misallocated within and among HHC hospitals because of the potential political consequences.[18] Confrontations between HHC and HSA (and thus the city) were avoided over a host of issues to protect the image of HHC as an effective and successful accomplishment in institutional change. Nevertheless, the Health Services administrator and the mayor did rigorously push the management of HHC to improve collections of third-party payments and to tighten financial controls.

The Health Services Administration and Its Administrator

     The Health Services Administration of the City of New
York was established by an executive order of Mayor Lindsay
in 1966. The new so-called superagency was supposed to
initiate, coordinate, and evaluate health programs of the City
of New York. Four operating agencies, the Department of
Health, the Department of Mental Health, the Department of
Hospitals (now the Health and Hospitals Corporation) and the
Chief Medical Examiner's Office were put under HSA. The
Health Services Administration was also supposed to monitor
the private sector and establish general health priorities for
the city. However, HSA could not really begin to function as
it should until January 1970, when Gordon Chase became the
third Health Services administrator. Prior to Gordon Chase's
arrival, HSA had practically no central staff, and the agency
did not have control over the budgeting and personnel functions
of its operating agencies.

     Chase systematically established a more effective agency.
He recruited and inserted many competent program managers
in HSA and its constituent agencies throughout the four-year
period. A General Counsel's Office was created where there
was none. The function of this office included providing legal
advice to the agency, drawing up legislative proposals and
the writing of contracts. Prior to Chase's arrival most HSA
contracts with providers of service merely said essentially:
"We promise to give you x dollars for services which will not
be specified in detail." With Chase's general direction, the
legal staff of HSA devised "performance contracts," which
related funding for services to specific performance (i.e.,
outputs and/or inputs) indicators.

     Chase also established a management services staff com-
prised mostly of management experts, industrial and information system analysts, auditors, industrial engineers, and
computer programmers. It worked on problems like improving
the operations of the city's Narcotics Register (a computerized
data bank on narcotics addicts) and computerizing the birth-
records system of the city to reduce average writing time for
birth certificates from six weeks to several days. Further,
the HSA public affairs and community relations function was
strengthened, and HSA consolidated the budget and personnel
functions of its line agencies. And finally, a substantial program analysis staff was developed under the general direction
of the then deputy administrator for program analysis, planning,
and budgeting, Robert Harris, and under the immediate supervision of Jeffrey Weiss, who was then assistant administrator
for program analysis.[19]

     During the first year of activities the program analysis
staff was responsible for the full range of analytic activities
of HSA, and for assisting in the development of HSA's program
budget for operations and its capital budget for facilities and

equipment. However, by July 1971 Chase and Weiss and ultimately New York City Budget Director Edward Hamilton decided
that the HSA program analysis staff could not properly devote
appropriate resources to longer-range policy issues and research
questions, to basic fact-finding, and to the capital budget. The
pressures for analysis of more immediate issues, for providing
analytic assistance to program managers who were developing
or changing programs, and for day-to-day "fire-fighting" were
consuming the time of the staff. Therefore, a second analysis
staff was created with responsibilities for developing the HSA's
capital budget, for analyzing longer-range issues, and for
upgrading HSA's data base and its understanding of fundamental
relationships which affected its programs and areas of responsibility. In July 1971 Irving Leveson was brought on as assistant
administrator to head the new Office of Health Systems Planning.
The Office of Health Systems Planning developed a capability to
take a more thorough look at proposed large-scale changes with
substantial long-run consequences. Greater attention was given
to issues of capital planning and budgeting and to consideration
of the interrelationships among expense and capital decisions
and among components of the health care system. The Office
of Program Analysis was reorganized to concentrate on program
analysis, evaluations, program development, review of the HSA
program budget for operations, and on day-to-day concerns of
interest to the administrator. Both of these staffs reported to
Jeffrey Weiss, the new deputy administrator for program analysis, planning, and budgeting.[20]
    The most important feature of the environment within
which these analysis staffs operated was Gordon Chase. Since
the primary function of these analysis staffs was to help the
Health Services administrator and his chief advisers make
better decisions, the administrator's style, his priorities and
values, and his method of operating and thinking had a pre-
dominant effect on the activities of HSA's Office of Program
Analysis, Planning, and Budgeting. Chase had four main
characteristics which very substantially affected the nature of
the analytic work developed in HSA.
    First, he was very oriented toward actual results. He
was not very interested in elegant papers or inputs per se.
Instead he liked to measure accomplishments in terms like
the number of addicts treated, the number of children with a
particular problem found (such as lead-paint poisoning), and
the number of abortions accomplished without medical complications. In view of his orientation and the great bureaucratic obstacles in a system which could stymie even the simplest
activities, Chase did not particularly appreciate strategic analyses which might fundamentally change a system, but would be
difficult if not impossible to effectuate.[21] Instead, he tended to
demand from his staff analytic efforts which focused on pro-

blems where it appeared a priori that some analytic effort would lead to a better decision which could be rapidly implemented.

Chase's second important characteristic was that he was not a health expert when he was appointed HSA administrator. He was not a physician and his prior experience was as problem-solver and administrator in the areas of foreign policy, economic development, civil rights, and human resources. The mayor selected Chase for two primary reasons: (1) Chase had a proven record as a top management expert, having come to the city from the federal government to effectively deal with serious management problems as the deputy administrator for management of the city's Human Resources Administration; and (2) the mayor was disenchanted with the performance of the two previous physician/HSA administrators.

In view of his background, Chase tended to focus initially on those "production" type problems and "social disease" problems (such as establishing a large number of methadone maintenance clinics) where firsthand medical expertise was not critical to the top agency decision-maker understanding the problem. Further, in those areas where he lacked prior knowledge (e.g., health services systems) he was open to advice and fresh ideas, and he was interested in learning about different ways to solve problems. While on the surface it might seem to some readers that receptivity is not a particularly unique characteristic, our own experience elsewhere in government indicates that it is difficult to find decision-makers, particularly at the city level, with this characteristic. One consequence of Chase's open-mindedness on those issues where he lacked prior knowledge was the fact that some individual analysts did have an opportunity to affect policy, and this is one reason why the best ones came to HSA in the first place.

A third characteristic of Chase was that he wanted results quickly. This tendency had the inherent risk of creating pressures that, if not properly channeled, could and sometimes did lead to sloppy, incomplete work; with the benefit of hindsight, some decisions based upon facts and assumptions would prove to be erroneous. But insistence on fast results also created badly needed pressures for action in a system with great inertia.

It was a political fact that Chase had only four years to accomplish whatever he could before his appointment would most likely terminate with a new mayor. There were enormous bureaucratic obstacles to change, and political pressures for achievement which were heightened by criticism of Chase's appointment by the public health community because he was the first non-physician to head a major public health agency in the United States. Chase's tendency to push for change as soon as possible was quite rational and understandable under these circumstances.

Finally, Chase was politically astute and sensitive to those considerations and actions required of him to both survive and accomplish something in a difficult environment. This characteristic was a major source of HSA's analytic staff's feelings both of accomplishment and frustration. Chase regularly exerted pressure on the bureaucracy to accomplish things that he wanted to get done. Some examples included setting up the largest methadone maintenance program in the country from scratch, establishing a significant alcoholism treatment program, establishing a gonorrhea screening program, restructuring mental health contracts to greatly increase services purchased, and strengthening prison health programs.

Chase was not very successful in solving those very difficult but often fundamental institutional problems which tended to carry a high political risk to either himself and/or the mayor from confrontations with powerful interests or the fear of political embarrassment or simply failure. Included in this category of problems were the issue of closing inefficient or unneeded hospitals (which was rarely done by anyone in New York), introducing incentives into the reimbursement of the municipal hospitals, and the problem of fundamental manpower misallocations at all job levels in the municipal hospital system. (This problem was closely tied to the very tough political problems of relationships with unions and affiliate institutions.) It should be emphasized that it is likely that few of the actions to deal with these problems would have had the support of the mayor. Furthermore, most of these fundamental institutional problems concerned the Health and Hospitals Corporation, which was not under Chase's direct administrative control and thus was critically dependent on the use of persuasion and the availability of active mayoral support.

CHOOSING THE ANALYSTS AND ISSUES

Some characteristics of the HSA's analysis staff are worth noting in order to better understand the nature of the analytic effort. Staff members tended to be well-educated and highly motivated, but with a few exceptions at the most senior levels, they did not have substantial prior experience or education in the health services area when they joined HSA. There were several reasons why there were few persons with health backgrounds on the HSA analysis staff. The salary structure would not support the hiring of many first-rate experienced persons with health backgrounds. Physicians were too expensive and typically lacked the training and inclination to do policy analysis. The young professionals in the labor market with health backgrounds (i.e., those with master's of Public Health degrees, etc.) tended to have training which did not prepare them well

for policy analysis positions,[22] and at that time many schools
of public health did not attract the best-quality students. Thus,
when presented with a choice between less capable persons
with health backgrounds and more analytic persons without
health experience or training, we often chose the latter. Generalized health knowledge was often superfluous when dealing
with highly particularized problems in a rapidly changing context like that presented by the City of New York. Specific health
knowledge could often be obtained by drawing on the experience
of program administrators and could sometimes be acquired
on the job, but analytic skills were typically better developed
in the universities.

During the second Lindsay administration, the analysis
staff of the Health Services Administration had the opportunity
to work on a wide variety of problems and issues. While the
program analysis staff was developing during the summer and
fall of 1970, and until they had the opportunity to learn more
about New York City's health care problems and the availability
of information pertaining to those problems, many of the issues
and questions they dealt with were thrust upon them by persons
or events external to HSA. Thus, they analyzed alternative
gonorrhea control programs (Chapter VI) because the incidence
of VD in New York was increasing rapidly, and the Health
Department had to take additional action concerning this problem. Similarly, the neighborhood family care center (NFCC's)
analysis (Chapter VI) was undertaken because a great many of
these facilities were in various stages of planning and construction by the city and future budget constraints would clearly
not allow the city to fund the operations of all the NFCC's that
were originally committed. Over time, however, as the program analysis staff acquired greater capabilities, it had much
greater leeway in defining the problems it wished to work on
or explore. The alcoholism analysis (Chapter VI) and the
benefit-cost study of alternative methods of treating heroin
addicts (Chapter III) are examples of analyses initiated by the
program analysis staff. Typically, given Chase's predilections
and the desire of HSA's program analysts to have an "impact, "
the studies during the first year of activity were program,
agency, or process evaluations (Chapter III) and papers dealing
with program development and implementation planning (Chapter VI).

With the addition of the health systems planning staff,
HSA developed a much more substantial capability to initiate,
define, and work on basic problems or programs. A greater
portion of the analysis staff's time was used in defining problems and issues and initiating studies (with the general or
specific concurrence of the HSA administrator), and proportionately less staff time was absorbed in responding to external
demands and the administrator's immediate requirements.

Consequently, most of the papers dealing with methodology and quantitative relationships (Chapter IV), system monitoring and description (Chapter II), and policy development and analysis (Chapter V) were initiated after HSA's Office of Program Analysis, Planning, and Budgeting had attained its full capabilities. It should be emphasized, however, that external demands and the administrator's priorities always took precedence over the analytic staff's own interests.

WHERE ANALYSIS HAD AN IMPACT

Since the principal reason for establishing the HSA Office of Program Analysis, Planning, and Budgeting was to provide the administrator of HSA and his key advisers and program managers with information which would lead to more and better decisions concerning the allocation of health resources, we thought that it would be instructive to students and practitioners of policy analysis if we indicated our views on the conditions under which policy analysis in HSA did and did not have an impact on decisions. The fact that the policy analysis function in HSA did have a considerable impact on certain decisions clearly does not provide evidence that the function had great social utility, since it might have facilitated the development and implementation of many poor decisions. Conversely, if the HSA policy analysis work had not influenced decisions this would not necessarily indicate that its work was not worthwhile, because the longer-range impact of many studies and processes are difficult to ascertain at the time they are undertaken. Thus the purpose of this discussion is not to give our view of the success of the policy analysis function of HSA, but instead to merely indicate how political, bureaucratic, and personality factors influenced the likelihood of analysis having an impact on decisions.

Policy analyses in HSA clearly had an important influence on the nature of many new categorical programs implemented by HSA during Mayor Lindsay's second term. Analysis occasionally influenced the actual decisions to undertake a program (e.g., gonorrhea screening). But its more important effect was to facilitate the design of a program after a tentative or firm decision had already been made on political grounds, judgment or the administrator's interest to do something about a problem. Examples here would include the alcoholism problem, methadone detoxification, tuberculosis, health clinic budget, reallocations, and prison health policy.

Analysis had a higher probability of influencing decisions in new categorical program areas because: (1) political forces usually had not formed strong positions in program areas where programs or policies did not exist; (2) the administrator was

interested in using analysis to help him devise and implement
new programs; (3) categorical programs were likely to be
implemented by the Health Department, which was administratively under Chase's direct control (as opposed to the
Health and Hospital Corporation), and the Health Department
did not have any powerful outside interest groups (like the
affiliate hospitals in HHC) to oppose or take strong positions
on programmatic issues; and (4) categorical programs aimed
at a particular type of health program required dealing with
strong internal pressures and entrenched groups but they were
unlikely to threaten the survival or role of existing health care
institutions, since categorial programs usually involved using
only a small portion of any single health care institution's
capabilities. Even here where analysis had a higher probability
of influencing decisions, the process of change could involve
difficult and protracted efforts.

 Policy analysis also had an impact on the definition and
restructuring of many preexisting HSA programs. These tended
to occur in circumstances where Chase had a strong personal
concern that people were not getting effective services.[23] In
addition, analyses had an impact when there were no strong
external political forces supporting preexisting programs, where
there were strong pressures for change from the mayor or
the Budget Bureau, or where glaring fiscal and program irreg-
ularities existed. Examples of instances where analysis did
affect preexisting programs would include some of the items
contained in the six-month status report on addiction (Chapter
III), the study of long-stay patients unnecessarily hospitalized
in municipal hospitals (Chapter I), and the neighborhood family
care center analysis (Chapter VI).

 In general, policy analysis had little impact on existing
operational programs within the purview of HSA where there
were major questions of cost-effectiveness, but where the city
administration or Chase were already committed. Thus analyses pertaining to the closing of unneeded hospitals in the municipal system had little real impact upon HSA policies during
this period (although HSA did get HHC to address the problem
of unneeded beds within some existing hospitals. See Chapters
II and V for some discussion of hospital planning issues.)[24]

 With the exception of a few analyses dealing with narrowly
drawn issues, the work undertaken by HSA's policy analysis
staff did not significantly influence the allocation of resources
within the Health and Hospitals Corporation.[25] Analyses which
had little or no impact tended to deal with fundamental problems
like the possible misallocation of physician and nursing resources
within and among HHC hospitals, the existence of unnecessary
hospitals, and the way the city's financing of HHC provided
that organization with no incentives for efficiency.

 There were several reasons why these policy analyses

had little impact on HHC activities. First, the analyses were intended initially for the HSA's administrator, who could only affect the decisions of HHC by persuasion or confrontation. Second, even if HHC central management wanted to make changes, HHC had great difficulty effecting change in a system dominated by bureaucracy, unions, medical politics, and community pressures.

Third, with the exception of a few members of its Board of Directors, HHC management and its Board of Directors appeared to be unwilling or unable to address the fundamental issues limiting the effectiveness of the Health and Hospitals Corporation. Thus, for instance, although it was acknowledged that HHC's hospital administrators were underpaid compared to their voluntary hospital counterparts, and although HHC and HSA top management tended to believe that HHC hospital administrators were a generally undistinguished group, no systematic effort was ever made to comprehensively establish and implement policies to upgrade the management of HHC hospitals. It was much easier to get the Board of Directors of HHC to agree on the least common denominator of trying to obtain more money from the city and other sources for the HHC, then it was to get the HHC board to agree to policies which would use the resources of HHC more effectively--although this was the fundamental reason for setting up the HHC.[26]

Fourth, constant crises of a financial and political nature forced top HHC management to devote an inordinate amount of time during its first three years to day-to-day fire-fighting.

The political and fire-fighting pressures were closely related to past and present failures of the city to take on fundamental problems of the HHC, with the result often being a highly constrained situation. The affiliation contract system had developed because mayors had been unwilling to pay competitive salaries for doctors in municipal hospitals. North Central Bronx Hospital, a source of enormous community pressure during its construction, was built outside of the community whose hospital it was to replace because of efforts by a previous hospitals commissioner to locate municipal hospitals next to their affiliates to facilitate staffing. The affiliation system was used to hire nonphysician personnel through voluntary hospital payrolls. Voluntary hospital employees were represented by Local 1199 of the Drug and Hospital Employees Union while municipal hospital employees were represented by District Council 37 of the American Federation of State, County and Municipal Employees. Pressures from District Council 37 led to promises from the mayor that nonphysician employees would be "rolled back" onto the city payroll. This would be accomplished primarily through the first new jobs available--those at the North Central Bronx Hospital. But integration of the operations of that hospital with its affiliate

Montefiore Hospital would be immensely difficult if employees
in the same jobs were represented by two different unions. To
this was added community hostility to the affiliate based on
accusations of lack of interest in indigent patients and their
problems. The "rollback" and "North Central Bronx" issues
are indicative of the types of problems that occupied a substantial part of the time of the top management of HHC during
the period.

In addition to its positive impact or lack of influence on
various policy and planning matters with the purview of HSA's
responsibilities, it is noteworthy that the existence of a substantial policy planning and analysis capability within HSA had
little impact on the past HSA practices of not reviewing the
HSA base operating budget on an annual, systematic basis as
part of the agency's budget process.[27] During the agency's
budget process, the Office of Program Analysis, Planning, and
Budgeting was encouraged by the administrator to continue
the past practice of focusing its analyses exclusively on new
program opportunities. In our view this was due to the fact
that the city gave agencies no real incentive to systematically
review existing programs.

Any "savings" generated by more efficient operations
usually accrued to the city generally rather than to HSA. Also,
the Bureau of the Budget permitted the agencies to initially
submit unconstrained requests for new funds; these would then
be reduced to more realistic levels by BOB without prior consultations with the agencies. These conditions were added to
the lack of mayoral backing in dealing with counterpressures
against the actions of BOB. Under these conditions, any HSA
administrator would be irrational if he undertook the political
and administrative problem of systematically reviewing his
base budget. Instead, malfunctioning programs which were
viewed as political or programmatic liabilities were examined
selectively on an ongoing basis.[28] Since these programs were
administratively with HSA (i.e., Health, Mental Health, or
Addiction Services), ad hoc analyses of problems and programs
in these areas did generally have an impact on the administrator's thinking and actions.

In summary, political factors, bureaucratic constraints,
and the administrator's interests and priorities influenced
heavily the scope, nature, and areas of "impact" of policy analysis in HSA. Policy analysis had a high probability of influencing decisions concerning new categorical programs because
political forces often had not formed, and these programs
would normally be implemented by the Health Department,
where the HSA administrator had direct administrative responsibility and control. In contrast, since the HSA administrator
influenced HHC policies by persuasion or confrontation, and
given the many constraints on effective action by HHC manage-

ment, HSA analytical activities had little influence on the policies and programs of the New York City Health and Hospitals Corporation.[29]

ORGANIZATION OF THE BOOK

In the following chapters we have included twenty-five selections. These range from memoranda to full reports. In some cases the complete manuscript is included; in others, only excerpts. The intent was to provide examples of analysis carried out in actual decision-making situations which did not permit the same degree of refinement that would normally occur in more academic environments. All of the work represented was performed within the Office of Program Analysis, Planning, and Budgeting of the New York City Health Services Administration. Because the focus of this book is on analysis at the corporate headquarters level of a large public agency we have not included any of the studies conducted in the Health Department, the Health and Hospitals Corporation, or RAND and other outside consultants. (A discussion of the experience in using consultants appears in the next section.) The diversity of HSA's interests covers some selections indicative of the analyses which are typical of these more specialized environments. But in order to give attention to matters which are of more general value and interest, we have not included any of the highly technical studies here. Many interesting HSA studies which are examples of the kind of work already shown could not be included in the space available.[30]

The intent was to cover a wide range of material. Areas covered include financing, costs, staffing, utilization, productivity, effectiveness, and organization and include topics of interest at both a local and national level. Issues discussed range from the central planning issues such as the appropriate number of hospital beds and national health insurance to local program questions such as alcoholism and home care.

We have also chosen examples of work at various steps in the development of policies and programs. We have roughly categorized the analytic process into five areas indicative of the stage of the work. System monitoring and description is a basic process, involving assessment of basic trends in measures which reflect major problems and resources and the structure and nature of the systems with which the analyst is concerned. Program, agency, and process evaluation includes a more systematic attempt to examine program objectives and functioning, effectiveness of alternatives, costs and benefits, organizational structure and efficiency, and to consider the merits of various alternatives. The area of methodology and quantitative relationships includes efforts to develop and test new techniques, to develop analytic models and approaches, and to measure and test cause and effect relationships. This area generally includes attempts to measure the effectiveness of policies involving major resource changes rather than individual programs. It includes the more formal and technical activities. Policy development and analysis is a broad area which covers efforts to assess the value of a range of alternative policies, usually with a substantial potential impact on a broad area of resource use. The area of program development and implementation planning concerns itself with the translation of the products of analyses of problems and alternatives into the development of specific program solutions and the structuring of their introduction so as to increase the prospects for effective action.

The selections in each chapter are preceded by a discussion indicating the nature of the materials presented and highlighting the context in which they were prepared, the significance of the studies, and the uses to which they were put. When appropriate, the relationships among the selections are indicated. The discussion takes place both with a view to detailing the value of each effort as an example of how analysis is done and also in order to make clear the value of the efforts in their own right to persons interested in the subject covered.

ADDENDUM: CONSIDERATIONS IN THE USE OF EXTERNAL ANALYTIC RESOURCES

The use of resources external to the public agency can be extremely beneficial under the right set of conditions. Under the wrong set of circumstances it can also be wasteful.[31] The traditional role of the consultant was to provide services at a level of effort or expertise too great to justify maintaining such resources on a continuing basis. The realities of bureaucratic life have also led to reliance on outside talent on a continuing basis when organizational constraints make it difficult to employ sufficiently skilled talent internally. Mayor Lindsay financed the New York City-RAND Institute for this reason.

RAND set up a New York office in January 1968 (subsequently rechartered as the New York City-RAND Institute). Contracts were with the individual city agencies. There was strong pressure, however, from the city's Bureau of the Budget for agencies to accept RAND regardless of their needs or the quality of RAND's work, and the realities of funding by BOB prevented a department from shifting funds for RAND to other uses. Antagonism developed with the agencies, who were suspicious of the prospect of having RAND provide information and analyses of their data to the Bureau of the Budget which might then be used to turn down the agency's budget request.

This experience demonstrates the value of using consultants at the initiative of the client agency. It is essential not only for the consultant to be accepted and its work to be accepted but also for the agency to be prepared to oversee the work of the consultant and to make effective use of its product.

A paradox arose as some agencies like HSA developed their own analytic capabilities. Internal expertise made it possible to both monitor and utilize the RAND work far more effectively. With an in-house capability to conduct and demand strong analysis one might expect that the use of consultants would have expanded further. But it was precisely as this capacity developed that some agencies (including HSA) cut back sharply on the RAND contracts.

The outside efforts of RAND were not a good substitute for a strong in-house capability, and RAND had to meet very different tests as to the quality of its work and its willingness to be responsive to agency interest to thrive as an adjunct to the in-house analysis staff.

Based upon the experience of the HSA analytic staff with the New York City-RAND Institute, for the research organization to gain an experience upon which sound recommendations could be based, and for the city to obtain results from the research which could be used, a number of demanding conditions would have to be met. The consultant would have to be highly responsive to the timing of its findings in order to make results available while they could be used. The consultant would have to present findings in a manner that made the reasoning as well as the recommendations clear to the client and be prepared to indicate specific actions necessary for follow-through and implementation. At the same time, the consultant would have to develop a strong knowledge of the local institutional framework and the factual background surrounding the choices being faced.

The client would have to provide clear access to the organization's information and processes, including taking the consultant into its confidence in sensitive matters. The client would also have to be willing to make an investment into longer-term behavioral and policy analyses in order to provide better answers on recurring questions that could not be addressed properly in a current decision cycle.

These conditions can never be perfectly met. There is a difficult balance between supervision of consultants to maintain responsiveness and allowing discretion to permit innovation. The client may tend to burden the consultant with tasks which do not challenge his talents. When the consultant becomes too isolated from the processes of the agency he is less likely to be able to judge accurately which of the many studies and

research approaches that might be selected will be most useful. The consultant may place excessive emphasis on over-
specialized technical research, which is geared toward the
academic incentives of individual researchers rather than
finding solutions to major problems. This especially was a
problem with the RAND Institute in its relations with HSA. The
vagaries of funding and organizational inflexibility may result
in the client staffing the project with inappropriate disciplines
for the problem at hand. Concerns about funding may also
produce unwillingness to take a strong independent stand when
supported by competent professional work. [32]
    In order to be effective the research organization must
be responsive to both short- and long-term needs. This may
require carefully tailoring organizational size, skill mix and
funding to the problems faced and it may require a free flow
of personnel in both directions between government and research
organizations. If responsiveness can be achieved, the nonprofit research organization can make a very valuable contribution to the solution of significant problems.

FOOTNOTES FOR CHAPTER ONE

1. Related discussions appear in Office of Program Analysis,
    Planning and Budgeting, New York City Health Services
    Administration, Staff Papers, 1971-1973, December 1973.
    This included detailed abstracts of many papers.
2. The analysis staff of HSA employed two dozen professionals
    and several consultants, including the New York City-RAND
    Institute. An analytic capability of this size was made pos-
    sible by the concurrent interest and support for analysis
    by the mayor, Budget Directors Fred Hayes and Edward
    Hamilton and Health Services Administrator Gordon Chase.
3. It is often necessary to redefine the problem presented
    even when the original problem is soluble because redefi-
    nition allows consideration of a broader feasible set of
    solutions than would be examined in the initial formulation.
4. It should be noted that there are two concepts of "short-
    term." One refers to the time frame in which the analysis
    must be conducted and the other to the length of time before
    the impact of programs and administrative actions can be
    felt. The point applies to both.
5. See the discussions and selections of phased replacement,
    the Capital Budget Message, and the transition issues
    paper in Chapter V.
6. Application of current scientific thought is more likely to
    be successfully carried out when the analyst is intimately
    involved in a significant work of his own in order to fully
    understand and be able to apply the state of the art.

7. Economic analysis has proved to be particularly useful in dealing with questions of public policy for a number of reasons. Economics is based on the problem of scarcity. The focus leads readily to examination of goals and alternatives for achieving them. Economics is decision-oriented. It gives prominence to the understanding of behavioral relationships that can be used to determine what the consequences of deliberate actions of government would be. Economics is concerned with major resource questions. It has developed concepts and methods for defining, measuring, and interpreting significant changes in production, manpower, facilities, and financing. Economics is concerned with broad market behavior. The actions of individuals are subject to large random variations and systematic influences which are often poorly measured and interact in complex ways. However, the average response of a large group of consuming or producing units to major changes in opportunities or incentives is often readily predictable. Thus economists tend to be more heavily involved in the policy development and analysis types of problems discussed in Chapter V.

8. See the discussion and analysis of heroin addiction in Chapter III.

9. This situation was recognized in 1972 when HHPC resolved to only approve new hospital construction in underserved areas and services.

10. This was the "B" agency under federal "Partnership for Health" legislation.

11. There were seventy-eight persons on the board and staff capabilities were limited. Its energies were directed toward efforts to create thirty-three local health planning districts from sixty-two districts in use by Community Planning Boards, more under control of the borough presidents than the mayor. Some related issues are discussed in the paper on transition issues in Chapter V.

12. See the discussion and analysis of employee health benefits in Chapter V.

13. The HHC was thought to be chronically underfinanced, and this was especially reflected in the need for preventive maintenance and routine housekeeping equipment and supplies, and in a general lack of capital intensive activities as compared to comparable voluntary hospitals.

14. Wallace Sayre and Herbert Kaufman, Governing New York City (New York: Russell Sage Foundation, 1960).

15. The Board of Estimate consists of the mayor, the controller, the president of the City Council, and the five borough presidents. Important functions include approval of all city contracts and approval with the mayor and City Council of the Expense and Capital Budgets.

16. During much of his term Mayor Lindsay was contemplating or actually running for President.
17. Also, as previously noted, some members of the HHC Board were very sensitive to the issue of the City's "interference" in the operations of HHC.
18. See Chapter II for a discussion and presentation of the Physician Staffing Study.
19. Beginning several years earlier the Lindsay administration had established large analytic units in the Bureau of the Budget, the City Planning Department, and the major superagencies (Human Resources Administration, Housing and Development Administration, Environmental Development Administration).
20. In practice there was always some overlap of responsibilities between the two staffs so that the best available person could be assigned to a particular task and because the problems themselves were so interrelated.
21. See, for example, the discussion of CHIP in Chapter V.
22. Several universities offering M.P.H. degrees have begun to restructure their programs and standards to provide more analytic training.
23. Chase was constantly deeply disturbed by accounts of addict deaths, prison suicides, and other personal tragedies which he felt could be avoided by administrative and program changes.
24. However, this is also an example of a case where HSA's studies contributed to a rethinking of the problem by agencies external to HSA, and the change in Health and Hospital Planning Council policies toward new hospital construction in 1972 was influenced by HSA analysts and their analyses.
25. HHC began to develop its own planning capability in the fall of 1971, about eighteen months after HSA's policy analysis staff was established. In fact, the first full-time director of the HHC planning staff came from the HSA policy analysis staff at Chase's initiation. It is our view that the HHC planning staff also did not have any substantial impact on most of the fundamental problems of the HHC because (with the important exception of the problem of collecting more funds from third-party payees) the issues were not addressed by top HHC management. Instead, the HHC Office of Program Analyses focused largely on analyses of highly operational issues.
26. See the memo by Robert Harris and the Program Guidance Letter in Chapter III for a further discussion of these points.
27. Despite the lack of incentive, HSA did undertake various reviews of Health Department programs throughout the year.
28. In addition to the activities of HSA's analysis staff, the HSA Office of Management Services reviewed and helped

improve many ongoing programs, such as reduction in
the average time required to obtain a birth certificate
from an average of six weeks to a few days.

29. We will not attempt to suggest what an analysis staff should
be like based on this experience. We have noted the way
in which opportunities to conduct analysis and for it to
have an impact depend on the interests of the leadership,
political constraints, the decision-making process, prospects for effective implementation, and the initial state of
knowledge. An analytic capability cannot be fully designed
in advance. It must be set up flexibly and evolve as
opportunities become clear and conditions change.

30. Among the more significant of these are a study of hospital
length of stay by James Posner for the Health Department,
the HHC bed-utilization study by Alan Leslie and others,
and the RAND nursing study by Allen Ginsberg and others.
Many HSA staff papers have also been omitted. These
include Ronald Rundolf's analysis of the distribution of
out-of-pocket costs and utilization in relation to income
and health status using the Population Health Survey, a
number of technical economic and statistical reports on
demand and utilization, less complete reports and memoranda, and three studies published separately: "Trends in
Physicians in New York City, 1959-1970," by Irving
Leveson and Gelvin Stevenson, New York State Journal of
Medicine, September 1974; "Medicaid Prepayment: Concept and Implementation," by James Hester and Elliot
Sussman, Health and Society, Fall 1974; and Hirsch Ruchlin
and Irving Leveson, "Measuring Hospital Productivity,"
Health Services Research, Winter 1974.

31. The Office of Health Systems Planning oversaw the work
of RAND, the Population Health Survey, and other consultants and developed plans to overhaul the letting of
hospital planning contracts. Many of these efforts were
eventually folded into the work of the office because of
barriers to efficient use of outside resources. The city processes were relatively reasonable in permitting the use of per
diem consultants where only direct labor services were purchased and where the persons required fell within artificial
salary constraints. However, the city's contracting process
presented so many difficulties in establishing fees, defining
products and marshalling contracts through the bureaucracy
that it was not possible to develop more responsive and lower
cost alternatives, such as small contracts for specific studies
with individual researchers in universities. The situation
with regard to planning contracts was somewhat different.
There was a history of letting architectural master planning
contracts for individual hospitals. These studies failed to
adequately consider the interrelationships among institutions

and often became adversary documents for the expansion of particular facilities. Rather than focusing on alternative courses of action, the work generally concentrated on the development of detailed plans for alternatives that had not been adequately considered. Agreement was reached that the Bureau of the Budget with advice from the Health Services Administration would disapprove new requests from the Health and Hospitals Corporation for master planning studies of municipal hospitals unless analysis of major alternatives had first been conducted. But the development of an alternative was hampered by the Bureau of the Budget's fear that a more complete analysis might also generate large-scale spending proposals.

32. A major argument of RAND for establishing its New York RAND Institute was that it would provide the continuity between administrations. Yet when in early 1974 the Beame administration set about to reduce analytic staffs throughout the city (by eliminating the "superagencies"), it also tried to phase out the New York RAND Institute contracts and finally reduced them to a minimal level. The RAND effort previously had been pared down to the most successful projects, and further cuts were probably not justified on substantive grounds, although they were expected from the new top management of the city, which was dominated by career bureaucrats who were not sympathetic to policy analysis.

II

System Monitoring

and

Description

HOSPITAL AND LONG-TERM CARE

Over the years a number of studies showed that a substantial proportion of long-stay patients in general care hospitals could be treated more appropriately and/or at lower cost
in other settings. In fact, the primary need in some cases was
not even medical attention. The most notorious example was
the "boarder babies"--children abandoned after birth or without a proper home situation to return to after medical treat-
ment--who would remain in the hospital month after month.
The largest group of long-stay patients unnecessarily hospitalized belonged in nursing homes or extended care facilities.
The problem of improper utilization was also prevalent in
nursing homes, and beds for placement could not always be
found as a result.

One of the most thorough studies of this subject was the
1961 examination of New York City hospitals by Frank Van
Dyke and Virginia Brown. The study demonstrated that while
the problem was of significant magnitude in the voluntary hospitals, in the municipal hospitals it was particularly severe.
It was in the municipal system that patients presenting social
as well as medical problems were most likely to appear. It
was in the municipal hospitals that patients considered least
desirable by the nursing homes--ones who were sicker and
required more care with less room for profit under allowable
reimbursement rates, or ones who were more difficult to
manage because of senility, mental health problems or low
education--were most likely to be found. It was there that the
pressure of demand would be least likely to force beds to be
made available to patients according to medical priorities.

Yet presumably there had been some progress over the

years, so there was a need for up-to-date information on the
size of the problem. In response to a direct request from
Mayor Lindsay in the fall of 1970, one of the first tasks of the
Office of Program Analysis was to replicate the Van Dyke and
Brown study for five municipal hospitals. The purpose of this
new study was to determine the extent to which HSA's previous
analyses of the city's "need" for new hospital beds were valid,
since those initial analyses had assumed that the then-existing
use of hospital beds was based on efficient medical care practices. The results of the extensive review of patient charts by
fourteen physicians were analyzed, and the main findings of a
much longer statistical analysis are presented here. The number of long-stay patients unnecessarily hospitalized had fallen
significantly from the 1961 levels, but the problem remained
enormous.

The study led to pressure from Gordon Chase, the Health
Services administrator, on officials of the Health and Hospitals
Corporation to reduce length of stay; a variety of administrative
actions resulted. Special efforts were made by the HHC to
reduce the number of boarder babies, to close empty maternity
beds, and to shift tuberculosis patients to outpatient treatment.
Regular reporting systems were set up to monitor these areas.
The long-stay effort blended into a more extensive effort to
increase occupancy rates in municipal hospitals.

A number of analyses were done by HSA and RAND on the
extent of low occupancy rates in particular hospitals and services. Occupancy rates had traditionally been low in maternity
and pediatric departments since large variability in demand
made it necessary to provide reserve beds to assure that peak
needs would be met. But the decline in the city's birth rate
since 1958 and the sharp drop under New York's abortion law
beginning in 1971 reduced the number of patients in relation
to beds.

Occupancy rates were particularly low in tuberculosis
wards, where more than a quarter of a century earlier, administration of drugs on an outpatient basis had replaced hospitalized treatment as the norm. The institutional remains of the
earlier system of tuberculosis hospitals did not vanish by themselves, and some patients continued to be treated on an inpatient
basis, albeit in decreasing numbers.

There were extra empty beds in specialized departments
which did not make their facilities available to handle the overflow of other departments. These problems were prevalent in
voluntary hospitals as well. Furthermore, there were substantial numbers of situations in which occupancy rates were
too low even in general services.

The Health and Hospitals Corporation had set up an Office
of Program Analysis under the direction of Alan Leslie, formerly of HSA, to go into these and other problems. A detailed

study of where the empty beds were and the adjustments necessary to close them was made by that office. A monitoring
system was set up to inform hospital executive directors on a
frequent basis of their utilization experience. Bed-reservation
systems were installed to provide current information on the
number and location of empty beds. Beds were ordered closed,
and the complex reshuffling of space allocations within hospitals
was carried out on a systematic basis.

In spite of these developments, very few beds were closed
until New York State introduced a reimbursement penalty for
excess empty beds effective January 1, 1974. Most of the
changes which did occur were "paper transactions" resulting
in no real economies.[1] The costs of heating, maintaining and
guarding largely unusued hospital areas were not great. The
major potential savings were in not having to replace beds
that were empty through new construction. While the delicens-
ing of empty beds may have had a minor impact on the number
of beds that would be approved for replacement, the more
important development was that attention began to focus more
directly on the number of beds needed in the system and on the
use of alternative sources of care.

At the same time as developments in individual services
and hospitals were being considered, the staff was attempting
to generate interest in the question of the number of hospital
beds and the number of municipal beds needed in the system.
The study of trends in general care hospital use, presented in
this chapter, built on the experience in dealing with long-stay
patients and empty beds in order to assess the need for hospital
use, presented in this chapter, built on the experience in dealing with long-stay patients and empty beds in order to assess
the need for hospital beds and long-term care facilities. The
census of municipal hospitals was declining, the number of
health-related facility and nursing home beds were expanding,
there were substantial approvals for new hospital construction,
length of stay was falling, and there was an increasing belief
that treatment could often occur at a lower cost outside of
hospitals. The mechanism for dealing with facilities policy
issues on a system-wide level was the Certificate of Need
Process.

As was indicated in Chapter I, the New York City Health
and Hospital Planning Council of Southern New York had the
responsibility for review of all general care and long-term
care construction proposals in an advisory capacity to the State
Department of Health. (Subsequently, a dual review system
including the New York City Comprehensive Health Planning
Agency was set up by the state.) New York had the first Certificate of Need Law in the country in 1964, allowing the state
to pass on the need for facilities before they could be built.
The Hospital Review and Planning Councils which had a similar

function under the Federal Hill-Burton legislation became the vehicle for this review. The Board of Directors of the Health and Hospital Planning Council of Southern New York represented diverse groups but was dominated by the large voluntary hospitals.

Several city government agencies including HSA had representatives on this board. For a brief time in 1971, these were organized into a Public Interest Caucus to prepare for the board meetings and present a block vote.[2] Pressure was exerted to change the guidelines to prevent further approvals for bed expansion except under exceptional circumstances. Similar pressure arose from the state, which became increasingly concerned about the budgetary implications of the wave of applications that had already been approved. In the fall of 1971 new guidelines were issued for New York City. The following year a moratorium was placed on further approvals of nursing homes and health-related facility beds.

At this point, interest in shifting away from costly institutional care began to grow rapidly. Two independent developments created a unique opportunity to reverse the approval of overexpansion of facilities. The first was the effect of the hospital rate-setting regulations under the 1971 Economic Stabilization Program. The result of the stringency of the regulations and the failure of hospitals to respond quickly to them, coupled with tightening credit conditions, was to make it exceedingly difficult for hospitals to pass New York State's financial feasibility test for mortgage money. As a result, few projects advanced. The other development was the strong reaction of local communities to the placement of nursing homes and health-related facilities in their areas. This reaction was brought about in large part by the placement of thousands of patients dumped from state mental hospitals without adequate provision for alternative services and the concentration of those patients in proprietary homes for adults and to a lesser extent in long-term care facilities. The result was a strong set of zoning restrictions dramatically reducing the number of projects which could advance.

AMBULATORY CARE

In spite of the growing interest among planning professionals in shifting treatment away from large institutions, there has been an increasing tendency for ambulatory care to be provided in hospital outpatient departments and emergency rooms. Nationally these account for one-fifth and in New York up to one-fourth of doctor's office and clinic visits.[3] In New York City as physicians moved increasingly into specialities, they tended to locate more in practices around and in hospitals and less in neighborhoods. This problem became increasingly serious in low-income and minority areas. Superimposed on this general trend was an unusually rapid growth in visits to both outpatient departments and emergency rooms of municipal and voluntary hospitals between 1969 and 1971. The study of the growth in hospital-based ambulatory care considered alternative explanations for the increase of 800,000 visits and concluded that the cause of the rise was the state's action in cutting Medicaid fees for physician's office visits by 20 percent in 1969. The cut came at a time when the fees had not changed since 1966 and were being eroded by rapid inflation. The effect was to induce private physicians to spend less of their time treating Medicaid patients. Less than two months after the study was reported in the press, the New York State Department of Health raised Medicaid fees by 50 percent.

Financial factors had appeared as important elements in the use of ambulatory care. But the New York experience did not provide as wide a range of policy changes as could be observed if attempts to encourage the use of services outside of hospitals in other areas could be considered. A particularly interesting opportunity arose with regard to the Swedish experience. Sweden had instituted the "Seven Crown Reform," in which the price of outpatient care to the patient was sharply reduced. Elizabeth Rodgers had just joined the HSA analysis staff after studying and working in England, so she had some familiarity with European systems and sources of information. As a result, it was possible to examine the Swedish experience at low cost in a short period of time. Fee increases instituted in Sweden in 1973 limited this opportunity to the period covered by the Rodgers study.

PHYSICIAN STAFFING

An early staff attempt to deal with the issue of municipal hospital productivity was an examination of the staffing of municipal hospitals by Smith Lanning. Estimated hours were compared to a measure of output developed for the study--Inpatient Day Equivalents. In this measure the American Hospital Association's measure of Adjusted Patient Days was adapted to take into account the mix of inpatient and outpatient services.

Wide ranges of physician availability were found. There was no available standard against which these could be gauged. Were a few hospitals too high in their use of physicians? Were most too low? It was clear that the data gathered by Lanning raised interesting questions. For example, why should the ratio of physicians to inpatient day equivalents be ten times higher at one municipal hospital's pediatric service than at another, supposedly comparable service? Were the data incorrect? Was one hospital financed at a relatively low level compared to the other? Could differences in case mix account for a significant portion of the difference in physician staffing? Were physicians at the relatively overstaffed hospitals spending a relatively higher portion of their time on research activities as opposed to patient care?

In late 1971, Chase, in his role as chairman of the board of the Health and Hospitals Corporations, asked the president of the HHC to comment on the Lanning study and suggested that the corporation with its affiliates explore the reasons underlying the wide disparities in physician staffing ratios, by specific type of service, among the then eighteen municipal hospitals.[4] After a long delay, the president of HHC responded with a HHC staff memo indicating some technical difficulties with the HSA physician staffing memo--but the reasons for the substantial disparities in staffing ratios among HHC hospitals were not given in the objections it raised. HSA staff subsequently recalculated its physician staffing data, making the adjustments suggested by HHC staff. These calculations did not change any of the fundamental disparities in the physician staffing data. The results were again sent by Chase to the president of the HHC. But still no significant actions were undertaken by the HHC in order to explain the possible misallocation of funding for physicians among HHC hospitals.

These physician staffing studies were treated very confidentially by the HSA and HHC, although members of the Board of Directors of HHC were briefed on their contents. This was due to the fact that the information was potentially politically explosive, since the local community boards and management and staff of the hospitals which appeared to have relatively few physicians on their staff would raise objections to the current affiliation funding allocations by the HHC. Thus, since HHC management apparently (as revealed by its lack of action) did not feel it was in a position during HHC's first three years to raise serious detailed substantive questions with its affiliated voluntary hospitals and medical schools, the data from the Lanning study and subsequent HSA and HHC studies of a similar nature were not even utilized to ask the appropriate questions.

FOOTNOTES FOR CHAPTER TWO

1. The state instituted occupancy rate standards of 60 percent in maternity, 70 percent in pediatrics and 80 percent in other general care services. To the extent occupancy was lower, reimbursement rates were reduced proportionately. Few services were actually closed as a result, and in spite of local opposition the state allowed offsetting increases in the

numbers of licensed general care beds in hospitals closing maternity and pediatric beds.

2. The HSA study of trends in general care use was one of several studies which were circulating at this time which made it clear that fewer hospital beds than had been approved were needed.

3. The number of doctor's office and clinic visits in New York City was 40-50 million in 1973.

4. Municipal hospitals obtained most of their physicians from affiliates under contract.

II-1 A STUDY OF LONG-STAY PATIENTS UNNECESSARILY HOSPITALIZED IN MUNICIPAL HOSPITALS

by Joyce de Terra, Alan Craig Leslie, and Elsa Marshal

THE 1961 AND PRESENT STUDIES

The Long-Stay Study of 1961

In 1961, the Columbia School of Public Health and Administrative Medicine, with the financial support of the Health Research Council of New York, conducted a "long-stay" study of ward service patients in nine municipal and voluntary general hospitals in New York City in an attempt to discover the extent of unnecessary general hospital care. Over a period of six weeks, internists of the study staff examined 611 patients, all of whom had been hospitalized thirty days or more, to determine whether the patients required short-term acute hospital care. In a follow-up visit, social workers and public health nurses on the study staff attempted to determine the factors preventing the discharge of those patients for whom no medical reason was found for their prolonged hospital stay.

The results of the study highlighted a condition long suspected: a large number of patients hospitalized on acute wards of general hospitals do not require general hospital care. The Columbia team found that 41 percent of patients surveyed, though requiring medical attention of some sort, did not require acute medical care. Their medical needs could have been met more adequately, and probably less expensively, in their own homes or by some other form of institutional or organized health care.

Unnecessary hospital care within the municipal system was found to be particularly severe. In each of the four municipal hospitals included in the study, 50 percent of the long-stay patients were in the hospital for nonmedical reasons. The

*Editor's Note: This study has been heavily condensed.

patients seen and the reasons for their unnecessary stays were found to be remarkably similar in the four hospitals, which varied in size and were scattered throughout the city. One important finding showed that in the municipal hospitals, three-fifths of the study patients over sixty-five and three-fifths of the children under five were hospitalized unnecessarily, compared to only two-fifths of the aged and one-fifth of the children under five in the voluntaries.

The Columbia group found that if adequate discharge planning had been conducted and if alternative facilities or programs were available, approximately 50 percent of the patients unnecessarily hospitalized might have been discharged to their homes or to substitute homes in the community. The remaining 50 percent needed care from a variety of long-term institutions or programs, including nursing home care, chronic care, and convalescent care. According to hospital personnel, one-third of the patients unnecessarily hospitalized were awaiting completion of discharge arrangements, one-third were recognized "disposition problems" that the hospital was unable to transfer or discharge, and the remaining one-third were not able to be discharged for various reasons.

The Present Study

In an effort to update the findings of the 1961 study, the Health Services Administration, in cooperation with the Health and Hospitals Corporation, undertook a survey of long-stay patients in five municipal hospitals. The methodology used followed in many respects that devised by the Columbia School of Public Health and Administrative Medicine in 1961 and in its subsequent long-stay studies.[1]

The Health Services Administration study was conducted over a period of four weeks in November and December of 1970 by fourteen physician-consultants (internists, surgeons, and pediatricians), some of whom had participated in Columbia's earlier long-term studies. A total of 191 patients, about evenly divided between the services of general medicine, general surgery, and pediatrics, were seen at the five hospitals. All patients had been hospitalized twenty-one days or more at the time they were seen. Census lists of long-stay patients were assembled on a ward-by-ward basis for all services at four of the five hospitals and updated shortly before the date of examination; the fifth hospital provided current lists of its long-stay patients.

In all cases, the participating physicians were asked to review charts of study patients and to examine the patients in order to determine whether at the time of review: a) active inpatient care in a short-term general hospital was required

(Group A); or b) inpatient care was not required at a general
hospital for medical reasons (Group B).[2] In making their
judgments, physicians consulted with hospital staff before and/or
after examining the patients. Physicians were also asked to
complete additional questions on the survey form analyzing
reasons for prolonged stay, health service needs, and discharge
prospects. Their efforts revealed that:

> --34 percent of patients hospitalized on medicine,
> surgery, and pediatrics wards at the study hospitals
> on a given census had been in the hospital twenty-
> one days or longer.
> --43 percent of this long-stay group had no medical
> reasons for their hospitalization on the study date.
> --71 percent of unnecessarily hospitalized long-stay
> patients were children under five years of age or
> adults over sixty-five years.
> --61 percent of the long-stay patients with no medical
> indication for their prolonged hospitalization required
> institutional care in alternate long-term facilities;
> 39 percent of the patients could have been returned
> to their homes or to foster homes in the community
> if appropriate health and social services were pro-
> vided.

FINDINGS

Why Group B Patients Are Still in the Hospital

In order to suggest appropriate alternatives, it is essential to know why patients with no medical reason for hospitalization remained in the hospital. Table 1 shows reasons for
this unnecessary hospitalization, as cited by study physicians
after consultation with hospital staffs.

In medicine, 63 percent of the patients are in Category 1,
awaiting transfer to another institutional facility, and 9 percent are still in the hospital because there has been an inordinately long turnaround time in laboratory testing leading to
incomplete diagnostic work-up, or else the decision on the
medical status of the patient has not yet been determined.

For the surgical service the highest percentage (60 percent) again were awaiting transfer to another facility, and 10
percent were awaiting another operation for which a date had
not been set.

In pediatrics, the spread into several categories is due
to complications arising from social and environmental factors.
In Category 4 (25 percent of the children seen in Group B), the
parents refused to take their child home; in Category 8 (18 percent of the children who should not be in the hospital) there
were no discharge plans made.

TABLE 1

Number and Percentage of Group B Patients
Unnecessarily Hospitalized, By Reason

		Medi-cine		Sur-gery		Pedia-trics		Total	
		#	%	#	%	#	%	#	%
1.	Waiting transfer to another facility	20	63	12	60	3	11	35	44
2.	Alternate facility refuses to accept patient	2	2	1	5	-	-	3	4
3.	Awaiting transfer to home care	1	5	1	5	-	-	2	2
4.	Family cannot care for or refuses to accept patient	1	3	-	-	9	34	10	13
5.	Awaiting discharge because patient's home is in need of repair	-	-	-	-	3	11	3	4
6.	Getting physiotherapy; no one planning for discharge or transfer	1	3	1	5	-	-	2	2
7.	Patient refuses to leave hospital	-	-	1	5	-	-	1	1
8.	Discharge plans incomplete or not formulated	2	6	1	5	5	18	8	10
9.	Diagnostic work-up incomplete; decision on medical status not determined	3	9	1	5	1	4	5	6
10.	Awaiting surgical procedure	-	-	2	10	1	4	3	4
11.	Awaiting equipment or supplies	1	3	-	-	-	-	1	1
12.	Hospital's social service lost referral forms	1	3	-	-	-	-	1	1
13.	Awaiting clearance by Bureau of Child Welfare for placement	-	-	-	-	3	11	3	4
14.	Treatment for an illness not requiring inpatient care	-	-	-	-	3	11	3	4
		32	100	20	100	28	100	80	100

TABLE 2

Type of Care for Patients Not Needing General Hospital Care

Type of Care	# Pts Needing this Care	% Pts in Service Needing this Care
1. Medicine		
Nursing home	19	59%
Chronic care	6	19
Home care	3	9
Home with Family support	4	13
Terminal care	-	-
Total	32	100%
2. Surgery		
Nursing home	8	40%
Chronic care	2	10
Convalescent home	5	25
Home care	2	10
Home with Family support	1	5
Terminal care	2	10
Total	20	100%
3. Pediatrics		
Chronic care	6	21%
Home care	6	21
Home with Family support	6	21
Foster care	9	32
Rehabilitation	1	4
Total	28	100%

Type of Care Needed

The type of alternative care needed (nursing home, chronic
care, convalescent, terminal, home care, home care with
family support, foster home, and rehabilitation) is given in
Table 2 for each of the three services. Well over half (59 percent) of those in medicine require nursing home care, again
reflecting their significantly higher age (seventy-one years)
as a group. Nursing homes are also the greatest individual
facility need in surgery, while in pediatrics the most pressing
need is for foster care facilities.

EXTRAPOLATION TO GENERAL MUNICIPAL HOSPITAL
POPULATION

Number of Patients Unnecessarily Hospitalized

Multiplying the total service percentages of all hospital
patient days of unnecessary hospitalization by the daily census
totals for the fifteen general care municipal hospitals for each
of the three services yields the projected number of patients in
all municipal hospitals for nonmedical reasons as of any given
day.

Medicine	296
Surgery	117
Pediatrics	139
TOTAL	552 patients

This is approximately 15 percent of total patients hospitalized in these three services on a census day.

Annual Number of Days of Unnecessary Hospitalization

The annual impact in terms of patient-days of the above
number of patients unnecessarily hospitalized as of a given day
is simply:

Medicine	296 x 365 = 108,040
Surgery	117 x 365 = 42,705
Pediatrics	139 x 365 = 50,735
TOTAL	201,480 patient days

Annual Number of Patients Unnecessarily Hospitalized

Dividing the mean duration of unnecessary hospitalization

by the mean length of stay of Group B patients as of the study
day yields as estimates by service of the percent of stay of
Group B patients which is unnecessary:

Medicine	43/72	= 59%
Surgery	21/69	= 30%
Pediatrics	201/336	= 59%[3]

The annual number of patients unnecessarily hospitalized,
of course, is annual days of unnecessary hospitalization divided
by mean length of unnecessary hospitalization:

Medicine	108,040/43	= 2512
Surgery	42,705/21	= 2034
Pediatrics	50,735/201	= 252[3]
TOTAL		4798 patients per year

Economic Cost to Society of Unnecessary Hospitalization

The annual economic cost to society of unnecessary hospitalization for all municipal hospitals is: $107.20 x 201,480 =
$21,599,000. The $107.20 per diem cost of hospitalization was
obtained by taking per diem costs in 1968 (latest available figures)
of all fifteen municipal hospitals, inflating them by an annual
rate of 10 percent (conservative), and calculating a city total
by weighting each hospital's per diem costs by the combined
size of the three services studied. Unfortunately, per diem
costs are available only by inpatient and outpatient categories
and not by services, so that we are unable to obtain annual cost
of unnecessary hospitalization by service. If, however, the
dubious assumption is made that per diem cost is roughly the
same for each service, the $21,599,000 is divided:

Medicine	$107.20 x 108,040 =	$11,582,000	54%
Surgery	$107.20 x 42,705 =	4,578,000	21%
Pediatrics	$107.20 x 50,735 =	5,439,000	25%
		$21,599,000	100%

These costs are for three services only. Not studied
were obstetrics-gynecology, tuberculosis, intensive care units
and psychiatry.

Interpretation of the Economic Savings

The $21.6 million in economic savings estimated as
benefits from elimination of medically unnecessary long-term
stays in three services of fifteen acute care municipal hospitals

represents <u>potentially</u> realizable savings. In order to realize
the full extent of these savings, hospital bed allocation among
services as well as total hospital bed complements may have
to undergo substantial change. In the short run, existing fixed-
cost structures and misallocation of hospital beds will preclude
full realization of the $21.6 million even if all necessary steps
are immediately taken to discharge patients whose stay is no
longer medically indicated. In economic terms, therefore,
such savings represent long-term (one year or more) average
cost savings rather than short-term marginal cost savings.

The other relevant factor that must be considered is
savings to whom. The paper calculates savings to society (or
the New York City public), but under current municipal hospital incentive schemes, third-party hospital reimbursement
schedules, and hospital service size (in number of beds), the
savings appearing on municipal hospital ledgers from discharging patients as soon as medically indicated may well be
negative. This problem can be overcome only with a suitable
combination of changes in reimbursement practices, service
size, and administrative incentives. Determination of this
combination will be undertaken in a following study.

And of course where unnecessary utilization is due to
lack of suitable alternatives for the patient, savings cannot be
realized until alternatives are created or utilized appropriately.

ANALYSIS OF ALTERNATIVES

Definitions

Before discussing the use of alternative facilities we
feel that the terms we have used should be adequately defined.
Because of various financing mechanisms which offer varying
types of coverage, terminology in the medical care field has
become somewhat confused and ambiguous. Different terms
are used to describe the same kinds of care but are altered to
fit the words used in the particular legislation paying for the
service rendered. And so we have our aged in "extended care
facilities," receiving "skilled nursing care" in a "long-term
care setting." The facility is usually not an "extension" and
we hope that all nursing care is "skilled."

(1) Nursing Homes: There are varying needs among the aged.
Some with minimal impairment of function are in need of a
communal residence with meal service; some require custodial
care, such as the aged blind or patients with senile psychosis,
who by state edict are no longer referable to state mental
hospitals; some are primarily in need of nursing care with
periodic medical supervision; and some are chronically ill aged

at various stages of debilitation, who need maintenance-type therapy. When the study physicians decided upon a "discharge plan of choice" they did so with only very general alternate facility categories in mind. For that reason, any patient over sixty-five who could not ultimately subsist on his own in the community was usually classified as in need of a "nursing home."

(2) Chronic Care: Chronic care refers to any facility offering long-term care and active treatment of chronic disease (renal, cardiovascular, orthopedic, neurological, or metabolic). Many of the pediatric cases seen with congenital malformation or brain damage and musculo-skeletal deformities belonged in such a facility.

(3) Terminal Care: The care of the terminally ill usually takes place in the chronic care hospital. The patients seen in our survey who were judged terminally ill seemed to have difficulty accepting their condition and were reluctant to leave the acute care hospital.

(4) Convalescent Care: We define convalescent care as short-term supportive (basically nursing) postoperative care of a patient while he is healing. Although none of our patients in medicine were placed in the category in need of convalescent care, it is our opinion that there are some patients recovering from asthmatic, nephritic, or cardiac conditions who would benefit from this kind of care. There are some experimental units in hospitals throughout the country where patients are responsible for their own personal care, take their own medicine, etc.

(5) Home Care: Hospital-based home care programs vary in services offered. In principle, this type of care provides for medical management of the patient in his home. It is set up to care for patients who cannot be treated on an ambulatory basis. Different hospitals provide different home services, but typically provided services include health aid, nursing, homemaking, housekeeping, physical therapy, speech therapy, and social service components. Usually nurses and health aides visit patients and administer treatments. The program has overall supervision by staff physicians, who confer with the visiting personnel and keep medical orders up to date.

(6) Home Care with Family Support: Where the discharge plan of choice was "home care with family support," the physicians felt that the patient ought to be at home with assistance from a member of his family in performing the activities of daily living.

(7) Foster Care: The Bureau of Social Services (HRA) is chiefly

responsible for the placement of children in need of foster care. The care of these children who for various reasons are no longer with their parents is undertaken in several types of foster homes while some children are placed with foster families. Foster care for the aged has been included within the category of old people who can subsist independently in a domiciliary type setting (i.e., the general category of nursing homes).

(8) Rehabilitation: There are very few facilities solely for the purpose of rehabilitation such as the Burke Institute, which offers intensive speech, occupational, and physical retraining. In our study sample, the patients who should have been getting intensive rehabilitation showed up primarily in pediatrics. We feel, however, that there are adults in medicine and surgery who ought to be in a rehabilitation facility such as Burke. In the acute hospital the patients who are referred for rehabilitation usually see a therapist only once or twice a week for not more than a half-hour. This lengthens their hospital stay inordinately.

Magnitude and Costs of Alternative Facilities

Table 3 is an extrapolation of our data on alternative care needed for the fifteen general care municipal hospitals. This yields the magnitude of the city's need by number of patients, as of a given day, who will need the alternative facility. Using the total number of days of unnecessary hospitalization and our table on need for a specific alternative by service, we also derived the number of days to be spent in the alternative facility per service. The greatest need in terms of number of days is for nursing homes, followed by chronic care facilities and home with family support.

Using the previous table on number of days of inappropriate facility usage (the number of days of unnecessary hospitalization) and our previously calculated per diem costs of $107.20 for all municipal hospitals, we compute the total cost of unnecessary hospitalization as before. We next determined the per diem cost of the different alternatives. If direct costs were unavailable, we used the Medicaid reimbursement rate.[4] We then computed the costs of the alternative facilities if all the days of unnecessary hospitalization were allocated to the appropriate facility needed. Subtracting the appropriate facility costs from the hospitalization costs yields economic savings for each of the individual alternative facilities if it was properly utilized.[5] Total economic savings to society is $15.9 million for these three services only. The assumptions behind these calculations are conservative; therefore the economic saving is likely to be much more. Again, the greatest savings would come from

TABLE 3

Magnitude of Need for Alternative Facilities

Type of Care	*No. of Patients	**No. of Days	
Medicine			
Nursing home	175	63,875	
Chronic care	56	20,440	
Home care	27	9,855	
Home with family support	38	13,870	
TOTAL	296	108,040	
Surgery			
Nursing home	41	16,790	
Chronic care	12	4,380	
Convalescent	29	10,585	
Home care	12	4,380	
Home with family support	6	2,190	
Terminal care	12	4,380	
TOTAL	117	42,705	
Pediatrics			
Chronic care	29	10,585	
Home care	29	10,585	
Home	29	10,585	
Foster care	46	16,790	
Rehabilitation	6	2,190	
TOTAL	139	50,735	
Total			
Nursing home	221	80,665	40%
Chronic care	97	35,405	18
Convalescent	29	10,585	5
Home care	68	24,820	12
Home with family support	73	26,645	13
Terminal care	12	4,380	2
Foster home	46	16,790	8
Rehabilitation	6	2,190	1
GRAND TOTAL	552	201,480	100%

*This column refers to the number of patients in general hospital population who on any given day in 1970 required stated facility.

**Number of days refers to the number of days of unnecessary hospitalization spent awaiting stated facility in 1970.

TABLE 4

Alternate Facility Care

Facility Type	Facility	Per Diem Costs	Capacity
Nursing Home[1]	Manhattan	26.53	3,671
	Bronx	27.11	2,405
	Brooklyn	22.60	3,885
	Queens	26.90	2,553
	Richmond	31.75	499
TOTAL		26.04	13,013
Chronic care	Coler[2]	45.00	916
	Goldwater	60.83	666
	St. Barnabas	84.00	415
	Calvary	74.30	111
	St. Agnes	65.05	100
TOTAL		57.80	2,208
Convalescent	Loeb Center for Nursing and Rehabilitation	75.00	85
TOTAL		75.00	85
Home care	Average costs of participating muni-cipal hospitals	7.54	
Home care with family support[3]		0	
Foster home	Department of Social Services approved homes	10.00	
Rehabilitation	Burke Rehab. Center	80.46	156
	New York State Rehab. Hospital	85.00	162
TOTAL		$ 83.00	318
Terminal Care	Same as Chronic	$ 57.80	

1. These include only proprietary nursing homes. Average per diem cost of municipal infirmaries is $40.76 and average per diem cost for private infirmaries is $30.50.
2. The listed Coler per diem cost is $34.59, but this cost was calculated in 1968 and we therefore inflated it to more accurately reflect current costs.
3. Some costs should be attributed to services provided by family members, but at this time we were unable to estimate the opportunity costs of such service.
4. Capacity figures are neither comprehensive nor complete but were given to indicate relative size of alternative facilities and any possible correlation between facility size and per diem costs.

TABLE 5.

Economic Savings Resulting from More Appropriate Use of Alternative Facilities

Type of Appropriate Facility	No. of Days of Unnecessary Hospitalization	Hospitalization Costs	Appropriate Facility Cost	Economic Savings
Nursing home	80,665	$ 8,647,000.	$2,101,000.	$6,546,000.
Chronic care	35,405	3,795,000.	2,046,000.	1,749,000.
Convalescent	10,585	1,135,000.	794,000.	341,000.
Home care	24,820	2,661,000.	187,000.	2,474,000.
Terminal care	4,380	470,000.	253,000.	217,000.
Foster Care	16,790	1,800,000.	168,000.	1,632,000.
Rehabilitation	2,190	235,000.	182,000.	53,000.
Home with family support	26,645	2,856,000.	-	2,856,000.
TOTAL	201,480	$21,599,000.	$5,731,000.	$15,868,000.

expanded use of nursing homes. The next two largest savings would be from greater use of home care and judicious discharge of patients to their own homes with family support.

FOOTNOTES

1. Much helpful advice was given to the Health Services Administration study team from both Frank Van Dyke and Virginia Brown of the Columbia School of Public Health, directors of the original study, and we are extremely grateful for their cooperation.

2. Where an evaluation could not be made because of lack of sufficient information, the patient was classified as Group C, but only four patients in our study had to be so classified.

3. If a cutoff date of two years is applied to duration of individual unnecessary hospitalization to reduce the effects of two pediatric patients with very long periods of stay, the number is 56 percent and 441 patients per year.

4. Table 4 gives examples of various institutions offering alternative forms of medical care with some per diem costs for each.

5. Table 5 shows realizable long-term savings from more appropriate use of alternative facilities. The economic savings column is derived by multiplying the number of days of unnecessary hospitalization time by hospitalization cost, and subtracting from this figure the cost of placing a patient in the appropriate facility.

II-2 TRENDS IN GENERAL CARE HOSPITAL USE IN NEW YORK CITY — 1950-1970

by Irving Levenson, Anita Altman, Harriet Grayson
Paul Grier, and Joanne Quan

SUMMARY

Some of the major points revealed in an examination of
trends in fundamental utilization aggregates are that:
1. While residents of New York City are about as likely to be
hospitalized as those of the nation, and bed availability is similar, the average length of stay in general care hospitals in
New York City is more than one-fourth above the national
average.
2. While the occupancy rate of the municipal system exceeded
that of the voluntaries by more than 19 percent in 1950, in 1970
it was lower by 10 percent.
3. Municipal hospitals have sharply reduced their length of
stay while the trend in voluntary and proprietary hospitals has
been upward.
4. As a result of shorter lengths of stay and higher occupancy
rates, the voluntary hospitals serve nearly one-third more
patients per bed than the municipals.
5. Changes since 1969 are greatly exaggerated as a result of
inclusion of statistics on abortions, but after adjustment the
directions of change are usually the same.
6. Current expansion plans approved by the Health and Hospital
Planning Council of Southern New York would result in a growth
of general care beds of 10 percent or 4,720 beds. The combined growth of general care and other hospital based beds,
nursing beds, and health-related facility beds is 35,000, or a
combined expansion of 41 percent.

7. By reducing average length of stay by one half of the excess over the national average as nursing homes become available and raising the average occupancy rate to 90 percent, the hospital system in New York City could admit the same number of patients as it does now with 20 percent fewer beds. Resources freed in this way could be used to provide ambulatory care, home care, and other services and to expand admissions when essential without much extensive growth of inpatient care.

LOCAL AND NATIONAL TRENDS IN GENERAL CARE HOSPITALS[1]

A decade ago the number of general care hospital beds per thousand population was one-third higher than the national average. Table 1 indicates that since 1960 the U.S. ratio grew by one-fifth to 4.2 while the New York City ratio remained approximately unchanged at its present level of 4.8. Currently the ratio of beds to population in New York City remains at one-seventh above the national average. Most of this remaining difference can be attributed to the fact that about one-tenth of inpatient days in the city are provided to residents of other areas. Thus the frequency of hospital admission of New York City residents is very similar to the rest of the nation. Trends in the number of admissions to hospitals in New York City and the United States shown in Table 1, parallel the changes in numbers of beds over the long term. Yet during the 1950's the national data show a more rapid increase in admissions than beds, presaging a growth in the number of beds, while the New York data show a smaller growth in frequency of hospital use than in bed availability in advance of leveling off of the bed supply. The difference in admissions is about the same size as would be expected based on use by nonresidents.

Table 2 reveals that general care hospitals in New York City had an occupancy rate about six percentage points higher than the national average in 1970 and had a higher occupancy rate in every one of the years shown. It is likely that this is the result of the general tendencies for urban hospitals and larger hospitals to maintain relatively high occupancy rates. Both series show substantial increases in capacity utilization during the most recent decade. The introduction of Medicare and Medicaid, the growth of private health insurance and other changes in the financing of services are believed to be a major factor.

In spite of the nearly identical frequency of hospitalization for New Yorkers as for the rest of the nation, the average length of stay in general care hospitals in New York City is more than 25 percent above the national average (Table 2). This is in part associated with a larger number of beds per capita and in part associated with higher occupancy rates. The

TABLE 1

General Care Hospitals Beds and Admissions per 1,000 Population
U.S. and New York City, 1950, 1955, 1960-1970[1]

	Beds		Admissions	
Year	U.S. (Complement)	N.Y.C. (Capacity)	U.S. Admissions	N.Y.C. Discharges[2]
1950	3.3	4.3	109.7	110.2
1955	3.4	4.6	115.7	118.1
1960	3.5	4.9	127.6	129.2
	(Complement)	(Complement)		
1960	3.5	4.7	127.6	129.2
1961	3.6	4.7	127.7	128.3
1962	3.6	4.7[3]	130.8	129.0
1963	3.7	4.8	133.9	132.4
1964	3.8	4.9	135.8	134.5
1965	3.8	4.8	136.5	133.1
1966	3.9	4.8	137.3	131.0
1967	4.0	4.8	136.4	127.6
1968	4.0	4.7	136.5	128.1
1969	4.0	4.7	140.0	127.4
1970	4.2	4.8	144.0	130.4

1. Only includes general care units in nonfederal general and
special hospitals.
2. Includes deaths.
3. Approximation based on 1962 bed capacity.

Source: Hospital Planning for the People of Southern New York
1964: Special Report 2, Hospital Review and Planning Council
of Southern N.Y., Inc.; Hospital Statistics of Southern New York
1969, Health and Hospital Planning Council of Southern New
York, Inc.; Statistical Abstract of the United States, 1970,

TABLE 2

Occupancy Rates and Average Length of Stay in General Care
Hospitals, U.S.[1] and New York City, 1950, 1955, 1960-1970

Year	Occupancy Rate		Length of Stay	
	U.S. (Complement)	N.Y.C. (Capacity)	U.S.[1,2]	N.Y.C.[1,3]
1950	75.9%	79.8%	8.1	11.2
1955	71.7	74.3	7.8	10.6
1960	74.3	75.7	7.6	10.4
	(Complement)	(Complement)		
1960	74.3	78.8	7.6	10.4
1961	75.1	78.7	7.6	10.5
1962	75.1	78.8	7.6	10.5
1963	76.0	80.0	7.7	10.4
1964	76.3	79.1	7.7	10.4
1965	76.0	80.5	7.8	10.6
1966	76.5	81.1	7.9	10.8
1967	77.6	83.2	8.3	11.3
1968	78.2	83.8	8.4	11.3
1969	78.8	83.6	8.3	11.3
1970	78.0	83.7	8.2	11.1

1. Excludes federal hospitals.
2. Excludes newborn.
3. Based on discharges.

U.S. Department of Commerce (Bureau of the Census); Hospitals, (Guide Issues), American Hospital Association. Population data for New York City were estimated by means of
linear interpolation for intercensual years.

average length of stay in New York in 1970 was 11.1, nearly
3 days above the national level of 8.2, and a similar difference
persisted in other years. Both in New York and the U.S., the
average length of stay declined sharply in the fifties, but rose
again to its 1950 level by 1970. The number of admissions per
bed rose from 1950 to 1960 and fell thereafter.

The reductions in length of stay in the 1950's are generally
attributed to control of communicable diseases and to deliberate
efforts to shift procedures to ambulatory and other bases. The
New York City Department of Hospitals began discharging
patients to proprietary nursing homes in 1952. The increases
in length of stay in recent years appear to be partially due to
the growth in insurance coverage for the aged and poor who
have particularly long stays as a result of greater health problems, and especially to the introduction to Medicare in July
1966.

TRENDS BY OWNERSHIP IN NEW YORK CITY

Table 3 shows that the growth of beds per capita in New
York City during the 1950's was particularly great in the voluntary sector. The voluntary, municipal, and proprietary hospitals roughly maintained their relative share of beds in general
care hospitals in the 1960's. There was some decline in the
municipals and a corresponding growth in the voluntaries, and
by 1970 the municipal system represented slightly less than
one-fourth of the total. Similar patterns appear in the data on
discharges (Table 4). Discharges per 1,000 population in the
municipal system fell from a peak of 28 in 1964 to 25 in 1970.

Occupancy rates, shown in Table 5, reveal large differences between sectors. Capacity utilization in the voluntary
and proprietary hospitals rose modestly in the 1950's and then
rose rapidly in the 1960's so that by 1970 their rates were about
10 percentage points above 1950 levels. The municipal hospitals, on the other hand, underwent a dramatic decline in the
1950's, with occupancy rates falling 20 points from 94 to 74
percent based on capacity. During the 1960's they were relatively stable, ending the decade 1-1/2 percentage points below
the 1961 peak rate of the decade. As a result of the changes,
the public and nonpublic sectors reversed their positions
between 1950 and 1970. While the occupancy rate of the municipal system exceeded that of the voluntaries by 19 percent
in 1950, it was 10 percent lower than the voluntaries in 1970.
Once again the changes are in part attributable to developments
in financing. The growth of public and private insurance made
it no longer necessary to obtain services at a municipal institution as a condition of receiving financial assistance. Yet
most of the changes in financing occurred after 1960 and the

TABLE 3

Hospital Beds per 1,000 Population in General
Care Hospitals in New York City by Ownership
1950, 1955, 1960-1970

Year	Municipal (Capacity)	Voluntary (Capacity)	Proprietary (Capacity)
1950	1.2	2.5	0.5
1955	1.4	2.7	0.6
1960	1.4	2.9	0.6
	(Complement)	(Complement)	(Complement)
1960	1.3	2.8	0.5
1961	1.3	2.8	0.6
1962	1.3[1]	2.9	0.6[1]
1963	1.3	2.9	0.7
1964	1.3	3.0	0.6
1965	1.3	3.0	0.6
1966	1.2	2.9	0.6
1967	1.2	2.9	0.6
1968	1.1	3.0	0.6
1969	1.2	3.0	0.6
1970	1.1	3.0	0.6

1. Approximation based on 1962 bed capacity.

Source: Hospitals and Related Facilities in Southern N.Y. 1971;
Hospitals and Related Facilities in N.Y.C. 1951-1961,
Health and Hospital Planning Council of Southern N.Y.,
Inc.

TABLE 4

Discharges per 1,000 in General Care Hospitals
in New York City by Ownership
1950, 1955, 1960-1970

Year	Muncipal	Voluntary	Proprietary
1950	26.4	65.8	17.9
1955	25.6	72.4	20.1
1960	27.7	80.5	21.0
1961	26.8	80.6	20.8
1962	27.4	81.4	20.2
1963	28.3	82.2	21.9
1964	28.4	84.8	21.3
1965	27.8	85.4	19.9
1966	26.9	84.5	19.6
1967	25.4	82.4	19.5
1968	25.2	82.8	19.5
1969	24.1	83.4	19.1
1970[1]	25.1	85.4	18.9

1. Adjusted for abortions.

Source: Hospital Planning for the People of Southern N.Y. 1964:
Special Report 2, Hospital Review and Planning Council of
Southern N.Y., Inc.; Hospital Statistics of Southern N.Y., 1971,
Health and Hospital Planning Council of Southern N.Y., Inc.

TABLE 5

Occupancy Rate in New York City General Care
Hospitals by Ownership
1950, 1955, 1960-1970

Year	Municipal (Capacity)	Voluntary (Capacity)	Proprietary (Capacity)
1950	93.6	74.8	71.3
1955	n.a.	n.a.	n.a.
1960	73.6	77.5	72.8
	(Complement)	(Complement)	(Complement)
1960	77.8	79.4	78.1
1961	78.4	79.5	75.0
1962	77.8	80.1	73.8
1963	77.3	82.2	75.6
1964	75.5	81.5	74.7
1965	77.4	82.8	75.4
1966	76.1	83.7	79.0
1967	74.8	86.4	85.4
1968	76.4	86.7	85.3
1969	75.9	86.6	84.7
1970[1]	76.9	86.6	84.5

1. Adjusted for abortions.

n.a. - not available.

Source: Hospital Planning for The People of Southern N.Y.
1974: Special Report 2, Hospital Review and Planning Council
of Southern N.Y., Inc.; Hospital Statistics of Southern N.Y.
1969, Health and Hospital Planning Council of Southern N.Y.,
Inc.; Hospital and Related Facilities in Southern N.Y., 1971.

extensive changes in the 1950's are not well understood.

The differences among providers in length of stay are equally marked. Table 6 indicates that the municipal hospitals have sharply reduced their long average length of stay while the trend in the voluntary and proprietary hospitals has been upward. However, both as a result of shorter lengths of stay and higher occupancy rates, the voluntary hospitals continue to discharge nearly one-third more patients per bed than the municipals.[2]

HEALTH FACILITY EXPANSION PLANS AND THEIR IMPLICATIONS

There are currently 82, 193 beds in hospitals, nursing homes, and health-related facilities in New York City. Major expansion in all of these types of facilities has been encouraged in the last six years by the availability of loans to public and private institutions at tax-exempt interest rates and low down payments through the New York State Housing Finance Agency and by reimbursement for interest, amortization, and depreciation in hospital daily charges through the Medicaid and Medicare insurance programs. There are 39, 932 beds planned which would result in a net expansion of the system to 122, 125 beds. This represents an increase of 48.6 percent. These changes are summarized in Table 7. The changes do not include construction plans of nearly equal magnitude of hospital beds to replace obsolete facilities.

General Care Beds

There are 37, 825 general care beds in the city. These represent 45 percent of all health care beds. A net expansion of 4, 696 beds is planned. Fifteen hospitals representing 2, 072 beds are either recently completed, under construction, or have financing guaranteed. The remaining beds have received approval from the Health and Hospital Planning Council of Southern New York.

This expansion program will have a substantial impact on the ratio of general care beds per 1, 000 population in the city. The current ratio is 4.8 and will increase to 5.4. An increase of about 900 beds is planned. In addition, current plans would produce an increase of 1, 300 beds in the municipal system other than general care. These changes would leave the municipal hospitals with approximately the same share of general care and other beds in the city.

TABLE 6

Average Length of Stay in New York City
General Care Hospitals by Ownership
1950, 1955, 1960-1970

Year	Municipal	Voluntary	Proprietary
1950	16.3	10.4	6.6
1955	14.7	10.3	6.9
1960	13.8	10.1	7.3
1961	13.8	10.2	7.4
1962	13.4	10.5	7.4
1963	12.8	10.4	7.6
1964	12.3	10.4	8.0
1965	12.7	10.4	8.2
1966	12.7	10.7	8.5
1967	13.2	11.2	9.2
1968	13.1	11.2	9.3
1969	13.2	11.2	9.5
1970[1]	12.8	11.0	9.6

1. Adjusted for abortions.

Source: Hospital Planning for the People of Southern N.Y. 1964:
Special Report 2, Hospital Review and Planning Council of
Southern New York, Inc.; Hospital Statistics of Southern N.Y.
1969, Health and Hospitals Planning Council of Southern N.Y.,
Inc.

TABLE 7

Summary of Expansion

| Type of Facility | Existing | Financed | Approved Expansion | | | Percent Expansion |
			Not Yet Financed	Total Planned	Total Projected Beds	
General Care	37,825	2,048	2,648	4,696	42,521	12.4%
Other Hospital Based	20,807	1,177	210	1,387	22,194	6.7
Mental Health	12,955	553[1]	100	653	13,608	5.0
TB	962	-46[2]		-46[2]	916	-4.8
Long-Term Care	6,890	670	110	780	7,670	11.3
Total Hospital Beds	58,632	3,225	2,858	6,083	64,715	10.4
Nursing Home Beds[4]	19,264	4,172[3]	9,560	13,732	32,996	71.3
Health-Related Facility[5]	4,297	1,220[3]	18,897	20,117	24,414	468.2

1. Assumes closing 100 existing beds at Metropolitan.
2. Reduction 46 beds at Bellevue.
3. Beds current under construction.
4. As of April 1972, there were 25,613 nursing home beds--a 33% increase in 1-1/2 years.
5. As of April 1972, there were 6,564 health-related beds --a 52.8% increase in 1-1/2 years.

Source: Hospital and Other Health-Related Facilities, 1971. Health and Hospital Planning
Council of Southern New York. Health and Hospital Planning Council, April 19, 1972.

Community Mental Health Beds

There are 12, 955 mental health beds in the city. Of
these, 2, 621 are short-term mental health beds. The municipal system is adding 629 beds. This represents an increase
of 23. 9 percent in the number of short-term mental health
beds in the city and 49. 1 percent in the municipal system.

Extended Care, Nursing Home, and Health-Related Facility Beds

By far the largest increase is in the number of these beds
which will be added to the system. Of the planned 39, 932 new
beds, 33, 489 beds are in the extended care, nursing home and
health-related category. This represents 83. 9 percent of the
growth of all beds. The impact of the increase of these beds
on the acute care hospitals will be substantial, particularly in
the municipal sector, where lack of available nonacute care
beds has prevented the reduction in excessively long lengths of
stay in many hospitals.

Some Implications

On the basis of a host of studies of the effects of variation
in bed availability, [3] we would expect that by itself the expansion
of general care hospital beds would:
  1. Result in a nearly proportional expansion of hospital
  admissions.
  2. Have no important long-term effect on occupancy rates.
  3. Produce a small increase in average length of stay.
We would expect the changes in nursing home and health-
related facilities to have the following impact:
  1. Substantial numbers of patients who would be treated
  in nursing homes in an absence of alternatives will be
  served in health-related facilities.
  2. The expansion of the number of nursing home beds
  and the availability of beds formerly occupied by patients
  more appropriately served in health-related facilities
  will provide an opportunity for a reduction in general care
  average length of stay of the order of magnitude that
  occurred in the 1950's.
When these expectations are considered together with the
utilization aggregates examined earlier, an interesting picture
emerges:
  1. If the hospitals in New York City could raise occupancy rates to 90 percent from the present level of 84
  percent, they could admit the same number of patients as
  currently with 7 percent fewer inpatient beds.

2. If the average length of stay in general care hospitals in New York City could be reduced by half of the excess over the national average as alternative sources of care become available they could admit the same number of patients as currently with 14 percent fewer beds. These general points apply to both the public and private systems, although even more so to the municipal hospitals because of their poor utilization statistics.

3. In combination it is possible for hospitals in New York City to admit the same number of patients as currently with about 20 percent fewer beds while 10 percent are scheduled to be added.

4. The expansion of beds can be expected to increase inpatient utilization and preempt resources which could be used to improve the provision of ambulatory care, home care, and other services. The construction costs, though high, may be important to deal with a serious problem of obsolescence of facilities, but this can be accomplished without so great an expansion of inpatient care.

FOOTNOTES

1. The New York City data in Sections I and II have been adjusted to exclude changes due to the 1970 New York State abortion law.

2. Editor's note: A section on the method of adjustment of the data for effects of abortion reform was deleted at this point.

3. For a review of the literature, see Irving Leveson, "Hospital Utilization Research for Capital Planning Decisions."

II-3 THE RECENT GROWTH OF HOSPITAL-BASED AMBULATORY CARE — November 1971

by Irving Levenson, Harriet Grayson, and Ronald Rudolf*

SUMMARY

About one in four ambulatory care visits in New York City is hospital-based. The use of outpatient departments and emergency rooms in both municipal and voluntary hospitals grew by 800,000 visits between 1969 and 1971. The timing of the changes which occurred indicates that changes in Medicaid coverage did not cause patients to make this shift in sources of care; rather, it was the response of physicians as their fees were cut. The increase in hospital-based ambulatory care was caused by the action of the State Health Department in cutting back Medicaid fees for noninstitutionalized providers by 20 percent in July 1969. The cut in the fee for a doctor's office visit from $5.00 to $4.00 resulted in a shift in medical activities to outpatient departments and emergency rooms, where costs typically run about $30.00 per visit (exclusive of diagnostic and pharmacy costs). The efforts to save money did not do so but instead substantially worsened the distribution of ambulatory care services. The growth in reliance on hospital-based sources was generally greatest in facilities nearest to large underserved populations, suggesting that the availability of services has become more unequal among population groups. The growth in hospital-based visits did not continue into 1972 in municipal facilities.

Improvements can be achieved by the establishment of more realistic fee scales for doctor's office visits under Medicaid. Fees can also be established which will facilitate the

*Brian Richter and Judith Tell assisted in the study. The cooperation of Dr. Stephen Rosenberg of the New York City Department of Health and Marvin Roth of the Health and Hospital Planning Council of Southern New York are greatly appreciated.

73

evolution of group practice clinics with better service levels
than in the Medicaid physicians' office, but lower cost than
hospital-based sources of care. These measures can relieve
some of the overcrowding at hospital clinics. This is an important first step toward making the services more comprehensive.

RECENT CHANGES

The nine and a half million visits to hospital outpatient
departments and emergency rooms represent about one-fourth
of the ambulatory care delivered annually in New York City.[1]
While Medicaid fees for physician office visits are set at $4.00
a visit, the cost of an average visit to a hospital outpatient
department or emergency room is typically about $30.00, even
after laboratory and pharmacy costs are excluded.[2] Between
1969 and 1971, the number of hospital-based ambulatory care
visits increased by 806,000. This study examines this change
in detail.

Table 1 presents the number of visits annually since 1965.
The introduction of Medicare in July 1966 and of Medicaid in
the same year caused a shift away from municipal hospital
ambulatory care. The decline in the total of hospital-based
ambulatory care until 1968 indicates that much of the shift was
in the direction of private physicians rather than voluntary
hospitals. Introduction of the health insurance programs slowed
the growth in emergency room use.

A dramatic reversal of the trend occurred after 1969.
The two periods are contrasted in Table 2. Between 1969 and
1971 the number of visits to municipal hospitals grew by
566,000, and visits to voluntary institutions increased by
240,000. Outpatient departments in all hospitals increased
their visits by 526,000, while emergency room visits grew by
280,000. These changes brought the level of hospital-based
ambulatory care to 9.5 million visits per year, surpassing
the pre-Medicare and Medicaid levels. (The 1969-71 increase
is substantially smaller, however, than the growth in the physical facilities for hospital-based ambulatory care which is
programmed for the next two years.) At the same time, as
the total expanded, emergency room visits grew to one-third
of the total for the first time.

The same pattern as found for all OPD visits can be seen
in the figures for general care visits to municipal hospital outpatient departments in Table 3. While the general care rise
between 1969 and 1971 was 250,000 visits rather than the
383,000 of the total, it is clear that the pattern is not caused
by the growth of expanding specialized services such as psychiatry
and addiction. It is also apparent that the changes were not
induced by supply factors. The growth in the number of hospital-

TABLE 1

Number of Hospital-Based Ambulatory Care Visits, New York City, 1965-1971
(thousands)

	1965	1966	1967	1968	1969	1970	1971
Voluntary							
Emergency Rooms	1,203	1,226	1,336	1,418	1,435	1,487	1,532
Outpatient Departments	2,941	2,768	3,096	3,127	3,056	3,117	3,199
Total	4,144	3,994	4,432	4,545	4,491	4,604	4,731
Municipal							
Emergency Rooms	1,435	1,506	1,503	1,427	1,451	1,585	1,634
Outpatient Departments	3,251	3,397	3,107	2,846	2,788	2,970	3,171
Total	4,686	4,903	4,610	4,273	4,239	4,555	4,805
Total							
Emergency Rooms	2,638	2,732	2,839	2,845	2,886	3,072	3,166
Outpatient Departments	6,192	6,165	6,203	5,973	5,844	6,087	6,370
Total	8,830	8,897	9,042	8,818	8,730	9,159	9,536

Source: Health and Hospitals Corporation, Hospital Statistics Service, "Hospital
Statistical Profile, 1965-1969, 1967-1971."

TABLE 2

Changes in Hospital-Based Ambulatory Care in New York City, 1965-1971

	Change in Number of Visits (thous.)			Percentage Change in Visits		
	1965-1969	1969-1971	1965-1971	1965-1969	1969-1971	1965-1971
Voluntary						
Emergency Rooms	232	97	329	19.3%	6.8%	27.3%
Outpatient Departments	115	143	258	3.9	4.7	8.8
Total	347	240	587	8.4	5.3	14.2
Municipal						
Emergency Rooms	16	183	199	1.1	12.6	13.9
Outpatient Departments	-463	383	-80	-14.2	13.7	-2.5
Total	-447	566	119	- 9.5	13.4	2.5
Total						
Emergency Rooms	248	280	528	9.4	9.7	20.0
Outpatient Departments	-348	526	178	-5.6	9.0	2.9
Total	-100	806	706	-1.1	9.2	8.0

Source: Same as Table 1.

TABLE 3

Outpatient Department Visits by Type of Clinic Visit
for New York City Municipal Hospitals, 1965-1971

(thousands)

Year	General Care	Physical Medicine & Rehab	Psychiatry	Chest	TB	Drug Addiction	Total[1]
1965	2,982	40	157	28	44	- -	3,251
1966	3,125	37	165	25	45	- -	3,397
1967	2,824	35	162	- -	62	23	3,106
1968	2,554	27	170	- -	60	34	2,846
1969	2,463	30	165	- -	66	64	2,788
1970	2,569	36	205	- -	67	93	2,970
1971	2,713	33	308	- -	61	57	3,171

1. Groupings of clinic visits may not equal total visits due to rounding error.

Source: Same as Table 1.

based physicians between 1969 and 1970 as reported by the
American Medical Association was substantially smaller than
in earlier years.

The growth appears to have been the result of a once-and-
for-all change. Recent data suggests it has stopped. The
changes in hospital-based ambulatory care was 429,000 between
1969 and 1970, and between 1970 and 1971 it was 377,000. However, data for the first six months of 1972 for municipal hospitals indicate a drop of 77,000 visits below the corresponding
period of 1971, a rate which if sustained would produce a
decrease of 154,000 or 6 percent for the full year. This compares with a gain of 250,000 in the preceding year.

The decline in municipal ambulatory care services may
have been the result of any of several factors. The price freeze
may have made staff reductions necessary. An attrition policy
was in effect under which few employees who left were replaced.
Improved collections may have resulted in less use of municipal
services. At this time we do not know how permanent the decline
is or what caused it and do not have similar data for voluntary
hospitals. Nevertheless, the data do suggest that the growth in
hospital-based ambulatory care has not continued.

Analysis of ambulatory care visits to each municipal
hospital provided further insights. There is some tendency for
the growth in municipal ambulatory care to be greatest in the
areas which already have the most inadequate services. Coney
Island Hospital, which is in the Gravesend Health Center District,
experienced a 27 percent increase in outpatient department
visits between 1969 and 1971. Queens Hospital, responsible for
areas of Jamaica, had an increase of 31 percent, while emergency room visits rose 23 percent. Bronx Municipal, serving the
Pelham Bay area, experienced an increase of 24 percent in outpatient department visits and 47 percent in emergency room visits
between 1969 and 1971. The changes at Kings County, which
serves many underserved areas, are not unusually large, but
that facility serves a particularly broad geographic area.

In order to determine the causes of these changes we
review the history of the Medicaid program in New York City.

THE MEDICAID EXPERIENCE

Medicaid went into effect in May 1966. Federal law
requires each participating state to include all welfare recipients
as eligible for Medicaid and permits the addition of a "medically
indigent" category to be defined by each state. Five basic health
services are mandated by Medicaid--physician care, hospitalization, nursing home care, laboratory and X-ray services, and
outpatient clinic services. Additional services are permitted
at the discretion of each state.

The New York State program began with a broad scope of services and liberal eligibility requirements for the medically indigent category. Both of these have been steadily reduced over time. The original eligibility ceilings and the levels after the reductions enacted by the State legislature took effect are as follows:

Family Size

	1	2	3	4	5	6
May 1966	$2,900	$4,000	$5,200	$6,000	$6,850	$7,700
April 1968	2,300	3,300	4,200	5,300	6,000	6,800
July 1969	2,200	3,100	4,000	5,000	5,700	6,400

A family of four earning up to $6,000 was eligible for Medicaid in 1966, while after July 1969 a family could not earn over $5,000 and remain eligible. In addition to lowering the eligibility ceilings in 1968 and 1969, the legislature modified the eligibility rules in April 1968 to exclude members of medically indigent families not on Public Assistance between the ages of twenty-one and sixty-five. An across-the-board decrease of 20 percent in fees of all noninstitutional providers was put into effect in July 1969. On January 1, 1971, all Medicaid recipients classified as medically indigent were required to pay 20 percent of all outpatient fees in cash, unless or until they "spend down" to the public assistance level of income net of medical expenses.

Both groups of recipients, those on public assistance (PA) and those classified as medically indigent (MA), increased greatly from the inception of the program, until about early 1968 when the eligibility ceilings were lowered and members of medically indigent families between the ages of twenty-one and sixty-five were excluded. The number of MA recipients showed a marked decrease at this time, although it has somewhat leveled off in recent years. The number of PA recipients of Medicaid services increased greatly between 1968 and 1970 after which it seemed to be leveling off. There is no growth in the total enrollment to account for the rise in hospital-based ambulatory visits. The number of physicians treating Medicaid patients has remained fairly constant over the years along with the number of other noninstitutional providers (podiatrists, optometrists, etc.). The decrease in fees put into effect in 1969 was associated with a small increase in the number of participating physicians.[3] The number of participating dentists has shown a steady decline.

Expenditures for MA recipients increased until 1968, after which they declined, probably due to the age restrictions passed by the state legislature. Expenditures on PA recipients have been increasing steadily since 1967. The fee cutbacks for non-

institutional providers have been totally ineffective as a means
of controlling total expenditures for Medicaid. Payments to
institutions amount to $951 million by 1971, while noninstitu-
tional providers received only $162 million. Between 1969 and
1971 payments to noninstitutional providers grew by 13 percent
while institutional payments rose nearly 8 percent. [4]
     A close examination of the timing of the changes in hospital-
based ambulatory care strongly suggests that the changes in
coverage had no substantial impact, but the reductions in fees
were of major importance. Table 4 shows the number of visits
to municipal hospitals by six-month periods for the last five
fiscal years. The changes beginning in the latter half of 1969
are notable. Monthly series on outpatient and emergency room
visits also show that the growth in visits began after mid-1969
and leveled off more recently. [5]

TABLE 4

Total Number of Outpatient Departments and
Emergency Room Visits in New York City Muni-
cipal Hospitals, by Six-Month Intervals,
Fiscal Years, 1968-1972

(thousands)

	Outpatient Departments	Emergency Rooms	Total
2nd Half 1968	1,384	728	2,112
1st Half 1969	1,400	702	2,102
2nd Half 1969	1,399	707	2,106
1st Half 1970	1,453	773	2,226
2nd Half 1970	1,517	812	2,329
1st Half 1971	1,696	816	2,512
2nd Half 1971	1,647	817	2,464
1st Half 1972	1,640	795	2,435

Source: New York City Health and Hospitals Corporation,
         Hospital Statistics Service

IMPLICATIONS OF THE HISTORICAL EXPERIENCE

The fact that the growth in hospital-based ambulatory care began after mid-1969 and probably only lasted through 1971 strongly suggests that the responsible factor was the 20 percent cutback in Medicaid fees to noninstitutional providers which took place in July 1969. The state policy intended to save money did not do so, but instead substantially worsened the distribution of services. This development is particularly unfortunate both with regard to the substantial unmet need which already exists and in view of the far higher costs of treating patients in an outpatient department or emergency room than in a doctor's office.

Fees continue to get farther out of date as the cost of living rises. The reduced fees work to increase the chances that as physicians retire in neighborhoods with large indigent populations, they will not be replaced. The expansion of hospitals will attract more and more physicians away from neighborhood practice.

These patterns can be reversed through a fee structure which makes more adequate services by Medicaid physicians financially feasible, coupled with monitoring to assure proper services are provided.

A policy of more realistic fees for physicians in the Medicaid program would provide an inducement for physicians to expand services to underserved areas and thereby improve the distribution of services. It is becoming critical to find an alternative to the present choice between the low cost but often inadequate service in the Medicaid doctor's office and the high cost, more extensive, but also often inadequate service in outpatient departments. One approach is the organization of Medicaid physicians into group practice clinics with broader services, internal quality control mechanisms, and reimbursement rates which permit more complete care. The setting of reasonable reimbursement rates is a key step in making this possible.

Restoring the balance of fees between private practitioners and group practices and hospital-based services of care can relieve some of the overcrowding in outpatient departments and emergency rooms. This is an important first step toward reducing fragmentation and making these services more comprehensive.

FOOTNOTES

1. The Population Health Survey reported 4.3 visits per person per year to all sources (including telephone calls in the

definition of a visit) for 1964.   Other studies show up to 5 visits.
2.   Based on data for thirty-seven ghetto medicine and municipal hospitals in a forthcoming RAND Study.   Costs in 1970
averaged $24.49 exclusive of diagnostic and pharmacy costs.
3.   This may have occurred because patients showed up at
more distant doctors' offices, creating pressures for service,
at the same time as other doctors left the program.   The number of doctors seeing any Medicaid patients is a poor indicator
of the supply of physicians to Medicaid patients, since a very
small proportion of physicians provide the great bulk of the
service.
4.   Editor's note: Several tables and graphs were omitted here.
5.   Editor's note: Detailed tables on geographic impact were
omitted.

II-4 FINANCIAL INCENTIVES TO ENCOURAGE OUTPATIENT CARE: THE SWEDISH EXPERIENCE

by Elizabeth Rodgers

SUMMARY

The response to reforms introduced in 1970 in Sweden's system of payment for medical treatment is examined for the purpose of extracting clues which might be applicable to the United States.

In Sweden, hospital care is essentially free to patients. Outpatient care is financed mainly by social insurance and a portion of the visit charge is paid by the patient. One of the aims of reform was to reduce inpatient care by encouraging use of outpatient services. The reform changed outpatient financing, lowering patient expenditures and eliminating economic transactions between patients and government-salaried physicians. Administration of social insurance contribution for medical care was simplified considerably, and outpatients were no longer required to apply for reimbursement.

During the first year of reform, the total level of outpatient visits increased. Total visits to clinics in 1971 increased 5 percent over 1969; visits to district medical offices increased 29 percent, and visits to private practitioners increased 8 percent for the same period. In the wake of the increase, however, waiting time for outpatient visits increased dramatically, from an average 33-day wait in 1969 for clinics to 60 days in 1971, an average waiting period of 8 days in 1969 to 19 days in 1971 for district medical offices, and from 15 days for private physicians to 17 days in 1971.

Within outpatient care, there was a shift from hospital clinics to district medical offices. Physicians at hospital clinics, formerly reimbursed on a fee-for-service basis for outpatient care, were made full-time salaried employees.

(DMO physicians continued on full salaries but were permitted to attend private patients after hours on a fee-for-service basis.) This shift in payment of physicians removed economic incentives to hospital physicians to deliver ambulatory care, while retaining patient incentives to obtain free hospital care in lieu of modestly priced outpatient care. DMO physicians, on the other hand, could now increase income by providing additional care. The combined effect appears to be a reduction in hospital physician time spent with each patient, an increase in hospitalization, and an increasing use of district medical offices.

There was also a sharp increase in return visits. It appears that hospitals have an incentive to increase the number of return outpatient visits rather than to increase the number of persons served.

The reform, contrary to intention, led to higher utilization of inpatient facilities. The number of days of hospital treatment reimbursed by social insurance rose from 18 million to 22 million. To some extent, the sharp increase was the result of detection by outpatient services. Another explanation is that the flat rate fee and the long waiting lines encourage district medical officers and clinic doctors to send expensive or time-consuming cases to the hospitals earlier than under the fee-for-service system. The total amount of illness appears unchanged for the period, since the number of cases of sickness cash benefit remained virtually constant from 1969 and 1970.

Costs have increased for most categories of health care and at a faster rate than in previous years. The reform has increased patient demand for more and higher quality outpatient care. With economic barriers removed, services are provided in a more equitable fashion. To the consumer of outpatient health services, waiting time has replaced price as the principal rationer of care.

SWEDISH MEDICAL CARE PAYMENT REFORM

In January 1970, Sweden introduced a system of payment for medical treatment by government-salaried doctors. The reform resulted in significant changes in both demand and supply and increased expenditures by social insurance and government sectors. Some changes in quality of care are indicated by changes in waiting time and length of visit. Administrative procedures were simplified at the outset, and long-run adjustments or innovations in delivery are beginning to appear.

The aim of the reform was to:
(a) decrease escalating medical care costs by giving a financial incentive to patients to increase out-

patient utilization relative to inpatient utilization.
    (b) simplify a cumbersome administrative pro-
cedure of reimbursement.

BACKGROUND

Structure

    Before discussing the reform, it is necessary to describe
the structure of Swedish delivery of care. The provision of
medical care in Sweden is largely public and is mainly provided
by county level government with contributions from the national
government and the social insurance fund.

Total Medical Care Bill, * 1969

Counties	67%
State	21%
Social Insurance	12%

    *net expenses for health and medical
care, operations and investment. [1]

    The primary responsibility of the twenty-four county
councils and three municipalities is to provide for the medical
and mental health of their residents. [2] Under this mandate, the
counties own and operate the 891 hospitals, [3] which are financed
through a local income tax and a token payment of 10 Sw. Cr.
($2.00) per patient day from inpatients. (Patients are later
reimbursed for this charge by social insurance.) Further, the
counties are responsible for appointing one or more physicians
as district medical officers in each of 750 local health districts.
Eighty percent of county budgets are spent on health care. [4]
    The district medical officers act as general practitioners
and public health officials, and are not affiliated with hospitals.
The counties, municipalities, and "other communes" contributed 67 percent of the net national expenses for health and
medical care, operations, and investments in 1969. [5]
    The state or central government provided 21 percent of
1969 net expenses for health and sick care. [6] The state has two
levels of operations: the Ministry of Health and Social Affairs
and the National Board of Health and Social Welfare.
    The Ministry of Health shapes national legislation, bud-
gets central government subsidy in the health field, and has
several administrative functions.
    The National Board of Health and Welfare has supervisory

functions: It is responsible for inspecting the quality of medical
care activities and has the power to create positions for public
employment of doctors. The board also has an investigative
function through its Medical Appeals Board, which hears mal-
practice or neglect cases, and a Certificate of Need function
through its Board of Medical and Social Welfare Buildings.[7]
The state also has created a Public Health Institute and a
National Bacteriology Laboratory.[8]

The National Health Insurance Board is the third major
institution concerned with health care. It spent 12 percent of
the 1969 total medical care bill.[9] Prior to 1970, the board
compensated insured members for 75 percent of their ambulatory care for part of medicines and for inpatient fees in public
wards. Over and above the health and sick care direct reimbursement, the insurance board also guarantees a certain
income in time of illness.[10]

In 1969 the Social Insurance Board was financed:

from employers' contributions	47%
from registered persons	40%
from state subsidies	12%
and from interest and other receipts	1%
	100%[11]

Supply of Outpatient Care

It has been possible to piece together a fragmentary
analysis of supply of 1969 outpatient care. There were three
principal sources:

	% total out-patient cases	No. of centers	Physicians
General hospital clinics	53%[12]	114[13]	4,660[14]
District medical centers	21%[15]	856[16]	1,250[17]
Private full-time practitioners	26%[18]		950[19]

Prices were charged by physicians on a fee-for-service
basis at time of delivery and patients were later reimbursed
by social insurance for three-fourths of a prescribed tariff.
The hospital physician was paid a lump-sum salary for inpatient
care, but there was financial incentive to treat outpatients on
a fee-for-service basis. This incentive is reflected in some
comparative utilization rates where a clear-cut outpatient alternative is possible. For example, a pre-reform 1963 study
showed that tonsillectomies appear to be performed in Sweden
only when outpatient adenoidectomies have failed to significantly
improve the patient's condition.[20]

On the other hand, incentives to hospitalize existed because
hospital care was free to the patient while ambulatory care was
not.

The Reform

The January 1970 reform aimed to decrease pressure on hospital care by making outpatient care more attractive. It changed outpatient financing to lower patient expenditure and to eliminate economic transactions between patients and physicians, increasing hospital physician salaries to cover outpatient care and eliminating fee for service.

Hospitals or clinics charged the outpatient 7 Sw. Cr. per visit, regardless of the scope of treatment or medications, and charged Social Insurance 31 Sw. Cr. per visit. Private patients continued to be reimbursed at 75 percent of a fixed fee schedule. In order to attract physicians to primary care, district medical officers were allowed to accept private patients after the required work hours.[21] Table 1 depicts the financial transactions before and after the reform. (In January 1973, following two years of rising costs, patient fees were increased from 7 to 12 Sw. Cr. per visit, and the social insurance contribution rose from 31 to 48 Sw. Cr. per visit.)

THE IMPACT OF THE SEVEN CROWN REFORM

Changes in Demand

The total level of outpatient visits demanded increased. While we do not yet have total figures, a survey conducted in late 1971 reveals the trend toward the increased number of visits and the dramatic increases in waiting time. Changes between 1969 and 1971 are summarized in Table 2. While total visits to clinics increased 5 percent, waiting time increased 82 percent, from a 33- to 60-day average wait. Total visits to district medical offices increased 29 percent, with waiting time increasing 137 percent, from 8 days to an average wait of 19 days.[22] Private practitioners absorbed some of the increased demand: an 8 percent increase in total visits and a 13 percent increase in waiting time from 15 to 17 days, at average fee of 40 Sw. Cr. per visit. There also was a shift, within outpatient care, toward greater utilization of district medical centers relative to hospital clinics.

The explanation for the shift in demand toward district medical officers seems to be found in both the long initial waiting time at clinics in 1969, a post-reform contraction in physician hours at clinics, and an increase in staff at district medical offices.

There was a sharp increase in return visits. Per visit reimbursement was fixed at 38 (31 + 7) Sw. Cr. to cover lab fees and X-rays. The increase in return visits may have been

TABLE 1

FINANCIAL TRANSACTIONS

Before Reform	After Reform
OUTPATIENT paid doctors' fee but was reimbursed 75% by Social Insurance. Final out-of-pocket cost was about 10 Sw. Cr. for routine visits, more for lab tests and X-rays.	OUTPATIENT paid only 7 Sw. Cr. per visit, regardless of scope of treatment, or medication. (Jan. 1973 fee raised to 12 Sw. Cr.).
Outpatient also paid 5-15 Sw. Cr. for medicines.	Covered in the one 7 Sw. Cr. fee.
INPATIENT paid 10 Sw. Cr. / day, but was reimbursed full amount by social insurance, unless pensioner after 365 days of benefit.	INPATIENT continued to be charged 10 Sw. Cr. with reimbursement by social insurance, unless pensioner after 365 days of benefit.
SOCIAL INSURANCE reimbursed outpatients for 75% doctor's fee, or about 30 Sw. Cr. for routine visits, more when expensive treatments required.	Pays hospital or county 31 Sw. Cr. per outpatient visit regardless of scope of treatment or medication. Reimburses patients of private doctors 75% of fixed fee schedule.
Reimbursed inpatients 10 Sw. Cr. per day, unless pensioner after 365 days of benefit.	Same
COUNTY COUNCIL paid doctors an inpatient salary, about 6,000 Sw. Cr., equal to about 1/2 annual income if doctor active with fee-paying ambulatory patients.[22] Financed hospital and district medical offices with local taxes, minimal central government subsidies and token inpatient fees.	Paid doctors full salary for 45 to 50-hour workweek and forbade hospital doctors from charging fees to patients. Salary based on years of training regardless of specialty. Financed hospital and district medical offices with local taxes minimal central government subsidies, token fees, and substantial contributions from social insurance. Research was now covered by salary equal to ambulatory care. District medical officers were permitted to supplement income by fee-for-service for care after official work hours.

TABLE 2

INCREASED VISITS AND WAITING TIME SINCE 1969[24]

	Clinics	DMO's	Private Practitioners
1.0 - Average Waiting Time in Days			
1.1 - 1969	33	8	15
1.2 - 1971	60	19	17
1.3 - Change in average waiting time - %	+82%	+137%	+13%
1.4 - 1971 waiting time, with various specialties:	Surgery	36 days	
	Ears	53 days	
	Psychiatry	69 days	
	Medicine	81 days	
	Gynecology	116 days	
	Eyes	165 days	
2.0 - Doctor's Time Spent with Patient			
2.1 - 1969	26	16	24
2.2 - 1971	21	16	22
3.0 - Total Visits per Week			
3.1 - 1969	235	110	86
3.2 - 1971	248	142	93
3.3 - Change in total visits per week	+5%	+29%	+8%
3.4 - Change in return visits	+13%	+25%	+6.5%
3.5 - Change in new visits	9%	+36%	+12.0%
4.0 - Doctor-Patient Contact			

Hours = $\dfrac{(2.1) \times (3.1)}{60 \text{ minutes}}$

	Clinics	DMO's	Private Practitioners
4.1 - 1969	101.83 hrs.	29.33 hrs.	34.4
4.2 - $\dfrac{(2.2) \times (3.2)}{60 \text{ minutes}}$ - 1971	86.80 hrs.	37.87 hrs.	34.1
4.3 - Change from 1969-71	-15%	+29%	-1%

associated with a decreased service per visit, which would be
equivalent to a price increase. The decrease in length of outpatient visits is consistent with this view. Inpatient care also
increased. The total number of bed days increased only 2 percent.[25] The number of days of hospital treatment reimbursed
by insurance rose from 18 million to 22 million.[26] While hospital admissions rose, the number of cases of sickness cash
benefit per 100 registered persons (paid from the day after a
person falls ill) remained virtually constant at 110 and 109 in
1969 and 1970 respectively.[27] It thus appears that while days
of sickness per person was constant, the reform led to significantly higher participation in institutional medical care.

Increased hospitalization may have arisen from a number
of sources. Increased screening and case-finding may have
been a factor, but two other factors are reported as well. The
long waiting times for ambulatory care may have resulted in
a shift of patients to hospitals for the more time-consuming
procedures. Furthermore, with a shift from fee-for-service
to salaried practice, physicians could no longer raise incomes
by seeing more ambulatory patients, and the relative incentives
shifted in favor of more frequent hospitalization.

Supply

The huge increases in waiting time (82 percent and 137
percent) do not seem to be explainable by the increased demand
(5 and 29 percent) to clinics and district medical offices alone.
Perhaps existing waiting lines of 33 and 8 days had already
created capacity production of care. The patient-contact hours
of doctors decreased at clinics, from an average of 102 hours
per week per clinic to 87 hours per week per clinic after the
reform, but there was a rise in reported hours at district
medical offices.

Andrews, Werko, and Bjorck report that the removal of
fee for service in outpatient care, the prohibition against doctors making specific personal appointments, and the introduction
of payment for research have all contributed to a reduced desire
among physicians to perform ambulatory care.[28] However,
Wilson points to the growing reliance on hospital clinics prior
to the reform as an indication that the shift away from personal
physicians predated the reform.[29]

District medical officers, with a 1969 waiting period of 8
days, were relatively more available than hospital-based physicians, and seem to have increased patient-doctor hours from
29.3 to 37.9 per week.

The increase in total demand and the relative shift in
demand for district medical officers are already being affected
by the supply pipeline. Total active doctors increased from

10,376 in 1969 to 10,949 in 1970. Medical school classes have
been increased from 457 admitted in 1960 to 896 admitted in
1969 and 956 admitted in 1970.[30] Furthermore, the training
now requires six months of public service, which has increased
the supply to the district medical offices. The number of active
doctors is expected to rise from the present 10,000 to 16,000
by 1975, and to 20,000 by 1985. The National Board of Health
and Welfare, which establishes new public service positions
for doctors, expects to double the number of physicians in outpatient clinics by 1975.[31] It seems very probable that the long
waiting period will generate the needed public support for more
staff and resources in the ambulatory care category.

The demand pressures have also been relieved by innovation in health manpower responsibilities. Nurses have been
upgraded in obstetrics and X-ray fields, and assistant nurses
have been given further responsibilities.[32]

Changes in Quality of Care

Since the reform, the average waiting time to see doctors
has increased as described; the reported number of minutes
spent with a patient has dropped slightly but remained at a high
level. Clinic patients see doctors for 21 minutes rather than
the 26 minutes reported before the reform; district medical
office patients' consultations last 16 minutes, constant since
1969, and private patients have 22 minutes with their doctors
compared with 24 minutes in 1969. These times compare favorably with Canadian experience, where length of time of visits
after introduction of Medicare fell to 16 minutes for office
visits and 11 minutes in clinics.[33] Full figures on lab tests
and X-rays are not available, but 51 percent of clinics reported
increases in tests and 38 percent had increased X-rays.[34]

Sweden reported post-reform increases in the number of
nonacute patients demanding emergency care. This could be
due to overflow from extreme delays in outpatient care as much
as from removal of economic barriers to care. The very
inexpensive care might attract patients who do not appear to
have reasonable cause, but it also enables anyone to come forward at an early stage of illness. The Swedes have instituted
the reform, believing the benefits from equal access to outweigh the costs of "unnecessary demands."

Administrative Impact

The administration of the social insurance contribution for
medical care has been considerably simplified. Outpatients
no longer must collect receipts and apply for reimbursement.

Patients pay the hospital cashier 7 Sw. Cr. at time of service, and social insurance pays the county council 31 Sw. Cr. for every patient treated.

Costs

The reform did not reduce costs the first year. In fact, for almost every category for which we have figures, the cost increased at a faster rate than the average for the four years prior to the reform. While we do not have the change in the total medical care bill 1969-1970, we can look at changes in social insurance, hospital running expenses, and council expenditures in the year following the reform.

Predictably, social insurance payments for outpatient care increased 11 percent, a rate much higher than the 6 percent average annual increase from 1965 to 1969.

Cost to social insurance for outpatient service rose from 300 million Sw. Cr. in 1969 to 432 million Sw. Cr. in 1971, an average annual increase of 20 percent. It appeared to level off in the first six months of the third year, when it rose at an annual rate of 2.3 percent. The increased expenditure by social insurance was financed by a redistribution of contributions. Employers' contributions in 1970 fell to 37 percent of total receipts, compared with 47 percent in 1969, prior to the reform. Registered persons contributed 50 percent of the total insurance receipts, up from 40 percent prior to the reform in 1969. State subsidies stayed constant at 12 percent, as did interest and other receipts at 1 percent. [35] Thus the social insurance increased both the absolute and relative contributions of registered persons, while the employers' contributions decreased in relative terms. The contributions of registered persons are based on their normal annual earnings, and are thus progressive. The fixed flat-rate payment at time of service, increased to 12 Sw. Cr. in 1973, is, however, regressive. The net distribution effect although unclear, is probably slightly progressive. The major change appears to be not reduced cost of care, but the reduction of economic hardship or actual barriers to ambulatory care in time of need.

Total medical care and medicine reimbursement (which included fees charged for hospital inpatient care) also increased at an increasing rate: 25 percent from 1969 to 1970, compared with a 17 percent average annual increase from 1965 to 1969. [36] This reflects the 22 percent rise in the number of days of hospital treatment reimbursed by social insurance (18 million to 22 million.) [37]

The social insurance expenditure per covered person rose

from 183.7 Sw. Cr. in 1969 to 227.1 Sw. Cr. in 1970, an increase
of 24 percent. While we do not have figures for number of persons covered in 1965, we know that the 1968 to 1969 (pre-reform)
increase was only 8.8 percent.[38]

Hospital bed days increased 2.1 percent, but running costs
rose 20 percent, compared with an average annual rise of 17
percent from 1965 to 1969. Running costs per bed day rose 17
percent, slightly higher than the 16.4 percent increase over
the four-year pre-reform period.[39]

The 1970 county council medical bill, which includes the
large share of hospital costs as well as district medical offices,
rose 21 percent, slightly less than the 24 percent average annual
rise from 1965 to 1969. This 21 percent annual rate of increase
was projected to continue in budgeted 1971 figures and estimated
1972 figures. Similarly, the projected annual increase for
total county investment and operations is 23 percent over the
1969-1972 period. The increased investment is projected to
expand joint service centers for district medical offices.

DISCUSSION

Publicly employed doctors were given fixed working
hours of 50 to 55 hours per week at a set salary. A Swedish post-reform survey of clinics and district medical
offices indicates that there was a decrease in the total number of hours clinic doctors spent with patients. Outpatient
cases were therefore severely rationed by more than 80 percent increases in waiting time at clinics.

Long-term efforts to remedy this shortage are begun.
Medical school classes have doubled from 1960 size, and nurses
are being upgraded to nurse practitioners in some areas. As
the number of personnel required increased sharply with the
added caseloads and reduced doctors' hours, the labor bill will
certainly rise. Outpatient costs from all these sources should
therefore rise substantially.

Hospital physician payment for outpatient care shifted
from fee-for-service to salary based only on years of training,
with the result that ambulatory specialists faced a drop in
salary and research salaries were relatively more attractive.
Indications are that physicians spent less time in direct patient
contact after the reform, but the government is increasing the
supply of physicians and trying to attract doctors into primary
care. It would appear, then, that the reform would increase
patients' demands for more and higher-quality outpatient care,
while giving physicians incentive to increase hospitalization of
difficult or time-intensive cases.

The reformed system is hallmarked by equity of access to care where waiting time has replaced price as the principal rationer of medical care. There is almost complete prepayment and the majority of physicians are now on salaries determined by years of training, regardless of specialty. The reform has succeeded in spreading equity, but has not controlled hospital cost inflation. In fact, in trying to discourage hospitalization, it seems to have built in incentives to hospitalize.

FOOTNOTES

1. Allman Halso och Sjukvard, 1969, Sverige Officiella Statistik, Social Styrelsen, Stockhom, 1972, p. 94, Table Cl.
2. Health and Medical Care Services: The County Councils in Sweden, Federation of Swedish County Councils, 1971.
3. Statistik Arsbok, 1972, Statistical Abstract of Sweden, Utgivare, Stetistika Centralbyran, p. 279.
4. Health and Medical Care Services.
5. Allman, p. 94.
6. Ibid.
7. "Organization of Medical Care," Fact Sheets on Sweden, Swedish Institute, 1971.
8. Health and Medical Care Services, pp. 3-4.
9. Allman, p. 94.
10. Social Benefits in Sweden, Trugghausa, Forlagsverksam-heten 1972, p. 24.
11. Statistik Arsbok, p. 262.
12. Allman, p. 59.
13. Ibid.
14. Health and Medical Care Services, p. 8.
15. Dr. N.B. Alyndgren, op. cit.
16. Health and Medical Care Services, p. 7.
17. Ibid., pp. 6-7.
18. J.L. Andrews, "Medical Care in Sweden Lessons for America," p. 11, in U.S. Senate Subcommittee on Health of the Committee on Labor and Public Welfare, Fact-Finding Visit to Europe and Israel, U.S. Government Printing Office, Washington, December 1972.
19. Ibid.
20. Ragner Berfenstam in The Swedish Health Services System, ACHA, Chicago, 1971, p. 173.
21. Alan Wilson, "Outcome of the Standard Medical Reforms in Sweden," Royal Ministry for Foreign Affairs, December 1972, p. 5.
22. Lars Werko, "Swedish Medical Care in Transition," Appendix J in U.S. Senate Subcommittee on Health, op. cit., p. 519.

23. Social insurance reimbursed public ward inpatient fees except for those on pensions after the 365th day of benefit. People over sixty-five utilize 41 percent of all bed days. (Ragnar Berfenstam, in The Swedish Health Services System, ACHA, Chicago, 1971, p. 169.)

24. Wilson, pp. 1-5.

25. Statistik Arsbok, p. 279.

26. Total bed days increased from 40.3 to 41.2 million bed days. This is a gross figure of hospital patient days, however, which apparently includes rest homes and institutions providing minimal health services. Ibid., p. 262.

27. Statistik Arsbok, p. 262.

28. Gunnar Bjorck, "One Man's Opinion, an Insider's View, Medicine in Sweden," Appendix 3, in U.S. Senate Subcommittee on Health, p. 472 ff.

29. Wilson, p. 3.

30. Allman, p. 90.

31. Health and Medical Care Services, p. 9.

32. Organization of Medical Care, p. 2.

33. Philip E. Enterline et al., "The Effects of Free Medical Care on Medical Practice: The Quebec Experience" (unpublished, 1972).

34. Wilson, p. 5.

35. Statistik Arsbok, p. 263.

36. Ibid., p. 262.

37. For those on pensions, only the first 365 days are reimbursed. Extrapolated from Allman, pp. 262-263.

38. Statistik Arsbok, p. 279.

39. Health and Medical Care Services, p. 20.

II-5   PHYSICIAN STAFFING STUDY — September 2, 1971

by Smith Lanning

SUMMARY

This study attempts to relate physician staffing levels to physician work load in twelve municipal hospitals. The physician hour is considered as the major unit of input. The patient day represents physician output. While the data available for this comparison are rather crude, several conclusions are quite evident:

1. The municipal hospital system is significantly over-staffed by physicians. For the twelve hospitals under study an average of 1.8 hours or 106 minutes of physician time per patient day was available from January to June 1970. (See Tables 1 and 2.) This includes the time of attending physicians, residents, and interns of affiliate and city hospitals. It excludes physician time required for outpatient and emergency care.

The required amount of physician time per patient day is a subject of some dispute. If one hour per patient day were sufficient time for patient care, education, research, and administrative duties, then the Health and Hospitals Corporation could do with a reduction of 43 percent in the current level of inpatient physician staffing. This amounts to somewhere between $15 million and $20 million in potential savings annually.

2. The apparent excess of physician time for inpatient activity is not explained by a dearth of time available for ambulatory care. In fact, the opposite seems true. From January to June 1970 the twelve municipal hospitals under study provided an average of 35 minutes of physician time for every emergency and outpatient visit (Table 3). In other words, physicians were seeing fewer than two patients per hour in clinics and emergency rooms combined. This is by no means an excessive work load.

TABLE 1

Average Physician Time: All Services
(Minutes per Patient Day)

Hospital	Total Minutes	Physician Attending	Resident	Intern	Total Hours
Cumberland	325	102	190	33	5.4
Lincoln	177	112	50	15	2.9
Metropolitan	131	46	51	34	2.2
Morrisania	123	40	58	25	2.0
Queens	98	32	49	17	1.6
Coney Island	97	33	46	18	1.6
Fordham	83	41	33	9	1.4
Bronx Municipal	79	21	43	15	1.3
Harlem	76	34	19	23	1.3
Sydenham	75	54	21	0	1.3
Elmhurst	75	25	36	14	1.2
Greenpoint	73	30	35	8	1.2
Total Average	106				1.8

Note 1: This data covers the period January to June 1970 with the exception of Lincoln Hospital. The data from Lincoln covers from January to December 1969.

Note 2: This data excludes chronic and extended care statistics.

TABLE 2

Average Physician Time by Service
(Minutes per Patient Day)

Hospital	Total Services	Medicine Only	Surgery Only	Pediatrics Only
Cumberland	325	276	325	528
Lincoln	177	250	167	153
Metropolitan	131	137	125	139
Morrisania	123	128	119	132
Queens	98	93	122	106
Coney Island	97	133	74	106
Fordham	83	74	74	101
Bronx Municipal	79	59	160	97
Harlem	76	82	179	59
Sydenham	75	57	95	61
Elmhurst	75	79	101	76
Greenpoint	73	70	91	70
Total Average	106	106	132	128

Note 1:   This data includes the time of attending physicians,
          residents and interns.

Note 2:   Data period - January to June 1970 except Lincoln
          which is January to December 1969.

TABLE 3

Ambulatory Visits: Average Physician Time

Hospital	Number of ER and OPD Visits[1]	Available Physician Minutes per Visit
Metropolitan	206,000	49.7
Elmhurst	156,000	46.2
Coney Island	124,000	44.3
Lincoln	363,000	39.3
Queens	144,000	39.1
Greenpoint	99,000	34.7
Morrisania	128,000	29.9
Cumberland	130,000	29.6
Sydenham	40,000	23.4
Fordham	111,000	21.0
Harlem	215,000	20.7
Average		35.4

1. The number of visits from January to June 1970 was estimated by dividing total ER and OPD visits for calendar 1970 by 2. In the case of Lincoln Hospital, actual visits for calendar 1969 were used.

3. There is an extremely wide variation in physician
time available per patient day from one hospital to another.
Cumberland Hospital pays for 5.4 hours of physician time per
patient day while Elmhurst pays for only 1.2 hours.
4. There are also wide variations in physician time available for a given service. For example, in surgery, Harlem
Hospital pays for 3.0 hours of physician time for every surgery
patient day. Coney Island and Fordham Hospitals provide 1.2
hours of surgery per patient. In medicine, Lincoln Hospital
provides 4.2 hours per medicine patient day, while the average
for medicine is 1.8 hours, and Bronx Municipal Hospital provides only 1.0 hours. (See Tables 4 to 7.)
    The above physician work load data represents an aggre-
gate picture of how much physician time is available for every
patient day. The most obvious question that the data raises is
how much physician time is really <u>received</u> by the patient.
Clearly the patient does not get 106 minutes of physician time
each day, the average available time for the entire system
(Table 1). Nor is it likely that he needs that much time.
    Aside from providing direct patient care, the physician
is also involved in educational, research, and administrative
activities. Much of that 106 minutes is probably going to these
indirect functions. And most likely the intern's time is divided
among direct patient care and indirect activities differently
from the resident's time, which is also different from the
breakdown of the attending physician's time.
    While we do not know how much time the intern, resident,
or attending physician spends directly with patients right now,
we do know that HHC is paying for too much intern, resident,
and attending time in total in certain hospitals and in certain
services. By simply comparing the physician availability at,
say, Elmhurst (a hospital generally considered to provide reasonable care) with physician availability at Queens or Metropolitan, we can conclude with reasonable certainty that Queens and
Metropolitan are overstaffed, <u>regardless of how their physicians
spend their time</u>.
    For example, there are more attending physician minutes
(46), more resident minutes (51), and more intern minutes (34)
per patient day at Metropolitan than at Elmhurst (attendings-25
minutes; residents-36 minutes; interns-14 minutes) from Table 1.
Furthermore, there are more minutes per medicine patient
(137), more per surgery patient (125), and more per pediatrics
patient (139) at Metropolitan than at Elmhurst (medicine minutes-
79; surgery minutes-101; and pediatrics minutes-76), according
to Table 2. If the excess physician minutes at Metropolitan are
spent on educational, research, and administrative activities,
then HHC must decide how much time they are willing to pay
for in these indirect activities and take measures to enforce
that decision.

TABLE 4

Medicine: Average Physician Time
(Minutes per Patient Day)

Hospital	Total Medicine Minutes	Attending Physician	Resident	Intern	Total Hours
Cumberland	276	73	161	42	4.6
Lincoln	250	170	38	42	4.2
Metropolitan	137	31	52	54	2.3
Coney Island	133	37	63	33	2.2
Morrisania	128	30	65	33	2.1
Queens	93	30	45	18	1.6
Harlem	82	27	23	32	1.4
Elmhurst	79	19	35	25	1.3
Fordham	74	24	41	9	1.2
Greenpoint	70	36	23	11	1.2
Bronx Municipal	59	16	28	15	1.0
Sydenham	57	54	3	0	1.0
Total Average	106				1.8

Note: Data period - January to June 1970, except Lincoln,
which covers January to December 1969.

TABLE 5

Surgery: Average Physician Time
(Minutes per Patient Day)

Hospital	Total Surgery Minutes	Attending Physician	Resident	Intern	Total Hours
Cumberland	325	111	185	29	5.4
Harlem	179	79	51	49	3.0
Lincoln	167	93	66	8	2.8
Bronx Municipal	160	27	86	47	2.7
Metropolitan	125	44	48	33	2.1
Queens	122	33	67	22	2.0
Morrisania	119	56	55	8	2.0
Elmhurst	101	44	27	30	1.7
Sydenham	95	51	44	0	1.6
Greenpoint	91	31	44	16	1.5
Coney Island	74	30	37	7	1.2
Fordham	74	58	9	7	1.2
Total Average	132				2.2

Note: Data period - January to June 1970, except Lincoln, which covers January to December 1969.

TABLE 6

Pediatrics: Average Physician Time
(Minutes per Patient Day)

Hospital	Total Pediatrics Minutes	Attending Physician	Resident	Intern	Total Hours
Cumberland	528	199	285	44	8.8
Lincoln	153	93	49	11	2.6
Metropolitan	139	40	29	70	2.3
Morrisania	132	37	44	51	2.2
Queens	106	31	47	28	1.8
Coney Island	106	31	75	0	1.8
Fordham	101	58	31	12	1.7
Bronx Municipal	97	19	41	37	1.6
Elmhurst	76	26	28	22	1.3
Greenpoint	70	31	39	0	1.2
Sydenham	61	61	0	0	1.0
Harlem	59	27	17	15	1.0
Total Average	128				2.1

Note: Data period - January to June 1970, except Lincoln,
which covers January to December 1969.

TABLE 7

Obstetrics/Gynecology: Average Physician Time
(Minutes per Patient Day)

Hospital	Total OB/GYN Minutes	Attending Physician	Resident	Intern	Total Hours
Cumberland	200	63	122	15	3.3
Lincoln	130	79	51	0	2.2
Metropolitan	119	51	68	0	2.0
Queens	110	49	38	23	1.8
Morrisania	109	30	64	15	1.8
Bronx Municipal	101	15	86	0	1.7
Fordham	88	44	34	10	1.5
Coney Island	87	33	33	21	1.4
Elmhurst	74	26	25	23	1.2
Sydenham	61	52	9	0	1.0
Greenpoint	55	20	35	0	0.9
Harlem	37	12	7	18	0.6
Total Average	96				1.6

Note: Data period - January to June 1970, except Lincoln,
which covers January to December 1969.

Simple comparisons of this type can and should be made. More important, we should probably move toward the establishment of some standards or standard guidelines for physician staffing. A very simple "first-cut" approach would be to select an exemplary hospital, such as Elmhurst, and to utilize Elmhurst's staffing level (75 minutes per patient day) as a standard for all hospitals to work toward. Probably more effective than this would be to select exemplary services at different hospitals (59 medical minutes at Bronx Municipal, 101 surgery minutes at Elmhurst, 59 pediatrics minutes at Harlem) and to utilize staffing levels of these services as "standards."

Combined with this approach should probably be some rules regulating the <u>physician mix</u> (among attendings, residents, and interns) and thereby the amount of physician education supported by HHC. For example, HHC might want to specify that the time of residents and interns should not exceed, say, 65 percent of total physician time available in the hospital. The level specified obviously would require further study and might well vary from one hospital to another.

Ultimately HHC will want to determine exactly how much physician time their patients really get. This would have to be determined from a field audit of the way a sample of physicians actually spend their day in the hospital. From this data a standard "from the base up" could then be derived by adding x amount of time for research and education and y amount of time for administrative activities to whatever time is found to be spent in direct patient care.

If this basic type of standard were coupled with an effective enforcement procedure, HHC might well be able to begin to control the elusive physician. The control procedure could consist of unannounced "observation audits" of the physician's daily tasks. The results of the audits would have to be tied directly to the affiliation contract to be effective, perhaps through a "deductibility" clause. Such a clause might call for penalizing the affiliate by the cost of that amount of physician time spent on patient care <u>in deficit</u> of the standard time to be spent on the patient care.

In addition to the above approaches to developing a standard for physician time required, a comparison with physician staffing levels at other hospitals should be made. Data on the Kaiser Permanente hospital system and the Veterans Administration hospitals would provide a guide of how much physician time is required for direct patient care.

METHODOLOGY

Allocation and Aggregation Assumptions

In order to compare physician input with work load as

measured by patient days, several allocation decisions had to
be made to match specific types of physicians. The raw data
on physician time (from the hospital expense report) was broken
into sixteen major physician categories corresponding to cost
centers.

While the unit patient day was used as the general measure for work load, two modifications were made. The first
was to weight intermediate care patient days at one-half the
value of general care days. This was done to account for the
fact that substantially less physician time is required to care
for an intermediate care patient than for an acute care patient.
The weighting factor of one intermediate care day equals one-
half acute care day is probably conservative in that an intermediate care patient actually requires less than half the physician
time required by an acute care patient.

The second modification was to include newborn days as
part of the work load of pediatric physicians. Since less physician time is typically required per newborn day than per acute
care day, each newborn day was considered to be equal to one-
third acute day in terms of the need for physician care.

Allocation of Intern Time--The total intern inpatient time
available was not divided among services, as were resident and
attending physician times. For purposes of this report the
total intern time was allocated at each hospital to the medicine,
surgery, pediatrics, and obstetrics/gynecology services.[1] The
allocation was based on a consideration of the following factors:

1. Number of internships offered by service by hospital
for FY 1970-71.
2. Relative dollar size of residency programs in medicine, surgery, pediatrics, and obstetrics/gynecology.
3. Relative size of average daily census in the medicine, surgery, pediatrics, and obstetrics/gynecology
services.

The allocation utilized in this report attempts to account
for the fact that rotating internships provide several months of
time in several different services. However, as it now stands,
the allocation of interns is crude and should be improved upon.[2]

FOOTNOTES

1. Dental intern time was treated separately and was allocated
to the surgery service.
2. Editor's note: Many tables of detailed data and methodology
have been omitted.

III

Program, Agency,

and

Process Evaluation

Since three-fourths of the city's tax levy dollars for
health services were being expended by the HHC in 1970, and
since the HHC mainly served disadvantaged persons, it is understandable that some members of the HSA analysis staff would
seek to push the HSA administrator to focus on the problems of
the Health and Hospitals Corporation. For the reasons outlined
in Chapter I and because of the newness of HHC, the HSA administrator did not press policy confrontations between the city
and the corporation during its first year. Further, since he
could more easily influence those agencies under his direct
control, the HSA administrator decided to devote most of his
time during his first year to his programmatic responsibilities
with the N.Y.C. Health and Mental Health Departments.

THE 1971 PROGRAM GUIDANCE LETTER

Given the actual and self-imposed constraints on the HSA
administrator's actions in 1970 concerning the HHC, the then
deputy administrator for program analysis, planning, and
budgeting of HSA, Robert Harris, sought to at least establish
the principle of HSA oversight over HHC. This led to an initial
Program Guidance Letter in July 1970, which had the full
approval of the administrator. The precedent was followed in
1971 by the Program Guidance Letter reproduced in this book. [1]
There are several noteworthy points about this letter.
First, the introductory section was deliberately "sugar-coated"
in order to make the more concrete suggestions or requests
more palatable to top HHC staff. For instance, the corporation
had not begun to "develop a strategy for ambulatory care" and
the central staff of the HHC had little to do with the implementa-

tion of the abortion program in its hospitals. This was done at
the individual hospital level, under the direct prodding of Gordon
Chase and Dr. Stanley Bergen, HHC senior vice-president.
Yet HHC was credited for these developments. Second, few of
the HSA recommendations in the letter were ever implemented
because of HHC management problems. Third, the letter was
probably counterproductive since it was leaked to The New York
Times and this increased the hostile feelings between certain
members of HSA and HHC staffs.

PROBLEMS WITH HHC--THE FUNDAMENTALS

The memorandum from Robert Harris, then deputy administrator, to Gordon Chase, administrator of HSA, is an example
of a "parting shot" by a policy analyst who resigned in part
because he could no longer in good conscience support the policies of the city in doing little to improve the performance of
HHC while continuing to claim success. This memorandum
has been included by the editors because we believe it gives the
reader some insights into the frustrations and role limitations
that are part of any policy analyst's job. At the same time it
presents a cogent, and in our view reasonably accurate, account
of the historical background leading up to the creation of HHC,
and an analysis of some of the problems with the HHC during
its initial year. Unfortunately, the prognosis for the future
of the HHC presented in this memo proved to be generally
accurate for the next three years.

THE BENEFIT/COST ANALYSIS OF HEROIN PROGRAMS

During the spring of 1970 when the HSA program analysis
staff was first formed, the problem of heroin addiction was
widely thought to be New York City's prime health and social
problem. The mayor and his top aides realized that this was
a multifaceted problem which might attain dimensions beyond
the control of local governmental initiatives unless rigorous
and innovative prevention and treatment programs were undertaken. The number of heroin addicts in the city was then
estimated at between 100,000 and 150,000, and the total addict
population was conservatively estimated to be growing at an
annual rate of at least 10 percent. Moreover, in 1969 the New
York City medical examiner recorded nine hundred deaths from
heroin overdoses, while the police commissioner was estimating
that heroin addicts were responsible for nearly half of all property crimes in the city.
When Alan Craig Leslie chose to undertake the benefit/
cost analysis of heroin addition problems and programs in the

fall of 1970, a great diversity of voluntary abstinence programs were available to addicts in New York City. These ranged from the large Phoenix House program patterned after the Synanon alcoholism program with its emphasis on encounter groups in residential therapeutic communities in which the addict is made substantially responsible for his own treatment to programs emphasizing professional psychotherapy such as Odyssey House.

There was an absence of good data in these programs, and it was hypothesized by some HSA analytic staff that these programs were just not doing the job. Further, Leslie believed that it could be shown that a multifaceted approach to the problem of treating heroin addiction would be more effective than any single approach, and he thought that his analysis might make a good case for this point of view. At that time, New York City was just beginning a city-sponsored methadone maintenance program which would ultimately have over 11,000 addicts in treatment by 1974. While most of the city's drug treatment programs were under the aegis of the city's Narcotics Addiction Agency, HSA had been given the responsibility of implementing the city's methadone program because the mayor regarded Chase as a "doer."

One reason we believe this analysis is of interest is because it represents the most ambitious effort by the program analysis staff to apply formal benefit/cost methodology to a problem. Moreover, the analysis contained several interesting conclusions which were helpful, but not decisive, in convincing those policy-makers like Chase to develop and implement heroin detoxification programs and an antagonist research program, at a time when the city had not yet implemented these programs. His analysis also indicated that the consequences of heroin addiction were so severe that even the most ineffectual approaches to the treatment and prevention of heroin addiction resulted in benefits which exceeded costs.

The Leslie analysis probably did not decisively influence policy directly. But this study, and the knowledge he gained from it, led to the recognition by the mayor and Chase that Leslie was the city's in-house staff "expert" on heroin addiction. Consequently, Leslie played a very substantial staff role in the further development and implementation of the city's drug antagonist and methadone maintenance programs.

We were unable to reproduce this analysis fully because of space limitations. Appendices dealing with the theoretical framework, the calculation of benefits, the cost/benefit evaluations of twelve program alternatives, the sensitivity analysis of the cost/benefit evaluations, and various statistical tables were all deleted. We have endeavored to give the reader a flavor for the rich content of these appendices by reproducing two of the twelve sections of Appendix C.[2]

SIX-MONTH STATUS REPORT ON ADDICTION

This report was written almost one year after Gordon
Chase was given administrative responsibility for the Addiction
Services Agency (ASA). The mayor assigned him this responsibility in addition to his other tasks. Since ASA encompassed
many high-priority programs which the administration believed
were not being run as effectively as they could be, and since
the mayor wanted to consolidate drug programs under one
administrator, Chase was given this assignment amid some
concern by the "drug-free" treatment community that he might
favor the Health Department's methadone maintenance programs over ASA's abstinence programs. For about one year
Chase was both HSA administrator and commissioner of ASA.
This dual role led to many implementation assignments to
HSA's program analysis staff, since Chase was ASA's policy-
maker and implementor.

This report to the mayor was developed for two reasons.
It reflected some real accomplishments, and Chase had regularly practiced the technique of keeping his boss, the mayor,
systematically informed of his accomplishments and problems.
Clearly this was one effective way to maintain the mayor's
support. Second, it was developed as a public relations document which would hopefully be reported by the press (with the
assistance of HSA press releases) so New York City's citizens
would read a favorable story about their city government
making progress in the fight against drug addiction. The materials used in the report, however, were developed as part of
a broad administrative monitoring effort directly concerned
with the management of the programs.

The memorandum provides a summary of some of the
ways in which HSA's policy analysts attempted to assist the
administrator in his efforts to implement program changes.
When the administrator assumed responsibility for ASA programs, a new section of HSA's analysis staff was constituted
to focus on addiction programs under a "director of addiction
studies." This staff assisted with program evaluations, it
helped develop quantitative program indicators, it developed
a program for pregnant addicts, and it did an analysis of the
nonnarcotic prescription drug abuse problem. The most useful function of the addiction studies staff was to provide the
administrator with the "quick and dirty" staff work he needed
to get some things done.

TUBERCULOSIS CLINIC STUDY

This brief analysis by Smith Lanning was undertaken at
the request of the new director of New York City's Bureau of
Tuberculosis Control, Dr. Lee Reichman. The objectives of

the study were to measure the productivity of the thirty tuberculosis clinics run by the Health Department and to evaluate
the effectiveness of certain aspects of the overall TB program.
In this case, a new, aggressive program director wanted some
assistance in detailing productivity measures, since he thought
that the productivity of his program could be improved; and he
hoped to use the savings from productivity improvements to
upgrade the quality of the program.

This study indicated that while the use of simple productivity measures (e.g., number of patients seen per hour)
to compare clinics which were presumably performing similar
functions did not provide any answers concerning relative productivity, these data did at least raise interesting questions
which required further administrative follow-up. Why, for
example, should physicians in one clinic see four times as
many patients in an hour as physicians in another? Another
question raised by the study concerned the need to continue to
see the 10,000 patients on clinic registers who were inactive
cases not receiving antibacterial drug treatment.

Here is an instance where the simple arranging of available data by the analyst proved quite useful. About 40 percent
of the TB clinics were ultimately closed or consolidated with
others, and the resulting savings were used to help defray the
costs of a new type of TB drug required for the program and
the costs of just maintaining program quality in a tight budgetary
environment.

The study did not present any conclusions which were not
known to Health Department policy-makers, but it was useful
as part of a set of activities to do something about known prob-
blems. Furthermore, this effort did substantially upgrade the
interpretation and presentation of previously available data.
This led to the establishment in the Health Department of a
special management information systems unit to undertake the
same function on a more systematic basis. Smith Lanning
went on to set up and direct this unit.

FOOTNOTES FOR CHAPTER THREE

1. The 1970 Program Guidance Letter, from the administrator
of HSA to the President of HHC, outlined the views of the HSA
administrator concerning the problem areas that HHC should
give priority attention to during fiscal year 1970. The 1971
Program Guidance Letter has been reproduced because it gives
the reader a better flavor for the problems than the 1970
Program Guidance Letter.
2. Dr. Leslie was awarded a Kennedy School prize because
his analysis was judged to be an outstanding example of a public
policy analysis. The entire paper was published by the Public
Policy Program, Kennedy School of Government, Harvard
University, Cambridge, Mass.

III-1 A BENEFIT/COST ANALYSIS OF NEW YORK CITY HEROIN ADDICTION PROBLEMS AND PROGRAMS — 1971

by Allan Craig Leslie

DEFINITION OF THE PROBLEMS

      The initial and often critical step in any formal decision analysis is specification of the decision boundaries of the particular problem being studied (i.e., should characteristic x be considered, should alternative y be evaluated, should interaction z be included). This paper will study the problem of heroin addiction in New York City, and in the process, two important boundaries will be imposed: geographical limitation to New York City and pharmacological limitation to heroin addiction. Another important but more subtle limitation will become apparent during discussion of alternative solutions to narcotic addiction--that is the cursory recognition that heroin addiction is not solely a medical problem or a generation problem or even a poverty problem, but rather one whose roots reach deep into the political and sociological fabric of our society. It is simultaneously part of our housing problems, our discrimination problems, our health problems, our alienation problems; the list is depressingly long, reflecting the great interdependence and complexity of urban society in this country and this century. Thus this paper incurs the terrible danger of treating a symptom of a disease rather than its underlying causes. While such action may be extremely beneficial, it may also be severely suboptimal, for though the whole is always equal to the sum of its parts, the individual part is not always representative of the whole.

      The necessity for imposing these limitations is simply to make the problem manageable or subject to analysis. Without exception the excluded aspects are either beyond municipal government control or devoid of informational content (i.e., nobody really knows anything about them). To extend the geographical boundaries beyond New York City, for example,

would permit consideration of national programs and legislation and international reduction of narcotic production and distribution (i.e., interrupting the primary narcotic flow from
Turkey to Marseilles to Canada and the northeastern United
States). It would also, however, require inclusion of national
and international differences in attitudes toward narcotics as
well as significant expansion of the political variables that
must be considered in implementing these alternatives (i.e.,
France will crack down on Marseilles' narcotic refinery operations if the United States modifies its NATO, tariff, or Berlin
policies, etc.). Moreover, expansion of the geographical
boundaries may not significantly alter New York City's decision
problem, for it still must treat its current addict population,
and the possibility of drastic changes in the supply of heroin
is essentially incorporated in the considered alternatives of
heroin legalization or substantial improvement of the narcotic
enforcement system.

The danger of restricting the scope of addiction to heroin
addiction alone is that heroin addiction is not independent of
amphetamine, barbiturate, cocaine, alcohol, or hallucinatory
drug usage. Indeed, the most common cause of failure in the
city's methadone or abstinence treatment programs other than
heroin readdiction is excessive use of alcohol and/or other
drugs. Moreover, removal of the heroin craving of many
addicts without significantly altering their environment, opportunities, and personality will almost inevitably lead to trans-
ferral of their addiction from heroin to drug x or drug y. Failure
to enlarge the scope of addiction in this paper from heroin to all
harmful addictive drugs including alcohol, therefore, leads to
suboptimality in actions taken, but this is partially justifiable
in that such enlargement requires significant expansion of currently unknown information about usage, effect, characteristics,
and consequences of these other drugs. Furthermore, heroin
addiction is presently the most serious type of addiction in New
York City, for while alcoholism and amphetamine usage are
more widespread in terms of numbers of people directly affected,
the criminal aspect associated with their usage is not nearly as
overwhelming as it is for heroin.[1] In addition, the growth rate
and expansion potential of heroin appears greater than for alcohol and most other addictive drugs.

MAGNITUDE AND GROWTH OF THE PROBLEM

Having defined the problem as heroin addiction in New
York City, it is necessary for planning and decision purposes
to determine the size of New York City's heroin addict population and its previous and projected growth rate over time.
Unfortunately, such information is either unavailable or biased.

The best addict information source is the city's Narcotics
Register, which in 1968 listed approximately 50,000 reported
heroin addicts, of which four-fifths are male, one-half black,
one-fourth white, and one-fourth Puerto Rican. The race and
sex characteristics of the addict population appear constant
during this period, while the number of youthful (under twenty
years) abusers is radically increasing, though much of this
change is attributed to changing reporting practices of agencies
supplying information to the register. Unfortunately, many
addicts, particularly the younger ones, are still not detected
or reported to the register by the various reporting sources;
the extent of this undercounting is indicated by the register's
failure to contain the names of nearly two-thirds of the 900
people certified by the city's medical examiner as having died
from heroin overdoses in 1969.[2] Limited neighborhood surveys[3]
also indicate a much higher prevalence than that reflected in
register figures; indeed, the figures generally used in public
and private by government, health, and community officials
for the true size of the city's heroin addict population lie
between 100,000 and 200,000, with 125,000 often being
quoted as a "best estimate." Only RAND and the Hudson Institute[4] have estimated addict populations of less than 100,000
(85,000 and 70,000 respectively) based on the belief that the
register does a more comprehensive job than given credit for
and that much of the register file is inactive in that many individuals are dead or duplicated (use of aliases by addicts being
frequent) or no longer addicted (i.e., addiction reports not
having been filed for them for five or more years)[5]. The point
to be made--other than that the city's heroin addict population
is currently very large and possibly of the magnitude of 100,000
or more--is that "hard" accurate information on its size (and
characteristics) is lacking and this is a serious deficiency that
should be (and partially is being) corrected by improved reporting and updating procedures for the Narcotics Register.
    Given an estimated heroin addict population of approxi-
mately 125,000, its distribution and growth rate are other
important parameters that must be determined before making
planning and resource allocation decisions. Appendix Table 4[6]
lists the distribution by borough of residence of newly reported
addicts to the Narcotics Register under twenty years of age, of
narcotic arrests, and of deaths from heroin overdoses. In
decreasing order Manhattan, the Bronx, Brooklyn, Queens,
and Richmond have the most serious heroin addiction problems,
while Appendix Table 5 lists the twenty (out of seventy-one)
individual neighborhoods with the greatest heroin addiction
problems, with East, South, and North Harlem, Bedford Stuy-
vesant, and South Bronx being the most acute problem areas.
    Equally alarming (and unquantified) as the size of the
city's addict population is its growth rate, which must be esti-

mated from growth rates of four relevant surrogate measures:
growth in the number of reports submitted to the Narcotics
Register, the number of certified deaths from heroin overdoses,
the number of reported cases of serum hepatitis, and the number of drug-related crimes. These statistics are presented
in Appendix Table 6, and the annual geometric growth rate
varies from 12 percent to 49 percent. Fortunately, a large
(but unknown) portion of the annual increases in these statistics
can be attributed to improved detection, diagnosis, and reporting practices rather than to increases in the underlying populations. Based on these statistics and visual neighborhood
surveys, however, it is not unreasonable to conservatively
estimate an annual addict population growth rate of 10 percent,
which, based on a current addict population of 125,000, implies
an additional 12,500 addicts per year. Moreover, the Narcotics
Register indicates a changing geographic and demographic distribution of the addict population, with the problem being more
widely distributed throughout the city and more concentrated
among younger people, though once again this change partially
reflects changing reporting practices. Appendix Table 7 indicates the geographic growth rates of reported addicts by borough
and health district from 1967 to 1968, with Queens experiencing
an 84 percent growth rate, the Bronx 66 percent, Manhattan 29
percent, Brooklyn 45 percent, and Richmond 84 percent. Based
on an overall addict population growth rate of 10 percent and the
preceding differential borough growth rates, the New York City
projected addict population by borough for 1975 is given in
Appendix Table 8. From this projection it can be seen that
while Queens and the Bronx experience greater annual growth
rates, the largest number of addicts will continue to remain
in Manhattan. The city's total addict population in 1975 is projected to reach the staggering level of 203,000. Moreover,
plotting of individual neighborhood growth rates reveals that
almost all have not yet "peaked out" in the number of potential
addicts, and that substantial addict population growth rates
could continue beyond 1975 in the absence of any major changes
in societal values and the size and nature of treatment programs.

CHARACTERISTICS AND MYTHOLOGIES OF HEROIN ADDICTION

Before beginning a cost/benefit analysis of alternative
treatment modalities for heroin addiction it is helpful and perhaps necessary to briefly discuss a few major characteristics
of heroin addiction and to dispel some of the more common
fallacies or misconceptions surrounding heroin addiction.
The first thing that becomes apparent in investigating
narcotic addiction--or, more specifically, heroin addiction--

is that a good deal remains unknown about its physical, psychological, and social characteristics. Several interesting and valuable case studies, often in the form of autobiographical novels such as Claude Brown's Manchild in the Promised Land and Malcolm X's autobiography, have been written, but few formal studies have been and are being undertaken to investigate the psychological, sociological, and physiological etiology and characteristics of heroin addiction. Moreover, the findings or conclusions of these studies are generally theoretically overly specialized and nonquantitative. England's recent (1965) legalization of heroin, however, is providing a valuable opportunity to intensively study the pharmacological and physiological basis of narcotic addiction. Based on commonalities found in these various studies, the following can be considered probable and operable manifestations of heroin addiction.

1. The physiological aspects of narcotic addiction are perhaps best known, yet even here the theory has not yet advanced beyond postulation of special narcotic receptors located in the brain. Moreover, the physiological basis for retention of addictive patterns after long periods of abstinence is still relatively unknown. The more commonly advanced (but unproven) theoretical explanation of such retention is Wikler's conditioning-reinforcement process, which combines elements of the experimental findings of Pavlov's dogs and Skinner's pigeons. Essentially Wikler proposes that once a person is addicted, specific environmental stimuli (the sight of a needle or a friend or a particular neighborhood) and internal psychological needs (often intended to avoid excess anxiety) trigger the craving for heroin. These stimuli-response patterns are not easily erasable as long as heroin provides a satisfactory response, and both stimuli and evoked response are often involuntary and even unrecognized by the addict himself. Furthermore, experiencing of withdrawal symptoms upon abstinence acts as a negative reinforcing stimulus resulting in heightening of the desire to "shoot up." This conditioning theory is partially supported by observable human behavior in other areas, yet, as will be shown, it has significant impact in the selection of competing treatment modalities and hence should be more carefully investigated.

2. Many behavioral scientists and psychologists feel the causes of continued addiction are primarily psychological rather than physiological and that initiation of drug use is essentially a psychological and sociological phenomenon. Psychological explanation for initiation of drug addiction, however, varies almost by individual addict and individual researcher, with alienation, thrill-seeking, social status, disruptive family background, and boredom frequently postulated causes. With respect to broader social factors, Irving Leveson has found from studies of differences in addiction rates among states that narcotic addic-

tion is positively correlated with measures of urbanization, city
size, relative poverty, alcoholism, and education (in the ghetto
the more educated are most likely to engage in antisocial behavior), with blacks having proportionately more addicts than whites
even when controlled for income level, a characteristic he attributes to perceived differences in "opportunities." In general,
however, comprehensive, reproducible, and quantitative studies
of the specific etiology of heroin addiction are lacking.

3. The multiplicity of addiction pattern and causative
factors makes it inevitable that the addict population is an
extremely heterogeneous population rather than the homogeneous
population it is commonly perceived as being. Unfortunately,
the Narcotics Register currently collects only name, birth date,
residence, sex, ethnic group, and drugs of abuse and thus fails
to collect a whole variety of important demographic and sociological characteristics of the addict population such as education,
income, and family status. A study done at Metropolitan Hospital in New York, using 253 randomly (given its already biased
addict population) selected addict patients, classified them on
the basis of criminality as evidenced by previous conviction
records and conventionality as judged by employment and family
records, behavior patterns, and general attitudes. Their
results are summarized in the following matrix, they clearly
refute the usual stereotype of the heroin addict as being enmeshed
in a drug culture on the periphery of the criminal underworld.

	Conventionality	
	High	Low
Low Criminality	23% (working addict)	21% (unmasked addict)
High	25% (two worlders)	30% (hustler stereotype)

4. Also contrary to common opinion, addicts--whether
middle class or ghetto poor--are first introduced to heroin by
their friends rather than by proselytizing salesmen (pushers).[7]
A survey of 100 addicts imprisoned in New York City's Riker's
Island found that 75 percent were introduced to drugs (and
heroin in particular) by street friends and only 16% by pushers,
while a recent profile of the city's Addiction Services Agency's
(ASA) patient population (1,166 sampled) revealed that 52 percent were introduced to drugs by friends of the same age, 33
percent by older friends, 3 percent by relatives, and 3 percent
by a pusher. In 88 percent of the cases the person(s) making
the introduction was an addict himself. The same profile also
revealed that stated reasons for drug experimentation were
curiosity derived from a friend's influence 60 percent, thrill-
seeking 24 percent, psychological problems 7 percent, curiosity engendered by films or printed material 5 percent, and

medical problems 1 percent. The importance of friendships in spreading heroin addiction lends support to the relevance to heroin addiction of the traditional cluster theory of statistical epidemiology, which says that once the number of disease carriers in a given neighborhood reaches some critical size the contagion spreads in a rapid and geometric fashion. [8] This has been actually observed in many New York neighborhoods or streets, where heroin addiction has reached epidemic proportions almost overnight. Thus prevention and treatment programs should aim at reducing the number of addicts to below this critical threshold size and/or reducing the heroin addiction contagion aspect of neighborhood friendship networks by reducing the seductive appeal of heroin. Numerous surveys have also indicated that a significant proportion (often a majority) of heroin users have experimented with other drugs, particularly marijuana, before heroin usage. The reader, however, is cautioned against making unjustified inferences of causality simply on the basis of similarity in addict characteristics, for the converse phenomenon does not appear to occur (i.e., the great majority of marijuana users do not use heroin).

5. Selection of heroin as the means of satisfying these psychological and sociological demands is understandable given the nature of heroin's action and the commonality among addicts of what they perceive as otherwise bleak, unexciting, and depressing lives. Intravenous injection of heroin (mainlining) rapidly produces a brief but extremely strong orgasmic "rush" followed by a short period of euphoria followed by a much longer period of drowsiness and withdrawal (the "nodding" phase). Contrary to widespread opinion, it is the initial, shorter periods of excitement that the addict primarily desires, rather than the longer periods of apathy and sleep. After a period of time, however, some heroin addicts experience a reversal of heroin-taking motivation from the positive one of enjoying a euphoric state to the negative one of avoiding withdrawal symptoms. This, of course, has important behavioral implications for selection of effective treatment programs for individual addicts.

6. Many people will also be surprised to learn that the physical harm incurred from heroin itself is minimal. Laboratory animal studies and human clinical studies conducted in England show that during chronic heroin use there is persistence of myosis, constipation, respiratory rate depression, and body temperature, blood pressure, and pulse rate elevation, but all such effects are relatively minor. There are also no severe or lasting physical effects from narcotics withdrawal. The great health dangers from heroin usage come not from the drug itself but from its purchase and administration. The illegality of the former brings one into contact with the criminal world and the fabled "drug culture." Increasing tolerance to the drug

(i.e., increasingly larger doses must be taken to achieve the same effect) rapidly necessitates daily payments averaging $20 to $50, thereby forcing many to turn to crime to support their habits. Injection of the drug incurs the dangers of hepatitis and tetanus, while the extremely varying concentration of heroin in street packages is responsible for overdoses in which death from heart stoppage or respiratory failure is almost instantaneous when the purity is far greater than one is accustomed to. Of 132 street packages of heroin recently sampled in New York City, 12 contained no heroin at all while the remainder were diluted in varying amounts with quinine so that heroin concentration ranged from 1 percent to 77 percent. A 1969 study of 1,031 narcotic-caused deaths in New York City conducted by the city's medical examiner revealed 9 percent were caused by tetanus, hepatitis, and sepsis, 80 percent by overdose, and 11 percent by suicide, murder, or accidental falls while under the influence of heroin. Indeed, drug abuse is now the leading cause of death for male residents of New York City aged fifteen to thirty-five, and doctors have roughly estimated that the life expectancy of a 20-year-old heroin addict is roughly that of a fifty-five-year-old nonaddict.

   7. An important operational difficulty stemming from uncertainty about the etiology and mechanism of addiction is determination of when a given individual passes through the stages of nonuser to addict. Addictive doses vary significantly by individual user and by method of ingestion. Skin-popping (subcutaneous injection) and sniffing (inhalation of heroin through the nostrils), for example, are less addiction-inducing than mainlining. The distinction between user and addict is particularly important in directing individuals to specific treatment programs (if a person is not an addict, methadone in the Dole-Nyswander maintenance dosage soon make him one, albeit a methadone addict). The usual test applied is evidence of withdrawal symptoms and a history of at least six months to two years of regular drug use (mainlining). Unfortunately, such evidence is frequently subjective and accepted without substantiating proof.

   8. Looking at the manufacture and distribution of heroin as an industry, albeit an illegal one, it differs from the traditional industry by having: (a) A marketing system that operates through small, highly personalized, face-to-face networks rather than relying on impersonal advertising and public stores. (b) An extremely large markup (3,000 to 8,000 percent) between first wholesale and final retail exchange. (c) A high degree of monopolization despite very low capital and technological barriers to entry. (d) A much larger proportion of employees involved in marketing than in production. In Chart 1 Mark Moore of the Hudson Institute gives a somewhat simplified picture of the typical heroin distribution network in the United

CHART 1

ONE MODEL OF THE HEROIN DISTRIBUTION SYSTEM

This chart is intended to present an oversimplified picture of how heroin is distributed in a large part of the market. The actual situation, of course, presents many variations.

Importers	Buy	10 - 100 kg.	(80-95% pure)	once every 4 to 20 months
Kilo Connections (and "Traders")	Buy	1 - 10 kg.	(80-95% pure)	2 - 8 times per month
	Sell	1/2 - 4 kg.	(40-45% pure)	2 - 4 times per week
Connections	Buy	1/2 - 4 kg.	(40-45% pure)	3 - 6 times per month
	Sell	2 - 15 ounces	(20-22% pure)	10 - 20 times per week
Weight Dealers	Buy	2 - 15 ounces	(20-22% pure)	1 - 2 times per week
	Sell	one bundle* (1/7 oz.) to one ounce	(10-11% pure)	2 - 4 times per day
Street Dealers	Buy	one bundle to one ounce	(10-11% pure)	3 - 6 times per week
	Sell	5 - 75 bags	(6-8% pure)	3 - 8 times per day
Jugglers	Buy	15 - 75 bags	(6-8% pure)	3 - 7 times per week
	Sell	1 - 10 bags	(6-8% pure)	3 - 15 times per day
Users	Buy	1 - 10 bags from street dealers or jugglers		1 - 3 times per day

*A bundle is 25 bags

States, which nevertheless indicates both the complexity and
(pyramidal) hierachical nature of the network with individuals
knowing only the "contact" immediately above and below them
in the hierarchy. Mr. Moore also theorizes that the demand
curve for heroin is not completely inelastic (i.e., the quantity
sold is not completely independent of price) but elastic at very
low price levels (which induce substantial experimentation
among nonusers) and very high price levels (addicts having
finite income sources including illegal ones and product sub-
stitutes such as cocaine becoming more attractive at high heroin
prices). The current supply of heroin the United States appears
rather large, for recent police capture of a very large amount
of heroin has not resulted in any noticeable shortage (panic) in
the streets.

In summary, a great deal of information remains unknown
about the physiological, psychological, and sociological aspects
of heroin addiction. The existence of narcotic receptors in the
brain has been postulated and psychological motivations for initiation of heroin usage basically include curiosity, thrill-seeking
and escape from the boredom and bleakness of ghetto life. It
appears that the heroin addict population is more heterogeneous
than commonly perceived, that the physiological dangers of
heroin usage are from its purchase and administration, that
the major sources of heroin introduction are older and peer-
group friends, that the drug is initially valued primarily for
its orgasmic rush, and that the spread of heroin addiction closely
follows epidemiological models. Finally, heroin addiction is
a particularly severe problem in the city's nonwhite ghettos,
and the drug is manufactured and distributed by a large and
complex criminal industry characterized by secrecy and a
pyramidal organizational structure.

SPECIFICATION OF PROGRAM GOALS

Given the aforementioned diversity in addict characteristics, drug use, and etiology, it is necessary to construct a
hierarchy of operational goals for narcotic treatment programs
rather than insisting on a single goal of complete opiate-free
behavior. Other possible goals (many of which have been
adopted by the Dole-Nyswander methadone program) include
reduction in crime rates, increases in employment rates,
improvement in general physical and mental health, and removal
from welfare roles as well as prevention of additional addicts.
The crude benefit/cost analysis of alternative treatment and
prevention modalities generated in this paper takes as its
objective maximum reduction in the number of man years of
heroin addiction with the earlier years in an addict's life more
highly valued than later ones for reasons soon to be shown. A

multiplicity of objectives, however, is implicit in this criterion, for the marginal value or benefit of preventing one additional year of heroin addiction is proportional not only to the age of the addict but also to the effect of his employment status, criminality, health, productivity, and emotional well-being.

SCOPE OF THE HEROIN ADDICTION PREVENTION AND TREATMENT PROGRAMS IN NEW YORK CITY

Given an objective of maximizing the number (or value) of additional years of heroin addiction prevented, there are several resource or budgetary constraints to be considered which essentially limit the possible magnitude of the anti-addiction programs. Among these constraints is a fiscal one, with federal, state, and municipal funds becoming increasingly scarce as the growth in the nation's fiscal crisis parallels growth in its narcotic addiction crisis (and its racial crisis, housing crisis, education crisis, etc.). The estimated funding of all heroin prevention and treatment programs in New York City for fiscal year 1970-71 is $80.6 million, of which 56 percent is state, 21 percent city, 13 percent federal, and 10 percent private (the distribution of these funds among individual programs is given in Appendix Table 9). It is probable that this total budget level will continue to grow by significant but not overwhelming amounts in the near future as narcotic addiction continues to receive top priority from government administrators and community leaders. New York State recently authorized $65 million for programs for youthful drug offenders but a 50:50 state-city matching requirement (the city can use federal funds as part of its share) has inhibited the obvious need. (The city, therefore, is currently asking for removal of this matching requirement.) In conclusion, in the absence of an emergency program, an annual growth rate of approximately 25 percent for the total annual narcotic program budget in New York City appears reasonable over the next five years, which would make the 1975-76 budget approximately $250 million ($200 million in 1970 dollars).

THE THEORETICAL FRAMEWORK

The Appendix develops in detail an addiction benefit/cost framework which is used to evaluate in an identical manner the following ten alternative treatment and prevention modalities for heroin addiction in New York City:
Methadone Maintenance
Phoenix House
Odyssey House

State NACC commitment
Antagonists (future form)
Heroin Maintenance (permanent)
Heroin Legalization
Increased Legal Enforcement
Detoxification (ambulatory, inpatient)
Involuntary Incarceration

In addition, Daytop Village, crisis intervention, genetic and personality manipulation, sociological change, and education and prevention programs are discussed but not evaluated because of lack of sufficient information. The assumptions underlying the theoretical framework are clearly specified and the overall lack of adequate data makes their number large and significant. Nevertheless, the resulting analysis is the first major attempt to apply a theoretical evaluation model to all possible heroin addiction reduction/treatment strategies and hence represents an important innovation capable of further refinement.

The Benefits Derived from Averting One Man-Year of Heroin Addiction

While the evaluation model compares alternative prevention/treatment modalities on the basis of total number of man-years of heroin addiction averted divided by program cost, the total benefit in dollars of individual programs is needed to compare the best addiction programs with housing programs, education programs, sanitation programs, etc., in order to make proper resource allocation decisions.[9] Thus the Appendix generates a total benefit per man-year of heroin addiction averted of $13,672, which is divided as follows:

Increase in employment earnings	$ 3,260
Reduction in premature deaths	1,510
Reduction in morbidity	410
Reduction in crime	3,954
Reduction in enforcement costs	1,640
Reduction in housing stock	164
	$10,938
Contagion factor (1.25)	2,734
Total	$13,672 per addiction year

The assumptions made in calculating benefits are almost all conservative and hence the above figures represent conservative estimates, with the "true" annual benefit perhaps being 10 to 20 percent higher than $13,672. The conservative approach, however, is taken to counteract the wildly unsupported and often ridiculously high figures mentioned by much of the communication media, as well as to establish the clear priority of heroin addiction programs under even the most conservative of assumptions.

Benefit/Cost Evaluation of Alternative Treatment/Prevention Programs

The ten quantifiable alternative treatment and prevention modalities for heroin addiction are carefully evaluated and compared in the Appendix, with the resulting benefit/cost ratio ($13,672 times program "success" rate times number of years of addiction remaining of the average program enrollee divided by program cost) being:

1.	Detoxification	20.7
2.	Antagonists (future form)	19.1
3.	Methadone	7.9
4.	Odyssey House	6.5
5.	Increased Enforcement	3.4
6.	Phoenix	3.0
7.	Heroin Maintenance	2.9
8.	State NACC	2.8
9.	Involuntary Incarceration	1.7
10.	Heroin Legalization	1.3

All programs have a benefit/cost ratio of greater than one, with variation among individual programs being very large. The Appendix contains a sensitivity analysis of the assumptions underlying calculation of individual program benefit/cost ratios, with some programs such as Odyssey House being much less reliable than other programs such as the methadone program, which has been carefully evaluated by a qualified independent body (Columbia School of Public Health).

Selection of a Multimodal Treatment/Prevention Program for Heroin Addiction

Based on the above calculations and an estimation of the addict population for whom the individual program is sufficiently attractive, a multimodal program embracing detoxification (primarily ambulatory detoxification), antagonist, methadone, and Odyssey House was selected as most effective and efficient. Those addicts for whom none of these programs was a success-ful modality were then assigned to a heroin maintenance pro-gram (rather than to a competing involuntary incarceration program which has a lower benefit/cost ratio) since its benefit/

cost ratio is significantly greater than one. Two major assumptions made in the selection of these five programs are: (a) That an antagonist form or delivery vehicle will be available within three years that will have a duration of action of a week or more. (b) That very careful and rigid screening criteria are used in the heroin maintenance program to prevent its existence from reducing success rates of other programs, since many individual addicts would be expected to prefer inexpensive, reliable heroin maintenance to any form of treatment.

Implementation of the Multimodal Program

Given a multimodal treatment/prevention program for heroin addiction, its implementation must clearly incorporate the reality that some programs are undesirable for or unacceptable to large segments of the addict population and that individual program success rates have been largely derived from treatment of carefully selected, unrepresentative segments of the addict population. This merely emphasizes the need for developing useful addict classification criteria for determination of preferable allocation plans among individual programs, but in the absence of such patient typologies, two alternative allocation plans are proposed and evaluated. Plan A is a simple hierarchial progression scheme whereby addicts progress from detoxification to antagonists to an Odyssey House model to methadone to heroin maintenance, with program successes siphoned off into the unaddicted pool. Plan B, on the other hand, uses heretofore undeveloped selective screening criteria (generated by regression analysis of historical data), so some addicts avoid some of the sequential steps of Plan A. Surprisingly, the two plans perform roughly equivalently, with a benefit/cost ratio of approximately 8.25. This extremely high ratio clearly indicates the relative desirability of shifting more financial and manpower resources into narcotic addiction from many far less attractive programs currently being undertaken by our government and private sectors.

WHO WILL PAY AND WHEN?

If the federal, state, and municipal governments decide to significantly reduce addiction in New York City by adopting Plan A or Plan B, the resulting time schedule of benefits and costs is given by Appendix Table 11. Plan B, utilizing selective screening criteria, has slightly lower costs and substantially higher benefits over earlier years (Years 1 through 7), with Plan A enjoying a similar advantage over later years (Years 8 through 14). This makes Plan B preferable in two respects:

Plan B:

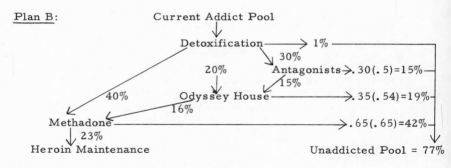

Cost of Plan B for 100,000 addicts:*

Detoxification	$	8.6 million
Antagonists		100.0 "
Odyssey House		300.0 "
Methadone		436.8 "
Heroin Maintenance		414.0 "
		$1,259.4 "

*cost of unsuccessful treatment same as in A

Benefit of Plan B for 100,000 addicts:

Detoxification	10 x 1,000x$13,762 = $		137.6 million
Antagonists	14 x 15,000 "		2,898.0 "
Odyssey House	11 x 19,000 "		2,876.3 "
Methadone	7 x 42,000 "		4,046.0 "
Heroin Maintenance	9 x 23,000	5,542	1,147.2 "
			$11,105.1 million

Plan A Versus Plan B Prior to Discounting

	Net Benefits	Benefit/Cost Ratio
Plan A	$10,937 million	8.65
Plan B	$ 9,844 million	7.85

politicians love to pass the costs of new programs onto succeeding administrations and if a discount factor of 10 percent
is applied, [10] Plan B has a significantly higher benefit/cost
ratio than Plan A. Thus timing considerations indicate a
strong preference for Plan B over Plan A.

Selection of Plan B, however, incurs a first-year cost
of $90 million or 112 percent of the current New York City
narcotic addiction budget of federal, state, city, and private
sources. The following three years require a 300 percent,
336 percent and 175 percent increase over current budget levels
respectively. While these costs are more than balanced by
resulting benefits, the problem remains of finding the necessary
funds from the various funding possibilities. Part (12 percent)
of the benefits, however, are from reduced enforcement costs,
and if 75 percent of this amount is quickly realized in terms of
lower municipal payroll costs, the money needed to be raised
for the first four program years is $46 million, $116 million,
$122 million and $8 million respectively.

Moreover, these calculations assume an almost overnight
implementation of the full program, which is an impossibility
considering the current unavailability of adequate antagonist
forms and the present illegality of heroin maintenance programs.
A gradual expansion to the desired program level, therefore,
is much more realistic; hence program costs would be significantly lower in initial years than that indicated in Table 11,
were it not for the existence of current programs considered
largely inappropriate by the analysis contained in this paper.
These programs comprise a majority segment of current narcotic program funding, and realistic political and bureaucratic
constraints may make it necessary to continue their existence
at lower or even current funding levels for a number of years.
The extent of this inefficiency, of course, is dependent on the
decisions of the city's top decision-makers, and this paper
will not speculate or discuss either this question or the related
issue of who (and how) should raise the required program funds.
Each is filled with complex legal, political, and distributional
components which need to be specified and analyzed in a further
paper. Finally, as an indication of existing misallocation of
funds, the 1970-71 estimates of program funding by federal,
state, local, and private agencies of narcotic programs in
New York City is compared to the cost breakdown of the multimodal program developed in this paper (remembering, however,
that the average proposed budget for the next eleven years is
$114 million versus $80 million currently being funded).

	Proposed	Current	Differences
Antagonist	8%	0%	- 8%
Detoxification	1%	6%	+ 5%
Methadone	35%	19%	-16%
Odyssey House	23%	4%	-19%
Heroin Maintenance	33%	-	-33%
Phoenix House		3%	+ 3%
State Narcotic Center		12%	+12%
Education/Prevention	minimal	56%	+56%

PROBLEMS OF IMPLEMENTATION

Public and private agencies in the City of New York are currently treating approximately 10,000 heroin addicts in a variety of ways (primarily methadone and voluntary/involuntary abstinence), yet the city's total addict population is estimated as being between 100,000 and 125,000 addicts. Moreover, present expansion plans of existing programs encompass only an additional 4,000 to 5,000 addicts, yet conservative estimates of the growth of the addict population during the next year exceed 10,000 addicts. Thus not only is the city currently treating a clearly insufficient number of its addicts, but it is also steadily losing ground in its efforts to combat narcotic addiction in the city.

This paper generates and evaluates a multimodal treatment/prevention program designed to have a significant impact on reducing the city's heroin addiction problems. As a major change in magnitude and scope from existing programs, it will inevitably encounter several serious problems of implementation which must not only be anticipated but confronted and hopefully overcome. These problems include:

(a) Manpower - Under existing law, any program distributing methadone (or heroin) must provide the services of a physician for medical screening and determination of proper dosage levels. A methadone clinic has an average patient capacity of 250 patients, and if under Plan B the annual methadone patient load is 42,000 addicts, this will require the services of 168 doctors. If similar physician and clinic size requirements also hold for antagonists and heroin maintenance, then an addition of 60 and 92 doctors respectively would be needed for an annual total of 320 doctor-years. Each detoxification clinic would also require a doctor by law (detoxification is achieved with gradually decreasing doses of methadone), but under Plan B, detoxification precedes (and does not overlap) the other treatment modalities.

In addition to finding the 320 man-years of physician service (a difficult task, since many doctors would be expected to

find such work uninteresting), the services of a large number
of counselors, nurses, and paramedical personnel must be
obtained, with shortages in the first two categories being probable. Beth Israel currently trains most of the professional
personnel in the city's methadone program, but with significant
expansion of the city's narcotic programs it should begin training
instructors to train others. Other steps that can be taken to
relieve personnel shortages are revision in staffing patterns
and use of private physicians in distributing methadone, though
the impact of each of these alternatives needs to be more carefully studied before initiation.

(b) Financial - As previously discussed, it is not felt
that the financial costs of a massive attack on the problem of
narcotic addiction need be prohibitive, particularly if savings
in enforcement and correctional costs are quickly realized.
Both the city and state appear to realize the seriousness of the
city's addiction crisis and have continued to grant it top priority
and increasing funds during a time of increasingly severe budgetary constraints. Furthermore, additional concentrated and
coordinated appeals by the governor and the mayor may be able
to elicit heretofore reluctant or scanty (13 percent of the city's
recent narcotic program budget) federal funds.

(c) Facility - The multimodal program would utilize hospitals (primarily the outpatient department), mobile units,
residential facilities or dormitories in the community, and
community storefronts. Negotiation for adequate hospital space
and facilities (including medical backup for facilities located
in the community) is rarely an easy task; location of suitable
community residences and storefronts is often a lengthy and
expensive process in many areas of the city. There is also the
problem of possible community resistance to location of treatment centers in their neighborhood, which will be discussed in
the following section. Site location and purchase problems,
however, can be adequately alleviated by sufficient advance
planning, which encompasses location of housing supply according to actual and projected addict-community demand followed
by constant monitoring of the desired area until a suitable building or site is offered for sale.

(d) Community Resistance - Some communities will
resist the locating of sizable nonhospital-based heroin addiction
treatment centers in their neighborhood out of fear that additional addicts will be attracted into the neighborhood, thereby
raising the general level of neighborhood crime. These fears
can be overcome only by an extensive and careful public education program which assures people that treatment facilities are
being simultaneously developed all over the city and that adequate
security provisions will be undertaken for each clinic. Use of
mobile units for ambulatory programs in low addiction areas of
the city may also reduce the fear surrounding development of

staionary clinics, which many residents may fear as being permanent.

(e) Time - In developing and analyzing two possible multi-modal programs (Plan A and Plan B), the constraint of time was virtually ignored. While public and governmental pressure is rapidly growing for substantial action now, it simply takes time to find, purchase, staff, and gradually build up to capacity the various treatment centers. In the case of heroin maintenance and antagonists, there will also be additional delays of a year or more and as much as three years respectively while required legal barriers and duration of action deficiencies are overcome. During this time, of course, attention should be focused on fully developing the other treatment modalities.

(f) All the above will require development of a heretofore understaffed central planning and decision-making body for narcotic programs in the city. Coordination with private and state programs is currently virtually nonexistent or inadequate, and responsibility for city policy and program management is fragmented among ASA (Addiction Services Agency), HSA (Health Services Administration), the Mayor's Office and to a lesser extent the Police Department and the Criminal Justice Coordinating Council. The Mayor's Narcotic Control Council is primarily a discussion and information generation and dissemination body (a valuable function) and not a decision-making body. Location of an overall decision-making, planning, and coordination body for narcotic programs of the city should be in a small central agency or in the Mayor's Office itself, with operating responsibility for specific narcotic programs being delegated to various city agencies. The Mayor's Narcotic Control Council should be expanded to include representatives of major state and private programs, with greater attempts made to coordinate these various agencies under city leadership.

(g) Political and Bureaucratic Impediments - The political pressures exerted against development of a major narcotic treatment program as envisioned in Plan B may be as great as those exerted in support of such programs. Aside from the obvious difficulties associated with heroin maintenance (including the possibility of attracting hard-core addicts from all over the country in a manner similar to that experienced by the city's pioneering welfare and abortion programs), other political problems include community resistance to location of treatment centers in their neighborhood; widespread fears, particularly in nonwhite ghetto areas, that prolonged methadone maintenance is a form of enslavement; rural and suburban unwillingness to finance reduction of urban problems; and obvious bureaucratic (and civil service/union) resistance to reduction or elimination of inappropriate existing treatment/prevention programs, many of which involve significant amounts of community participation and commitment (RARE, AWARE, etc.). The heroin main-

tenance problem may be politically insurmountable in the
immediate future; hence the less satisfactory alternative of
increased law enforcement may be substituted for it. The other
problems, however, should be met by public education programs,
generation of sufficient treatment alternatives, incorporation of
community groups in locating and operating local treatment
programs, and above all, strong political leadership and commitment from the mayor and his cabinet.

(h) Addict Recruitment - Presently no treatment program
in the city finds it very difficult to attract sufficient numbers of
addicts to fill their capacity, but this can be expected to change
as narcotic programs significantly expand in size and type.
Addicts may soon have to be actively recruited to enroll in particular treatment programs, and this will require careful and
accurate dissemination of program information through public
communication media, the schools, the courts, and the prisons.
Storefronts should contain distributable detailed information on
the location, admission requirements, and treatment orientation of all existing modalities. It may even occur at some
future date that as the untreated addict population is steadily
reduced to its "hard-core" element, development of financial
incentives for the addicts may have to be required to induce
them to undergo treatment. Finally, operation of effective
treatment programs will in itself be the best form of advertise-
ment, since knowledge of their existence and effectiveness will
spread quite rapidly through the various street channels of
information used by the addict population.

RECOMMENDATIONS

1. Based on the analysis contained in this paper, a major
multimodal heroin treatment/prevention program should be
quickly initiated (and expanded), one which encompasses detoxification, methadone, and Odyssey House programs with increased
enforcement of narcotic laws with special emphasis on the arrest
and conviction of large-scale pushers. Simultaneously, the
legal barriers to heroin maintenance should be overcome to
permit enrollment of verified "hard-core" addicts with prolonged addiction histories and demonstrable reluctance or
inability to give up heroin. Antagonist research programs
designed to extend their duration of action should be fully funded,
and as soon as successful, should be developed as a major
treatment/prevention modality. The overall benefit to the citizens of New York and to society in general of undertaking the
preceding has been shown in this paper to substantially outweigh
incurred costs.

2. A good deal more useful information about narcotic
addiction must be collected to allow more accurate and com-

prehensive analysis of the problem and its solutions. Included among such badly needed information are quantitative measures of individual program costs and effectiveness (particularly education programs), more accurate measures of New York City's addict population (size, distribution, growth, and socio-logical and etiological characteristics) and generation of rele-vant patient typologies. Development and implementation of standard experimental design criteria and monitoring (similar to that conducted by Columbia University's School of Public Health for methadone) of all experimental treatment and pre-vention programs should also be undertaken.

3. Greater coordination and cooperation among and within federal, state, city, and private programs is needed to insure widespread application of beneficial innovations, communication of relevant evaluation information, and geographical distribu-tion of facilities in accordance with need.

4. Finally, all involved should more carefully examine the etiology of drug addiction, for therein lies the only true or permanent solution to the city's drug crisis. In some cases, it is merely boredom and thrill-seeking by overly pandered and protected children and adults, but in most cases it is the result of serious interrelated material, opportunity, and psychological deprivations encompassing poverty, discrimination, inadequate educational opportunities, broken homes, and the survival penalties and characteristics of ghetto life. Remedial changes in these causative factors are far more complex, costly, and comprehensive than those proposed in this paper for reduction of one of its manifestations. Failure to recognize, analyze, and attack these deeper causes, however, makes it inevitable that at best the narcotic programs will provide some additional time or relief before another manifestation appears with equally or perhaps greater harmful consequences for society. Removal of a cancer must always be complete, or the remainder will quickly subdivide and multiply, ending eventually in the painful death of the patient.

CONCLUSION

The seriousness of the city's heroin addiction problems is clearly indicated by an estimated addict population of nearly 125,000 addicts, an annual addict population growth rate of 10 percent, and an actual and opportunity cost of $13,762 per addict-year or $1.7 billion for 1970. Judged by the magnitude of these statistics, the current public and private narcotic treatment and education programs are inadequate and growing at an insufficient rate. Moreover, evaluation of the cost and effectiveness of these programs indicates that the scarce financial and manpower resources given to narcotic addiction programs can be more optimally allocated.

FOOTNOTES

1. The primary focusing upon heroin addiction, however, has another element, the implications of which must be recognized and confronted, and that is heroin's status as largely, but not exclusively, a problem of the ghetto, which in today's cities often means a problem of the city's nonwhite population. Other drugs, particularly the hallucinogenic ones, are largely a problem of disaffected middle-class white youth, while alcoholism is more widely distributed throughout our society. Thus giving heroin addiction first priority has specific political and racial connotations that must be faced rather than ignored or disguised.

2. In estimating total addict population size, use of an extrapolative factor of 3 may be too large, for the register is particularly poor at listing very young addicts and 224 of the deaths from heroin overdoses in 1969 were teenagers.

3. A disputed study reported to Congress by former NIMH Director Stanley Yolles claimed 18,000 hard drug addicts in a forty-block area of Harlem with a total population of 60,000 people.

4. "Development of an Issue Paper on Narcotic Addiction in New York City" by John Surmeier, February 1969, an internal unpublished RAND document and a series of multiauthored reports by Hudson Institute for New York State. The latter estimate is based on derivations from reported crimes against property and from neighborhood implications of various estimated addict population sizes.

5. Based on random sampling, Mary Snow of the New York State Narcotic Control Commission estimates that 25 percent of the register file is "inactive."

6. Editor's note: The factual and methodological appendices of this report were deleted due to space limitations. However, Appendix C, parts 1 and 4, was retained to give the reader a flavor for the type of material contained in Appendices A through F cited in this report.

7. This distinction between pusher and friend is somewhat blurred when the two are the same. Furthermore, the pusher finds it economically as well as socially desirable to introduce friends to heroin, for he then creates new customers.

8. Whether heroin addiction is a contagious disease in the epidemiological sense is presently disputed, though statistically it appears to be adhering to epidemiological patterns. It is not, however, infectious in the traditional sense, and behaviorally the host actively seeks out the agent rather than avoiding or being unaware of it. Furthermore, the condition of the host and his environment are often the prime causative factors rather than the agent itself.

9. This, of course, is an idealization, since other programs are rarely evaluated in a benefit/cost framework.

10. The discount factor is applied to reflect society's time preferences, not inflationary or deflationary changes.

APPENDIX C

Benefit/Cost Evaluation of Alternative Treatment and
Prevention Programs

Before evaluating the various program alternatives according to the previously developed theoretical framework, it is
necessary to comment on the quantity and quality of the underlying information. Simply, it is far too little and far too poor.
There is an extreme lack of communication of known information on narcotic addiction programs, with federal, state, city,
and private agencies funding and/or operating programs but none
acting as central coordinators and few even recognizing the
need for such coordination. Most importantly, few individual
programs actually implement an evaluation and monitoring
system which will provide the information needed for proper
analysis of costs and effectiveness, and most of these programs
are pervaded by an unwarranted amount of secrecy. The net
result is that series after series of experimental programs and
innovations are tried without evaluation and continued or dis-
carded without rationalization. Finally, most programs are
biased in patient selection, avoiding if possible those with mixed
drug histories, severe medical or psychological problems and
records of extreme antisocial behavior, as well as imposing an
age limit of below forty and above twenty-one. Thus they avoid
the rather sizable proportion of the addict population which is
most difficult to treat and probably the one with the highest
crime, unemployment, and readdiction tendencies. Thus it is
very misleading to automatically extrapolate program success
rates to the entire addict population or to compare effectiveness
of programs with radically different population characteristics.
In the absence of the previously discussed patient typology
classifications this danger can be reduced only by qualitatively
incorporating differences in program addict characteristics.

Methadone

Methadone is an addictive drug which when taken orally
blocks the euphoric action of heroin for twenty-four hours.
Administered orally, it has no side effects, is mildly tran-
quilizing, extremely inexpensive, exhibits no tolerance behavior,
and induces withdrawal symptoms when withheld. Its two disadvantages are: the euphoric effect produced when administered
intravenously (thereby creating some abuse potential) and the
suspicion that by reducing anxiety and preventing extremes of
depression or elation the emotional growth and maturation of
the patient may be seriously retarded. It also appears that
the addictive property of methadone makes it a very prolonged

treatment, for of 350 patients withdrawn from the Beth Israel methadone program for voluntary or disciplinary reasons, nearly all became readdicted to heroin or asked to return to the program.

Pioneered in 1964 by Drs. Dole and Nyswander of Rockefeller University, the methadone program has achieved remarkable success; as of November 4, 1970, of the 4,376 admissions to the Dole-Nyswander program 80 percent remain under treatment. The group's annual arrest record has dropped from 18 percent to 3 percent arrested, and there is a marked increase over time of their employment rate (from 30 percent initially to 68 percent after one year, 72 percent after three years, and 78 percent after four years, with an additional 3 percent to 5 percent in school) and a corresponding decrease in those on welfare. There are now methadone facilities for approximately 5,000 addicts in New York City, with an additional 2,500 being constructed over the course of the next year. The waiting list for these various programs exceeds 5,000 patients.

Despite recent relaxation of entry restrictions from an age range between 21 and 40 to one of 18 and older and recent acceptance of patients with mixed drug histories, major health problems, and histories of mental illness, its mean age remains 33.3 years (versus 27.9 for those addicts recorded by the Narcotics Register) and based on its current racial composition of 39 percent white, 19 percent Puerto Rican, and 42 percent black (versus 25 percent, 28 percent, and 47 percent respectively for the Register), Irving Leveson has computed the average number of remaining years of addiction as 7. Thus y_1 is taken as 7 and p_1 as approximately .75. Because of its addictive nature, methadone is not considered desirable for very young or highly motivated addicts, whom, it is hoped, can avoid prolonged addiction. Moreover, methadone is not an attractive modality to young addicts who firmly believe they can hustle without becoming addicted and to addicts with long addiction histories who refuse to give up the pleasure of a heroin rush. Dr. Dole has estimated, therefore, that methadone is an appropriate treatment modality for 50 percent of the current addict population.

The average cost of the current methadone program has been estimated at $1,500 per year, but actual expenditures are closer to $2,000 per year, which includes cost of the drug and its administration and a variety of social, vocational, and psychiatric counseling services. Moreover, it appears hospital overhead is not adequately incorporated in this figure (clinic visits are twice daily during the two-to-five-week induction period, gradually evolving to once or twice a week after a period of half a year or more; only 10 percent require any hospitalization during induction), but counteracting this is the likelihood that substantial economies can be achieved by fewer

and more streamlined supportive services and improved distribution (eventually using private physicians).[1] Thus a future
annual average program cost of $1,000 appears reasonable,
and in expectation of these economies, an average cost of
$1,300 per year is assumed.

*   *   *

Narcotic Antagonists

Narcotic antagonists, primarily (currently) naloxone and
cyclazocine, represent a relatively new treatment modality
which has been tested in only a few limited experimental programs. Closely resembling methadone in their pharmacological
action and method of administration, they have a lower abuse
potential, and most importantly, are physiologically non-
addicting. This nonaddictive property makes them a preferred
chemotherapeutic modality for both very young addicts and highly
motivated addicts who may need only a minimum level of treatment, as currently appears inevitable with methadone. For
these segments of the addict population, therefore, antagonist
treatment offers the very real possibility of successful withdrawal from the program after two to three years of chemo-
therapy accompanied by the usual social, medical, vocational,
and psychiatric counseling. This possibility is increased by
the yet unproven belief that antagonists act differently from
methadone by blocking the euphoric effect of heroin rather than
by satisfying the craving for heroin as does methadone, and
that this negative reinforcement makes possible "erasing" the
addiction process proposed by Wikler. Unfortunately, the nonaddictive property of antagonists is paradoxically the greatest
impediment to their widespread application. The current duration of action of naloxone and cyclazocine is twenty-four hours
or less, and because of their nonaddictive nature it is extremely
difficult to get patients in a voluntary program to appear daily
to receive their dosage. Methadone patients will appear daily
for their methadone partly because they are addicted to it and will
experience withdrawal symptoms if they don't. The city, however, is initiating a major research program to significantly
extend the duration of action of antagonists to a week, a month,
or even a year or more. Such a technical breakthrough will
enable antagonists to become an important treatment modality
for several sizable segments of the addict population.[2] Moreover, if the duration of action reaches a period of several
months or more, antagonists will become a potentially valuable
prevention (immunization) modality for heroin addiction.
Because of their special desirability as a treatment
modality for teenagers, the probable antagonist program mean
age will be several years younger than the methadone average.
Taking the mean age as twenty-four years and the number of

years of addiction remaining, y_4, as 14, the program cost can be reasonably estimated at \$2,000 per year for two and a half years (higher than methadone costs because of greater counseling needs and the higher cost of the drug) and the success rate as .50 (lower than the methadone program rate because younger addicts are characteristically harder to treat).[3]

FOOTNOTES

1.   Another possible methadone maintenance program would simply distribute methadone with few if any supportive services. Its annual cost per patient would be \$500 or less, but its probable success is unknown (ARTC is researching this problem) though undoubtedly less than .75.
2.   With such long duration of action, addicts who fail to appear on schedule can be sought out directly or indirectly through friends and relatives to be given their doses of the particular antagonist drug.
3.   The analysis of the antagonist alternative is based solely on use of an antagonist of duration of a week or more.   Such a drug is currently unavailable but development is likely within three years.   Until then, antagonists are not a feasible treatment modality.

III-2 SIX-MONTH STATUS REPORT ON ADDICTION — July 23, 1973

by Gordon Chase

The following is a status report on where we are in the fight against drug abuse and addiction in New York City. We have built up a tremendous treatment capacity--twice the number of persons in treatment as the next twelve major cities with drug problems combined. We have solid proof that these programs, both drug-free and methadone maintenance, actually work in reducing crime and in allowing the individual to lead a more productive life. We are reaching addicts we never reached before, in the streets, in hospitals, in schools, and most importantly, where they intersect with the criminal justice system. All the indicators available to us show a decrease in narcotic addiction and a drop in addict-related crime. We have mounted a comprehensive program of control as well as treatment to curb the growth of the soft drug problem before it reaches epidemic proportions, but in no way will we neglect the remaining steps we must take against hard-core narcotic addiction: constant monitoring and evaluation to insure program productivity and effectiveness, and securing meaningful employment of thousands of ex-addicts to complete their rehabiliation.

I. INDICATORS OF NARCOTIC ADDICTION

The first half of 1973 has seen a continuing build-up in the number of drug abusers and addicts reached by treatment programs. Evidence has also emerged which appears to indicate a leveling off and a decline in the level of narcotic addiction. Four major indicators, each reported independently, support this hypothesis: addict admissions to correctional institutions, non-transfusion serum hepatitis cases, addict-related crime, and narcotic overdose deaths.

A. Addict Admissions to Correctional Institutions

During the first five months of 1972, 10,039 addicts were admitted to the four largest NYC Correctional Institutions (the Adolescent Remand Shelter and the Bronx, Brooklyn, and Manhattan Houses of Detention). For the same time period this year, the combined total had dropped to 6,072 addict admissions, a decrease of 40 percent, while the number of nonaddict admissions remained relatively constant. Fewer addicts were admitted to the prisons in all major arrest categories, including theft, robbery, and burglary, which are generally considered addict-related crimes.

B. Non-Transfusion Serum Hepatitis Cases Reported to the Health Department

Monthly reports of non-transfusion serum hepatitis cases, which occur almost entirely in heroin addicts, had been rising steadily since 1965 and reached a peak of 167 in January 1971; since that time, there has been a decline, with the May 1973 figure a low of 12. The combined total for the first five months of 1973 was 100 cases--the lowest for seven years, and an 80 percent decrease from the 474 cases reported during the first five months of 1972.

C. Addict-Related Crime Reported to the Police Department

Complaints of those crimes generally considered addict-related have tended to decrease from the first five months of 1972 to the first five months of 1973, continuing on the sharp decrease from 1971. On the other hand, complaints of those crimes generally considered nonaddict related have increased for the same time period.

Addict-Related Crime: First Five Months of Each Year

	1971		1972		1973
Robbery	37,821	down 18.8%	30,712	down 3.8%	29,532
Burglary	75,807	down 20.2%	60,523	down 2.3%	59,121
Motor Vehicle Theft	32,245	down 18.5%	26,272	up 6.7%	27,999
Grand Larceny	34,266	down 34.1%	22,597	down 14.1%	19,409
Petty Larceny	45,591	down 19.0%	36,946	down 12.3%	32,397

D. Overdose Deaths Reported to the Chief Medical Examiner

Overdose deaths, which had leveled off during 1972, declined during the first quarter of 1973. Although some cases are still pending, it is estimated that the first quarter of 1973 will show a 20 percent decrease from the same period last year,

from 257 to a maximum of 205 (a 20 percent decrease) and a
minimum of 180.

II.   CURRENT STATUS OF TREATMENT PROGRAMS

A major achievement has been the virtual elimination of
waiting lists for all treatment modalities, so that every addict
who wants treatment can get it. We are now expanding as rapidly
as we can identify addicts, and we have begun to deploy our
resources in more effective ways, by consolidating some programs, expanding others, increasing productivity and funding
new modalities.

A.   Census

As of May 31, 1973, New York City had a total of 56,522
persons in treatment--22,373 in drug-free programs and 34,149
in methadone maintenance. This represents 45.2 percent of an
estimated 125,000 addicts. A recent survey of the next twelve
largest cities with major addiction problems showed a combined total of 222,400 addicts but only half as many persons in
treatment as New York--28,176. For individual cities, proportions of addicts in treatment ranged from Baltimore, with
24.6 percent to Los Angeles, with 6.7 percent. We continue to
maintain a balance between methadone maintenance and drug-
free programs, and at the present overall growth rate of 3
percent per month, we can estimate that 60,000 to 65,000 persons will be in treatment by the end of the year.

Treatment Modality	May 1973 Census
HSA Methadone Maintenance	10,774
Other Public Methadone Maintenance	14,853
Private Methadone Maintenance	8,522
Methadone Maintenance Subtotal	34,149
HSA Residential Drug-Free	3,058
HSA Ambulatory Drug-Free	5,400
HSA Youth Centers	2,697
NACC Drug-Free	8,213 estimated
Private Drug-Free	3,000 estimated
Drug-Free Subtotal	22,373
Total in Treatment	56,522

B. Increased Productivity

We are requiring increased productivity in existing programs by reducing funding in some areas while expanding in others.

1. Drug-Free Programs

Funding levels of thirteen programs have been cut for a gross savings of approximately $981,000. $443,000 of these funds has been applied to other programs for fiscal year 1974, leaving a net reduction of $538,000 for expansion or new programs. We have also increased the contractual capacity of six programs by 315 treatment slots without increasing funding.

2. Ambulatory Detoxification

We are consolidating the city's nine ambulatory detoxification clinics to five, converting the closed clinics, where possible, to other purposes. Two such units at Harlem and St. Mary's Hospitals will become new Methadone-To-Abstinence or Low-Dose Methadone clinics. This will not affect our capability to detoxify heroin addicts, however; in conjunction with the mobile van outreach program we are extending the clinics' hours of operation until 9 P.M., and in one case, until midnight.

C. New Methadone-to-Abstinence and Low-Dose Methadone Programs

By the end of calendar year 1973, we plan a total of 1500 Methadone-To-Abstinence (MTA) slots and 200 Low-Dose Methadone (LDM) slots--both innovative components of a third major treatment modality that combines some of the best features of methadone maintenance and drug-free programs.

1. Methadone-to-Abstinence

Those patients previously reluctant to commit themselves to an indeterminate dependence on methadone can now be served by MTA programs. Two such programs are currently in operation: Kings County in Brooklyn, and SERA in the Bronx, for a total of 650 slots. Five additional clinics are scheduled to open this fall for 835 more slots.

2. Low-Dose Methadone

    LDM programs will test the hypothesis that 40 milligrams of methadone daily is a sufficient dose to prevent recidivism in selected patients. Two clinics with a total of 200 slots are scheduled to open this fall: Greenpoint and St. Mary's Hospitals, both in Brooklyn. In addition, the MTA programs at Joint Diseases Hospital and New York Medical College in Manhattan will also test the low-dose theory.

III. EVALUATING AND IMPROVING PROGRAMS

    During the last six months we've been able to show conclusively that our programs, both drug-free and methadone maintenance, work using such measures as reduction in arrest rates during and after treatment. We have installed comprehensive information, monitoring, and evaluation systems in many of our programs, and we expect to have completed installation in all of them this fall. A major effort, and one that will continue for the remainder of this calendar year, is the use of these systems to improve program effectiveness.

A. Management Information System

    A Management Information System (MIS) comparable in sophistication to that used in our methadone maintenance and ambulatory detoxification programs has been installed in over 40 of our 120 drug-free programs, and should be fully operational in all programs by the end of the summer.
    This system will enable us to trace changes in employment, schooling, means of support, and legal and medical problems of all those we serve. MIS data, including intake, attendance, and termination reports, will be used to generate a frequent city-wide census and critical evaluative data.

B. Evaluation

    Each of our programs has been evaluated at least once and we are starting on our second cycle. At the same time, we've taken steps to use evaluations as a guide to prompt remedial action, and we are looking for ways to implement standards in privately operated programs.

1. HSA Programs

    ASA's Operations Unit discusses each evaluation with the drug-free program involved, and within one month provides the program with a detailed Findings and Recommendations report including timetables for compliance. Other evaluative tools are used to review drug-free program performance prior to refunding, including District Directors' reports and budget analysts' recommendations. Our methadone maintenance and ambulatory detoxification clinics receive periodic evaluative visits from central staff analysts whose recommendations are implemented on an ongoing basis.

2. Non-HSA Programs

At the request of the Department of Social Services, we have reviewed 100 drug-free programs not under contract to us to determine their adequacy for addicted welfare recipients. Of these, 24 were found acceptable. We have also extended our methadone data system to private maintenance programs-- a crucial element in insuring that the standards established by regulatory agencies for these programs are met--and we are considering our own on-site inspections.

C. Urinalysis

Approximately 75 percent of all HSA-funded programs now require urinalysis for drugs at intake and thereafter at least once a month. All remaining HSA-funded programs will be participating by October.

D. Fiscal Audits

We have strenthened auditing procedures in our own programs and are in the process of reviewing the procedures of other city agencies responsible for non-HSA programs.

1. HSA Programs

During the last six months we have installed new bookkeeping, disbursement and state claims procedures as well as reorganizing fiscal and technical assistance operations.

2. Non-HSA Programs

We are reviewing the procedures used by the Human Resources Administration to audit those drug-free programs with which it contracts and those bills submitted to appropriately authorized providers of care. Additionally, Medicaid bills submitted by all methadone maintenance programs are audited by both the Department of Health and the Department of Social Services.

E. Quantitative Program Indicators

We are developing a system which will use a number of data sources to rate our programs quarterly according to ten quantitative measures. The indicators, including retention rate, spending rate, cost per client, percent of "dirty" urines, decline in arrest rate, and employment ratio, will aid in monitoring and upgrading performance.

F. Pregnant Addicts

All HSA programs, both drug-free and methadone maintenance, give priority to pregnant addicts. Guidelines for serving this important population are now being developed, requiring pregnancy tests for all women, specifying how prenatal and postnatal care should be provided and coordinated and requiring detailed reporting and close monitoring. We will also attempt to implement similar guidelines in non-HSA programs.

G. Technical Assistance and Training

We have developed the capacity to train program staff in a broad range of clinical and management skills and, in the next year, we expect to provide up to fifty hours of training for 1500 persons. Training is offered in two formats.

1. All Program Staff

All staff members are currently offered a twelve-hour course in Adolescent Development and a six-hour course in Basic Pharmacology. Also planned are a twenty-four hour course in Introduction to Counseling Skills, a fifteen-hour course in Management of Drug Programs, and a nine-hour course in Basic Issues and Approaches in Drug Abuse Treatment.

2. Skill Training

Based on an assessment of skill deficiencies in individual programs, staff will receive up to fifty hours of instruction in specific areas, including intake and screening, clinical skills, and program management.

H. Addiction Research and Studies

The ASA Research and Evaluation Unit conducts, both with its own staff and via contracts with social science research firms and universities, detailed research and evaluation studies of addicition treatment effectiveness. Approximately twenty different such studies are under way or have been completed.

One unique effort, now in its final stages, involves field track-
ing of a sample of 150 former addicts who were enrolled in
drug-free treatment during the last six months of 1970. In
addition to a lengthy field interview, we will use arrest, employment, and welfare data, and a recent urine sample, to determine
outcome success for this representative sample.

IV. METHADONE DIVERSION

In an attempt to minimize the potential for illicit methadone diversion, we are focusing on improving policies and procedures for dispensing methadone in both HSA and non-HSA
facilities.

A. Decreased Dosage Levels

It is believed that much illegal methadone diversion takes
place when patients use only a portion of their take-home doses
and sell the rest. To insure maintenance at the minimum
required level, we have scrutinized our own clients closely,
and asked that non-HSA clinics do the same.

1. HSA Methadone Maintenance Programs

In August 1972 69% of our maintenance patients were on
stabilized daily doses of 100 milligrams or more. By May 1973
this percentage was reduced to 46.5. Over the same nine-month
period, the percentage of patients receiving more than 100 milligrams daily decreased from almost 20 to less than 2. It is
program policy that written justification for all doses over 100
milligrams must be entered in the patient's record; the program
director's approval is required for all doses over 120 milligrams.

2. Non-HSA Methadone Maintenance Programs

We have asked all other programs to provide data on
prescribed methadone dosages and urged them to follow our
lead in keeping doses at the minimum effective level.

B. Increased Federal Responsibility

We believe federal supervision has improved substantially,
through tightened FDA approval mechanisms for all programs.
Standards have been established; the scientific training and
experience of all professional employees is scrutinized and
regulations govern organizational structure, medical and rehabi-
litative sources and procedures for dispensing, administering,
and accounting of methadone.

C. Security Provisions

To prevent methadone diversion due to theft, we are
installing burglar alarms in all our out-of-hospital clinics. More
frequent audits of our clinics and of hospital pharmacies are
being conducted, and special audits will be made when irregulari-
ties are indicated. We have requested Police Department cooperation in storage and shipment of medication to selected HSA
clinics where this is a problem, and we will continue to work
with the police to prevent diversion.

V. SCHOOL DRUG PREVENTION PROGRAMS

During the last year, we have reshaped the concept of
school drug prevention programs. We've gone from a didactic
information-oriented approach directed at the general student
population to one of counseling and intervention targeted at a
high-risk population of present and potential drug abusers. We
are in the process of developing new techniques to identify drug-
prone youth and evaluating the impact of different drug prevention techniques on these young people. We have taken an
activist role in administering school programs, allocating funds
according to performance and need, insuring staff qualifications
and installing information, monitoring, and evaluation systems.
Combined service levels of these programs for school years
1972-1973 include 373,180 youngsters in individual or group
counseling, 76,877 parents in counseling sessions or workshops
and 26,877 teachers in training sessions.

A. SPARK Program

SPARK, our largest school program, serves all of the
city's 94 high schools, with a total of 256,000 students. The
program's major activity is individual counseling; it also provides various kinds of group sessions, leadership development
and referral.

1. Levels of Service

In each semester of the 1972-1973 school year approximately 16,700 youngsters were seen for individual counseling;
6,500 participated in formal group sessions and 5,300 in
informal rap sessions.

2. Measures of Program Effectiveness

An evaluation of the SPARK program's effectiveness was
completed for the first time during the last six months. In
comparing current student records with those for the year prior

to SPARK participation, we found a 28 percent improvement in
school attendance, a 49 percent decrease in disruptive behavior,
a 39 percent decrease in subjects failed, an 8.4 percent increase
in grade average, and a 66 percent decrease in unsatisfactory
citizenship.

B. Public School District Drug Prevention Programs

Programs serving 31 public school districts, or a total of
844,000 youngsters, concentrate on individual and group counseling, family counseling, alternative schools that include intensive remedial instruction and after-school youth centers.

1. Information System

A new information system installed in all district drug
prevention programs in April 1973 indicates levels of participation in program activities, measures the degree of student
interest in those activities, and monitors levels of service by
program staff.

2. Levels of Service

The May 1973 service level report indicates that 8,138
students were seen in individual counseling sessions, 50,219 in
rap sessions, 23,186 in discussion groups, 8,440 in intensive
group sessions, and 3,781 in training activities.

3. Administrative Improvement

Funding levels previously unrelated to number of students,
degree of drug abuse, or quality of program have been reallo-
cated; eleven districts were increased because of program
excellence and three were cut for poor performance.

C. Nonpublic School Programs

Nonpublic schools funded for drug prevention programs
include the Archdioceses of New York and Brooklyn, $245,945
and $298,500 respectively, and the Hebrew Day Schools,
$256,730. We would like to increase the low funding in this
area, with per capita spending at $1.50 to $6.70 as compared
with $14.00 in SPARK and $15.00 in the public school district
programs.

D. Centrally Operated Youth Centers

During the last six months sixteen youth centers operated
by ASA have been reorganized, intensified, and upgraded. Previously offering actual treatment but underutilized, the centers

now gear their efforts toward prevention, return to school, or alternative training and employment. Young people in need of long-term treatment are referred to appropriate programs. With the new approach, a census of roughly 350 at the end of 1972 has been nearly doubled to 635.

1. Conversion to Chronic Truant Centers

Four of the youth centers located in areas of high drug abuse (two in Brooklyn, one in Queens and one in Manhattan) were converted to intensive programs focusing on the chronically truant high-school-aged population--a target group of 65, 000- 70, 000 city-wide. We are planning additional Chronic Truant Programs in Central Brooklyn, the South Bronx and Central Harlem.

2. Staff Expertise

All of the centers had been using a group pressure approach with little staff expertise. Now the "growth contract" technique is used to foster individual commitment to change by rewarding positive behavior. Staff workshops in counseling and group dynamics are held, and Hunter College School of Social Work has been asked to place graduate students in the centers to increase professional staff.

VI.   OUTREACH AND REFERRAL

As part of our commitment to reach the hard-core addict population previously resistant to treatment, we have nearly doubled the number of outreach units in the last six months, increased the number of weekly referrals into treatment nearly fivefold, and tightened procedures to insure that referrals actually begin treatment. Further expansion is planned, bringing the total number of outreach units to 37, with particular emphasis on links with the criminal justic system.

A. Placements into Treatment

From January 1, 1973, through June 30, 1973, we placed 9, 338 persons into treatment; 6, 223 into long-term programs and 3, 115 into ambulatory detoxification. During the week ending December 29, 1972, 14 referral units placed 57 addicts into treatment. By the end of June, with 27 referral units, the weekly number had increased fivefold to approximately 300 placements.

B. Expansion of Outreach Efforts

We are continuing to increase our outreach efforts with
the planned addition of fifteen new units. The concurrent elimination of five underutilized units will give us a net total of thirty-
seven. Three of the planned areas of expansion will allow us
to intersect the addict as he comes into contact with the criminal
justice system throughout the city in courts and prisons and, on
a pilot basis, in police precincts. Other expansions will reach
addicts in hospitals and on the streets.

1. Court Referral

In cooperation with judges and district attorneys, the
Court Referral Project places addicts in treatment programs
as an alternative to prison. The Queens court referral unit
just opened will make the project--already operative in the
Bronx, Manhattan and Brooklyn--city-wide.

2. Police Referral

A new pilot program referring addicts directly from
police precincts to treatment programs will begin with units at
Queens Central Booking and the 30th and 34th Precincts in the
Washington Heights section of Manhattan.

3. Prison Referral

In cooperation with the Department of Correction, the
Prison Referral Project places addicts in treatment upon their
release from city detention facilities. Now operative on Rikers
Island, the project will be expanded by five new units serving
the non-Rikers Island facilities, including two in Queens, one
in Manhattan, one in Brooklyn and one in the Bronx.

4. Hospital Referral

Referral units currently located at Harlem, Kings County
and Bronx Municipal Hospitals refer hospital patients identified
as addicts into treatment programs. Three additional units are
planned, bringing the total to six.

5. Mobile Vans

Three mobile vans now circulate throughout the city,
primarily placing hard-core heroin addicts into ambulatory
detoxification programs. Three additional vans are planned

bringing the total to six. To meet the special demands of the
addict population, an extension of hours is also planned, with
three vans and one ambulatory detoxification clinic operating
until midnight.

VII. THE SOFT DRUG PROBLEM

Non-narcotic prescription drug abuse, and particularly
abuse of barbiturates and other sedatives, is an increasing
problem. Many of these drugs are physically addicting.
Unlike narcotics, their untreated withdrawal syndrome can
result in death. And, unlike narcotics, they are most often
legally produced and then diverted into illegal channels. We
are conducting an ongoing investigation of the scope of the
problem, and we have mounted a six-point program to begin
to deal with it.

A. Scope of the Problem

Our initial report on non-narcotic prescription drug
abuse indicates a building danger in various segments of the
population. We are continuing to investigate this problem as
well as the problem of mixed addiction involving alcohol.

1. Multiple Addiction

The proportion of alcohol or other non-narcotic drug
abusers has increased from an estimate of under 10 percent
five years ago to 58 percent last year among narcotic addicts
admitted to Morris Bernstein Institute for inpatient detoxification.

2. Abuse of Barbiturates and Other Sedatives

There has been a 20-fold increase in the proportion of
drug users with exclusive sedative abuse among detainees at
the Spofford Juvenile Center, from .7 percent in 1968 to
14 percent in 1972. Of New York City public school students
aged ten to nineteen sampled in a 1972 study, 10 percent reported
having abused barbiturates. In a 1973 survey of students who
identified themselves as pill abusers, the drug most often used
was the nonbarbiturate sedative methaqualone (Quaalude), cited
by 40 percent. Secobarbital (Seconal), a barbiturate, was
second in order of mention, cited by 30 percent.

B. Program to Deal with Soft Drug Abuse

HSA's program is aimed at increased use of our police
and surveillance authority to identify and prevent diversion of

soft drugs, and at increasing the capability of hospitals and
treatment programs to deal with soft drug abusers.

1. Pharmacy Audits

A special Drug Auditing Division has been established
within the Health Department's Division of Environmental
Health Services, expanding capacity to check pharmacies for
evidence of drug diversion and to prosecute violators in criminal court. Thirty pharmacies were audited last year. With a
total of sixteen inspectors beginning July 1, annual auditing
capacity will be increased to 280 of the city's 2,200 pharmacies, with concentration on high-risk targets.

2. Medicaid Data

The first in a continuing series of quarterly reports will
be generated this summer, using Medicaid data to identify doctors who overprescribe abused drugs and pharmacies that over-
dispense them. Offenders will risk suspension from Medicaid
if they cannot justify their actions.

3. Health Code Changes

Because federal and state controls on non-narcotic prescription drugs are inadequate and often lag behind abuse trends
in New York City, we have submitted and the Board of Health
has approved for publication amendments to the Health Code
giving the Commissioner of Health authority to place prescribing
restrictions on abused drugs.

4. Federal Controls

We are assisting the Federal Bureau of Narcotics and
Dangerous Drugs in the preparation of testimony to intensity
controls on barbiturates and methaqualone. With the Mayor's
Committee on Prescription Drugs, we are continuing to push
for stricter controls on other sedatives and stimulants.

5. Inpatient Detoxification

We have identified problems in the admission of non-
opiate addicts for inpatient detoxification and moved to correct
them. We are implementing city-wide standards for comprehensive detoxification from all drugs so that any addict can be
admitted to a nearby hospital for withdrawal. First targets for
the comprehensive service are a total of sixty beds in Queens
and Metropolitan hospitals.

6. Psychiatric Backup for Treatment Programs

We are adding psychiatric components to existing drug
programs to enable them to treat the new multiple drug abusing
population with its higher incidence of psychopathology. The
first two components are planned to serve a total of 2,000 program clients in the Bronx and northern Manhattan.

VIII. EMPLOYMENT OF EX-ADDICTS

The last and most difficult task we have undertaken to
alleviate the drug problem in New York City is to secure meaningful employment for thousands of ex-addicts. During the last
six months we have identified the job-ready population in our
treatment programs in need of placement, installed the capacity
to screen this population in the context of specific opportunities,
and begun to develop an adequate supply of jobs in both the public and private sectors.

A. Identification of Job-Ready Ex-Addicts

We have identified at least 8,000 ex-addicts in HSA treatment programs who are job-ready and seeking employment.
Perhaps another 8,000 ex-addicts in non-HSA treatment programs
are job-ready. Many of these ex-addicts lack marketable skills
and will need opportunities with heavy training components.

1. HSA Drug-Free Programs

Information returned from our drug-free programs indicates roughly 3,000 ex-addicts who are job-ready but currently
unemployed and seeking work or training. Another 6,000 are
believed to be gainfully occupied in jobs, training programs or
as homemakers.

2. HSA Methadone Maintenance Programs

An estimated 5,000 ex-addicts in our methadone maintenance programs are job-ready but unemployed; 4,500 are
considered gainfully occupied.

B. Screening of Job-Ready Ex-Addicts

We have established six screening units to verify each
ex-addict's job readiness and to refer him or her to particular
openings. These central screening units have the advantage of
not advocating for any particular treatment program and therefore determining job-readiness more objectively. Each unit
can screen up to 50 ex-addicts per day.

1. ASA Screening Units

   We operate five screening units ourselves: two in Manhattan, two in Brooklyn and one in the Bronx.

2. Vera/PACT Screening Unit

   A sixth unit, the third in Manhattan, is currently operated by the Vera Institute of Justice and will shortly be taken over by PACT, a nonprofit private business organization.

C. Job Development

   More than 5,000 jobs or training slots have been committed for the coming year and placement will begin this summer.

1. Public Sector Jobs

   We have had our greatest success at developing jobs within the public sector. A total of 3,500 to 4,000 ex-addicts will be employed by city agencies within the next year. HSA will hire 400 ex-addicts in the next six months as part of a Supported Work Program we are sponsoring in conjunction with the Human Resources Administration. The Vera Institute of Justice will hire 3,000 ex-addicts within the next twelve months to work under contract to various city agencies. Finally, a few hundred additional job openings have been identified by city agencies for direct hiring of ex-addicts.

2. Private Sector Jobs

   At least 1,500 jobs in the private sector will be available to ex-addicts within the next year. The Human Resources Administration (HRA is contracting with PACT to develop 1,000 private sector jobs in the next twelve months; PACT has already contacted the hundred largest firms, and over one-third of these have agreed to hire ex-addicts. HRA is also contracting with the Association of Personnel Agencies of New York for placement in training as well as private sector jobs.

III-3   TUBERCULOSIS CLINIC STUDY — June, 1971

by Smith Lanning

Patient visits in Table 1[1] include only those visits to physicians. Physician-hours consist of the time of all per-session physicians and one-fourth of the time of the physician in charge at each clinic. This portion of the time of the physician in charge is our best estimate of the average time he spends in the capacity of a clinician.

The table indicates that the average number of visits to a physician is 3.6 per physician-hour, or one visit every 16 minutes. At least initially this would appear to be a reasonably high level of activity for any physician.

The number of visits varies quite substantially from one clinic to another, reaching a high level of 8.2 visits per hour at Williamsburg-Greenpoint and a low of about 2 visits per hour at Morningside. The clinic cost per visit varies greatly from clinic to clinic, too. The average cost is $11.34. The highest-cost clinic (Jamaica-West) provides a visit at $23.32, and the lowest cost per visit figure of $8.29 is provided by the Bedford clinic.

There are many reasons for the variations in cost and volume from one clinic to another. The physicians in one clinic may be providing a higher quality of treatment than in other clinics, thereby consuming more of their time per patient. Patient needs may be greater or more complex than in other clinics. Or the clinic may not have sufficient supporting staff.

Even with these complexities we would like to move toward being able to answer the question whether these conditions do in fact explain the entire differences in the activity figures. The value of asking such a question is suggested by the fact that $238,000 a year could be saved if we could increase the volume of the ten clinics with lower than the average number of visits per physician hour to the city average of 3.6 visits. This is 15 percent of those costs directly related to clinic acti-

vity and under the control of the Bureau of TB. (This assumes
that these clinics could adjust their session schedules and personnel assignments accordingly.)

   We can explain many of the variations from clinic to clinic
in terms of (1) the productivity of physicians (number of patient
visits per hour), and (2) the staff complement of each clinic
(number of support hours per physician hour). Ultimately, it
would be helpful to develop some overall guidelines or standards
for both the productivity of the physician and the support available per physician hour. With such guidelines the efficiency of
each clinic could be measured periodically, compared with its
counterparts, and appropriate staff and session adjustments
made.

   Whether 3.6 visits per hour is the proper standard for
average physician productivity is a question which requires
further investigation. The figure could be too high or too low.
Since some clinics see as many as 6 or 8 patients per physician hour, 3.6 visits is probably not too high. The exact level
will require careful consideration of the specific tasks required
of the physician in the patient visit.

   A rough standard for the number of support personnel
hours per physician-hour is helpful in judging the adequacy of
staffing patterns in each clinic. The average figure in 1970 was
3.7 support-hours (public health nurse, public health assistant,
clerk) for every clinician-hour. The support figure varied from
2 to 8 per hour among the clinics. If the time of X-ray technicians were added to this figure, the support-hours would probably reach roughly 4.7 per physician-hour. This would appear
at first glance to be high. If it were found that 3.0 support-hours
per physician-hour were adequate to handle a standard volume,
clinic costs could then be reduced substantially by bringing the
more highly staffed clinics in line with this figure.

OTHER COSTS

   In addition to those costs directly identifiable with patient
visits to a physician, such costs as those for roster clerks,
X-ray technicians, nurse field visits, lab work, TB control overhead, and a portion of the overhead of Department of Health are
also related to clinic activity. Table 2 divides all costs related
to TB clinic visits into direct costs, or that portion directly
involved in providing service to the patient, and indirect costs,
or those costs which are in support of the direct service costs
and are not directly a part of service rendered.

   The total cost of a visit to a TB clinic is about $26.13.
This is not much lower than the $32 charge for an outpatient
visit in municipal hospitals. And it appears to be as or more
expensive than a visit to a private physician. The table indi-

cates that <u>48 percent of this cost is made of indirect costs</u>.
This is due largely to clerical costs and the many layers of
supervision now existing in the Department of Health (the program bureau, the district health office, the Bureau of Nursing,
and executive management). The means of allocating costs to
the Bureau of TB are very rough, and these figures should be
combined as indicators of the basic proportion of direct and
indirect costs rather than actual costs.

While most of the indirect costs are not under the control
of the Bureau of TB, some are. Roster clerks, for example,
are not found in most TB clinics, and their total cost is estimated to be about $150,000 per year. Depending upon the need
for a full-time roster clerk in each clinic, there may be a
means to increase the responsibility of each roster clerk from
one to two clinics. The Bureau has already done this in some
cases. A similar potential for savings exists in the use of
X-ray technicians, now one or more for each clinic.

EFFECTIVENESS

To this point we have concerned ourselves with the measurement of volume of activity without addressing the effectiveness of that activity. To some extent, the effectiveness of the
entire TB control program is reflected in the incidence level
of the disease. This level has declined from 60 cases per
100,000 in 1960 to 31 cases in 1971. This measure is too gross,
however, to help directly in determining the effectiveness of a
particular part of the TB control program or a particular clinic.

A measure of the percentage of persons with active TB
who are converted to inactive status over a certain time period
would be much more helpful. This information is presently
gathered on a sample basis for the entire program at widely
spaced intervals of time. A recent study indicates that the percentage of patients who are converted to inactive status is about
10 percent less than is medically feasible over a two-year
period. This would suggest a need for improved follow-up procedures of patients with active TB.

To assist us in locating the relatively less effective areas
of the program, the above percentage measures must be available on a clinic-by-clinic basis and in timely fashion. A similar
percentage measure of those patients on chemoprophylactic
treatment who actually complete the treatment process would
also be helpful. Finally, a cost per case treated and a cost per
preventive prophylaxis administered by clinic would be extremely
useful to have. The bureau, in conjunction with federal project
management, is attempting to develop some of this data at the
present time.

With the lack of the above data it is still possible to review the effectiveness of certain segments of the program. In particular, the bureau is concerned with the advisability of maintaining some 10,000 patients on clinic registers who are inactive cases not receiving antibacterial drug treatment. The bureau has found that physicians typically prefer to continue to see these patients each year largely for continuity in record-keeping. An additional 9,000 patients who are contacts and associates of patients with active TB are also seen once or twice a year without receiving antibacterial drug treatment. These two categories of patients account for between 20,000 to 40,000 visits to physicians each year. This is 11 to 22 percent of the total number of visits. The number and proportion of these patients varies widely from one clinic to another. A change in policy toward these patients would clearly enable the bureau to free up sizable resources for potentially more productive uses.

The bureau has also done some work on the issue of the cost-effectiveness of preventive treatment. This is a difficult issue to quantify, since many of the benefits of the prevention of a disease are intangible, such as the value to a person of not contracting TB and the accompanying but lesser value to his family and associates of his remaining in good health.

The importance of reviewing the cost-effectiveness of preventive treatment is illustrated by the fact that roughly 15 percent of all visits to physicians are for purely preventive treatment. Aside from the personal benefits, prevention saves the cost of hospitalization which would otherwise have been incurred by the diseased patient. The cost of hospitalization is an average of about $6,300 per case of active TB treated (70 days of hospitalization at $90^2 a day = $6,300). An additional $240 to cover outpatient service of twenty visits at $12 per visit bring the total treatment cost to $6,540.

The benefit of preventing a case of active TB consists of this $6,540 cost of hospitalization plus one-fourth of that amount to include the cost of the fact that four newly active cases of TB result in one additional active case. This gives us a figure of $8,175 as a rough indicator of the quantifiable portion of the benefit of preventing a case.

The cost of preventing a case depends on the number of visits in the preventive process, the number who complete this process, the incremental cost per visit, and the number of these patients receiving preventive treatment who would otherwise have contracted the disease. If six clinic visits are required to complete the preventive process, the incremental cost per visit is $12, and 80 percent of these patients who begin prevention actually complete it, then the Bureau of TB should provide preventive treatment to all groups of patients for whom one active case is prevented for every 90 people receiving preventive treatments. For those groups for which more than 90 preventive prophylaxes would be required to prevent one active case of TB, the cost would outweigh the benefits included in the above analysis. The personal benefits from not contracting TB are not included in this analysis and would have to be before any decisions were to be made on its basis.

As the length of hospitalization for TB patients declines, the benefits of preventing a case also declines. This suggests that the bureau review its preventive program on an ongoing basis to assure that it is directed at appropriate segments of the population.

IMPLICATIONS

The analysis suggests several areas in which further attention would appear warranted:

1. The wide variations in clinic output indicate the potential value of creating a standard for physician productivity. The time required to resolve what a fair standard is appears to be warranted by the improved capacity to schedule sessions and staff support according to the real needs of each clinic.

2. The need to continue to see the large segment of 20,000 patients on the clinic registers who are inactive cases, contacts, or associates not receiving drug treatment deserves further review. A definite plan to eliminate some or all of these patients could emerge from the review.

3. As suggested above, a review of the existing assignment of roster clerks and X-ray technicians. might also lead to an improvement in operating efficiency.

4. The cost-effectiveness of preventive treatment deserves further analysis to determine the appropriateness of continuing preventive services to certain segments of the population.

5. The role of hospitalization of patients with active TB varies from 60 percent of all active patients in one district to 20 percent in another. The high cost of hospitalization suggests the value of reviewing the manner in which districts decide when and how long to hospitalize TB patients.

FOOTNOTES

1. Editor's note: Tables I and II were omitted due to space limitations.

2. The hospitalization cost of $90 a day is an estimate of the incremental cost of providing an extra day of TB care. It assumes that of a total hospitalization cost of about $120 a day, roughly 75 percent or $90 is the variable or incremental cost of an additional patient day.

III-4 PROBLEMS WITH THE NEW YORK CITY HEALTH AND HOSPITALS CORPORATION — May 27, 1971

by Robert Harris

As you know, there are many things that irritate HSA staff in day-to-day dealings with HHC. Most are of the Mickey Mouse variety (e.g., they do not provide information we request, they provide misleading information, they do not honor commitments on such things as space and construction, they are personally abusive and obnoxious, etc.). The whole nonsense business that we have gone through on budget swaps,[1] for example, is incredible. And we have not seen the end of it.

We discuss these issues frequently, and I fear that those discussions have obscured some other points I have tried to make. They are all quite minor problems in the overall scheme of things. What concerns me greatly is mounting evidence of very serious fundamental problems that threaten to make the promise that we saw in HHC unrealizable. While we have discussed these piecemeal over the past few months, I would like to explore them somewhat systematically, if briefly. While highly critical, the intent of this memo is constructive, since it still remains possible to do something about the problems.

EXPECTATIONS FOR HHC: HISTORICAL BACKGROUND

We all know that, by and large, health care delivery in the United States is terribly inefficient and wasteful of resources, (the Glazer piece from The Public Interest which I sent you a few weeks back highlights this). Many simplified diagnoses of the industry's illness are available. The diagnoses and prescriptions are so well known as to be cliches. Yet it is very difficult to do much about it because of the fragmented nature of the industry. No one controls all of the components--and no one can force them to work together.

New York City is in a unique position with respect to

grappling with these problems. Here, and nowhere else in the
country, government controls enough of the industry to (perhaps)
make it work. Forty percent of hospital capacity is owned by
the city, and the city directly or indirectly provides funds to the
rest of the system--through affiliation contracts, Charitable
Institutions Budget, Ghetto Medicine, etc.[2] Coupled with the
funds that flow from the state, and at least some cooperative
state officials, the city has enormous potential financial leverage.
In addition, there is a great deal of moral power that you have
barely tapped. Going public on some of the abuses of contracts,
etc., has potential for forcing change. Moreover, the city has
indirect regulatory handles on the private sector (e.g., at least
five members of the Board of the Health and Hospital Planning
Council of Southern New York are ex officio city members,
who carry disproportionate weight in debate). And of course
we have CHP in the wings.

One main reason why the city could not do much with this
latent power in the past lies in the fact that the bureaucracy of
city government makes it virtually impossible to do anything.
It is very difficult on a routine matter to thread your way
through the Departments of Personnel, Purchasing, Public
Works, Budget, etc., and then deal with municipal unions, the
ladies,[3] etc., without losing sight of your original objective in
in the quest to retain your sanity. The development of a corporation was viewed by many as a way out of the mess of city bureaucracy in running our hospitals; you may recall that the idea of
a corporation was originated by and strongly pushed by Fred
Hayes for that reason.

A corporation unshackled from operating constraints
imposed by the old-line city bureaucrats, that had direct control over 40 percent of the hospital beds in the city, and that
provided $140 million of medical school financing could swing
immense weight in the overall health delivery system. Operating
under policies laid down by HSA (see enabling legislation), the
Corporation could start reshaping the way in which medical
care is delivered in New York City. If HHC knew what it wanted
to do, it could move quickly and with clout. It was to be a big
fiscal drop.[4] It could easily (in concept):

1. Experiment with any number of organization schemes
to improve delivery of care (e.g., vary input mixes of
professional and nonprofessionals, substitute capital for
labor, etc.). Group practices, health maintenance organizations (HMO's), and the like could be developed to
expand services in areas of high need at relatively low
cost.
2. Consolidate specialty care clinics in outpatient departments to both reduce costs and improve the quality of
patient care.
3. Reallocate beds to meet patient needs rather than to

preserve medical empires and serve research and teaching needs of medical schools.

4. Reduce costs without letting quality deteriorate by managing resources carefully and forcing affiliates to focus much more on patient care rather than research or education.

5. Close down beds that are not really needed.

6. Etc., etc.

It could do those thing in its own hospitals, and if it did them well, it would show by example what is possible. Such changes could then be pushed into the private sector by the exercise of some of the powers HSA has. A freewheeling operating agency (HHC) operating with HSA (with its regulatory, administrative, and moral clout) would be a very powerful agent of change. This prospect was one of the great attractions of HSA when we were recruiting last year.

In addition, at a minimum, a corporation could be expected to do a better job of traditional hospital administration than a traditional city agency. Thus even if HHC did nothing innovative in the health delivery system area it could be expected to save money or increase output for the same amount of money. Or perhaps simply reduce waiting time in outpatient departments. This achievement alone would be a great one.

RESULTS TO DATE

Alas, HHC has done none of the above. Nor has it, in the first year, geared up to do any of the above in the future--except for the minimal possible result of faster payment of bills and the like. It has instead expended enormous energy on such objectives as:

1. Establishing petty bureaucratic autonomy from the city and HSA, while remaining financially dependent.

2. Demanding huge budget increases to reflect its greater efficiency.

3. Accelerating low-grade press agentry (e.g., a credo that is pure B.S., a fancy bound budget that is technically incompetent and also heavily larded with pure B.S. such as a promise of $200 million more services for less tax levy,[5] etc.).

4. Making the board feel powerful and important despite the fact that it is powerless and should have no real function other than reviewing management performance in the implementation of city policy.

In the process, the HSA administrator has been forced into the position of behaving as though he is Chairman of the Board DESPITE being Health Services Administrator of the city, rather than BECAUSE he is. This had the effect of of excluding HSA (your staff) from the policy-making and moni-

toring role which was envisaged by the proponents of a corporation, which was explicitly spelled out in legislation, and which
you planned on last year. The HSA staff has been forced to
close its eyes to things that it should have some say over by
legislative authority and by virture of the fact that HHC is
spending lots of city money and we are the City Health Agency.

The affiliation contract issue is an interesting case in
point. As you know, HSA staff members were specifically
excluded from working on the affiliation contract task force by
HHC staff, despite the overriding importance of the contracts
to the city and your great interest. The reason given was that
HHC staff was going to develop all of the necessary facts and
figures to negotiate tough contracts on their own, with help
from AMS.[6] It now turns out that no facts and figures were
developed. While a tough model contract (as drafted by an
outside law firm) will be helpful, the numbers that go into the
blanks in the model contract are crucial--and nonexistent.
Negotiations are going on based on subjective judgments of
performance--largely based on Stan Bergen's knowledge. As
you know, he is leaving.

As a result of this, and many similar encounters, HSA
staff would rather avoid major issues involving HHC than deal
with HHC. Dealing with HHC on any issue generally involves
doing a lot of work that they should do and being rewarded with
abuse or being ignored. Actions adopted by the board are
frequently contrary to common sense, as well as contrary to
HSA views of the correct way to proceed. (As an example,
look at the corporation's vocal pushing of nurse housing--an
expensive and probably ineffective solution to the problem sold
to the board by staff before any analysis was done. As another
example, look at the retrenchment from the status quo with
respect to community boards.)

The top HSA staff has become terribly estranged from top
HHC staff (by HHC desire and action). The HHC staff has also
alienated the Bureau of the Budget, the Department of Personnel,
the Corporation Counsel, and other responsible city agencies.
This is a very high cost indeed for the illusion of independence--
given that HHC's independence has not helped it improve anything. The hostility toward HHC from all of these services
cannot be completely without foundation. As evidence of the
failure to bring about improvement, review HHC's draft progress
report that you gave me a few weeks ago. Specific failures were
outlined in some detail in my memo of March 17, 1971, on
"Evaluation of the HHC: The First Nine Months, " and the attachments to that memo. The most recent failure occurred in
reviewing budget options. The board, prompted by HHC staff,
adopted an absurd and noncredible public posture.[7]

I trust that you are aware that the general consensus of
informed opinion around the city is that HHC is another version

of the Department of Hospitals except that it is more expensive,
less credible, and less responsible (based on unsolicited views
transmitted to HSA staff by a large nonrandom sample of knowledgeable outside observers with whom we deal on other matters).
This reputation does not help recruitment.

THE FUTURE

I fear that a pattern has been set that will persist for
some years. My reasons for feeling this are simple:
    1. HHC has not adequately dealt with the collections pro-
blem this year. [8] This is a major failure and symptomatic
of a more basic problem. The collections problem is
easy compared with any substantive health care delivery
problem. The world's most incompetent accountants
could solve it if given enough time--so the fact that it has
"improved" does not warm my heart. It damned well
ought to start improving after nine months of disaster
because the people working on it are not the world's most
incompetent accountants. But it has taken much too long
for me to have any faith in them being able to tackle a
hard problem. And remember, we (including you) have
only their word that it has been "solved." We have no
evidence of a real solution except for an assertion that
the new management system will be installed by October.
Informed rumor is that this is not true (again). And, of
course, in the stalling process this year, they have made
it seem like a great accomplishment to be only about
$60 to $90 million in the hole instead of $100 million.
(The exact magnitude of the budget deficit depends upon
the amount of cash balance HHC needs to operate, since
it will, by June 30, reduce its cash balance to approximately zero.)
    2. HHC--in its maiden year--has attracted very few first-
rate doers and thinkers. (How many can you name with a
straight face?) Yet it needs lots of both to change anything.
It has a generally mediocre staff, with few exceptions.
Recruiting good guys will be harder in the future, because
only good guys can recruit good guys. The contagion
effect is strong. Stan Bergen could perhaps do a great
operations job--but he needs good staff support from both
planners and implementers in great depth to have more
than a surface impact. Fighting fires does not improve
the system, no matter how good a fire fighter you have.
To date Stan has been fighting a holding operation. [9]
    Operationally improving a system requires detailed
staff work. To date the only studies that might lead to
change have been done by non-HHC staff: The ambulance

study--based on early studies by the city administrator's
office and others and pulled together with recommendations
by HSA staff; our work on blood supplemented by a Health
Department survey; the patient Bill of Rights program
developed by HSA; review of hospital facility needs done
by HSA; long-stay patient study and on-going follow-up
studies on home care and long-term care, etc.
3. HHC has set a pattern of dealing with the city that will
make it difficult to get the kind of city support it needs
and should have. (E.g., continuous attempts to flim-flam
the Budget Bureau have made BOB very cautious about
giving HHC more money. One cannot give no-strings
money to people one does not trust.)
4. HHC pronouncements have little credibility, e.g.,
when Joe English announced the closing of eight hospitals,
it was buried away in the back of The New York Times
(see editorial in the April 20 Times for their assessment
of this possibility). Yet the truth could have been made
horrible enough to achieve the political objective while
remaining credible publicly.
    In short, my views of HHC reflect the opinion that a great
opportunity has been lost for substantive reform of the health
care delivery system--and possibly irretrievably lost. My
frequent negativism does not reflect a schtick, or an irrational
feeling that HHC "cannot do anything." I have simply observed
that HHC has done very little (see their own progress report
which I noted earlier). It is also not geared up to do much more
in the future, and it will be increasingly difficult to recruit
first-rate managerial and analytic talent.

WHAT TO DO

    These conclusions, I venture to say, have been reached
by many others. I am merely the least soft-spoken member of
your staff on the subject. Having reached these conclusions,
and expressed them frequently, it is incumbent on me to make
some constructive suggestions. What can be done to partially
salvage the situation? It is unrealistic to try to ignore HHC--
tempting as that thought is. It is simply too large and obtrusive
to be able to make believe it isn't there. The following are a
few steps in the right direction:
    1. A major step that we must take is to develop the kind
of formal relationships between HHC and HSA we let slip
last year. (We did this because of the feeling that we were
working toward common goals, etc., and dealing with men
of good will. That turned out not to be true.) The program
guidance letter[10] that we have drafted is a first step in this
process. Actively forcing HHC to face up to the issues

may help force it to focus on some of the things it has
screwed up this year. Our draft focused on input problems
because they are primary.

2. <u>The chairman of the board must take control of the
board even if it involves a confrontation</u>. This can be
done on issues where you are right on the merits--count
the votes. And the risk involved in confrontation is,
really, small. HHC is too important to let the feelings
and sensibilities of a few stand in the way of making it
work. A viable chairman of any corporation cannot be in
the position of being whipsawed by a runaway board on one
side and a weak corporate staff on the other. Only when
he is in firm control of the board (at least on issues where
he is right) can the staff be shaped up.

3. <u>Some staff changes are called for in HHC</u>. I think you
know what they are. A few deletions and a lot of additions
are needed, <u>and you must make sure it happens</u>. Joe
English has some real talents that are needed in his job.
But he is lacking in technical knowledge of all sorts, and
more seriously, he seems unaware of the kind of support
that he needs in his central staff. The board (chairman)
must intervene and recruit a top management. The lack
of a good top management at the end of a full year is
inexcusable.

RECAPITULATION

In short, who has been made healthy by HHC? The answer
is essentially no one. Costs are higher, efficiency and ration-
ality (or lack thereof) unchanged, and the future prospects would
seem to be more of the same. It is very, very sad.

FOOTNOTES

1. <u>Editor's note</u>: Prior to the creation of HHC, the Hospitals
Department routinely included some HSA items in the Hospitals
Department budget. These funds were to be transferred to HSA
from HHC, but they never were, due to obstructive tactics of
HHC.

2. <u>Editor's note</u>: The Charitable Institutions Budget funded the
city's share of Medicaid funds, and Ghetto Medicine is a subsidy
program for voluntary hospital outpatient departments.

3. <u>Editor's note</u>: "The ladies" refers to various female health
lobbies.

4. <u>Editor's note</u>: A device to avoid the city's bureaucratic rules.

5. City funds.

6. American Management Systems, consulting firm retained by HHC.

7. Editor's note: HHC threats to close hospitals were not believed by the press.

8. Editor's note: This refers to an inadequate third-party billing system which caused a substantial revenue shortfall.

9. Editor's note: Stanley Bergen, M.D., Senior Vice President, resigned several months later.

10. Editor's note: See the program guidance letter in this chapter.

III-5 PROGRAM GUIDANCE LETTER — July 7, 1971

by Gordon Chase

On July 30th of last year, I sent you a memorandum giving some general guidance as to the main priorities for the first year of operation of the Health and Hospitals Corporation. Over the past year, the corporation has done quite well in accomplishing some of those things discussed in last year's Program Guidance Letter which, on behalf of the city, I felt to be most important to focus on immediately. There is still, however, plenty of ground which has to be covered.

Community Participation in the management of the eighteen municipal hospitals is on the way to becoming a reality; the corporation has established the first community relations service in the history of the municipal hospital system. I expect you to continue your efforts to organize your community boards into meaningful and useful forces and to have them all in place and operating before June 30, 1972.

Progress in the area of improving your Receivables Collections has been substantial. The crucial importance of implementing a system to maintain and hopefully even improve upon this performance cannot be stressed enough, if the corporation is to obtain the needed revenue to make the municipal hospitals a truly first-class provider of health care.

The corporation has begun to develop a Strategy for Ambulatory Care which will relate the neighborhood family care center (NFCC) program with current ambulatory care services being provided by municipal hospitals; in addition, the new comprehensive family care centers to be opened at Sydenham and Coney Island during fiscal year 1972 will be most welcome advances. I am still very concerned, however, with the need to rationalize hospital outpatient services and emergency rooms. As I pointed out last year, long waiting lines, complex systems, lack of adequate patient referral systems and medical record systems, and unnecessary overspecialization of clinics all lead to both a

167

failure to provide high-quality medical care and demeaning
experiences for patients.

In the area of <u>Improvement of Selected Programs</u>, the
abortion program, begun and so well run during the corporation's very first year of operation, is perhaps one of your most
outstanding successes to date. Your attention over the next
year should be focused on achieving similar success with other
programs of a community nature, such as venereal disease
control, lead poisoning, drug addiction, and alcoholism.

Despite our building program and your major renovation
programs, we are still a long way from bringing the municipal
system up to the standards of the best voluntaries. We must
continue to press ahead in the area of <u>Physical Plant</u>.

Although tough negotiations lie ahead, you have developed,
for the first time since their inception almost ten years ago,
meaningful draft <u>Affiliation Contracts</u> which would ensure a
high level of professional medical service, accountability of
the affiliates, and the responsibility of the corporation to
decide what services will be delivered where. The next step
is to translate this affiliation contract into a reality.

<u>Prison Health</u> is another service in need of improvement
which, while we have developed a plan (and taken some steps)
to deal with this problem, is still in need of our continuing attention. We at HSA will continue to lead this effort until HHC is in
a position to take it over.

The corporation has made substantial progress toward
solving part of your <u>Staffing Problem</u> by adding more than 1,000
registered nurses to your work force over the last year. Considerable progress has also been made in recruiting comptrollers
at each of the hospitals, personnel directors, and collection
staffs. A similar major effort is needed to strengthen your
management capabilities further at the central corporate staff
and hospital levels.

Improving such administrative staff will directly affect
your problems of <u>Organization</u>. However, as I pointed out last
year, you must install a good management information system,
including accurate financial reports, to ensure the proper management of the municipal hospitals.

Wide variations among hospitals in average lengths of
stay, costs per inpatient day, and costs per outpatient visit
still remain to be addressed. As I pointed out last year, these
inequities are in need of <u>Immediate Managerial Improvement</u>.
Additional areas for you to focus the corporation's managerial
efforts on are delineated below.

This program guidance memorandum is being issued at a
time when the fiscal year 1972 HHC budget has just been settled.
I recognize that analysis needs to be done in order to determine
how to fund new or expanded programs out of the corporation's
base budget. I realize that this task will require tremendous

effort in the next few months by the HHC Central Office. None-theless, we cannot afford to slight the fiscal year 1973 budget preparation process because of this situation. Rather, we must integrate our work on both the fiscal year 1972 and the fiscal year 1973 budgets. This guidance is issued with this goal in mind.

Five major topics are covered by this memorandum:
1. Format of the fiscal year 1973 Budget Submission
2. Allocation of the Base Budget among Institutions and Services
3. Financial Information, Control, and Procedures
4. Management Staffing
5. Specific Issues and Programs to Be Analyzed

I would like by August 2, 1971, a detailed plan indicating the steps that the corporation expects to take during the next fiscal year to deal with the problems outlined in this memoran-dum. The corporation's plan should indicate what will be finished by when, what problems can be anticipated for each area, the specific means that will be used in each area, resource commitments, and designation of staff members who will have general and specific responsibility for each area.

In developing your plan, I would like you to note particu-larly the financial and management reports discussed below. These are of extreme importance.

As the attached timetable indicates, I think it is impera-tive that you develop this one-year plan by August 2.

If you note the attached timetable, you will see that there is very little room for slippage, since HSA must review the budget prior to its submission.

I. FORMAT OF THE FISCAL YEAR (FY) 1973 BUDGET
SUBMISSION

The FY 73 submission should, much as the FY 72 submis-sion did, contain analyses of total expenditures and revenues and the major policy and program issues. It should also include budget requests for each institution and for the Central Office.

While budget requests for each institution can certainly be presented by major programs, other presentations should also be made this year. Perhaps the most important extension from the FY 72 submission should be to prepare a budget request at a greater level of detail than the FY 72 submission. While such a breakout is perhaps not as useful from a broad policy standpoint as a program budget, it is more important from a management and control standpoint. Internal management and control deserve primary emphasis throughout the FY 73 budget cycle. This includes starting with a careful analysis of how the institutions are organized, how they should be organized, and how the cost center structure should relate to the organization.

The budget submission should also have available supporting backup documents. The Central Office base budget should be broken down into meaningful service levels for purposes of analysis. Particular effort should be devoted to exploring ways to reduce the Central Office base. Each institution's submission should include an analysis of what part of the recommended program is to be carried out by the affiliates.

The base budget request should contain each of the following items. In all cases, the underlying figures and assumptions should be clearly presented so that they can be understood by all concerned parties.

1. A zero-base analysis of one hospital and/or one program.

2. A projection of the impact of inflation on the base budget. (Analyses of wage changes should be forwarded under separate cover and kept confidential lest they prejudice collective bargaining negotiations.)

3. An analysis identifying which costs are directly variable with changes in work load.

4. A projection of changes in work load broken down at least by program.

5. Revenue projections.

II. ALLOCATION OF THE BASE BUDGET AMONG INSTITUTIONS AND SERVICES

Because of time constraints and lack of financial data, last year's budget request contained no analysis of the $617 million base. Clearly, this base must be understood--an immediate analysis of the base must be undertaken. This analysis should be extended to identify further reallocation of the base which ought to be made in FY 73. In particular, the following questions should be answered:

1. Which services and institutions are net revenue producers?

2. For which services and institutions would patients most likely be able to receive treatment elsewhere should the service or institution be closed?

3. What is the relative benefit of nonmedical activities such as social services?

4. What types of services could benefit from consolidation at a smaller number of institutions?

III. FINANCIAL INFORMATION, CONTROL AND PROCEDURES

A. Expenditure Reports and Expenditure Control

Expenditure reports and expenditure control go hand in hand. I am aware that this year the corporation could not effectively control the expenditures of individual institutions because it did not know how much each institution was spending. I understand that for the past several months expenditure reports by institution have been prepared and circulated to the institutions. Please send HSA by July 9 a copy of all reports prepared to date.

It is my understanding that the financial management data-processing system being developed will allow much more detailed expenditure reports beginning next year. Please forward copies of all such reports to HSA. Likewise, you should prepare a set of procedures explaining to the hospitals exactly what actions will be taken when these reports indicate that they are over-spending their budgets. You should also concentrate on developing procedures to give hospitals interim budgets at the beginning of FY 72. (It will probably be some time after the beginning of the year before the final allocation of your total budget to each institution is complete, so interim budgets will be necessary.) I would like to receive a copy of such procedures by July 15.

I would also like to receive by July 15 a copy of a manual you should prepare explaining to the hospitals how your new expenditure reporting system will operate. This is a necessity if they are to have time to understand it before it goes into operation. While you should concentrate on explaining in detail the extent to which controls will be imposed, be careful not to claim that you will control hospitals in ways you cannot enforce.

B. Collection Reports

Before October of this year, I would like to receive a monthly report stating both (1) how much cash was collected from sources outside New York City and (2) the amount of receivables created both during the preceding month and for the fiscal year to date. This should be compared with a plan for collections. In the interim I would like whatever cash flow reports you can make available on a regular basis.

You should develop rigorous definitions of receivables and cash collections to avoid the confusion which ensued this year. (Likewise, you need to develop rigorous accounting definitions to explain the corporation's budget: e.g., what is an encumbrance, or what is a refund?)

I understand that you have underway plans for further
reforms in the collections area and some plans for beginning
to automate portions of the system. By July 15 I would like to
have a short paper describing these plans and indicating your
schedule for accomplishing the various tasks.

IV. MANAGEMENT STAFFING

The corporation should prepare a management staffing
plan for improving the corporate organization. This plan should
consider including project managers for such corporate-wide
activities as blood management, security, and patient screening
in the emergency rooms; regional line managers as suggested
by the Piel Commission; corporate managers of ambulatory
care, home care, and long-term care. Also, the management
staffing plan should consider appropriate incentives for corporation personnel and steps for management training and development. Specific attention should be given to building a capable
middle management staff at each hospital.

V. SPECIFIC ISSUES AND PROGRAMS TO BE ANALYZED

There are obviously many issues in need of analysis, only
some of which are suggested below. These analyses are all
relevant not only to preparation of both FY 73 base and discretionary budget requests, but also to final allocation of the FY
72 budget. I would like to see, as part of your one-year plan,
your specific ideas as to what analyses you feel that you should
focus on.

A. Security

It is important to analyze each hospital's particular
security needs and to recommend solutions.

B. Ambulances

During the past year, an analysis was begun of the ambulance situation in the city. An effort should be made to complete
the study.

C. Staffing Needs

The corporation seems well on the road to conducting a
useful analysis, in conjunction with RAND, of the nursing short-

age problem in the city and how to deal with it. That type of
analysis is also needed on the problems of physician staffing,
we need to appraise the current staffing patterns in our hospitals
to see if, in fact, we do have a maldistribution of our most
expensive manpower.

D. Capital Construction

On the basis of the staff study which painted a rather pes-
simistic picture of alternative capital financing mechanisms, we
obviously need to sort out our priorities for future capital construction. Although this is a more long-range problem, it is
important that the analysis that is currently being conducted on
this issue be continued in order to suggest a way out of our present dilemma and to avoid future miscalcuations of how much
we can or should build.

E. Hospital Utilization

Some comprehensive analyses are needed in the whole
area of the utilization of our hospitals. What do we do about
empty TB beds where there is a dire need for psych beds?
Where are we going to get beds for new services such as alcoholism and addiction? What are we going to do about the fact
that at least 15 percent of the patients in municipal hospitals
do not belong there? Should we allow physicians in our hospitals to admit private-paying patients as a means of filling empty
beds and as a means of moving us further away from a two-
class delivery system?

F. Drug Addiction

HSA has developed an analysis of the drug addiction problem city-wide. Analysis is needed to suggest what the corporation can further do to combat this problem.

G. Incentive Budgeting

A viable incentive budgeting scheme will be important if
the corporation is to become financially more independent of the
city. A program for periodic performance evaluation and goal-
setting should be initiated this year. If the hospitals are to be
accountable, then their individual budgets must be tied to such
performance measures as improvements in their collections or
reductions in average lengths of stays over the long run. Similarly, there is a need to develop a plan of rewarding managers
for their performance.

IV

Methodology and
Quantitative Relationships

THE EVALUATION OF THE HEALTH INSURANCE
EXPERIMENT

In 1972 the battle lines were being drawn for a second round of debate on the issue of national health insurance. HEW staff under Secretary Eliott Richardson had developed the "MEGA proposal" with its recommendation of maximum liability health insurance to cover medical expenses beyond a given dollar limit. This set the stage for the introduction of the second Nixon Bill in January 1974. At the same time-congressional staffs were preparing for introduction of what subsequently became the Kennedy-Mills Bill and for the Long-Ribicoff Bill, modifying earlier proposals of the principal sponsors for comprehensive national health insurance and for catastrophic health insurance.

The issues of eligibility and coverage and efficiency had become clear also. Would the program have compulsory coverage to assure that all persons receive services in time of need, or would it be voluntary to avoid the costs of coverage for those with less interest, knowledge, or foresight? Would there be one plan for all or would there continue to be a separate plan for the poor? Health insurance for the poor was more comprehensive and government-run, so that the question of one plan for all depended on the way in which the issues of comprehensiveness and role of government would be resolved for the general population.

The most fundamental coverage and efficiency question was whether to have relatively complete coverage for high-cost illness episodes in order to reduce the patient's risk of a very high bill or whether to make the patient share significantly in the cost, increasing his financial risk in order to provide an incentive to avoid unnecessary expenditures. This issue required both assessment of consumer preferences and a clear understanding of the effectiveness of coinsurance rela-

tive to other methods of cost control. Secondly, there was the
issue of the extensiveness of the list of services to be covered,
and finally the question of the role of the health insurance
industry in administration of the plans.

Underlying these discussions was the issue of cost. Both
Medicare and Medicaid had turned out to cost a great deal more
than originally estimated and to have significant unanticipated
effects on the delivery of health services. There was a great
desire to avoid surprises of that magnitude.

The cost issue had three components which were often
badly confused. The first was the issue of how large the direct
costs associated with changes in insurance would be. Included
here are the costs of previously uninsured expenses such as
newly insured services and patients' shares of costs which
become insured. Second was the question of the indirect cost
effects. These consisted of (1) increases in utilization as a
result of health insurance lowering the out-of-pocket costs of
the consumer and (2) increases in the unit costs of services
stemming from insurance effects or demand pressures on
available resources and the efficiency of administration. In
addition were the costs of previously covered services--the
majority of health expenditures which were already being
financed by health insurance programs under public and private
auspices and through tax provisions affecting health insurance
premiums and medical care expenditures. It was the consolidation of these sources that would greatly increase the dollars
for health appearing in the federal budget. The latter category
did not represent a cost to the public but simply a change in
accounting. But those who opposed either national insurance
or a large role for the federal government persistently added
the costs of previously covered services of any plans to its
real costs.

While all this was going on, President Nixon was proceeding to substantially dismantle the Office of Economic Opportunity
in spite of strong opposition from Congress. With OEO rapidly
being stripped of its operating responsibilities as programs
were cut or transferred to other agencies, officials were anxious to find a way to solidify OEO's position in the area of
research and development. This required finding initiatives
which would draw on past strengths, be highly visible, and
involve substantial resources. A social experiment to play a
major role in the national health insurance debate met these
conditions. The Negative Income Tax Experiment that OEO
had overseen was phasing out. Colleagues at RAND were looking for a visible way to expand research activities in health
economics, and the administration and Congress were looking
for the guidance of professionals to help resolve the complex
issues in the formation of national health insurance policy.

It is in this climate that the RAND Corporation, after

extensive discussions with OEO, published its proposal for a
health insurance experiment in November 1972. It was not
difficult for the experiment to be misinterpreted as a study of
the effects of national health insurance. RAND was conducting
a housing allowance experiment which was designed to give
careful attention to both supply and demand effects and in its
health work was studying the impact of various national health
insurance proposals.

The range of issues which analysis of the economic issues
of health insurance would have to deal was broad, and there
were many key issues outside the province of economics per se.
Yet RAND proposed to study only the demand effects of national
health insurance for a tentatively approved budget of $32 million.
Failure to take into account supply together with demand could
lead to gross overestimates of the expansion of utilization
which would take place.

The proposal was advancing through the federal bureaucracy without any independent outside evaluation. It was doing
so in spite of great doubts as to whether the answers would be
available before the major decisions on national health insurance had been made. It was doing so in ways which led too
many people to believe it would provide far more complete
answers than it ever could. It was doing so amid increasing
concerns that the study might be used as an excuse to delay the
enactment of health insurance legislation while awaiting results
that could at best provide only a small part of the answers to
the questions enumerated above.

Since we shared these concerns, in November 1972 regular meetings were held between Jeffrey Weiss, Irving Leveson,
and James Hester to develop a strategy for setting forth and
circulating a critique. Hester and Leveson completed a rough
draft in January 1973 and copies were circulated to key policy
analysts in Washington.

Interest was aroused quickly and started to spread. In
February a revised draft was completed and mailed to thirty
health economists. In March, HEW convened a group of high-
level consultants to evaluate the proposal. They were nearly
unanimous in their concern for the objections raised, and a
majority recommended against going ahead with the experiment.
Joe Newhouse from RAND prepared a response to the Hester-
Leveson paper, and Hester and Leveson prepared a rejoinder.
Over the strong objections of staff and consultants the study
was tentatively approved by the Assistant Secretary of HEW
for Planning and Evaluation.

During this period there were significant changes in the
proposal. There was a built-in evaluation after the initial
experience with the first site. Furthermore, the experiment
no longer excluded all persons with incomes over $12,000 and
now could be useful for estimation of the demand effects of a

much wider range of health insurance plans. Other refinements were made, but fundamental methodological objections
which reduced the value of the effort far below its cost were
too inherent in the approach to have ever been changed. The
debate succeeded in arousing professional interest on these
questions.

The March 1974 issue of Inquiry carried papers by Newhouse and by Hester and Leveson incorporating and refining
the original material. Included were papers by Larry Orr,
who oversaw development of the effort in OEO, and an independent methodological paper by Kisch and Torrens on health
status assessment. The September issue carried a comment
on Hester and Leveson by Newhouse. There will be many
more papers on the experiment with a strong methodological
bent. It could be unfortunate if the experiment drew too much
attention from the issues in the national health insurance debate
itself.

RESEARCH ON THE BEHAVIOR OF HEALTH SYSTEMS

The Office of Health Systems Planning represented a
major change in the way in which analytic efforts would be
carried out in HSA. Sufficient resources were available to
engage in in-depth analyses of pending policy issues. Many
of these would be oriented toward capital outlay decisions.
Capital construction carried with it long-term commitments
toward operating expenses requiring examination of various
considerations of program content and feasibility. While in
the context of a single community within New York City one
could examine the extent of the problems and alternative programs and solutions, decisions over whether to build a facility
were carried out in an environment of competition among communities as to where programs would be located. The kinds
of matters which formal research was best able to address
would therefore provide "planning factors" to be utilized in
discussions that dealt simultaneously with a large number of
complex considerations.

A sizable volume of formal research on U.S. health care
problems had been accumulating because of a substantial increase
in national resources devoted to health services research and
development during the period 1966-74. Few of the great
many persons with which the office had to deal could be expected
to be familiar with the nature of that research, its strengths
and weaknesses, its uses and its implications. If the office
were to have an impact in a climate which made it necessary
to deal with many people, it would be necessary to establish

mechanisms for communicating approaches, ideas, and findings on a regular basis.

Several mechanisms were set up to accomplish this purpose. Soon after the office initiated activities in July 1971,
a program of extensive production and distribution of research
reports was developed. In January 1972 a series of semiweekly
seminars. was begun to bring together staffs of various government agencies and interested parties in universities and research
organizations to exchange ideas and to keep informed of the
progress of research several months before formal reports
would be available. In June 1972 a first annual report of the
Office of Health Systems Planning was circulated to provide
detailed information on the activities of the office. A 1973
annual report was developed containing another paper on the
work of the office and abstracts of the dozens of staff papers
that had been completed. The effort was well received in
draft form, and the project was expanded to include the Office
of Program Analyses and published as a monograph entitled
Health Services Administration Staff Papers 1971-1973 in
December of that year.

The paper "Hospital Utilization Research for Capital
Planning Decisions" by Irving Leveson is an early effort to
pull together the content of research studies that were being
used by the office. It was begun in order to provide senior
staff of the Health Services Administration and the Health and
Hospitals Corporation with early and thorough information on
the kinds of approaches being used, the reasons for the office's
interest in particular pieces of information and studies, initial
findings from some of our own work, and the relationship of
the work of the office to the body of published research. The
paper was circulated in draft form five months after the office
was set up.

An initial thrust reflected in the paper is the analysis of
utilization data as a means of assessing the number of hospital
beds needed. This was the subject of an intensive technical
study subsequently by Irving Leveson and Regina Reibstein. [1]
It was not possible to find a performance measure such as
occupancy rate to determine when there was an oversupply of
beds, even with elaborate efforts at reinterpretation of the
statistics. The approach which evolved was that one could
decide the direction in which the system should be moved by
exploring the success of alternative systems using less hospital beds, more ambulatory care, and prepaid group practice.
Rather than expect the system to regulate itself or signal its
inefficiency, one would instead use direct administrative control over the number of beds to move deliberately toward a
system that reduced cost by replacing less emphasis on hospitalization.

THE ANALYSIS OF HOSPITAL PRODUCTIVITY

The modern general care hospital produces a wide range
of services including inpatient treatment, treatment in outpatient departments and emergency rooms, diagnostic and
pharmacy services, extended care, and home care. These are
intertwined with research and teaching activities in complex
ways. The provision in these institutions of more than one-
fourth of the $100 billion spent on health care in 1974, the
rapidly rising costs of both inpatient and outpatient services,
and uncertainties over the effectiveness of incentives facing
not-for-profit enterprises--all lead to heightened concern over
the performance of hospitals in meeting public goals.

A major factor limiting performance of the hospital sector
is the absence of generally available measures of cost and
productivity. This is of no less concern in New York City,
where a system of public hospitals has a $900 million budget
and the two-thirds of the patients who use voluntary hospitals
face facilities ranging from the most prestigious to the most
obsolete.

Hirsch Ruchlin's study, "A Comparative Analysis of
Hospital Productivity in the Municipal and Voluntary Sectors,"
takes advantage of the availability of detailed information for
New York City in order to construct more complete measures
than is generally possible with data available elsewhere. This
is used to compare productivity in the municipal and voluntary
hospital sectors and to examine changes over time, using a
variety of output and input measures.[2]

The paper is the first of a series of three reports ema-
nating from the exploratory HSA hospital productivity project.
A second paper focuses on the methodological issue of the
information gained from adding refinements to a basic output
measure. The third presents a multivariate statistical analysis
of hospital productivity. Primary emphasis is placed on
examining the effect of behavioral, structural, and policy variables on productivity variation.

One of the more interesting findings is that occupancy
rates appear to be positively related to productivity for municipal hospitals and negatively related to productivity for voluntary hospitals. There may be two different phenomena operating.
The occupancy rates of municipal hospitals are very low.
Productivity would tend to be reduced when utilization is low
because fixed costs are high relative to variable costs. There
are indications that low occupancy is a more general measure
of inefficiency in public hospitals as well. Voluntary hospitals
with very high occupancy rates, on the other hand, tend to be
prestige institutions with reputations for high-quality care.
It is in these institutions especially that measured outputs may
not adequately reflect the quality of care delivered, with the

result that the use of additional inputs appears to result in lower productivity. The implications of these two situations are very different.

Another interesting finding concerns the effects of the affiliation contracts by which city hospitals purchase professional services. Hospitals tend to divide themselves very sharply according to the percentage of their physician costs in the affiliate budget: eight of the hospitals cluster around 30 percent and seven are close to 100 percent. The difference in the level of productivity of hospitals with costly near total reliance on affiliates and the productivity of hospitals with limited affiliation arrangements is far from statistical significance because of the great variations in productivity among hospitals within each group. However, the mean difference is about 30 percent. Such a potentially important magnitude requires close examination.

FOOTNOTES

1. "The Economics of Hospital Utilization under Insurance," paper presented at the annual meetings of the American Statistical Association, New York, December 1973.
2. The editors regret that space constraints led to deletion of a number of interesting methodolocial sections from Ruchlin's paper. Among the deletions were important caveats and alternative interpretations to the main findings of the study.

IV-1   THE HEALTH INSURANCE STUDY: A CRITICAL APPRAISAL

by James Hester and Irving Levenson *

        The federal government's initiation of Medicare and Medi-
caid programs in the mid-1960's stimulated a chain reaction in
all phases of the health care system. Many of the developments,
such as the rapid inflation in hospital costs, were not anticipated
at all or were greatly underestimated. The combination of long
response times in adjusting supplies of both practitioners and
facilities and the continual modifications of the programs have
prevented the health system from settling into equilibrium, so
the final consequences of the programs are not clearly understood even today.
        Most of the national health insurance proposals now under
consideration would produce changes potentially much greater
than Medicare and Medicaid. In evaluating the alternatives and
designing new programs, the key question is how to estimate the
likely impact of alternative proposals on the health system--
how would they affect utilization of different levels of care,
sources and prices of various types of service, numbers and
distributions of providers, etc? The papers by Newhouse and
Orr discuss some of these policy issues and argue for the use
of a major controlled experiment--the Health Insurance Study[1]--
to help resolve them.
        Social experiments represent an important tool for policy
analysis in general, and for exploring the consequences of alternative health policies in particular. The proposed project is an
ambitious attempt to extend the use of social experiments now
under way for income maintenance[2] and housing allowances[3]
programs into the area of health policy. However, in designing
such an experiment, it is crucial to understand at the outset
precisely which questions need to be answered, which of these

*The authors wish to thank Jeffrey Weiss and Gelvin Stevenson for
their valuable comments and suggestions.

can potentially be resolved by small-scale social experiments, and how well any particular experiment is likely to provide these answers.[4] It is essential that the issues selected be amenable to small-scale experiments, and that the experiment be designed to maximize the probability of producing reliable results. If this is not done, the damage from false hopes raised and then dashed by unrealistic expectations, and from delays in seeking alternative approaches to obtain needed data can easily outweigh whatever benefits are produced by the experiment. This paper undertakes a critical examination of the Health Insurance Study from this perspective.

FUNDAMENTAL ISSUES

In general, the scope of the proposed experiment appears impossibly broad, encompassing too many and too wide a range of objectives. As currently described, it will explore (1) the sensitivity of utilization of health care to price; (2) the effect of health care on health status; (3) the effect of health maintenance organizations on utilization, quality of care, and health status; and (4) the influence of physician work load on pattern of practice, mix of services, and utilization. The compromises required among competing objectives in constructing the sample of consumers, selecting sites, acquiring data and controlling for key parameters, together with the progressive complexity in actually implementing the design, could pose a serious threat to the value of the experiment. Some difficulties will be overcome by improvements as the study progresses, but others are so fundamentally tied to the basic parameters that they cannot be avoided.

The emphasis in the descriptions and discussion of the experiment make it clear that not all of these objectives carry equal weight. The principle intent of the Health Insurance Study is to estimate the effect of different levels of health insurance coverage on the demand for medical services. In simplest form, the question is how much will a national health insurance program with very low coinsurance and deductibles stimulate major changes in the volume and type of health care demanded? What are the consequences of varying the levels of coinsurance and deductibles on utilization for major types of services, substitution between services, program costs, etc.? The following discussion highlights the major problems that the Health Insurance Study faces in trying to provide meaningful answers to this question. The problems include the size of the experimental changes, the time span of the experiment, the influence of different regulatory settings, and some details of the design of the experiment.

The strongest arguments against the experiment reduce

to a single issue: What information can an experiment that generates only small-scale changes in demand for health care provide about health policies that could produce substantial shifts in the composition and level of demand, and thus in the health delivery system itself? The experiment will measure the effect of different levels of insurance on the demand for health services of 500 families at each site. If the programs under study were extended to the entire population in the area, the utilization patterns found in the experiment would be likely to change substantially as the price of health care increased, as existing facilities and providers were overloaded, as the new financing stimulated redistribution of the location or specialties of providers, etc.

Our main concern is how well the experiment can provide reliable information on changes in patterns of use, cost, and quality of medical care that accompany major changes in demand without exploring responses of the total health care system supplying those services. We are convinced it cannot, and our reasoning, in detail, follows. While some useful information can be obtained from the experiment, there is a real question as to whether the $32 million cost is justified. After allowing for reasonable expectations as to the results of the experiment, it is apparent that much additional research remains to be carried out to develop a more complete set of answers to the range of questions on which intelligent policy decisions depend.

Basic Flaws in Experimental Design

The Health Insurance Study is primarily structured to answer the following question: If a small fraction of the people in a given area have their medical care costs reduced for a period of three to five years, how will their use of medical care change? Economic theory tells us that consumption of health services will tend to increase as the effective price goes down due to improved insurance coverage. The study intends to verify the sensitivity of different income groups to price changes, and the role of price relative to other demand factors such as waiting time and health status. The sensitivity to price is in question because providers have a major input into decisions regarding health service utilization. Also, at the time they are actually using the services, most consumers are unaware of both the total costs and out-of-pocket cost after insurance.

The experiment is designed to estimate the shape of the demand curve for health services in the presence of a relatively fixed total supply. At each site, the supply of services available to the participants in the experiment is highly elastic (because of their small numbers), but the total capacity, organizational structure and incentives for the health delivery system in the area are constant. However, a full-scale national health insurance program should produce just the reverse conditions. In the short term, the supply of services available will be relatively inelastic. The greater demand will produce smaller increases in quantity and larger increases in price than in the experiment because resources cannot be shifted as easily among industries as among individual consumers of the same product. In the long term, the new equilibrium pattern of consumption will depend upon the response of the supply system to the new demand; i.e., upon the complex interrelationships between supply and demand in the context of whatever regulatory mechanisms are established.

Relying upon the experiment to estimate the level and composition of demand that would be produced under a national program requires three key assumptions which may turn out to be valid, but which cannot be assumed a priori: first, that the total change in demand is small; second, that the length of time over which adjustments occur is comparable to the lifetime of the experiment; and third, that the key administrative and regulatory restrictions are reproduced.

Small Changes in Total Demand

One of the basic characteristics of the experiment is that it will not produce any significant change in the composition or level of demand for medical care at a site. With a total of 2,000 families distributed over four sites, the experiment will affect only 500 families or approximately 2,000 people in any one area. The physicians and other medical staff will not see a perceptible change in the number of people coming to them for care; those with better financing will simply replace others in the area.

The experiment may generate substantial changes in the behavior of individual families. However, there will be no way of estimating how this behavior would be modified by the consequences of the large-scale increase in total demand that would occur if the same health benefits were extended to all residents of a large area. The following are some of the specific consequences that a small-scale experiment would not duplicate.

Expansion of Supply System   Utilization could easily increase in the experiment if families with increased insurance coverage displaced other families seeking to use existing medical resources. Yet if a similar increase in insurance coverage took place in an entire city or the nation, the ability of utilization to increase would depend on the ease with which the industry could expand the quantity of services supplied and the nature of the expansion.

If supply is relatively fixed as a result of restrictions in building hospitals or training doctors, for example, the increase in
utilization will be relatively small. If the supply of manpower
and facilities were increased concurrently, the results would
be quite different. If the supply system does expand under a
national program, the details of the change, e.g., organizational form, controls on cost and utilization, etc., will be
important determinants of the ultimate use and cost of the
program.

Cost The less the quantity of services supplied responds
to changes in demand, the more prices are going to bid up as
consumers compete for a limited number of services. The
higher prices of services would result in less of an increase in
demand when insurance reduced the patient's out-of-pocket share
of costs. The extent of these changes may be very different
depending on the policy toward rate regulation that is followed.

Changes in Quality of Care Changes in the degree of
insurance coverage can have important influences on the intensity and quality of care. Hospitals may more readily increase
the sophistication of services when a whole market is more
fully covered by insurance. This pattern may be significantly
modified by rate regulation. Increases in demand with a relatively fixed supply may create pressures that affect the tho-
roughness of medical examinations, or the way in which priorities
are set among patients and diseases. These in turn may
influence the individual's ability to get care, or the quality of
counseling and referral.

Redistribution among Providers The implications of a
national financing plan for redistribution of demand among
providers make the supply system response to alternative plans
a crucial issue. A national health insurance program could
remove one of the major bottlenecks hindering the expansion of
neighborhood health centers and other innovative organizations
for delivering medical care. A related issue is the effect of
changes in demand on the increase in number of providers and
the resulting impact on hours of work and location of practice.
The exact nature of this redistribution would be affected by the
nature of the insurance proposal. [5]

Technology and Innovation If a large-scale change in
demand takes place and it persists for a long time, new methods
of producing and delivering services tend to develop in response
to the new opportunities. Financial markets will adapt their
practices to the needs of the industry and suppliers of drugs
and equipment will take advantage of new opportunities. Changes
in techniques and organization can take place, with results that
can have far-reaching implications.

Short Lifetime of the Experiment

If the response of the supply system is accepted as a key
aspect of the experiment, then a three- to five-year lifetime

becomes far too short. Some changes could be made during this
time period; but most changes would not be made unless the
providers had assurance that the new funds, which provided the
impetus for the changes, would last long enough to justify major
investments of time, energy and funds. Because the response
of the housing supply system, particularly through private
financiers, was a crucial issue in the housing allowance experiment, the designers of that experiment guaranteed that the
allowances would be continued for fifteen years, even though the
formal experiment would be completed much sooner.

Regulation

The changes in utilization, supply, and costs will depend
heavily on the exact system of state and local regulations within
which the experiment operates. Examples of possible effects
are many, and a number of them have already been mentioned.
There may be a smaller response in states that have strong
certification-of-need laws, since such efforts to limit cost by
controlling the supply of hospital beds may limit the expansion
of facilities. Expansion may be less likely where strong cost
control legislation exists. Laws restricting the composition
and organizational form of medical providers, regulating the
types and functions of medical personnel, etc., have already
caused gross differences in the evolution of the medical system
and will continue to do so. The evolution of Professional
Standards Review Organizations, regulations requiring preadmission screening of hospital patients, and successors to the
Economic Stabilization Program may have profound effects.

The extent of such changes imply that specific effects of
regulatory conditions cannot be omitted from the analysis without great danger of serious error in estimating behavior from
data that ignore the impacts. They also increase the possibility
that the experiment itself will be disturbed by forces that it was
not designed to statistically control.

Further Issues

Some further issues need additional work if the experiment
is to function as intended. One involves the consumer's knowledge of his insurance coverage, which is generally incomplete.
In the experiment, it can be expected to be extremely poor
because of (1) the limited duration of the experiment; (2) the fact
that participants--neighbors, fellow employees, family doctor
and other providers of service--will not simultaneously be
becoming familiar with the plan; (3) the likelihood that some
rules will first be evolving during the experiment; and (4) the
complexities of comparing the new plan with previous coverage
when the plans may not be similar and when the changes in
coverage were not made at the participant's initiative. As a
result, the degree of adjustment to changes in insurance terms

can be expected to be a good deal smaller than if there were a large-scale change that persisted.

Second, the size of the sample is not likely to permit clear differentiation of the effects of varying provisions. The authors have made significant efforts to overcome the problems, but they continue to be serious. Medical care use varies a great deal among individuals. Only one-tenth of the population will be hospitalized in a given year--and there are only 500 families on any one site. There are sixteen categories of enrollees according to inpatient coinsurance rate, outpatient coinsurance rate, maximum expenditures as a percent of income, and HMO membership. With an average of 125 families in each plan, containing about 50 hospitalized persons if reflective of the general population, the opportunities for comparisons among subgroups become quite restricted. To make comparisons, it becomes necessary to pool the data and assume that more effects are linear additive so that the subgroup designations can be represented as variables in a multivariate analysis. In order to improve the efficiency of the estimates, the researchers hope to be able to reduce the price combinations to four variables. However, this method rules out interaction effects among coinsurance for inpatient and outpatient services and income limitations on expenditure; and these may be quite important. Furthermore, the HMO category still represents one--not four--of sixteen categories; and there is no indication of any ability to identify differential effects of HMO enrollment.[6] There are a great many other interaction effects that may be important, the testing of which will be severely limited by sample size considerations.

Finally, a major objective of the experiment is to explore the relationship between utilization of health services and health. However, the state of the art of measuring health status is quite primitive.

Grossman's outstanding study had enormous methodological difficulties in obtaining robust estimates of the relationship of medical care to overall health status across individuals with a sample size of 1,770.[7] The sample here is larger; and for some models of health determinants, it may be possible to pool several years of data to increase sample size further. However, an approach using information from existing sources, such as the National Health Survey, to study relationships for specific diseases is likely to be far more useful.

The issue of the effect of health services on health status is an important one, but it is separate from the question of the influence of level of insurance on use of services. The analysis of the relationship between health services and health does not depend on the experimental variations in level of coverage, which are the central rationale for the Health Insurance Study. The

combination of health examination data and information on the
time sequence of events offer interesting new data. However,
one must be cool to the prospects for major gains from this study
in either developing the missing measures of health status or
relating marginal shifts in utilization to changes in health.

Some Alternative Approaches and Sources

In his paper, Larry Orr makes some points that bear
repeating before several alternative approaches and sources are
noted. It is quite correct that it is often not possible to obtain
sufficient information on coinsurance and deductibles to make
reliable tests from information generated from household surveys. Surveys provide only the crudest information on out-of-
pocket costs and do not provide accurate data on insured
expenses. Insurers are reluctant to release the data they do
have; and often they have the wrong data. Furthermore, the
longitudinal data supplied by the experiment offers numerous
advantages. However, the importance of the specific opportunities that do exist, and the possibilities of expanding such
alternatives at far lower cost should not be underestimated.
The most extensive source of household-based information is the National Health Survey. In its cumulative experience,
information on millions of persons has already been collected.
Longitudinal data and special questionnaires have been developed
in various forms. Attention to problems of methodology and
data quality have been excellent. The primary sampling units
provide a possible unit of observation for which hundreds of
sites could be analyzed. [8]
The most obvious approach would be to integrate the
National Health Survey household data with information on local
institutions, resources, legal framework, and other factors.
Analysis would require the development of a method of providing access to individual observations from the household
study. Information on changes in coverage in insurance plans
in local areas developed from independent sources could be
matched with data on utilization and other characteristics.
Availability of health resources and methods of regulation could
be compared among a large number of geographic units. The
effects of the introduction of Medicare and Medicaid could be
thoroughly explored.
Improved use of the National Health Survey would require
substantial efforts in HEW to make data available to outside
researchers and to give priority in grant awards to proposals
addressing these questions. A decisive change in this direction
would be far less costly than efforts that involve new collection
of statistics that are similar to data collected for more than

a decade. Furthermore, improved accessibility of data of this
kind would be a general resource, useful for a wide range of
analyses and not limited to any one set of studies.

In addition to the survey data, substantial opportunities
exist to observe the effects of changes in health insurance
coverage among defined populations without setting up a new
plan. Examples of "natural experiments" of this kind include
the Weisbrod and Fiesler's before-and-after study of effects
and changes in utilization under Blue Cross in St. Louis, and
the Kansas Blue Cross/Blue Shield outpatient experiment
analyzed by Hill and Veney. [9]

CONCLUDING REMARKS

The basic flaws in the Health Insurance Study come to light
if one stops to consider what a similar experiment ten years ago
would and would not have revealed about the consequences of
the implementation of the Medicaid program on a national scale.
Suppose $32 million had been spent to test the response of 2,000
poverty-level families scattered over four sites under a half-
dozen combinations of limits of coverage and copayments.
Perhaps we would have gained some insight into the general
magnitude of the changes in demand, but so many effects are
tied into the nature of the supply system and the administrative
framework that it is quite doubtful that the experiment would
have yielded results of much use in choosing among alternative
plans.

If the scale of the experiment were significantly stepped
up and concentrated in one area, it would allow a better test of
administrative feasibility under one set of conditions, but would
still not provide an effective indicator of the crucial supply
system response. The reasons for this lie in the role of the
duration of the experiment, administrative regulations, and
other conditions in shaping that response. Most importantly,
many effects would not occur unless changes actually took place
on a national scale at the same time. Evolution in training
and medical practice, and of organizational forms would
depend particularly on national forces. The Health Insurance
Study seeks to provide data on key policy questions. However,
most of the answers can only come from detailed study of situations in which major changes have taken place in a large market.
Social experiments can play an important role, but we have been
unable to avoid the conclusion that the experiment cannot ful-
fill its promise because of basic limitations that cannot be
removed by refinements in the course of its evolution.

FOOTNOTES

1. This paper was published in Inquiry, March 1974, along with
Joseph Newhouse, "A Design for a Health Insurance Experiment,"
Larry Orr, "The Health Insurance Study: Experimentation and
Health Financing Policy" and Arnold Kisch and Paul Torrens,
"Health Status Assessment in the Health Insurance Study," and
an "Introduction" by James Veney. The editors are grateful to
the editors of Inquiry for allowing reproduction of that paper.
An earlier version of Newhouse's paper, "A Design for a
Health Insurance Experiment," was published in November 1972,
by the Rand Corporation (R-965-OEO). An earlier draft of our
critique commenting on this first version was circulated in
January 1973.
2. Harold Watts, "The Negative Income Tax Experiment."
Paper presented at the annual meeting of the American Statistical Association, New York, December 1973. An excellent
discussion of the limitations of the experiment can be found in:
Davis Elesh; Jack Ladinsky; Myron J. Lefkowitz; and Seymour
Spillerman, "The New Jersey-Pennsylvania Experiment: A
Field Study in Negative Taxation." In: Kenneth Boulding, et al.
(eds.), Transfers in an Urbanized Economy (Belmont, California: Wadsworth Publishing Company, Inc., 1973), pp. 181-201.
3. Ira Lowry, et al., Testing the Supply Response to Housing
Allowances: An Experiment Design (Santa Monica: The Rand
Corporation, 1971) WN-777-VI.
4. For a general critique of the feasibility of social experiments,
see: Alice M. Rivlin, Systematic Thinking for Social Action
(Washington, D.C.: The Brookings Institution, 1971), pp. 108-
119; and Donald A. Schon, Beyond the Stable State (New York:
Random House, 1971), Chapter 7.
5. The great range in quality and organization forms of the
sources of medical care for the medically indigent provide good
reason to suspect that the supply system will be an important
determinant of the response of the consumers in the experiment.
A ghetto family with access to only a crowded hospital outpatient
clinic or emergency care room is likely to have a change in use
for services quite different from that of a lower middle-income
family in suburban areas with private doctors more readily
available.
6. The uncertainties as to the ability to identify HMO effects
are a good deal greater than the sample size discussion indicates.
The definition of an HMO allows for wide variations in the structure of the delivery system, e.g., in form of physician reimbursement, extent of group versus individual practice, access
to hospital beds, etc. These differences produce variations in

utilization patterns within the HMO classification that could be of the same order as the variation between HMO and non-HMO.

7. Michael Grossman, The Demand for Health: A Theoretical and Empirical Investigation, Occasional Paper 119, National Bureau of Economic Research (New York: Columbia University Press, 1972).

8. See: U.S. Department of Health, Education and Welfare, Public Health Service. Health Statistics from the U.S. National Health Survey, The Statistical Design of the Health Household, Interview Survey Series, A-2 (Washington, D.C.: GPO, July 1958).

9. B.A. Weisbrod, and R.J. Fiesler, "Hospitalization Insurance and Hospital Utilization," American Economic Review 51: 126-131 (March 1961); and Daniel B. Hill and James E. Veney, "Kansas Blue Cross/Blue Shield Outpatient Benefits Experiment," Medical Care 8:143-158 (March-April 1970). A review of a number of such studies can be found in Paul B. Ginsburg and Larry M. Manheim, "Insurance, Copayment, and Health Services Utilization: A Critical Review," Journal of Economics and Business 25:142-152 (Spring 1973).

IV-2 HOSPITALUTILIZATION RESEARCH FOR CAPITAL PLANNING DECISIONS: EVIDENCE AND OBSERVATIONS WITH SPECIAL REFERENCE TO NEW YORK CITY — April, 1972

by Irving Leveson

INTRODUCTION

Changes in the number of patients treated can be brought about in a number of ways. New facilities can be constructed, existing structures can be occupied more fully, inpatient turn-over can be increased, and alternative forms of care can be substituted. Implicit in these decisions are major changes in the scope and intensity of services and changes in the population served.

Over the years formal research has built up a substantial body of evidence which can contribute significantly to under-standing of the complex forces which interact in the health care system. Recognition of these forces is essential for sound deci-sions concerning health care facilities, utilization, service mix, and patient priorities.

Research on utilization of health systems is widely scat-tered and requires careful interpretation. Interpretation is facilitated by the development of frameworks to structure infor-mation. Formal analysis is most useful when combined with more casual observations and experiences with which it must be consistent to be of practical use. Furthermore, formal research is most thoroughly understood not in the abstract, but when its application to problems of real concern is demonstrated. For these reasons, in preparing a "state of the art" paper on utilization of hospital and other services, a number of specific questions have been selected for in-depth discussion and a variety of types of information are considered.

An undercurrent in the material is the importance of supply factors in accounting for observed utilization patterns. This emphasis departs greatly from the usual attention to demand forces and suggests a level of control on the part of providers of service which hitherto has not been sufficiently taken advantage of in planning health care systems.

AVAILABILITY AND UTILIZATION OF FACILITIES

Historical Determinants of the Supply of Facilities

Analysis of supply determinants is useful primarily from the point of view of assessing the courses of action which are necessary in order to generate a desired supply response.

Auster, Leveson, and Sarachek found in interstate comparisons for 1960 that there was a strong negative relationship between per capita hospital facilities and population growth, implying a long lag between population changes and adjustments in the capital stock. Availability of facilities was also strongly related to the amount of property income per capita in the area.[1] Sander Kelman examined the capital stock adjustment process in detail. His interstate analysis revealed an average lag of nine years between the creation of a shortage and a bed being put in place to fill any part of the shortage. During the first nine years, on the average only 24 percent of the new demand was filled. The speed of adjustment of the capital stock to shortages was greater for the richer states than for the poorer states. The Hill-Burton program did not have a statistically significant effect on the rate of adjustment in spite of its stated objective of equalizing bed-to-population ratios.[2]

Demand and Use

Little work has been done directly on the demand for health facilities. Kelman has estimated the determinants of the desired capital stock and found insurance coverage to be a particularly powerful variable.[3] More generally, the demand for facilities and equipment has been treated as a derived demand derivative from the demand for medical care.

The most powerful factor explaining observed differences in hospital use rates in the population is the number of beds available. The evidence on this relationship is overwhelming. In their 1959 monograph, Roemer and Shain cite work of others to report that "studies in Saskatchewan, where hospitalization prepayment covers the entire population, show the rates of hospitalization to vary directly with the supply of beds in local area," and that "the hospitalized days utilized per 1,000 persons per year among the 48 states in 1951 were found to vary directly with the supply of beds per state." Reporting their own work, they note that "examining 1957 data, we have shown a high correlation to persist between the bed supply of each state and its

over-all utilization rate" and "these findings are further con-
firmed in a county-by-county analysis in New York State."[4]
Roemer and Shain further note that occupancy rates vary little
with bed availability.

The interstate findings on admissions and occupancy rates
were corroborated by Rosenthal.[5] In a subsequent study
Dr. Roemer details the case of a relatively isolated hospital in
an upstate New York county that underwent a 42 percent expansion in beds and after three years had a 28 percent higher number of patient-days.[6] He cites further evidence published in 1960
for Massachusetts by Rubinstein, Mason, and Stashio and for
England by Forsyth and Logan.[7] The relationship of hospital
utilization to bed availability has been reaffirmed in extensive
econometric studies of variations among eleven regions in
England and across states in the United States.[8] An HSA study
in progress of major hospital openings and closings further finds
a rough proportionality between changes in patient-days and beds
in hospitals undergoing change while nearby hospitals seem
unaffected. Roemer's Law, as the tendency for bed availability
to determine hospital use has become known, is now widely
accepted. Yet throughout all of the research to date there is little
in the way of explanation of the reason for the phenomenon.
Roemer and Shain, and later Feldstein in his British study, state
that the availability of beds is a factor in the demand for medical
care--that is, that supply somehow interacts with demand.
Feldstein includes some discussion of waiting lists for beds as a
possible mechanism deterring use when beds are scarce, but he
relies on bed availability itself as the explanatory variable in the
empirical analysis. Feldstein also provides an interesting but
inconclusive exploration of the way the behavior might be generated from a hospital decision-maker's utility (preference) function.

Roemer and Shain explicitly considered the possibility that
a conclusion of causality is spurious, anticipating the criticism
of Rosenthal and Klarman.[9] If variations in supply occur in
response to variations in demand, supply would be greater where
demand was higher and there would be a tendency for beds to be
filled when they are built. If that were the case, supply changes
which took place completely independently of demand changes
would lead to unfilled beds. The wide range of conditions under
which supply variations are observed lead Roemer and Shain to
reject this interpretation. But what then do we mean when we say
demand depends on availability of beds? In formal terms, unless
price changes sufficiently, for the quantity demanded to vary when
supply varies implies that a shortage exists. What is the source
and nature of any such shortage and what behavior would it imply?

The answers to these questions are anticipated in the title
of the Roemer and Shain monograph itself. The authors have
chosen the title "Hospital Utilization Under Insurance" and show

particular interest in the evidence derived from circumstances under which insurance coverage is most complete. Yet no formal model to indicate the reason we should expect such behavior under insurance has been previously developed, nor has the nature of the behavior been shown to be related to the extent of insurance coverage. Here we suggest the outlines of a theory that would yield predictions of observed relationships. A complete formal exposition is beyond the scope of this paper.

A Causal Mechanism

Consider a model in which the desired stock of capital is determined by the desired quantity of medical care, a quantity which is primarily determined by income and insurance coverage. As long as the actual stock of capital is less than or equal to the desired stock, the actual stock is the level used (subject to adjustments because of queuing). If the desired stock of capital exceeds the actual stock, changes in supply of capital will automatically be directly associated with changes in utilization, since demand is present to support any level of activity within the range. This model is consistent with Kelman's findings of a large gap between the actual and desired capital stock which is not readily closed.

But why should there be shortages of beds which persist for long periods of time? Here the answer lies in the nature of insurance coverage, as Roemer and Shain correctly sensed. Contrast a case where there is no insurance coverage with one in which only 20 percent of the cost of hospital care is paid by the patient. If the cost of a hospital stay is $1,000, the patient paying full costs will have an incentive to undertake treatment only if the value of the expected benefit of that hospitalization is at least $1,000. If the patient only pays 20 percent of the cost, he may be willing to undertake care even when the expected benefit is well below $1,000, though above $200. The result is that as insurance coverage becomes more extensive, the quantity of services desired may far exceed the capacity of the industry to provide services. And since the quantity of the facilities is determined not only by historical circumstances but by a set of deliberate regulatory mechanisms and the availability of financing, the availability of beds may not be allowed to anywhere near approach levels at which benefits are as low as out-of-pocket costs. The consequence is that within the range of variation observed, beds are always filled. Beds are built because demand is there, and insurance provides the basis of the demand. Some of the mechanisms which limit the expansion of beds can in fact be viewed as deliberate means to protect the interest of the consumer, who ultimately bears the full cost in his insurance premiums.

Roemer and Shain cite as an example of the effect of bed availability the . 5 beds per 1, 000 population at that time in Iran, the 4. 0 beds in the United States and 7. 5 beds in Saskatchewan. We would expect that the difference between the United States and Iran is attributable to differences in income, while the higher rate in Saskatchewan is the result of the extensive insurance coverage in the province. Of course, these are the variables found important in studies of the demand for hospital care and the desired capital stock.

OCCUPANCY RATES

The Nature of the Problem

Increasing occupancy rates is one of the most obvious means of economizing on capital. Yet relatively little is known about which factors are important determinants of existing patterns or how occupancy rates would change in response to alternative courses of action. Studies of hospital costs show that per diem cost tends to be reduced by increases in occupancy rates or in length of stay. In Ingbar and Taylor's study of 72 Massachusetts hospitals in 1958-59, the incremental cost of a patient-day when occupancy rates were increased were not much above half of average costs, so that the potential economies through increased capacity utilization are possible.[10] Occupancy rate patterns, however, do not show the responsiveness to this potential one might hope to see. From studies in other subject areas, it is thought that unit costs rise extremely rapidly, with further increases in output when operations are very near "full capacity."

Before reviewing the evidence of forces which determine occupancy rates, one should clarify some conceptual points. Occupancy rates of medical facilities are an approximation to the economic concept of capacity utilization. This concept relates the actual rate of production of output per unit of time to the maximum rate which could be produced with a given set of productive resources. Occupancy rates, however, use a measure of the quantity of physical capital as the denominator (i. e., physical capital rather than potential output of service) and hence do not assume that a sufficient staff is available to permit empty beds to be filled. A means of overcoming this problem suggested by RAND is to look at the highest occupancy rates achieved during the year as a measure of the true ability to produce. Another problem is that occupancy, in treating the patient-day as the unit of output, does not take into account the intensity of care.

In measuring capacity we would prefer not to define a maximum point in practice. Rather than deal with capacity as fixed, it is useful to imagine unit costs as increasing more and more rapidly as maximum output is approached. Practical

levels of capacity utilization thus take into account cost by
defining a full capacity point somewhat short of maximum output. In the case of general care hospital beds the rule of thumb
is usually in the neighborhood of 90 to 93 percent for large urban
facilities.

A difficult problem of interpretation arises in trying to
understand patterns in observed occupancy rates. Consider,
for example, the case of a short-term general hospital for
which demand has fallen to a permanently lower level. The
hospital might adjust by increasing the average lengths of stay
of the same patients it would have served without the fall and
by filling beds with patients who might otherwise have gone into
long-term care institutions. It may close down some units or
convert space to other uses. As a consequence, the observed
difference in occupancy rates before and after the fall in demand
might be small or nonexistent, and it would not be possible to
correctly infer the effect of the demand change on occupancy
without also looking at the numbers and types of patients served.
Similar problems arise with regard to other sources of change
because of the forms that adjustment takes. It therefore becomes
exceedingly difficult to determine the implications of alternative
decisions for occupancy rates without a complete model and a
detailed set of observations. Frequently the adjustment to
change is passive, with the number of patient-days restored
and little thought given to choices in providing service. Guidance
over the way in which hospitals adjust to occupancy rate changes
is essential in order to assure that the desired outcomes are
achieved.

The Evidence

A great deal of work on occupancy rate has gone on in the
field of operations research. Queuing analysis views the hospital as facing a rate of arrivals of persons demanding service
which can be assumed to be randomly distributed over time.
The hospital then selects an occupancy rate corresponding to the
proportion of patients which it is willing to have to turn away.
One of the most widely used propositions derived from this
approach has been the notion that occupancy rates must be greater
in larger hospitals in order to have a given chance of rejecting
patients. This can be seen by considering one large hospital
that is the same size as two smaller ones. If demand is random,
the peak arrival rate at one of the small hospitals will not always
occur at the same time as at the other. If the institutions were
combined, it would be possible to assign patients overflowing
one section to empty beds in another. It is apparent that this
size difference in occupancy rates is dependent upon the small
hospitals being unwilling or unable to send patients if needed
from one hospital to another because of factors like geography,

poor cooperation among institutions, limitations imposed by the
nature of physician admitting privileges, and separation of markets because of factors such as religion and veteran status.
The applicability of the assumption that hospitals act independently in large city systems has been widely assumed but only
partially demonstrated. [11]

In fact, by limiting itself to the assumption of independent
demands for different facilities the analysis has been most useful in documenting the potential savings where services are
fragmented and a coordinated utilization policy is possible.
This is done by comparing the current institution with results
under the assumption of complete cooperation, in which case
the whole system can be treated as a single institution. Unfortunately, this type of analysis has rarely been used to explore
the nature of interactions among institutions and their implications for restructuring arrangements.

The primary difficulty with the queuing analysis is that it
fails to consider the factors entering into the choice of the proportion of patients turned away, but characteristically only
determines the implied occupancy rate once that decision has
been made.

The decision as to optimal occupancy must rest not only
on such factors as cost behavior with rising occupancy rates
but also on such basic considerations as institutional functions
and objectives. It is apparent that the most extensive variation
in occupancy rates in New York City is by type of institution.
Hospitals of medical schools and prestige teaching hospitals tend
to have low occupancy rates. These may reflect the fragmentation of authority among medical specialties, which can block
the advantages of size, a problem that is particularly severe in
the New York City municipal system at the present time. They
may also reflect a desire for turning away cases a small percentage of the time so as to minimize the chances of losing
cases of particular teaching significance.

The studies of Roemer, Rosenthal, Feldstein, and others
discussed previously do not show much variation in occupancy
rates across broad geographic aggregates. Comparisons of
diverse boroughs and neighborhoods within New York City for
large voluntary teaching hospitals also suggest variation in
occupancy rates of only a couple of percentage points under normal circumstances. The range of forces potentially operating
to determine occupancy rates can be seen from an attempt to
explain why occupancy rates are typically ten percentage points
lower in the New York City's municipal hospitals than in comparable voluntary hospitals.

Municipal Hospital Occupancy Rates

The tendency for New York City's municipal hospitals to

have lower occupancy rates than voluntaries may arise from greater fluctuations in arrival rates. This could come about because of a large number of emergency cases or if the voluntary hospitals refused to treat some cases at times when peak loads came in both municipal and voluntary systems. The municipal hospital would then require lower occupancy rates to have the same frequency of turning patients away. This factor may have some validity. However, the lower occupancy rate in the municipal may also reflect a greater unwillingness to refuse treatment at all, a posture that would well be consistent with the traditional mandate of the institutions.

A test of this hypothesis comes from the HSA analysis of the effects of major hospital openings and closings on utilization of nearby facilities. If municipal hospitals accept patients more readily, we might expect them to experience a greater increase in patient census than voluntaries when nearby facilities close. Preliminary findings suggest that there is little response from either type of institution.

Another hypothesis which has been advanced is the notion that demand is less for municipal than voluntary hospitals because of differences in real or perceived quality, stigma, patient desire for separation by social class, and the like. Yet the difference in occupancy rates has persisted for a long time, and it is not clear why a difference in demand should not have resulted in a rapid enough downward adjustment in the capacity of the municipal system to bring occupancy rates up to the level of comparable voluntaries. It is noteworthy that in the unusual circumstances of the Great Depression there was a large rise in municipal hospital occupancy rates in order to take advantage of the availability of subsidized care only in those institutions. [12] The effect of the introduction of Medicare and Medicaid was to reduce the occupancy rates of municipal hospitals practically imperceptibly. [13] If demand was the main factor, we might also expect to find substantial variations among municipal hospitals in occupancy rates in a way which is systematically related to the availability of alternative sources of care. Crude observation of neighborhood differences do not suggest this to be the case.

It has also been suggested that demand is limited because of staffing factors. The staff effort argument contains two parts. First is the question of adequacy of staff. Between 1969 and 1970 the municipal hospitals added 1,000 nurses. No major change occurred in physician availability. During the period, occupancy rates rose substantially. Preliminary analysis suggests there was no tendency for occupancy rates to rise most in the hospitals in which the greatest increase in nursing occurred. Furthermore, there is no obvious tendency for the municipal hospitals which are most well endowed with physicians to have above average capacity utilization at a given time. The second

argument suggests that the physicians have less incentive to
keep occupancy rates high than they would under a fee-for-service
arrangement. The impact of this factor is not clear at the
present time, but the RAND study shows that occupancy rates
during peak periods do indicate that substantially higher rates
of service are in fact achieved with present staff. Furthermore,
Sydenham Hospital, the one municipal which has physicians with
private practices, has occupancy rates which are clearly no
better than those of other municipals.

The most compelling evidence on the causes of low occupancy rates in municipal hospitals comes from an examination
of occupancy rate patterns by type of service. Many municipal
hospitals are operating at capacity rates in excess of what is
considered practical full capacity in their general medical and
surgical units. Yet specialty departments show occupancy rates
which are typically less than 75 percent. It would appear that
fragmentation is greater in the municipals than in the voluntaries,
and this is the major reason for the difference in occupancy.

The conjectural nature of these observations should be
borne in mind.

PATIENT TURNOVER

Some Determinants

Reductions in the average length of stay offer an opportunity to economize on physical facilities, since with high patient
turnover the costs of capital may be shared among a greater
number of patients. Even more important, however, is the
potential for savings in operating costs.

Costs per patient-day tend to be substantially lower the
longer the average length of stay for a given set of patients.
This is the result of a greater intensity of care in the earlier
days of a stay. Ingbar and Taylor's data suggest that an additional day cost only about half an average day.[14] Reducing the
average length of stay will tend to raise the cost per patient-day
because of the increased proportion of days which are early
stay days. Often costs per day are further increased as a
result of an increase in the intensity of care in the first days of
hospitalization, which is brought about in order to permit a
shortening of the length of stay. However, on the average the
proportionate reduction in length of stay tends to be longer than
the increase in cost per day. Consequently, a decline in average
length of stay produces a reduction in cost per case.

If length of stay were determined by medical technology
alone, the average length of stay would depend only on the distribution of patients according to type and severity of illness.
There would be no opportunity to reduce cost per case by reduc-

ing average length of stay without substantially compromising health. In fact, there is considerable evidence to indicate that this is not the case. Length of stay varies with both supply and demand factors which reflect opportunities rather than technology.

Martin Feldstein's studies for the United States and England indicate that length of stay is strongly influenced by the availability of hospital beds in relation to population. A 1 percent increase in bed availability tends to produce a rise in average length of stay of about 1/3 percent.

K. K. Ro examined variation in length of stay adjusted for case mix among 9,000 patients in twenty-two Pittsburgh area hospitals in 1963. While hospital characteristics tended to play a minor role, length of stay tended to vary substantially with such socioeconomic characteristics of patients as insurance coverage and income.[15]

Studies of the determinants of length of stay have typically examined the total activities of a set of hospitals adjusted for diagnostic mix. Some attempt has been made to examine the separate effects of economic forces on length of stay for different types of cases. However, a substantial amount of variation in length of stay is associated with variation in case mix. Case mix is itself an important decision variable, the implications of which have barely been explored.

Length of Stay in New York City

Large variations not related to the number of beds available occur in average length of stay in general care beds. In New York City, which has practically the same number of beds per capita as the nation, the average length of stay is nearly one-fourth above the national average. New Yorkers have only four-fifths of the chance of obtaining a hospital admission as others. Reduction in length of stay may be an effective means of avoiding the need for costly new construction.

A number of explanations for a high length of stay are possible. Municipal hospitals may be responding to their low occupancy rates. In addition, there may be more of the types of patients who require long stays in New York. However, when we make the comparison excluding the municipal hospitals (omitting the first factor and overcompensating for the second), the length of stay is still moderately higher than the national level.

While estimates of the effect of insurance on length of stay which are readily applicable to the problem are scarce, greater insurance coverage and government payment in New York City appear to be major contributors to the high length of stay. A further possibility is the extensive role of medical schools and the prevalence of teaching hospitals in New York City. Prestige teaching hospitals tend to have particularly high lengths of stay because of the methods of treatment used. The existence of extensive insurance coverage probably contributes heavily to the ability to engage in extensive types of treatment which are associated with long stays.

Refinement of these observations will depend on the development of more detailed information on utilization by method of payment and type of provider along lines which are anticipated.

SUBSTITUTION OF LONG-TERM CARE

Possibilities for shifting the treatment of patients now served in general care hospitals to nursing homes and other long-term care facilities are extensive, as examinations of medical records have consistently shown. The Rochester study found that 15 to 20 percent of the patients in a short-term general hospital did not require hospitalization for medical reasons.[16] The Van Dyke and Brown study of long-stay cases in New York found unnecessary hospitalization in about one-third of all long-stay cases in municipal hospitals and one-fourth in voluntary hospitals. A follow-up study of municipal hospitals ten years later found unnecessary hospitalization of one-fourth of all long-stay cases.[17]

If we wish to compare the costs of treating long-stay patients in general care beds with the costs in long-term care institutions there are two choices which must be addressed. If the alternative is to substitute an entire stay in a long-term care facility, the appropriate comparison is between the cost of treating a long-stay patient in a short-term care facility with the cost of treating the same patient in a long-term care facility.

It may often be more appropriate to provide relatively intensive care in the early days of a stay of a long-stay patient. This would involve providing services in a short-term hospital initially and in a long-term institution subsequently. In that case, appropriate cost comparisons among institutions would apply to the latter part of the stay of a long-stay patient. Rough comparisons of this kind suggest that long-term care facilities may not be more attractive than short-term care for the long-stay portion.

The average cost per patient day in nursing homes is typically one-fourth to one-third of the cost per patient-day in short-term general hospitals. While the cost per patient-day of treating a long-stay patient in a short-term general hospital is typically about half of the cost for all patients, the cost for the latter days of the stay are somewhat lower. But these cost comparisons do not necessarily mean that short-term general hospitals provide the same service at higher cost. Rather, they may reflect a different treatment response. If that is the case,

it may be possible to reorganize a short-term general hospital--
that is, by converting a portion of the facility to long-term care
and thus providing comparable treatment when costs are comparable.

Cost studies indicate that incremental costs per patient-
day of serving a given type of patient with a given average length
of stay are lower if services are expanded by raising occupancy
rates. This would suggest that long-stay cases could be used to
fill empty beds when occupancy rates are low at a cost which is
comparable to long-term care institutions even without adjustments for extent of services. It further implies that long-term
care facilities are more economical when occupancy rates are
near full capacity. This hypothesis requires closer examination.

If short-term hospitals cannot adapt so that their long-stay
cases do not receive unnecessarily intensive treatment, a shift
to long-term care institutions would nevertheless be desirable.
The same would be true if it were impossible to avoid having
the costs of long-stay cases inflated by cost spill-overs from
other areas.

SUBSTITUTION OF AMBULATORY CARE FOR INPATIENT CARE

Evidence on the possibilities for substituting ambulatory
care for inpatient care comes from a variety of sources. One
type of evidence relates to the response of utilization to relative
prices in the context of a demand model. Another is based on
comparison of utilization in different geographic areas which
differ in the availability of ambulatory care. A third applies to
the experience of particular hospitals differing in the quantity
of ambulatory care provided. Additional results come from
utilization experience under prepaid group practice.

Karen Davis and Louise B. Russel have examined the
response to relative prices in an analysis across forty-eight
states in 1969.[18] Use of outpatient department services was
found to be highly sensitive to the price of inpatient services.
When price was measured by the average room charge, a 1 percent increase in the price of inpatient care was associated with
a 1-1/2 percent increase in OPD visits. Similarly, in the
demand equation for inpatient care, a 1 percent increase in the
price of outpatient services was associated with a 1/4 percent
increase in inpatient use. The fact that the ratio of the elasticities of 1 to 6 (.25 versus 1.5) is roughly the same as the
national ratio of costs of outpatient and inpatient care implies
that on the average patient choices between outpatient and inpatient care in response to the relative prices they face result in
the allocation taking place within a fixed total budget. The
response of length of stay to outpatient price was found negligible.

Martin Feldstein has estimated the effect of physician
availability on hospital admission rates for Medicare enrollees

in an interstate econometric mode.[19] He found that a 1 percent
increase in private physicians per capita was associated with
a .2 percent reduction in admissions per enrollee. The model
permitted an estimate of the overall effect on hospital costs.
Taking into account the direct cost of the physician services, the
greater tendency to use extended care facilities where physicians
are more available, and the implications of this for shorter
lengths of stay and higher costs per patient-day with short stays,
the effect of a 1 percent increase in physicians per capita is
still to reduce total costs by .07 percent.

Leveson has developed a model which explicitly indicates
the mechanism by which availability of ambulatory care influences
inpatient utilization and provides preliminary tests by income
group.[20] The impact on ambulatory care is seen as the resultant
of a case-finding effect which raises demand for hospital care
and a preventive effect which reduces it. Comparisons are
made among region and family size groups in a national survey
for 1970 and 1971. No negative relationship is found in general,
but there is a strong tendency for out-of-hospital physician
expenditures to be negatively related to inpatient expenditures for
the $7,500-$10,000 income range in that year.

As indicated earlier, K. K. Ro found in a sample 9,000
discharges from twenty-two Pittsburgh area hospitals that when
other factors were controlled for, presence of an outpatient
department was associated with a 25 percent lower average
length of stay.[21] Lave and Lave found in comparisons among
sixty-six Pennsylvania hospitals that hospitals with health centers had 14 percent fewer common diagnoses, a greater proportion of complex surgery, and a higher average subject complexity
index.[22]

Studies of the experience of Kaiser Permanente and other
comprehensive prepaid group practice arrangements have found
that modest expansions in ambulatory care have enabled 10 to
20 percent reductions in hospital use when incentives to reduce
hospitalization are included in forms of greater physician remu-
neration.[23]

MIX OF SERVICES

The Approach

The availability of health manpower and facilities and the
extent of insurance coverage have an impact on the level of
intensity and sophistication of services as well as on the quanti-
ties of service provided. Studies of variations in use with bed
availability and insurance coverage provide basic information
on these forces by identifying categories of service which are
most readily forgone when resources are tight.

We would prefer to jointly classify activities according to

method of treatment and type of illness in order to examine this question. Presently available data, however, permit separate consideration of diagnostic categories but do not distinguish treatment methods. These data are difficult to interpret because of the absence of information on the number of persons who could potentially be given a particular service. Thus we may find that utilization in one diagnostic category responds little to bed availability because the population is already saturated with services, while in another, lack of response implies adequate controls over tendencies toward inefficiency when the system is loose. The appropriate test of the effect of bed availability and insurance coverage is to examine their impact on admission rates. While some information of this kind is available, most of the data refers to responses of length of stay. Nevertheless, it is possible for some interesting common tendencies to emerge.

Evidence from Studies of Bed Availability

Martin Feldstein examined the elasticity of beds used with respect to bed availability in a regression analysis across regions for England in 1960.[24] Separate estimates are provided for the impact of availability on admissions and length of stay. Table 1 reproduces Feldstein Table 7.10, showing elasticities which indicate the percentage change associated with a 1 percent change in beds per capita. Particularly high elasticities for both components were noted for acute respiratory infections and arterio-sclerotic heart disease. Above-average elasticities were also found for abdominal hernia (female), hemorrhoids and varicose veins (female).

The interpretation of these data are not possible without additional information on the success of treatment. We would expect to find low elasticities where practically all cases of a given type are being treated even when beds are scarce. Feldstein attributed the low elasticity for malignant neoplasms, for example, to a practice in England of maintaining terminal cancer patients in the hospital "after there is no longer any hope of helping them." He was also concerned about the low elasticity for tonsillectomies, suggesting that the procedure is performed with little regard for other priorities when beds are scarce.

A look at the more detailed calculations by diagnosis and sex shows particularly high admission elasticities for the following categories:

infections and parasitic disease
allergic, endocrinal, metabolic, and nutritional (female)
ear and mastoid
urinary
skin and cellular

Table 1

Elasticities by Diagnostic Category*

Disease (1)	Beds Used** (2)	Admissions** (3)	Mean Stay (4)
Acute appendicitis	0.15(0.36)	-0.16(0.33)	0.31(0.14)
Acute upper respiratory infections	2.57(1.00)	1.53(0.52)	1.04(0.74)
Peptic ulcer	0.85(0.52)	0.29(0.40)	0.56(0.51)
Abdominal hernia (female)	1.39(0.44)	0.52(0.22)	0.87(0.44)
Hemorrhoids	1.14(0.62)	0.70(0.48)	0.44(0.24)
Tonsils and adenoids	0.55(0.46)	0.23(0.38)	0.33(0.38)
Arteriosclerotic heart disease	2.22(0.70)	1.14(0.51)	1.08(0.99)
Malignant neoplasms	0.58(0.30)	0.68(0.29)	-0.10(0.20)
Varicose veins (female)	1.40(0.70)	0.78(0.41)	0.62(0.67)
Males	1.03(0.14)	0.66(0.13)	0.37(0.15)
Females	0.97(0.11)	0.63(0.17)	0.34(0.21)
All Persons	--	0.65(0.15)	0.35(0.15)

*Elasticities calculated with respect to total number of beds per 1,000 population.
**Per 1,000 population, 1960.
Figures in brackets are standard errors of responsiveness index values.

      acute upper respiratory infections
      bronchitis
      cerebral paralysis
      arteriosclerotic heart, including coronary
      other (than acute) and unspecified appendicitis
      other digestive diseases
      Smaller but still relatively high responses of admissions
to bed availability were found for diseases of:
      bones and organs of movement
      other allergic, endocrinal, metabolic and nutritional (female)
      hemorrhoids
      varicose veins
      peptic ulcer (female)
      Roemer provides comparisons of length of stay for a relatively isolated hospital in an upstate New York county which

underwent a 42 percent expansion in bed capacity. Length of stay changes in twelve of fifteen major diagnostic categories which exhibited increases were:

Major Diagnostic Grouping	Length of Stay 1957	1959	Percent Increase
Infections and parasitic diseases	7.0	7.8	11%
Allergic, endocrinal, metabolic and nutritional diseases	7.7	10.9	33%
Diseases of the blood and blood-forming organs	6.5	12.4	91%
Diseases of the nervous system and sense organs	9.8	13.7	40%
Diseases of the circulatory system	15.5	18.2	17%
Diseases of the digestive system	9.8	9.1	-7%
Diseases of the genitourinary system	7.3	9.1	25%
Complications of pregnancy, childbirth, and the puerperium	3.3	4.1	24%
Diseases of the skin and cellular tissues	7.9	15.9	101%
Disease of the bones and organs of movement	10.9	12.5	15%
Symptoms, senility, and ill-defined conditions	10.8	13.8	28%
Accidents, poisoning, and violence	7.2	8.1	12%

The increases were most extensive in diseases of blood and blood-forming organs, diseases of the nervous sytem and sense organs, and diseases of the skin and cellular tissue. Respiratory diseases showed no change, while deliveries, mental diseases, and congenital malformations showed decreases.[25]

Evidence from Studies of Health Insurance Effects

Data comparing utilization of health services by persons who differ in health insurance coverage require more complex interpretation. Persons will to some extent be most likely to acquire insurance the greater their expectations that services will be used--the so-called moral hazard effect. In addition, insurance coverage, by lowering the out-of-pocket cost to the user, results in greater use of services. We are primarily concerned with the price effect, but the evidence will also be influenced by differences in moral hazard effects for different types of services. Variations in use in different diagnostic categories will tend to be influenced by the characteristics of the persons among whom various illnesses are prevalent. Nevertheless, the results are quite interesting and not that inconsistent with the data on effects of bed availability.

Hyman Joseph examined the effects of insurance coverage

on length of stay for the twenty-two most frequent diagnostic
categories for twenty-seven Iowa hospitals in November 1965
to April 1966. When other variables were controlled for, length
of stay for seven disease categories has found to be statistically
significantly related to insurance coverage. These categories
were:

ICD No.	Category	Sensitivity to Insurance (Price Elasticity)
492	Primary atypical pneumonia	1.88
500	Acute bronchitis, bronchitis	.44
510	Hypertrophy of tonsils and adenoids	.09
541	Ulcer of duodenum	.33
584	Cholelithiasis, colic	.20
660	Delivery without complication, stillborn	.14
820	Fracture of neck of femur, hip	1.38

The two categories with particularly high sensitivity of
length of stay are ones for which alternative locations for major
portions of the recovery process are available. For primary
atypical pneumonia many cases are treated entirely without
hospitalization.[26]

FOOTNOTES

1. Richard Auster, Irving Leveson, and Deborah Sarachek,
"The Production of Health, An Exploratory Study," Journal of
Human Resources, IV, No. 4 (Fall, 1969), pp. 411-436, and
unpublished appendices. The amount of capital stock per patient-
day was found not to differ with variations in length of stay.
2. Unpublished Ph.D. Dissertation, University of Michigan.
This is not to say that Hill-Burton has no effect, but only that
its effect is not large enough to be observable in broad aggre-
gates. Some unpublished work by Kent Nash comparing selected
Southern counties suggests that the effect may be sizable in
some cases.
3. Op. cit.
4. Milton I. Roemer and Max Shain, Hospital Utilization Under
Insurance, Hospital Monograph Series No. 6, Chicago: American
Hospital Association, 1959, p. 13. The cited studies are G. W.
Meyers, "Hospitalization Experience of a Government Hospital
Care Insurance Plan," Canadian Journal of Public Health, 45
(September 1954), pp. 372-380 and 45 (October 1954), pp. 420-
429; L. C. Reed and H. Hollingsworth, How Many Hospital Beds
Are Needed? Washington: U.S. Government Printing Office,
1953; and M. Shath and M.I. Roemer, "Hospital Costs Relate to
the Supply of Beds," Modern Hospital 92, No. 4 (April 1959),
pp. 71-73, 168. The close relationship of patient-days to beds

across counties holds within New York City both then and at the present time.

5.   Gerald Rosenthal, The Demand for General Hospital Facilities, Chicago: American Hospital Association, 1964.

6.   Milton I. Roemer, "Bed Supply and Hospital Utilization: A Natural Experiment," Hospitals 35 (November 1, 1961), pp. 36-42.

7.   A. D. Rubinstein, H. R. Mason and E. L. Stashio, "Hospital Use in Massachusetts, 1945-55," Public Health Reports 75 (January 1960), pp. 51-54; and G. Forsyth and R. Logan, The Demand for Medical Care, London: Oxford University Press, 1960.

8.   Martin Feldstein, Economic Analysis for Health Service Efficiency: Econometric Studies of the British National Health Service, Amsterdam: North Holland Publishing Co., 1967; "An Aggregate Planning Model of the Health Care Sector," Medical Care, (November-December 1967); "An Econometric Model of the Medicare System," Quarterly Journal of Economics 85 (February 1971), pp. 1-20; "Hospital Cost Inflation: A Study of Nonprofit Price Dynamics," American Economic Review 61, No. 5 (December 1971), pp. 853-872.

9.   Op. cit.; and Herbert E. Klarman, The Economics of Health, New York: Columbia University Press, 1965, pp. 193-141.

10.   Mary Lee Ingbar and Lester D. Taylor, Hospital Costs in Massachusetts: An Econometric Study, Cambridge: Harvard University Press, 1968. The estimates somewhat bias downward the ratio of marginal to average costs by standardizing for some services which may vary when length of stay and occupancy rates change. See Table 4.8, p. 69. Also see Martin Feldstein, Economic Analysis for Health Service Efficiency, op. cit.

11.   Some interesting work on this question has been done in the 1972 RAND study for the Health Services Administration.

12.   Paul N. Worthington, "The Basis for Municipal Capital Outlay on Health Care Facilities in New York City," unpublished master's thesis, Hunter College, 1964.

13.   Byron Bruce Zellner, "Capacity of the New York City Hospital System," discussion paper, New York City Department of City Planning, July 1, 1971.

14.   Op. cit. Also see Feldstein, Economic Analysis for Health Service Efficiency, op. cit.

15.   "Patient Characteristics, Hospital Characteristics and Hospital Use," Medical Care 7, No. 4 (July-August 1969), pp. 295-312.

16.   U.S. Public Health Service, Research in Hospital Use: Progress and Problems, Department of Health Education and Welfare, Publication No. 390-E-1, Washington: U.S. Govern-

ment Printing Office, 1961. For a discussion of some of the
earlier evidence see Roemer and Shain, op. cit.
17. Frank Van Dyke, Virginia Brown, and Anne-Marie Thom,
"Long Stay" Hospital Care, New York: Columbia School of
Public Health, 1963; and Joyce De Terra, Alan Craig Leslie,
and Elsa Marshall, "A Study of Long-Stay Patients Unnecessarily
Hospitalized in Municipal Hospitals," New York City Health
Services Administration, 1971.
18. "The Substitution of Hospital Outpatient Care for Inpatient
Care," The Review of Economics and Statistics, May 1972.
19. "An Econometric Model of the Medicare System," Quarterly
Journal of Economics 85 (February 1971), pp. 1-20.
20. "The Econometrics of Reduced Hospitalization," paper
presented at the annual meetings of the Econometric Society,
New Orleans, Louisiana, December 1971, revised in October
1972.
21. Op. cit. Only "hospital" variables were controlled for.
Patient variables are examined in a separate analysis only.
22. Judith R. Lave and Lester B. Lave, "The Extent of Role
Differentiation among Hospitals," Health Services Research
6, No. 1 (Spring 1971), pp. 6-14. The hospitals with health
centers were all teaching hospitals in Alleghany County.
Variables for teaching states and location were included, but no
tests were made for interaction effects.
23. See Report of the National Advisory Commission on Health
Manpower, Washington: The Commission, 1967, pp. 64-70; and
Herbert E. Klarman, "Analysis of the HMO Proposal--Its
Assumptions, Implications, and Prospects," paper presented at
the Annual Symposium on Hospital Affairs, University of Chicago
Center for Health Administration Studies, April 30, 1971.
24. Martin Feldstein, Economic Analysis for Health Service
Efficiency, Amsterdam: North-Holland Publishing Company,
1967.
25. Milton I. Roemer, "Bed Supply and Hospital Utilization:
A Natural Experiment," Hospitals 35 (November 1, 1961),
pp. 36-42.
26. Hyman Joseph, "The Measurement of Moral Hazard,"
Journal of Risk and Insurance (forthcoming). Less clear-cut
information is provided by Gerald Rosenthal's study of the effect
of insurance coverage on length of stay in a sample of 16,000
admissions to 68 hospitals in five New England states in 1962.
The 28 largest age-sex diagnostic categories were examined.
When the "price" to the patient was measured by out-of-pocket
costs as a percentage of the total, while negative elasticities
predominated, the elasticities were typically smaller than -.1
and many categories had positive signs. When the measure of
price was the average daily room charge, elasticities were
typically about -3 but there was no obvious pattern or consistency

among categories. See "Price Elasticity of Demand for Short-Term General Hospital Services," in Empirical Studies in Health Economics, ed. Herbert Klarman, Baltimore: The Johns Hopkins University Press, 1970, pp. 101-117.

IV-3   A COMPARATIVE ANALYSIS OF HOSPITAL PERFORMANCE IN THE MUNICIPAL AND VOLUNTARY SECTORS

*by Hirsch S. Ruchlin**

SUMMARY

This study develops a methodology for measuring hospital productivity, analyzes the relative productivity of the municipal and voluntary sectors in New York City during the period 1969-1972, and illustrates the use of productivity estimates in the health planning process.

Productivity is estimated by quantifying the volume of output produced by hospitals relative to the volume of resources utilized in generating the output. The elements of institutional output included in this study are: number of inpatients treated; number of ambulatory care visits provided; days of home care provided; number of interns, residents, registered nurses, and health paraprofessionals trained; and by approximation the volume of research underway. Resources utilized in the production process include labor, supplies, and materials, and plant assets and equipment. Two refinements are introduced into the quantification procedure: the volume of inpatient care is adjusted in an attempt to reflect varying case severity across hospital sec-

*The author is associate professor in the Department of Health Care Administration, Baruch College-Mount Sinai School of Medicine, City University of New York. He wishes to express appreciation to Harriet Grayson, Brian Richter, Ronald Rudolph, and Carolle Sulmers for invaluable assistance and to various agencies which provided data and evidence, especially the New York City Department of Health, the New York City Health and Hospitals Corporation, the Associated Hospital Service of New York, the Health and Hospitals Planning Council of Southern New York, and the United Hospital Fund of New York.

tors, and an intensity of care measure is developed as a proxy for quality of care improvements over time.

The following inferences emerge from this study:

Viewing the four-year period in its entirety, neither hospital sector appears to enjoy a clear productivity advantage.

Over time the voluntary sector improved its productivity pattern; the reverse is true for the municipal sector.

The voluntary sector appears to treat a more severe (costlier) patient population.

The municipal sector exhibited a greater percentage increase in intensity of services provided than the voluntary sector.

The voluntary sector appears to exhibit greater labor intensity per adjusted patient-day than its municipal counterpart.

Average length of stay, expenses per adjusted patient-day, bed size, and age of plant assets appear to be related to institutional productivity patterns.

Within the municipal sector no relationship existed between productivity and proportion of the medical staff consisting of interns and residents.

Hospitals with a higher proportion of medical staff paid for by the affiliation budget had higher productivity, but the difference was not statistically significant.

No relationship emerged within the voluntary sector between productivity and number of attending physicians/bed.

The results reported in this study must be regarded as tentative, and in some cases speculative, due to:

The possibility that the quality proxy adopted may still underestimate actual quality.

The case-mix adjustment having been based on data that reflected the attributes of select population groups-- the poor (Medicaid patients) and the elderly (Medicare patients).

The absence of an adjustment for the quality of the education environment and a rigorous measure of research.

STUDY METHODOLOGY

The Definition of Hospital Output

The medical care literature clearly indicates that a hospital's mission and function consists of three major activity areas: the provision of patient care services, the provision of educational services, and the conduct of research. Thus hospital output is defined as the sum of these three activities weighted by their proportion of hospital revenue (cost).[1] Weighting is employed to reflect the fact that each activity would generally not be accorded equal importance in different institutions or settings.

Patient Care Services

Patient care services include inpatient care, ambulatory care, and home care. Ambulatory care entails the provision of clinic care (visits) and emergency room care (visits). The quantity of inpatient care provided is estimated as the sum of the number of cases treated per year, adjusted for case severity. Two alternate proxy specifications for case severity are suggested. The first specification is guided by the recognition that different resources and resource use levels are required to treat patients admitted to each of the medical service areas. The best indication of this fact that was available for use in this study was the recommended registered nurse staffing for each medical service area. Consequently, the number of admissions in each medical service area was multiplied by a recommended registered nurse staffing ratio, where the ratio reflects recommended staffing vis-a-vis the general medical-surgical service.[2] Thus admissions to medical areas requiring more nursing care are accorded greater importance (higher arithmetic values) than admissions to medical areas requiring less care. The second specification incorporates an adjustment for the costliness of treating the type of patients hospitalized as reflected by an institution's diagnostic case-mix profile.

The quantity of ambulatory care is estimated as the weighted sum of the number of clinic and emergency room visits; each visit type (clinic and emergency room) was multiplied by a statistic reflecting the intensity of registered nurse staffing in these two areas.[3] Additional refinements reflecting the type of clinic within the outpatient department was not made due to lack of data. The volume of home care services provided was quantified as the sum of the number of days of home care provided by each institution. Each of the three patient care services (inpatient care, ambulatory care, and home care) was weighted (multiplied) by the proportion of hospital patient care revenue (cost) incurred from the provision of each of these services.

Quality of Care Considerations

Recognizing that there are two dimensions to the amount of patient care services offered--quantity and quality--and that the procedure outlined above reflects only quantity, a proxy quality adjustment is introduced. Quality is two-dimensional, possessing both objective and subjective elements. No attempt is made to reflect the subjective element. The objective aspect of quality is approximated by annual changes in the intensity of services provided. Intensity of services reflect the provision of more services (both from a quality and quantity vantage point) per adjusted patient-day. [4] Service intensity is measured as the percentage increase (or decrease) in real expenditures for patient care (gross expenditures deflated for rising labor and supplies costs). This adjustment is limited to the longitudinal analysis, because over time, variations in expenditures across hospitals are more likely to reflect quality-related changes than efficiency changes. At a point in time (a cross-sectional analysis), the reverse is more probable.

Education

A hospital's educational activities consist of medical education, registered nurse education, and the training of health paraprofessionals. Consequently, educational output is approximated as the weighted sum of the number of students trained per year in each area. The weighting factor by which the total number of students trained was multiplied is based on the importance of each type of trainee as reflected by their average salaries commanded in the market. [5] Thus greater weight is given to medical education, and to a lesser extent to nursing education, than to the training of paraprofessionals.

Research

The volume and value of research activities underway in any institution is the most difficult component of institutional output to measure. To a large extent research, education, and patient care, respectively, are joint products. Furthermore, very little agreement exists as to what is actually research in a hospital environment. Attempts can be made to approximate the dynamism of a research-oriented environment by quantifying the number of scholarly articles authored by staff, or the number (or dollar value) of research grants and contracts. However, data on each of these activities is not readily available. [6] Consequently, it was decided to use the extent of an institution's commitment to education (as reflected in the volume of medical, nursing, and paraprofessional training offered) as a proxy for the institution's commitment to research. [7]

The Quantification of Output

Aggregate hospital output is quantified as the weighted sum of the volume of patient care and educational services rendered. To overcome the arithmetic difficulty inherent in adding entities expressed in different units (inpatients treated, outpatient visits, number of students), each output component, and subcomponent in the case of patient care services, was first converted into an index based on the average value for all hospitals in the study sample, then weighted, and then aggregated with the other components.

Hospital Inputs

The inputs used in production consist of: labor, supplies, and capital. The value of the labor input is approximated by aggregate payroll costs;[8] similarly, the value of supplies, materials, and purchased services used in production equals the amount expended on non-payroll operating expenses (excluding depreciation). The economic (as opposed to accounting) value of capital and equipment utilized in production was not readily ascertainable; consequently, it was approximated by first estimating the value (replacement cost) of each sector's net plant and equipment assets,[9] and then calculating an annual utilization (flow) rate based on the net asset estimate.[10] All dollar values were converted into constant (base year) dollars; the dollar amount of the three input components for each sector were then summed and converted into an (input) index based on the average dollar value for all hospitals in the study sample.

Productivity

Having quantified both output and input, productivity was calculated by dividing the value of the output index for each sector by the value of the input index for that same sector.

By converting to indices, one obtains a measure of performance relative to a hypothetical average institution.

The productivity values here are to be interpreted as follows: A productivity value greater than 1 implies that a sector produces a greater percentage of an industry's total output than it consumes of an industry's total input. Conversely, a productivity value less than 1 implies the production of a smaller percentage of an industry's total putput than it consumes of the industry's total input.

STUDY SAMPLE AND DATA BASE

Study Sample and Data Sources

The study population for this report consists of a sample of twenty-eight short-term general hospitals; fifteen of which constitute the municipal sector, and thirteen the voluntary sector. The choice of voluntary hospitals was dictated exclusively by data availability considerations. A wide range of bed sizes was represented.

Three major data sources were tapped for use in quantifying the productivity estimates; statistical data on general hospital activities derived from individual hospital annual uniform statistical reports, hospital financial (cost) data derived from individual hospital annual uniform financial reports (voluntary hospitals) or year-end cost analyses (municipal hospitals), and admission diagnosis data collected by the Medicaid Audit Program of the New York City Department of Health. Statistical and financial data were available for a four-year period only, 1969 through 1972. Consequently, the study is limited to these four years.

Data Refinements

The legalization of abortions, the unique status of one municipal hospital with regard to attending physicians, and the attempt to capture the economic ramifications of a medically severe case mix necessitated both a number of adjustments in the basic data and the construction of new variables. [11]

Case Mix and Resource Absorption

The medical, nursing, and ancillary service resources required to treat a specific patient load depend, to a large extent, on the particular diagnostic case mix of a given institution. The derivation of a proxy resource absorption statistic was based on the assumption that resource absorption depends on two factors: relative cost per patient-day and relative average length of stay. Base-line diagnosis distribution data per hospital were obtained from the Medicaid Audit program of the New York City Department of Health. The Health Department data aggregated the diagnoses into eighty categories, based on H-ICDA codes. [12] Detailed length of stay and cost per day data by diagnosis were available from the National Center for Health Statistics and the Social Security Administration respectively. [13] These two data sources were used to derive relative length of stay and cost per day values for each specific diagnosis category identified in the New York City Health Department study relative to all diagnoses reported in that study. In those cases where a precise diagnosis match could not be obtained from all the data sources used based on ICDA codes, a "second-best" match was made with the aid of a registered nurse and a physician.[14] Multiplying the relative cost per day statistic by the relative length of stay statistic yields a resource absorption measure indicating the relative costliness of treating a patient in a given diagnostic category. As the Medicaid Audit Program data was available for calendar year 1972 only, the application of the resource absorption adjustment was limited to the last study year.[15]

PRODUCTIVITY PROFILES

Five distinct productivity indices were calculated, based on the methodology outlined in the previous sections. The formulas used in computing each index appear in Table I. One can view Index I as embodying a crude approximation of hospital output. Indices II and IV improve on this first approximation of output by incorporating education (and research) into the output measure and adjusting for case mix, respectively. Indices III and V are variants of Indices II and IV; they give equal weight to the direct patient care and the nonpatient care element of hospital output. The productivity indices per sector for the period 1969-1972 appear in Table 2.

Cross-Sectional Patterns

At any given point in time the municipal sector appears to display greater relative productivity than the voluntary sector. The productivity indices presented in Table 2 for the municipal sector are above 1.0, while the productivity indices for the voluntary sector are below 1.0. However, the productivity differential between sectors is not very large. The addition of the education (and the imputed research component) inherent in Index II appears to widen the performance gap between both sectors; the value of the productivity index of the voluntary sector decreases. The adoption of a weighting schema that gives greater weight to nonpatient care activities further accentuates the difference between the two hospital sectors.

The addition of a diagnosis specific case-mix adjustment (Indices IV and V, 1972 data) leads to an increase in the voluntary sector's productivity index (0.992 versus 0.973 and 0.934 versus 0.923);[16] an opposite effect is noted in the municipal sector. However, the proxy case severity adjustment is apparently not great enough to reverse the performance patterns noted above.

Table 1

Productivity Indices

Index Number	Formula	Weight Values
I	$\dfrac{y_1 \text{ (Weighted Inpatient Care Index)} + y_2 \text{ (Weighted Outpatient Care Index)} + y_3 \text{ (Days of Home Care Index)}}{\text{Input Index}}$	$y_1 = .80$ $y_2 = .19$ $y_3 = .01$
II, III	$\dfrac{z\,[y_1 \text{ (Weighted Inpatient Care Index)} + y_2 \text{ (Weighted Outpatient Care Index)} + y_3 \text{ (Days of Home Care Index)}] + (1-z) \text{ (Students Educated Index)}}{\text{Input Index}}$	II: $z = .87$ $(1-z) = .13$ III: $z = .5$ $(1-z) = .5$
IV, V	$\dfrac{z\,[(\text{Resource Absorption Adjustment}) (y_1) \text{ (Weighted Inpatient Care Index)} + (y_2) \text{ (Weighted Outpatient Care Index)} + (y_3) \text{ (Days of Home Care Index)}] + (1-z) \text{ (Students Educated Index)}}{\text{Input Index}}$	IV: $z = .87$ $(1-z) = .13$ V: $z = .5$ $(1-z) = .5$

Table 2

Productivity Profiles -- Voluntary and Municipal Sectors

Year	Sector	Productivity Indices				
		I	II	III	IV	V
1969	Voluntary	0.992	0.863	0.862		
	Municipal	1.006	1.019	1.056		
1970	Voluntary	0.957	0.942	0.901		
	Municipal	1.035	1.047	1.081		
1971	Voluntary	0.986	0.969	0.923		
	Municipal	1.011	1.024	1.063		
1972	Voluntary	0.990	0.973	0.923	0.992	0.934
	Municipal	1.008	1.023	1.064	1.001	1.052

Longitudinal Patterns

Some interesting longitudinal patterns emerge over the four-year period 1969-1972. If output is defined solely as including patient care elements (Index I), one notes an absolute decline in the value of the productivity index of the voluntary sector during the period 1969-1970 and a continuous increase in the value of its productivity index during the periods 1970-1971 and 1971-1972. The trend in the municipal sector is the reverse of that reported for the voluntary sector. The value of the productivity index increased from 1969 to 1971 and declined continuously thereafter. When nonpatient care elements are incorporated in the definition of output (Index II), one notes a continuous increase in the value of the productivity index of the voluntary sector during the four years under study. With regard to the municipal sector the value of the productivity index increased during 1969-1970, but declined from 1970 to 1972.

An analysis of the annual percentage change in the various output and input elements that jointly determine the productivity profile of each sector provides some explanation for the reported productivity trends. As can be seen from the data reported in Table 3, the municipal sector experienced a greater increase in the number of (weighted) inpatients and outpatients treated during 1969-1970 than the voluntary sector, concomitant with a smaller increase in total inputs utilized in the production process. Hence a widening productivity gap between the two sectors over this period. During 1970-1971 the reverse was true: the voluntary sector experienced the greater percentage increase in patient

Table 3

Percentage Increase in Output and Input Elements,
Voluntary and Municipal Sectors, 1969-1972

		Percentage Increase			Annual Compounded Change,
Output/Input Element	Sector	1969-1970	1970-1971	1971-1972	1969-1972
Patients Treated (Unweighted)	Voluntary	5.2	0.1	0.3	1.8
	Municipal	4.4	-0.2	-4.1	-0.4
Patients Treated[1] (Weighted)	Voluntary	4.4	3.6	-0.9	2.4
	Municipal	5.0	-0.5	-3.9	0.1
Clinic and Emergency Room Visits (Unweighted)	Voluntary	4.3	7.0	3.1	4.8
	Municipal	6.8	4.9	6.2	6.0
Clinic and Emergency Room Visits[1] (Weighted)	Voluntary	5.1	7.1	2.4	4.9
	Municipal	7.9	4.7	2.0	4.8
Days of Home Care	Voluntary	-11.7	-4.0	14.4	-1.0
	Municipal	-8.8	0.9	1.8	-2.2
Students Trained	Voluntary	5.7	7.6	3.1	5.4
	Municipal	4.1	5.8	2.2	4.0
Total Inputs	Voluntary	7.6	8.2	4.0	6.5
	Municipal	1.7	5.1	2.1	4.6
Payroll Expenses[2]	Voluntary	5.4	8.2	1.4	4.9
	Municipal	5.3	5.1	-3.1	2.3
Non-Payroll Operating Expenses[2]	Voluntary	13.5	9.5	9.1	10.7
	Municipal	-4.5	24.5	13.4	10.5

1. Weighted based on relative registered nurse staffing per service area.

2. Based on constant dollar values.

care output and the smaller percentage increase in inputs. Over
the period 1971-1972 the voluntary sector experienced a smaller
decline in (weighted) inpatient care and a greater increase in
outpatient care than the municipal sector. Even though the
voluntary sector also exhibited a greater increase in input utilization than the municipal sector, its superior performance (in
a comparative sense) with regard to the volume of output produced more than compensated for the increased resource utilization and led to an improvement in aggregate productivity.
Over the entire study period (1969-1972) the voluntary sector
displayed greater growth in both weighted output and input elements; however, the rate of input utilization increase exceeded
that of output production.

   Three additional observations of interest emerge from the
data appearing in Table 3. First, while the municipal sector
had relatively more education output, the voluntary sector
experienced a greater growth in education output than the municipal sector in every period under study. Second, with but one
exception, utilization of supplies and materials (non-payroll
operating expenses) increased much more rapidly in each period
in both sectors than the utilization of labor (payroll expenses).
Third, the weighting of the volume of inpatient and outpatient
care produced resulted in some noticeable changes in output
growth. On an unweighted basis, the growth of inpatient care
during 1969-1970 was greater in the voluntary sector and the
growth of outpatient care during 1971-1972 was greater in the
municipal sector. The reverse is true when weighted units are
compared.

The Effect of the Quality Adjustment

   The introduction of an intensity of services adjustment as
a proxy for changes in quality of care over time had no major
effect on the overall relative productivity patterns reported above.
As can be seen from Table 4, the municipal sector still maintained a slight relative productivity advantage. It is worthwhile
to recall that the intensity of services adjustment is an absolute
one; it reflects annual changes over the previous period for the
given sector (i.e., 1970 as compared to 1969 for each sector,
etc.).[17] Thus the data in the 1971 cells for Indices I and II and
in the 1972 cells for Indices I and IV indicate that both sectors
were productive in that the volume of adjusted output, exceeded
the volume of input.

   One interesting point emerges from a longitudinal analysis
of the data appearing in Tables 2 and 4. Whereas the direction
of productivity changes over the periods 1969-1970 and 1970-1971
remain the same, a different pattern emerges for the period 1971-
1972. The introduction of a proxy quality adjustment reversed

Table 4

Productivity Profiles -- Voluntary and Municipal Sectors,
Quality Adjustment Included

Year	Sector	Productivity Indices				
		I	II	III	IV	V
1969	Voluntary	0.992	0.863	0.862		
	Municipal	1.006	1.019	1.056		
1970	Voluntary	0.982	0.965	0.914		
	Municipal	1.021	1.035	1.075		
1971	Voluntary	1.048	1.023	0.954		
	Municipal	1.098	1.100	1.106		
1972	Voluntary	1.014	0.994	0.935	1.018	0.935
	Municipal	1.087	1.091	1.103	1.068	1.090

what initially appeared to be an improvement in the productivity
of the voluntary sector. This reversal is directly traceable to
the fact that the percentage increase in intensity of services
provided by the voluntary sector during the period 1971-1972
was small compared to its own performance in the previous
period (1970-1971). However, in absolute terms, the intensity
of services provided in the voluntary sector exceeded that provided in the municipal sector in every period under study.

It should be recognized that although the quality proxy
adjustment adopted here appears to be superior to other efforts
reported in the literature to measure quality, [18] it is still possible that low productivity values and unfavorable productivity
differentials result from quality-related factors not captured
by our proxy measures. However, the proxy adopted is the
best that could be estimated with the data that was available for
this study.

The Effect of an Alternate Valuation of the Municipal Sector
Capital Stock

The construction costs for three municipal hospitals
currently nearing completion (Lincoln, North Central Bronx,
and Woodhull) approximate $110 per gross square foot. Adopting
this figure as being representative of the replacement cost of
municipal facilities, and revising the respective municipal and
voluntary input indices results in some interesting changes in

relative productivity profiles. The value of the productivity gap between sectors is narrowed in each year. In most instances, the voluntary sector appears to be more productive than the municipal sector.

In the final analysis the question of whether a significant productivity differential exists between hospital sectors depends on which productivity measure is chosen. If we assume that municipal hospitals experienced the same capital costs as voluntary hospitals, they appear to be more productive. However, if we assume that the municipal sector has to pay more for its capital assets or that municipal projects embody more capital per square foot than voluntary projects (a condition which our capital measure does not detect) then one can claim that in some instances the voluntary sector is the more productive one.

PRODUCTIVITY PROFILES AND HEALTH PLANNING

I will now illustrate the potential use of the productivity measures in two areas of the health planning process: (1) validating simplistic indicators of hospital performance, and (2) clarifying some relationships between institutional characteristics of the industry and performance.

Rather than continue the voluntary/municipal dichotomy in the analysis presented in this section, I pooled the output and input data for the twenty-eight hospitals into one hypothetical system and developed institution rather than sector specific averages as the base for index number construction. As Productivity Indices II and IV are more comprehensive than Productivity Index I and embody more conservative weighting factors than Productivity Indices III and V, they are utilized in the analysis presented in this section. [19]

Productivity Indices and Conventional Measures of Hospital Performance

In the absence of refined measures of institutional performance, many analysts of hospital efficiency have relied on costs per adjusted patient-day, occupancy rates, and average length of stay as productivity surrogates. Of these three measures average length of stay exhibits the closest association with our measure of institutional productivity. The inverse relationship prevailed for all four years under study, and was characteristic of institutions in both sectors. [20] This relationship remained in effect when a resource absorption adjustment was included in the output measure (Index IV). [21] As the calculation of the resource absorption measure was based partly on length of stay factors, the resultant inverse relationship between a productivity measure entailing a resource absorption correction and length of stay is indeed noteworthy. The least efficient institutions are characterized by relatively long lengths of stay while the most efficient institutions have shorter length of stay profiles:

The average length of stay/productivity relationship is to be expected because the dominant output component is based on number of patients treated. Greater output volume can be achieved by decreasing average length of stay, ceteris paribus. Had patient-days been used as the primary output measure, a different relationship would probably have emerged.

No discernible relationship appears to exist between aggregate institutional productivity and occupancy rate.[22] However, a different productivity/occupancy rate relationship appears to exist for each sector. Among voluntary hospitals, characterized by relatively high occupancy rates, facilities with higher occupancy rates exhibited lower productivity values. An opposite pattern existed for municipal hospitals. On balance, the prevailing relationships in the two sectors offset each other.

Over the four-year study period a consistently negative relationship existed between expenses per adjusted patient-day and institutional productivity.[23] This inverse expense/productivity relationship also prevailed when an adjustment was made for resource absorption. While the reported inverse relationship prevails in both hospital sectors, the extent of the relationship was stronger in the voluntary sector.

Institutional Characteristics and Productivity

In the course of this study data has been gathered on a number of institutional characteristics which may be related to productivity. These characteristics are: bed size, age of facility,[24] number of attending physicians per bed (voluntary sector only),[25] ratio of interns and residents to total medical staff (municipal sector only), and percent of medical staff costs paid for by the affiliate hospital (municipal sector only).[26]

There is no strong relationship between institutional size, as measured by number of beds, and productivity.[27] The absence of any relationship prevailed throughout the study period and remained in effect when a resource absorption adjustment was included in the productivity calculations. However, if the two largest municipal facilities are omitted from the analysis, an inverse relationship seemed to emerge. This relationship, if valid, implies the existence of diseconomies of size within the study sample.

The older facilities appear to be more productive.[28] This situation is explainable by noting that hospitals with an older plant will exhibit lower depreciation expenses, and, ceteris

paribus, lower input costs. However, one should not conclude
that new capital is not a productive resource. Even if one
accepts the hypothesis that plant capital is not economically
productive (but is desired for safety or appearance considerations), it is possible that new capital equipment is productive
and can be utilized in newer plants. Unfortunately, data limitations prevented the disaggregation of plant and equipment capital.
    The data indicate the absence of any systematic relation-
ship between the number of attending physicians per bed and
productivity.[29] No systematic relationship appears to exist
between the intensity of physician services, defined as the proportion of interns and residents to the total medical staff, and
productivity.[30] Interesting patterns which require further
exploration emerge between the degree of utilization of affiliate
physicians by municipal hospitals, defined as the percent of
physician costs paid for by the affiliate budget, and productivity.[31] Two clusters emerged when these two variables were
plotted. The lower cluster appears to include all facilities
which utilize a small portion of affiliate physician input. The
majority of institutions in this group have a relative productivity
value less than one. The reverse is true of the upper cluster,
which contains institutions utilizing a very high proportion of
affiliate physician input.[32] The mean difference is about 30
percent, but it is far from statistically significant. In a test of
the difference between means, the t ratio is less than 1.

FOOTNOTES

    1. Revenue data was not available for the municipal hospitals
included in the study. For these institutions, cost data was used.
    2. The staffing ratios in terms of registered nursing hours per
patient-day, by medical service area, are: medicine, gynecology,
rehabilitation, psychiatry, and chronic care = 3.8; newborn = 3.2;
obstetrics = 4.8; pediatrics = 4.5; premature = 6.3; extended
care = 2.3; intensive care = 12.0. (The New York City Health
and Hospitals Corporation, "Nursing and Clerical Service Levels"
New York: The New York City Health and Hospitals Corporation,
September 1973, mimeo.)
    3. The weights used were: emergency room = 0.6, outpatient
clinic = 0.4. These weights were computed from data presented
in the Health and Hospitals Corporation report, "Nursing and
Clerical Service Levels."
    4. This approach was suggested by Stuart Altman and Joseph
Eichenholz in their paper "Control of Hospital Costs under the
Economic Stabilization Program," presented at the December
1973 American Economic Association Meetings. The number of
adjusted patient-days are calculated as total inpatient days plus
equivalent outpatient visits. Equivalent outpatient visits equal

the number of outpatient visits divided by the ratio of inpatient revenue per day to outpatient revenue per visit.

5. As reported in the 1970 Census of Population, earnings for physicians, registered nurses, and health technologists and technicians (chosen as a proxy group for all health paraprofessionals) were $36,952, $14,770, and $8,940 respectively, yielding the following relative weights: 1, 0.4, 0.24. (U.S. Bureau of Census. Census of Population, 1970. Subject reports. Final Report PC(2)8B, Earnings by Occupation and Education. Washington, D.C.: U.S. Government Printing Office, 1973, Table 1.)

6. Had such data been available, many difficulties would have arisen, minimizing its value. Among the difficulties to be encountered in this area are the allocation of "credit" for articles written jointly by staff from different institutions, two or more versions of the same basic research findings, the quality of the journal in which the article appeared, the receipt of funds by a medical school for research to be conducted in part or entirely at a hospital affiliate, and the receipt of funds by one hospital for research conducted in part or entirely at its affiliate hospital.

7. In effect, the education component of output was weighted by the joint proportion of revenue (cost) devoted to education and research-related activities.

8. The payroll data used contained an imputation for the value of services rendered by members of religious orders.

9. Gross plant assets were valued at $65 per gross square foot. Equipment value was estimated as 20 percent of gross plant assets. For a discussion of hospital construction costs, see Health and Hospitals Planning Council of Southern New York, Construction Costs of Health Facilities (New York: Health and Hospitals Planning Council of Southern New York, May 1972). Although the Health and Hospitals Planning Council report included a municipal project, Health and Hospitals Corporation officials claim that current construction costs for municipal hospitals are approximately $110 per gross square foot. In recognition of this fact, the valuation of the municipal capital stock was recomputed, utilizing $110 per gross square foot as the relevant replacement cost. The effect of higher construction costs for municipal facilities on institutional productivity is explored in a subsequent section.

10. The assumed utilization rate--8 percent--was drived by imputing a 6 percent return on capital and a 2 percent annual depreciation allowance. The latter statistic is based on an assumed useful life of hospital capital of fifty years and a declining balance method of depreciation. This latter assumption was dictated by the vintage of hospital capital currently existing in New York City.

11. Editor's note: Sections on data refinements were deleted.

12. A significant degree of heterogeneity may still exist within

some of the eighty diagnostic categories. Data availability
factors precluded a finer disaggregation.
13. U.S. Department of Health, Education, and Welfare,
Public Health Service. Inpatient Utilization of Short Stay Hospitals by Diagnosis, U.S., 1968. Vital and Health Statistics
Series 13, No. 12 (Washington, D.C.: U.S. Government Printing Office, 1973); U.S. Department of Health, Education, and
Welfare, Social Security Administration. Short Stay Hospitals
Under Medicare, 1969: Use and Charges, By Major Diagnosis,
1969. DHEW Pub. No. (SSA) 74-11702 (Washington, D.C.:
Office of Research and Statistics, Social Security Administration), August 17, 1973.
14. The instructions given to these two health professionals
was to select the closest diagnosis among those for which data
exists which resembles the diagnosis for which a match is being
sought in terms of medical, nursing, and ancillary service
requirements. Initially, the physician and nurse each prepared
a match list independently of the other (the correlation between
their matches was 0.98). In the rare instances where disagreement occurred, the opinion of the nurse prevailed, as she had
greater familiarity with hospital-based patient care.
15. Editor's note: A section detailing defects in the data used
for calculating resource absorption was deleted.
16. The calculated case-severity resource absorption adjustment is: voluntary sector = 1.026; municipal sector = 0.967.
17. Changes in intensity of services provided by sector over
the study period were:

	Voluntary	Municipal
1969-1970	2.8	-1.3
1970-1971	6.8	8.6
1971-1972	2.9	7.8
1969-1972	4.0	4.8

(annual compounded change)
18. See, for example, Harry I. Greenfield. Hospital Efficiency
and Public Policy (New York: Praeger, 1973), p. 22, where
quality is approximated by the number of services offered.
19. The capital input used in calculating these indices is based
on a $65 per square foot valuation. Although municipal hospital
construction may entail higher costs, we assume that these
additional costs do not yield commensurate productivity improvements but rather reflect bureaucratic and political factors which
are unique to the municipal sector. (See Eli Ginzberg et al.
Urban Health Services: The Case of New York. New York:
Columbia University Press, 1971, Chapters 3-4.)
20. The correlation coefficient between these two variables is
-0.62.
21. The introduction of a resource absorption adjustment did,
however, weaken the degree of association between productivity
and average length of stay ($r = -0.58$).
22. The correlation between these two variables is 0.35.

23. The correlation between these two variables is -0.54. This relationship is to be expected as the productivity indices are output per unit of input measures, which in turn is the reciprocal of a cost per day measure.

24. Age of facility data was compiled as part of the capital stock variable construction.

25. Number of total attending physicians per hospital were obtained from the Medical Directory of New York State. The number of full-time salaried physicians per institution was deducted from this total to arrive at the number of attending physicians. The term "attending," as used here, implies a nonsalaried relationship between physician and hospital.

26. Based on the physician staffing study in this volume.

27. The correlation between productivity and affiliation is -0.25.

28. The correlation between these two variables is 0.42. As the capital stock at replacement cost valuation was undertaken with 1969 as the base period, 1969 data is used here.

29. The correlation between these variables is -0.02. This analysis is limited to the voluntary sector since, with one exception, municipal hospitals do not permit either nonsalaried or salaried physicians to admit their private patients. Data availability limited the analysis to 1971.

30. The correlation between these two variables is -0.14. Data availability considerations limited this analysis to municipal hospitals, and to the 1971 period.

31. The correlation coefficient between these two variables is 0.44.

32. Editor's note: Space limitations necessitated deletion of a substantial ensuing discussion of further implications of the findings of this analysis.

V

Policy Development

and Analysis

These studies concern issues involving the broad allocation of resources and/or questions relating to the incentive effects of different alternative policies. Although the HSA policy analysis staff contained analysts with a variety of formal educational backgrounds and experiences, the studies in this chapter were done primarily by economists. This is because the economists on the staff were particularly trained to consider issues involving the efficient allocation of scarce resources and the nature of various behavioral relationships among complex social systems.

THE NATIONAL FINANCING OF HEALTH CARE

During the period 1970-1974, health care policy-makers of the City of New York closely followed national events regarding the consideration by the Congress of alternative national health insurance plans. In his 1970 health message President Nixon proposed a plan which received a great deal of coverage by the press and some consideration by the Congress. Since the Nixon Plan would, if enacted, substantially influence the manner in which the nation financed health services for the poor, and since New York City already expended about $500 million in city tax dollars on health services for the poor, New York City officials were particularly concerned about how the Nixon health insurance plan would affect its citizens and its municipal budget.

Gordon Chase asked the program analysis staff of HSA to develop quick estimates of how particular national health insurance proposals would affect the city. Furthermore, Chase was interested in using the media to publicly criticize or praise the features of various health insurance proposals. Since New

York City already had a relatively generous Medicaid program in effect, and a unique system of municipal hospital services, all but the most generous of health insurance proposals (i. e., the Kennedy-Griffiths Plan) were likely to have adverse effects upon the city's finances.

The paper by Jeffrey Weiss and Lynda Brodsky grew out of an effort to develop a systematic framework to consider the drawbacks and advantages of various national health insurance plans. Apart from their short-run effects upon the city's budget, HSA analysts were also concerned about the long-term effects of various national health insurance plans upon the principal problems of the health care system. And they thought that their "quickie" analysis, which was primarily concerned with New York City, might be of interest to those health experts interested in national health issues. At that time, no published analysis had systematically indicated the various policy conflicts inherent in efforts to achieve the multiple objectives for national health insurance plans.

Thus Weiss and Brodsky selected the Kennedy plan to illustrate the trade-off effects of the provisions of this plan against the objectives of national health insurance. Proposed plans for the national financing of health care aimed to eliminate the problems of a maldistribution of health services and resources, an inefficient medical care delivery system, rapidly rising costs and prices, and inadequate catastrophic insurance. Because these objectives cannot necessarily be advanced simultaneously, as this analysis clearly indicates with respect to the Kennedy plan, one must decide upon an ordering of objectives. After priorities are established, the various detailed issues such as eligibility requirements, benefits covered, reimbursement rules, and financing mechanisms can be considered more rationally.

THE CITY HEALTH INSURANCE PLAN (CHIP)

Although it was clear by 1972 that prospects for the enactment of some form of national health insurance by the Congress were exceedingly small, some members of the staff were intrigued by the possible incentive effects of a "generous" National Health Insurance Plan upon the Health and Hospitals Corporation. A prime cause for the sometimes poor or indifferent care offered by the municipal hospitals was thought to be the fact that HHC had a captive population in the medically indigent who had to use public hospitals if they wished to receive free care. One solution to this problem might be a health insurance plan which would provide the medically indigent with the means to select alternative services. It was believed that this would result in the HHC losing patients to private physicians and voluntary hospitals, and there would be substantial pressure in those HHC facilities which remained open (after an exodus of patients) to improve their services.

Furthermore, the then-existing mechanism of financing the HHC consisted of essentially the city giving the HHC an annual payment to cover the difference between its projected expenditures and its projected third-party receipts. This city payment was not related to the effectiveness of HHC operations because (1) no firm procedures or guidelines were established to determine the basis for the payment; and (2) the city and HHC went through an annual political exercise which essentially focused on the determination of a single budget number for the HHC without regard to the needs or performance of individual hospitals. This process resulted in a recurring midyear HHC fiscal crisis with neither the city nor HHC able to assign specific responsibility (at the individual hospital level) to the reasons for the fiscal shortfall. The mayor was thus faced with the unpleasant prospect of covering the HHC deficit or forcing the HHC to make across-the-board reductions in services.

The proposal from Jeffrey Weiss to Gordon Chase for a new city-HHC financial relationship (CHIP) was a response to this set of problems. This memo was based upon the staff work and deliberations of a joint City Budget Bureau-HSA study group which met during the first six months of 1972.

The initial intent of this joint study group was to develop proposals for a mandatory city-wide health insurance plan covering all citizens of the city. One reason for HSA-BOB staff interest in this issue was that Mayor Lindsay was a potential presidential candidate in 1972 and it was thought that a city health insurance proposal would be of interest to him in his possible role as a candidate. Another reason for our interest was the expectation that the city's existing subsidy to HHC would provide the basis for a city health insurance plan. However, it soon became apparent that legal, technical, and empirical obstacles precluded the possibility of developing any such plan. In particular, HSA analysts could not determine the highly specific financial and service implications of alternative health insurance plans for various groups of employees and employers, because its data from the city's "Population Health Survey"[1] proved to be too inaccurate for this purpose. We knew that the mayor could never publicly announce a proposed mandatory plan without giving some indication of its total cost to the city and employers, and without indicating who would gain and who would lose through the adoption of his plan.

Consequently, the joint study group lowered its goals and attempted to develop the general arguments and guidelines contained in the CHIP memo with the more narrow objective of rationalizing the way HHC was subsidized by the city. However, when Chase received this memo, he was greatly disappointed since he had presumed that HSA staff (at its own initiation) were working on a city health insurance plan, and Weiss did not clearly inform him about the methodological difficulties which led to the change in program objectives and design. Chase never seriously considered the ideas contained in this proposal for this reason and because a priori he did not have confidence that the changes proposed in the CHIP memo would make much difference in HHC's operations. At the same time, the Bureau of the Budget personnel involved in this effort circulated the CHIP memo to the deputy mayor and other policy-making officials in the Budget Bureau. The response they received was that "these ideas are very interesting and probably right, but the politics of the situation are such that it would be impractical to surface these very large issues concerning the HHC with only eighteen months remaining in the mayor's term." These responses were not surprising; the HSA-BOB staff knew from the start that they were addressing an issue which had a potentially high substantive payoff, but a very low probability of being seriously considered by top policy-makers--for very good political reasons on their part. The effort was undertaken with a small chance of a possibly very great impact.

N.Y.C. EMPLOYEE HEALTH BENEFITS

In the spring of 1973 executives of the Health Insurance Plan of Greater New York (HIP) approached James Hester, a senior member of the HSA program analysis staff, and requested his assistance in getting the administrator interested in the then-ongoing contract negotiations between the City Department of Personnel and HIP. The HIP executives hoped that Chase might intervene on behalf of HIP and somehow induce the city's negotiators to agree to more generous contract terms for HIP. While Chase thought that it would be inappropriate to intervene in ongoing contract negotiations between the responsible city agency and the health insurance carriers which insured the city's more than 300,000 employees, he was interested in some of the longer-range issues raised by the current negotiations.

Chase therefore persuaded the deputy mayor to add the Health Services administrator to the Health Insurance Directorate, an ad hoc small group of high level city officials concerned with the city's policies toward its insurance carriers. In practice, the director of the city's Department of Personnel dominated this group and determined its actions. HSA and the Health Department had not previously been deeply involved in reviewing the city's health insurance policies for its own employees, because HSA had enough difficulties attempting to deal with

problems within its own bureaucratic jurisdiction, and because
of the preeminent position of the city's director of personnel.
(It was feared that the then city director of personnel might
use his bureaucratic powers to delay or stop agency efforts to
hire key people if he was offended.)

In this instance, the urging of a respected analyst (Hester)
and the nature of the issues convinced Chase that he should take
on the risks involved in intervening in another agency's traditional area of responsibility. Chase's high standing with the
mayor made it possible for him to engage in this effort to inter-
ject HSA's general substantive concerns into what was at that
time viewed as a routine negotiation between the city and its
health insurance carriers.[2]

The focus of the research of James Hester, Edward
Salsberg, and others was to explore the use of the city's
employee health benefits program as an explicit tool for shaping
the quality of health services available to its own employees
and to the residents of the city as a whole. Since one out of
every seven New York City residents had their health insurance
purchased by the city's employees and employees' dependents
health insurance plans, New York City clearly had substantial
potential leverage with its health insurance carriers. A major
issue of the city-HIP negotiations in 1973 was whether HIP
should be given additional funds to pay for hiring additional
full-time physicians to upgrade the quality of its services.[3]

We have presented the introduction to the very substantial
Hester-Salsberg Interim Report on the N.Y.C. Employees
Health Benefit Program (with some tables deleted), and a
shortened version of the study's recommendations. The actual
report contained a great deal of empirical information which
could not be presented here.

This report did have one impact upon the city's ultimate
offer to HIP and its other health insurance carriers in the fall
of 1973. The deputy mayor decided that Chase's arguments
concerning the merits of supporting HIP efforts to employ additional full-time physicians did have merit, and additional funds
were allocated for this purpose (i.e., recommendation number 2)
despite the contrary views of the then director of the department of personnel. In exchange, HIP agreed to institute certain quality and management controls.

POLICY DEVELOPMENT AND THE PLANNING
ENVIRONMENT

The physical development of many of our large cities took
place primarily in response to the rapid increases in population during the waves of immigration which ended in 1925.
Construction lagged behind population growth, and the boom

continued into the early 1930's. Many of the facilities which
were built during this era are coming due for replacement
at about the same time. While incomes have grown, the rise
in construction costs has far outpaced the rise in the general
prices. As a result, the share of income which is necessary
for replacement alone is nearly as large as was necessary for
new construction. Furthermore, there is no longer the luxury
of building on vacant land.

Health facilities face a major obsolescence problem
because of large changes in technology and financing. In many
instances, this obsolescence is compounded on top of a problem
of physical deterioration. Obsolescence arises from three
sources--changes in medical technology, changes in construction technology, and changes resulting from the growth in
incomes and third-party financing and thus an upgrading of
standards. These forces manifest themselves in problems of
inadequate space, antiquated support systems, and insufficient
flexibility for the future. As a consequence of these developments, many structures of relatively recent vintage are func-
tionally obsolete.

An effective facilities policy contains several components.
These include economically extending the use of existing facilities for a longer period of time through maintenance and renovation. They include serving more patients with a given set
of facilities by increasing occupancy rates, reducing average
length of stay, and developing less costly alternatives in areas
such as ambulatory and long-term care. In New York City,
they include consideration of the appropriate size of the municipal relative to the voluntary sector. A facilities policy must
further assess the scale of effort required for alternative
replacement strategies and set forth a course of action to be
undertaken should various levels of funding for construction of
replacement facilities become available.

The study of "Phased Replacement of Municipal Hospital
Facilities" by Irving Leveson and Julie Northup (February 1972)
takes some basic steps toward outlining the funding requirements for a feasible strategy and development of a set of priorities. Attention is focused on the age of facilities and its
implications for a phased replacement strategy. This consideration gives emphasis to circumstances where both physical
deterioration and obsolescence are most acute, and provides
"ball park" estimates of the ability of alternative financial
resources to deal with the problem. The study was done as a
successor to a previous study which examined the size of the
obsolescence problem independently of resource availability
and alternatives to new hospital construction.

The excerpts from the Capital Budget Message of the
Health Services Administration delivered in October 1973
illustrate how these principles and analyses are incorporated

into a formal process in which policies are established and budgets negotiated. The message reflects an increasing emphasis on gradual renewal of existing facilities over complete replacement construction in a manner which is integrated with consideration of specific decisions facing the city and the development of planning processes within which they are to be considered. The transition issues paper which follows devotes substantial space to consideration of several specific major facilities decisions which had to be addressed. It was in the context of dealing with issues such as these that the aggregate policy toward hospital construction within the municipal system would have to be shaped.

"Transition Issues in Health Services" by James Hester and Irving Leveson represents an extensive effort to clearly lay out the issues for the new administration of Mayor Beame which took office on January 1, 1974. The paper dealt with eight issues, five of which are included here. These issues had repeatedly been raised in memoranda and Program Guidance Letters as well as at numerous meetings among heads of agencies. But with many new people coming in it was necessary to have a rapid method of bringing them up-to-date and putting the diverse written materials in proper context. It was further hoped that the transition issues paper itself would provide the basis of future policy statements.

The transition issues paper was developed at the request of Gerald Frug, the former first deputy administrator of HSA, who served as Health Services administrator from October 1, 1973, until January 7, 1974. There were a number of other documents prepared with similar purposes in mind. A paper dealing with the organizational structure of the Health Services Administration and its constituent agencies was also requested by the administrator. Several longer transition papers dealing with selected issues were prepared at the initiative of the analysis staff directors. The Capital Budget message report was far more extensive than in the past. Many file memorandums were prepared to expand the written record available to the staff in both HSA and various interested agencies. "Health Services Administration Staff Papers, 1971-1973" was in part a response to the requirements of orderly transition.

It is difficult to evaluate the impact of the transition issues paper, of the many documents prepared with the transition in mind, or of the entire transition process that included a variety of discussions with the new officials. The new health commissioner/Health Services administrator Dr. Lowell Bellin was simultaneously trying to absorb facts, sort out priorities, evaluate people, and assess the rapidly changing political situation.

The inescapable fact of the period (January-May 1974) is that the policy advice given the Beame administration could only have an impact within the climate that the new

mayor had himself created. That climate was represented
by the placing of a former controller and budget director in
City Hall (i.e., Abe Beame) and by the appointment of a
deputy budget director as the chief deputy mayor. It was
represented by the increased power given to the city's overhead agencies. And it was represented by a major policy
focus on administrative questions rather than major substantive problems. Among these was the issue of "dismantling
the superagencies," including HSA. One casualty of these
priorities was the analysis staff of HSA, which relegated
to a minor role; thus most the analysts gradually
resigned.

LONG-TERM CARE POLICY

"Perspectives on Long-Term Care" by Byron Bruce
Zellner is an early "think piece" on one of the most intractable
areas of health policy. The reason for the difficulty, the
author explains, is the close substitution between nursing home
services and housing, food, social services, etc., outside of
institutions. The high degree of substitution leads to a degree
of discretion which makes it even more impossible to define
overall "need" than for other institutional services.
The issue is a reflection of a more general problem of
attitudes and the resulting policy toward the aged in this country. Even as we make progress against the problem of poverty
among the elderly through increased benefits under Social
Security and private pensions, disability benefits, and health
insurance, the problem of organization of services and eligibility remains. Attempts in this country to develop communities for the aged in which the availability of homemaker services,
community dining, medical services, and type of housing are
varied within a single complex as the aging process advances
have gained little ground even on an experimental basis. The
seriousness of the problems only becomes clear when considered against the short life expectancy of persons put in
nursing homes which cost $15,000 per year in New York, the
segregation of the aged in mental hospitals, and the displace-
ment of the aged from their own homes by public and private
relocation in the process even of building homes for the aged.

FOOTNOTES

1. The "Population Health Survey" consisted of a sample of
5,000 N.Y.C. households surveyed during most years from
1964 through 1970. This survey contained information comparable to the National Health Survey.

2. It might be of interest to the reader to note that the new mayor as of January 1974, Abe Beame, who as a long-time city employee had strong ties to the city personnel director, removed Chase's successor from the Health Insurance Directorate in 1974.

3. HIP physicians treated both private fee-for-service patients and HIP patients. The physicians received fixed per capita annual payments per HIP patient, and it was often claimed that this led to reduced attention to HIP patients relative to fee-for-service patients.

V-1　AN ESSAY ON THE NATIONAL FINANCING OF HEALTH CARE*

by Jeffrey Weiss and Lynda Brodsky

WHAT ARE THE PROBLEMS?

During the past two years, interest in a major expansion of federally financed health insurance has decidedly heightened, and it is clear that this will be an increasingly important issue over the next few years. President Nixon and Senator Kennedy, among others, have proposed plans for a major expansion of federally financed health insurance. Some of the proposals for extending federally financed health insurance imply or presuppose major changes in the nation's health care system, and all of the proposed plans will add billions of dollars to the nation's expenditures on health.

These plans are all designed to help solve one or more of the problems with out health care system. These problems are: (1) a maldistribution of health care services and resources; (2) an inefficient medical care delivery system which is characterized by unnecessarily high health care costs, a lack of emphasis on preventive medical care, and poor quality control; (3) rapidly rising medical care costs and prices; and (4) inadequate catastrophic health insurance for most Americans.

The inability of the poor to purchase health services on the same basis as more affluent citizens is reflected in a number of statistics which have been well documented and do not require elaboration. Though cultural considerations may be partly responsible, a lack of purchasing power by the poor is the primary reason for disparities in the consumption of health services among income groups in this country. That the United States

*This paper was originally published in The Journal of Human Resources, Vol. 7:2, Spring 1972. The editors are grateful to the editor of The Journal of Human Resources for allowing reproduction of this paper.

lags behind seventeen other countries in life expectancy for males and twelve other countries in infant mortality may be traced in part to this inequity. [1]

A variety of factors account for the inefficient health care delivery system in this country. For one thing, our system consists of several hundred thousand independent producers who provide medical services, dental services, short-term general hospital care, and the like, with little or no coordination. Within specific geographical areas, this has created an "unbalanced" system--a surplus of some services and shortages of others. Secondly, the increasing specialization of the medical profession has contributed to a lack of concern for the whole patient and has made it difficult for the individual to secure health care. Then, the fragmented, "cottage" nature of the health services industry has resulted in relatively little research being devoted to ways to improve the effective utilization of health care resources. With the possible exception of drugs, major technological innovations in the health care industry have tended to be quality-improving rather than cost-saving.

The most important factor underlying health care inefficiency is the health insurance system, which has caused providers and consumers of health care to pay less attention to health care prices as out-of-pocket costs have become increasingly small relative to the total cost of health care for any given illness. Health insurance plans have generally reimbursed hospitals on a "full cost" basis and have accepted the "prevailing" fees charged by physicians, so that very weak constraints have been placed upon the rate of increase in hospital costs and charges and physician fees. There is overwhelming evidence that much unnecessary surgery is clearly related to the availability of health insurance coverage. [2] Private health insurance plans typically contribute to unnecessary medical care utilization by not covering preventive health care services, by reimbursing surgical services much more fully than medical services, by covering laboratory tests and X-rays on an in-hospital basis but not on an outpatient basis, and by not covering lower cost alternatives to expensive acute care hospital stays, such as nursing homes and home care visits.

Rapidly rising medical care prices and costs are due to several important factors:

1. The aggregate demand for health care has risen sharply throughout the post-World War II period as population has increased, incomes have risen generally, the proportion of elderly persons in the population has risen, and people have become more aware of the benefits of health care through increased education and technology.

2. The supply of health care services cannot adjust rapidly to changes in demand. It takes many years to increase the supply of physicians, dentists, pharmacists, and other key health

care personnel. Technical innovations, which might have had
the effect of increasing health care resources, have not occurred
to a significant degree.

3. The organizational and insurance factors discussed
earlier which encourage inefficiency also encourage inflation.

The fourth principal problem with our health care system
is the lack of adequate health insurance to protect most Americans against financial catastrophe if they become seriously ill.
Today, about 65 million Americans do not have any form of
major medical insurance. About 100 million are not covered for
physician services. Furthermore, the typical health insurance
policy still pays only a relatively small portion of the average
health care bill. In 1969 health insurance paid for 38 percent of
consumer expenditures on personal health care. Even under
Medicare, the average person still must pay 55 percent of his
health care expenditures.

HOW CAN NATIONAL HEALTH INSURANCE AFFECT THESE
PROBLEMS?

We know enough about the health care system to state
clearly that any national health insurance scheme will have a
very uneven effect on the four problems just discussed. There
is one major reason for this conclusion: The objective of controlling health care costs and prices conflicts with the objective
of improving the distribution of health care services and, in the
short run, with the objective of improving our present inefficient
and fragmented medical care delivery system.

No national health insurance plan would be very likely to
substantially redistribute health care services and resources.
First, the powerful financial incentives necessary to promote
a redistribution of services and resources conflict with the
objective of controlling medical care costs and prices. Thus,
the incentives will probably be mild and will work over a long
period of time. Second, the ability to pay for medical care
services will not be sufficient to induce many physicians and
other health practitioners to practice in our urban ghettos or
rural poverty areas. New institutions, like neighborhood family
care centers, might be needed to help attract these practitioners,
and new recruitment devices, such as a national medical corps
in lieu of military service, may also help. Moreover, there
will continue to be considerable disparities in the distribution
of health care services and resources as long as there are great
disparities in income among the population.

Both the Kennedy bill (S.3) and the Nixon administration's
bill (S.1623) provide significant incentives to encourage the
establishment of prepaid group practices--health maintenance
organizations which will care for the health needs of a defined

population for a fixed sum of money per year. Even assuming that institutions which are responsible for the total care of the patient and which provide a broad range of services (like the Kaiser health plan in California) are desirable alternatives to our present inefficient medical care delivery system, these institutions will be slow to develop.

For one thing, many physicians and consumers prefer solo practitioner arrangements to prepaid group practice arrangements, and thus they will have to be induced with rather substantial financial incentives.

Second, the successful operation of these institutions requires capable management. It took many years for the Kaiser health plan to acquire the degree of managerial proficiency which it now possesses, and indeed, we think that the unique feature of Kaiser is its managerial capability. If this is the case, one could expect that the rapid development of prepaid group practices would not lead to substantial immediate gains in the quality of medical care or to controls over medical care costs, since the requisite managerial skills do not generally exist in the medical care sector. Health care administrators generally share a large portion of their decision-making responsibilities with the medical staffs of their institutions, boards of directors, and, increasingly, community representatives. This necessary dilution of authority and responsibility, combined with a traditional lack of emphasis on modern managerial practices, results in a rather weak managerial capability in even our largest and best health care institutions.

An adequate national health insurance plan could bring rapidly rising medical care costs and prices under control. This would necessitate either controlling prices directly by establishing acceptable prevailing fees and charges for different services or controlling them indirectly by limiting total medical care expenditures (under the plan) by society. A ceiling on total expenditures for a particular health care product, such as hospital care, can be effected if the national health insurance plan covers most expenditures for that product.[3] However, direct or indirect price control in the health care sector would result in greater queues for services; therefore, the various pros and cons of this method of rationing services versus reliance upon prices to ration services would have to be considered.

Pressures on costs and prices would be reduced over the long run if health insurance provided incentives for low-cost modes of treatment. For example, a preferable national health insurance scheme should eliminate current incentives to use acute care as opposed to alternative lower cost forms of institutional or home care.

A successful national health insurance scheme should readily solve the problem of inadequate catastrophic health insurance for most Americans. Since the magnitude of the

financial loss necessary to cause a "financial catastrophe" for
a given family or individual presumably varies with the level of
income, such a plan would cover a large proportion of medical
expenses for low income people and a smaller proportion of
expenses for higher income people. The bulk of medical care
expenses not now covered by insurance is not a substantial
financial burden to most American families. Therefore, it is
anticipated that this objective can be accomplished without putting very much additional pressure on rising medical care costs
and prices and that the total additional costs of achieving this
objective will not be prohibitive. To protect against financial
catastrophe requires a health plan which covers the large medical bills infrequently incurred by a relatively small portion of
the population. A very adequate plan of this type could probably
be provided for about one-third the cost in federal revenues of
the very comprehensive health insurance plan provided under the
Kennedy bill. To illustrate this point, it is sufficient to note
that just adding a $100 family deductible to the Kennedy plan would
cut its cost in federal revenues by $5-8 billion and would result
in a substantial savings in administrative costs. The only financial catastrophe coverage which could conceivably put added
pressure on medical care costs and prices is in the long-term
care area, where most services are not adequately covered by
health insurance and where individuals can incur prohibitive
financial burdens.

SOME STRATEGIC CHOICES

In choosing among the wide array of possible national health
insurance plans, one must first decide on an ordering of objec-
tives--a decision which will clearly influence the nature of the
plan. The options are:
    1. To provide adequate catastrophic health insurance
coverage for the population. The implementation of this objective would require the smallest expenditure of federal funds,
but it would not get at the fundamental defects of the health care
system. This objective is emphasized by the American Medical
Association in its proposal to finance health insurance through a
federal tax credit scheme.
    2. To provide adequate catastrophic health insurance
coverage for the population, with adequate cost controls. This
strategy has the advantage of not only minimizing federal expenditures on health but also greatly affecting the total health care
expenditures of society. None of the major national health
insurance plans is aimed solely at this set of objectives.
    3. To provide for adequate catastrophic health insurance
coverage with strong price and cost controls, while emphasizing
the objective of redistributing health care services. This is the

basic strategy outlined by President Nixon in his health message of February 1971, and it would clearly be a great deal cheaper for the federal government and society than strategy number four below. However, services would not be redistributed as rapidly.

4. <u>To pursue a strategy designed to redistribute health care services and provide adequate catastrophic health insurance protection, with some minimal degree of control over costs and prices</u>. The disadvantage of this particular strategy, which underlies the Kennedy plan, is that it would be extremely costly to implement and it would probably lead to a much more rapid rate of price inflation than exists today and/or extensive rationing of some services by providers.

SOME QUESTIONS

Once a basic strategy is selected, the answers to several of the questions listed below are evident. However, answers to some of the questions require additional research, while other answers may be provided only with great uncertainty.

1. <u>Who should be covered</u>? Coverage of the entire population, for a basic set of benefits, is consistent with all of the objectives discussed above. However, some elements of the population must be excluded from obtaining certain "luxury" benefits (where supply is very limited) such as dental care, if weight is given to the objective of controlling inflation and the total costs of the plan.

2. <u>What benefits should be provided and for how much</u>? The answer to this question depends greatly upon the strategy selected. If there is great weight given to the objective of redistributing health services, many benefits would be covered which might not be covered under a plan which emphasized cost control. Similarly, premium payments, deductibles, and co-insurance--which promote "cost consciousness" of consumers and producers--would more likely characterize a plan that emphasized cost control and the efficient utilization of resources than one directed at redistributing health services.

3. <u>How should the providers of health services be reimbursed</u>? The federal government could "fix" the fees and charges of providers either directly, by negotiating fee and charge schedules, or indirectly, by negotiating fixed per capita, annual rates of reimbursement. An advantage of fixing fees and charges is that the government and the public would get more for their health care dollars. On the negative side are the opposition of providers to fixing their fees and charges and the difficulties inherent in reasonably administering a negotiated fees and charges policy.

Providers of care could be reimbursed on a fee-for-service

basis or on a per capita basis. Under the latter method of payment, providers agree to furnish health services for a fixed
cost per patient. A presumed advantage of this type of reimbursement is that it would reduce the incentive to prescribe unnecessary
services--a danger under a fee-for-service contract. Difficulties, however, would arise from the fact that the incentive for
practitioners to work hard is diminished and from the direct
opposition of many practitioners who oppose any policy which
might limit their incomes.

    4. What types of incentives should there be for changing
the structure of the health care system? If the development of
prepaid group practices is desired, the method of effecting this
change must be selected. Reliance on the free market has
resulted in relatively little formation of prepaid groups. If this
is primarily due to the aversion of physicians to alter their
current structure of practice, the level of compensation necessary to coax physicians to change might be so high so as to offset
the presumed advantages of such groups. Alternatively, the
absence of change may be due to the inability of physicians to
meet the high initial costs and the administrative difficulties of
setting up prepaid groups. In this case, loans and/or grants,
combined with technical assistance, may be in order. Another
approach would be to provide financial incentives to consumers
to use prepaid groups in expectation that the decreased demand
for solo practice would encourage physicians to combine.

    5. How should the national health insurance plan be
financed? A major issue here is the relative emphasis given to
financing out of general revenues as opposed to payroll taxes.
Also, there is the issue of whether or not a separate Social
Security-type trust fund should be established for the plan. While
financing out of general revenues is more progressive, a plan
which relied more heavily on regressive payroll taxes might be
more politically acceptable. An advantage of a separate trust
fund is that in earmarking funds, it would guarantee monies for
health. The great disadvantage of the trust fund is that it would
probably tend to lessen the competition for funds between health
and other socially important purposes; consequently, there would
be less pressure to control total health care costs. If the experience under Social Security and Medicare is any guide, the Congress seems more willing to increase earmarked payroll taxes
than taxes generally.

    6. How should the national health insurance system be
administered? One important issue is the role of private insurance companies under the national insurance plan. The Kennedy
plan leaves their use to the discretion of the administering
agencies, while other proposals would retain a large role for
private insurance companies. It would appear that the paper-
processing and bill-paying role of private insurance companies
does not really conflict with any of the objectives of a national

insurance plan; thus under any plan some private insurance
companies could be retained for this function. However, if some
importance is given to the objective of controlling medical care
costs and prices, the policy-making and medical care audit
functions of the private insurance carriers must be reassigned
to institutions which will protect the public interest.

Another issue is the relative emphasis given to local, state,
regional, and national administration. The specific form of
administration selected will clearly depend upon the objectives
of the plan. For example, the AMA plan would not control
medical care costs or restructure the health care system, and
its administration would be similar to the present arrangements.
In contrast, the Kennedy plan does seek both to control medical
care costs and to restructure the system, and the administrative
apparatus established under the proposed legislation clearly
reflects this fact. The Kennedy plan provides for a national
administrative agency under the Department of Health, Education, and Welfare, ten regional agencies, and a hundred or so
local agencies.

7. How much emphasis should be given to financing the
insurance plan as contrasted with financing the creation of the
additional resources necessary to provide services under the
plan? If redistributing services and restructuring the system
have some priority, clearly a substantial effort should be made
to increase the output from health professional schools, to create
new institutions, and to affect the distribution of health manpower. Many of our health professional schools are in bad
financial shape, and this, combined with evident current health
professional manpower shortages, indicates that increased
federal funding is required now to increase the supply of health
resources in anticipation of a national financing plan.

AN ILLUSTRATIVE CASE--THE KENNEDY PLAN

While grids comparing in descriptive terms the various
features of different national health proposals are plentiful,
there is not a single published analysis of how any one proposal
will help solve the multiple problems of our health delivery
system. In Table 1, we have very crudely (and quickly) analyzed
the various features of the Kennedy plan to ascertain the direction
of effect of these features upon the problems of our present
health care system. To facilitate this analysis, the problems
have been recast as objectives to be accomplished by the Kennedy
plan. Moreover, the objective of political feasibility has been
added, for if a program is not politically feasible, the other
objectives will never be realized. The total cost of a plan and
the degree to which it interferes with existing systems are considered, in this analysis, to be inversely related to the plan's

Table 1

Effect of Provisions of the Kennedy Plan on National Health Insurance Goals

Provisions of the Kennedy Plan	Redistribute Access to Health Care Services	Promote a More Effective System	Stop Rising Costs and Prices	Insure Against Catastrophe	Political Feasibility
I. Eligibility					
All U.S. residents	+	+	-	+	?
II. Benefits					
Hospital; no limit	+	+	0	+	0
Nursing home; 120 days	+	+	-	+	-
Home health; no limit	+	+	-	+	-
Physician; no limit	+	+	-	+	0
Psychiatrist; if private, 20 sessions	+	+	-	+	-
Psychiatrist inpatient; 45 days	+	+	-	+	-
Optometrist; no limit	+	+	-	0	0
Podiatrist; no limit	+	+	-	0	0
Glasses; no limit	+	+	-	0	0
Lab work; no limit	+	+	-	+	-
Approved drugs for inpatient, group patient; or chronic patient	+	+	0	+	0
Ambulance; no limit	+	0	0	0	0
Dentist; under 15 years old, then all	+	+	-	+	0
III. Administration					
Structure					
Health security board under HEW	0	?	0	0	+
10 regions	0	?	0	0	+

100 subregions	o	o	o	?	o
Local	o	o	o	?	o
Powers and Duties					
Establish policy, regulations, standards, evaluate performance, gather data	o	o	+	+	−
Assess regional needs	+	o	+	+	?
Approve institution budgets	+	o	+	+	−
Approve providers	+	o	o	+	−
Payment authority (may use private insurance co.)	o	o	o	+	?
Monitor standards	o	o	+	+	−
Technical assistance	o	o	+	+	o
Coordinate expenditure levels	o	o	+	+	−
Citizen ombudsman	+	o	+	?	?
Health priorities	+	o	o	+	−
IV. Policies					
Organization of Services					
Resource development fund to assure availability of benefits by loans and grants	+	o	+	+	?
Preferential payment to groups	o	o	?	+	−
Training programs for new and old fields, minorities	+	o	+	+	?
More benefits to subscribers	o	o	−	+	−
Rules on use of specialist and private physician	o	o	+	+	o
Payment					
Budgeted by region	+	o	+	+	?

249

Table 1 (Continued)

Budgeted by health category	+	+	+	0	–
Budgeted for following year	0	+	+	0	–
Distributed on per capita basis	+	0	+	0	0
Paid to groups first	0	+	+	0	–
Negotiated rates for fee-for-service physicians	0	–	+	0	+
V. Financing					
Health security trust fund	0	0	0	0	+
1% tax on earned and unearned income up to $15,000 (employee share)	–	0	+	0	?
2.5% tax on self-employed income up to $15,000	–	0	+	0	?
3.5% tax on wages (employer share)	0	0	+	0	?
50% of costs financed from federal general tax revenues	+	0	–	0	?

Note: The entries on the table indicate whether the option described will have a positive, neutral, negative, or uncertain effect on achieving the goal. Often the combined effect of two features will differ from their individual effects. For example, broad benefit coverage will have a negative effect on controlling price increases because it will increase demand without increasing resources. A provision to increase resources, however, will lessen the negative effect on this goal. In all cases, the effect of the features listed are their individual effects without regard to other provisions of the bill.

political feasibility. This latter "interference" criterion
generally assumes that provider preferences will have more
weight than consumer preferences with political decision-makers.
Thus, for example, we indicate that preferential payment to
groups under the Kennedy plan will not be viewed favorably by
the Congress.

The direction of the effect of any major provision of the
Kennedy plan upon each objective is entered in Table 1 as positive (+), negative (-), uncertain (?), or neutral (0). While our
estimates of the effect of the various features of the Kennedy
plan are admittedly rough, we believe it is important for a start
to note that a given provision of this plan, or any other plan,
will not necessarily affect all objectives in the same way.

Without going into great detail, we will discuss the general
principles used to determine the direction of the effect of each
provision. A positive effect on the redistribution of health care
is due to the altering of incomes or preferences of physicians
and hospitals; to the assessing of regional needs and other methods
of monitoring services; and to the provision of minority group
training programs, which have a redistributive effect because
they reach those who will presumably be highly motivated to
treat low-income groups and because they provide income to
low-income individuals. Inclusion of certain benefits such as
psychiatric and dental services will also have a strong redistributive effect since low-income groups do not generally have
access to these services.

The efficiency goal is advanced by including benefits which
allow for a more rational utilization of resources, such as inclusion of home care; however, limitations on certain benefits may
lessen efficiency by encouraging the substitution of less appropriate alternative services. For example, a limitation on the
number of nursing home days allowed may induce longer hospital stays than necessary. Any measures which intervene with
the independent behavior of provider units by introducing an
allocative overview are likely to eliminate inefficiencies. For
example, many more hospitals do open heart surgery in this
country than is justified on medical and efficiency grounds.
Finally, incentives to consumers and providers to improve
utilization will have a positive effect on efficiency.

It is interesting to note that the comprehensive benefit
coverage of the Kennedy plan may have a paradoxical effect on
efficiency. Because it does not discriminate against the use of
any type of service in its reimbursement, the range of benefits
will permit a more rational and efficient utilization of all health
services. However, at the same time, it will increase the
consumption of all health services relative to other goods and
services because insurance reduces out-of-pocket costs. The
result is efficiency internal to the health care system, but perhaps external inefficiency dependent upon society's desire to

increase the supply of other services, such as education and recreation, which cannot be provided because the necessary resources are devoted to health.

Some of the provisions which advance the efficiency goal also advance the anti-inflation goal because improved utilization will reduce upward pressure on prices. However, the effect of including some benefits is inflationary because of resource constraints. Regressive methods of taxation from employee income tend to limit health inflation since these tax revenues will increase less rapidly than incomes generally. The plan's provision for prospective budgeting also has an anti-inflation effect because it can put a harness on the freedom of health institutions to escalate costs. In the long run, however, the effect of any of these detailed provisions upon the anti-inflation goal is likely to be small relative to the effectiveness of the President and the Congress in resisting "unwarranted" demands by providers for substantial annual increases in their compensation.

To insure against catastrophe, the more complete the benefits, the more complete the insurance. The cost to the consumer of certain services, however, should never reach catastrophic magnitude. Podiatry service is an example of this. Coinsurance lessens the protection against catastrophe but could be scaled down with increasing expenditures to leave no coinsurance and no substantial financial burden. As can be seen in Table 1, other provisions of the Kennedy plan do not affect the objective of providing catastrophic insurance.

The inclusion of a benefit is viewed as less politically feasible if it is likely to be interpreted by legislators as a costly addition of a luxury nature. Incentives to providers and consumers to change the existing structure of health care delivery are regarded as politically unpopular because there are vested interest groups to protect the existing structure. In addition, most of these incentives take the form of increased regulation, which is certain to be politically unpopular among providers. There are more question marks for this goal than for others because where some people will benefit at the expense of others, it is difficult to readily determine the net political effect.

In general, the Kennedy plan points out the inverse relationship between political feasibility and all other goals. This is particularly true for promoting a more effective system and political feasibility because there are perceived vested provider interests in maintaining an ineffective system. The goals of increasing the effectiveness of the health care system and controlling the rising costs of health care are seen to be generally complementary in the long run. This is so because as an effective system improves utilization, it will reduce the excess demand on certain services which puts pressure on costs and prices. Further, the goal of redistributing access to health care services can be adverse to the anti-inflation goal since increased expen-

ditures by the poor for a relatively fixed supply of services in
the short run will be inflationary. On balance, the Kennedy bill
advances most goals, but in its present form it is possibly too
costly and too destructive of the present system to be politically
feasible.

WHAT NEXT?

At this point, it is obvious that an evaluation of the effect
of national health insurance plans is exceedingly complex. It is
difficult to appraise even the direction of the effect of some of
the features of the Kennedy plan upon the various goals associated
with a national health insurance plan. And it is clearly a major
task to determine the combined effect of many specific provisions upon a particular goal. While it is likely that billions of
additional public dollars will be allocated for some program in
the near future, almost no serious attention is now being given
to the behavioral issues associated with various plans.[4] The
burden is clearly upon the federal government to promote a
major analytical effort to evaluate proposed and alternative plans,
using the rich body of existing information about our health care
system and additional data from systematic experimentation.
Unless a research program far more extensive than the fragmentary efforts now underway takes place, national health insurance
could be as disappointing as Medicare and Medicaid with respect
to achieving desired social objectives.

FOOTNOTES

1. Differences in environmental factors and life styles may be
more important than the maldistribution of consumption of health
services in determining differences in life expectancy among
industrialized nations.
2. See, for example, A. Donabedian, "An Evaluation of Prepaid
Group Practice," Inquiry 6 (September 1969).
3. See, for example, M. I. Roemer, Medical Care Under Social
Security (Geneva: International Labour Organization, 1969).
4. A good example of this disregard for behavioral responses
is an HEW study estimating the costs of various national health
insurance proposals. Apart from its unspecified calculations,
the report's rigid nonbehavioral forecasting assumptions were
biased in favor of the Nixon plan and against the Kennedy plan.
It ignored the potential impact of the Kennedy plan's administrative cost control features upon future health care prices. See
A Study of National Health Insurance Proposals Introduced in the
92d Congress, A Supplementary Report to the Congress (Washington: Department of Health, Education, and Welfare, July 1971).

V-2 A PROPOSAL FOR A NEW CITY-HHC FINANCIAL RELATIONSHIP (CHIP) — August 9, 1972

by Jeffrey H. Weiss

INTRODUCTION

This memorandum discusses the need for a new city-HHC
financial relationship and describes one program of reorganiza-
tion (to be called the City Health Insurance Plan; referred to as
CHIP hereafter). Since the essential point of the paper--that a
philosophy of management and financing based upon hospital-
directed incentives must be adopted--will have its advocates and
adversaries independent of voluminous documentation, only a
broad outline of a possible course of action is presented here.
If CHIP is accepted by the relevant parties, a detailed implementation plan can be worked out. The proposal can perhaps
best be conceptualized as creating ties between the HHC and
the city analogous to those being developed between the various
agencies and the city by the budget-reform experiment. [1]

Much of the work underlying this memorandum was performed by Lynda Brodsky, Harry Rosen, Suzanne Schwimmer,
and Chuck Atkins of our program analysis staff. Comments and
information were solicited from relevant HSA, HHC, and DSS
staff. Valuable suggestions also came from Evan Davis and
Joe Feite of the General Counsel's Office in the Bureau of the
Budget.

THE FUNDAMENTAL ISSUE

A prime cause for the often poor quality of care offered by
municipal hospitals to their patients is thought to be the availability to the HHC of a captive, impotent population--the non-
Medicaid poor who must use public hospitals if they wish to
receive free care. The only efficient solution would appear to
lie in a federal-, state-, or city-financed health insurance plan

254

which would provide the poor with the means to select alternative facilities.

In the absence of federal and state action, HSA's program
analysis staff devoted considerable effort to analyzing the technical and political feasibility of a city-financed health insurance
plan for all its citizens. After considerable discussion and
analysis, this unrestricted policy was found to be untenable.
The recommendation which follows is thus aimed at patching up
the current system's inadequacies rather than drastically changing it: it in effect institutionalizes and regulates the until now
de facto principle that all who use municipal facilities are
insured. There is, however, a secondary benefit. Looking
toward a future which undoubtedly will contain some form of
national health insurance, steps not unlike the ones outlined in
this proposal are inevitable. CHIP would thus serve to prepare
the city system for this eventuality.

THE PRESENT SYSTEM

The present mechanism of financing the HHC consists
essentially of giving the corporation a lump-sum tax-levy payment to cover the difference between its budget and the anticipated payments from cash collections and third-party payers
(Blue Cross, Medicaid, and Medicare). This amount, though
renegotiated annually, is poorly correlated with need or the
effectiveness of the HHC's operation, for several reasons. First,
no firm procedures or guidelines have been established, with the
result that the determination is largely influenced by the political
climate and the funds available for "controllable" programs city-
wide. Second, substantive aspects of the individual hospital
budgets are obscured because the city and the HHC focus essentially on the determination of a single budget number. It has
consequently been difficult to induce the individual hospitals to
support HHC's efforts to develop adequate cost and collections
data, and there has been very little incentive, if any, for the
individual hospitals to maximize third-party payments or cash
collections and to use the resources at their disposal effectively.

The implication for efficient management and planning is
obvious--midyear financial crises have repeatedly strained city-
HHC ties.[2] Unable to assign accountability, both parties have
suffered: the city has been forced to disburse additional funds to
cover unexpected shortages; the HHC has been compelled to
make drastic across-the-board reductions in service and personnel.

One further problem with the current city system of financing the Health and Hospitals Corporation is that it does nothing
to promote the development of effective subsidiary HHC institutions, which was one of the primary reasons for establishing the

HHC. Local boards will have little real power until they have some degree of control over individual hospital budgets which are based upon the revenues collected by each hospital.

THE CHIP SYSTEM PROPOSAL

The essential features of CHIP are as follows:

1. City payments for service would be determined on a per diem or per visit basis (in much the same way as Blue Cross payments are now determined). Once the rates had been set, the HHC budget would be approved by the Board of Estimate in much the same manner as the Charitable Institutions Budget is now approved. Linking payment to service would be one step toward removing the hospital system from the political process. It might, moreover, encourage the review of existing purchase-of-service agreements and facilitate ground-breaking efforts in other areas (e.g., the copayment schedules for OPD services might be reexamined and thought given to the issue of copayment for inpatient services).

2. These per diem or per visit rates would be established prospectively and written into a contract between the city and the HHC. The contract would (1) spell out what costs would and not be covered; (2) establish the rules concerning any future increases in rates (these rules would conform with the state cost-control law and any federal wage-price guidelines then in effect); and (3) define the steps to be taken by the HHC and the city if the agreed-upon rates were exceeded (these steps would include required cutbacks in services at specific hospitals when costs exceeded certain upper boundaries, or the replacement of management personnel). The city would be legally bound to pay the specific rates, while the individual hospitals and the HHC would be bound to perform the services within the prescribed cost limits. Surpluses would presumably be retained by the individual hospitals--a strong, positive, incentive to both increase collections and control expenditures.

3. The city would only assume payment for patients after all other sources of funds had been proven unavailable. This would provide a substantial negative incentive to individual hospitals and the HHC to pursue other sources of funds.

4. As an incentive for managerial efficiency and for increased community input, the CHIP plan would strive for a decentralization of accountability: each individual hospital administration would be held responsible for the operation of its hospital, including collections. In contrast to the present system of financing where financial difficulties are discussed only in terms of the gross budget of the entire corporation, such decentralization disaggregates any fiscal crisis to the point where program trade-offs can realistically and substantively be made.

The successful implementation of these essential features which comprise the CHIP plan is dependent upon certain technical capabilities which are being developed or can be developed over the next several years. The foundation of the entire system is a capability for budgeting and cost accounting in each of the corporation hospitals, because each aspect of a hospital's operations will have to be costed out before any submission is made for a rate. The HHC has made substantial progress in this area over the past two years, and it would seem that another two years should allow enough time for the rudiments of an effective budgeting and cost accounting system to be in place in each municipal hospital. In addition, the city requires the development of an effective utilization review system to guard against patient overutilization of corporation hospitals. The development of a utilization review system for Medicaid is now underway, and it is anticipated that this system could be used for CHIP as well when it is completed in about one year. The last crucial technical element is the conversion of Medicaid payments from a single corporation-wide rate to separate rates for each hospital. These Medicaid rates could be the same or different from CHIP rates. Without this modification, a major part of hospital revenues would still come from a centralized budget process not linked directly to performance or to delivery of care. Ideally, a separate Medicaid rate arrangement could be negotiated with the state during the period in which CHIP was being implemented. However, if an acceptable agreement were not worked out, the corporation could achieve the same result by receiving the Medicaid funds centrally and then disbursing them to the hospitals on a separate per diem or per visit rate basis. It should be noted that both Blue Cross and Medicare now reimburse HHC with distinct rates for each hospital.

It is recognized that some ingredients of the CHIP plan could be implemented by the HHC without the city's participation-- namely, the decentralized budgeting process and the associated technical systems, and the empowerment of the community boards. However, adoption of the CHIP proposal would in effect serve to encourage and facilitate the resolution of those pivotal issues.

THE MEDICAID-CHIP BILLING PROCESS ILLUSTRATED

The Medicaid-CHIP billing process would begin, whether the point of entry to the system was an HHC inpatient admitting office, an emergency room, or an outpatient clinic, with an interview at which information pertinent to a determination of collection status would be obtained. The patient's records could then either be flagged for potential Medicaid, Medicare, or other third-party, or CHIP submission, or else simply sorted according to eligibility or noneligibility for CHIP.

The first processing activity would be an application for Medicaid coverage for those determined eligible by the initial interview. Administrators would, of course, be aware that this activity would result in revenues that would contribute directly to their hospital's programs, and that failure to apply for as many eligible patients as possible would not result in a subsidy through CHIP. Submissions for CHIP payment would be audited and not paid if the patient proved eligible for Medicaid.

At the end of the hospitalization or following the visits, the appropriate billing forms would be filed for those patients covered by Medicaid, Medicare, Blue Cross, Workmen's Compensation, or private insurance. For all patients not covered by the above third parties but within the eligibility limits established for CHIP, Medicaid billing forms would be sent to a central processing unit. The basic intent is to require indentical information for Medicaid and CHIP.

It is presumed that Medicaid bills would continue to be processed in the same manner, with full examination of every bill before payment is authorized. But since CHIP can establish its own standards, independent of the state, only a small statistical sample need be scrutinized for appropriateness of services rendered, accuracy, and completeness. Deficient bills would be returned to the hospitals for clarification or reinvestigation. Ultimately, a determination would be made as to the ratio of deficient to adequate bills in each hospital, and CHIP reimbursements to the hospitals would be diminished by corresponding percentages.

Again, it is assumed that Medicaid's payment method will continue, but a periodic advance system, used by Medicaid for the voluntaries, is proposed for CHIP. The city would pay out in advance a percentage of the expected revenues of each hospital based on projected work loads and the predetermined reimbursement rates. These advances might be made quarterly with a final reconciliation of reimbursement with actual activity occurring after the final quarter of each fiscal year.

The accounts of patients found to be not eligible for CHIP and whose bills proved uncollectable after agreed-upon efforts by the HHC could be turned over to the city for audit and further collection effort, if deemed necessary.

COST OF CHIP

The estimated annual administrative costs for CHIP are as follows: $500,000 for a city-operated fiscal audit; $300,000 for a medical-utilization audit; another $300,000 for the city rate-making agency; and $1.5 million for the CHIP bill processing. If the corporation then spends an estimated $2 million per year in additional personnel for a decentralized cost-control budgeting system, and an additional $2 million for physical renovations and equipment (amortized over a ten-year period), the total cost for administering CHIP would be $4.8 million per year.

But, as mentioned previously, CHIP should give individual hospitals substantial positive incentive to increase collections. While the amount of collections improvement potentially attributable to CHIP is, of course, impossible to predict, it should be noted that an increase in Medicaid collections of just 2 percent would be sufficient to pay the annual costs of CHIP. More important, there is clearly little effort now being devoted to collections from individuals for the required cash portion of Medicaid, Medicare, and private insurance, and for the copayments from city-charge patients on OPD services. The potential increase in cash collections from individuals are estimated for Medicare alone to be about $6 million, or more than the administrative costs of CHIP.

TIMETABLE

It is clear that a modification in the city-HHC financial relationship would have far-reaching effects; refinements would continue to be necessary long after the basic system had been installed. Key milestones can, nevertheless, be identified:

1. establishment of an implementation task force (personnel for the task force might be drawn from HSA, BOB, CHP, HHC, DSS, and local hospital boards);[3]
2. development of more reliable accounting and medical record systems in each hospital;
3. strengthening of relevant city department operations (i.e., HRA's ability to handle an increase in paperwork, and HSA's audit and rate-setting capabilities);
4. setting of detailed ground rules under which CHIP would reimburse HHC hospitals on a per diem or per capita basis;
5. negotiation with Blue Cross on the problem of rates not covering HHC costs for Blue Cross patients and/or estimation of and planning for any special city subsidies.

It is estimated that the rudiments of the CHIP system could be in place and operating by July 1, 1974, since the lead items of HSA inpatient audit, HRA processing, and HHC accounting and budgeting systems are all underway. The HHC might, in fact, be in a position to start the decentralized budgeting component, on a trial basis, during the fiscal year 1973-74. As was emphasized earlier, the CHIP system would continue to develop after its initial implementation date. Declining rates paid for hospital stays that exceed an acceptable limit for a given disease category or separate rates by service within hospitals are possible later refinements. During the experimental period, staff reductions or reductions in service need not necessarily occur if there are cost overruns.

SOME PROS AND CONS OF THE CHIP PROPOSAL

There are imposing hurdles associated with implementing the CHIP plan, but its advantages for the city and its citizens appear to substantially outweigh any possible drawbacks. These drawbacks include the great initial efforts required to establish CHIP and make it work, and the possible controversies created because the CHIP plan would affect various power relationships among the parties serving or being served by the HHC.

The prime advantage of CHIP to the city and its citizens is that it would promote an improved use of resources by the corporation due to better fiscal incentives. This should in turn result in an improvement in the quality of care delivered. Moreover, insofar as CHIP encouraged decentralized control, it would provide some counterforce to the unions and affiliate institutions--both active opponents of change in the present system. Finally, because of the detailed rate-setting mechanism proposed, the city would have somewhat greater policy leverage over specific health care issues affecting the corporation. It is anticipated that ultimately sufficient distance would be established between the city and the HHC to permit the same fiscal ties between these two parties as exists between the HHC and Blue Cross or Medicare.

From the HHC's stance, all of the above--decreased interdependence, improved care, decentralized control--would not be inconsistent with their goals. However, a substantial transfer of power from HHC central and the affiliates to individual hospital managements and local hospital boards would pose a significant challenge to the administrative capabilities of the HHC, as would the need to improve collections and the financial and management information systems.

In summary, it should be stated that this CHIP proposal is not presented as a panacea for all the various problems of the HHC. Better financial incentives are not likely to promote much improvement in the system if capable management does not exist at the HHC central and individual hospital levels to respond correctly, intelligently, and decisively to the proper incentives. But it is unlikely that even the best management could substantially alter the utilization of the resources of the HHC without a revision in the city's financial relationship with the HHC; without, in other words, establishing incentives for individual hospital

management and the corporation as a whole. Lastly, insofar
as CHIP would encourage the rapid development of the administrative and informational capabilities of the HHC and its hospitals, it can perhaps be regarded as the necessary precursor of
any national health insurance plan.

FOOTNOTES

1. Editor's note: An experiment designed to test the results of
delegating some of the city's Budget Bureau's powers to agencies
like HSA.
2. A case in point is the suit now being brought by the HHC
against the city, charging default on payment of the minimum
tax-levy support prescribed by the founding legislation.
3. Editor's note: BOB - Budget Bureau of the City of New York;
CHP - Comprehensive Health Planning Agency; DSS - Department
of Social Services.

V-3 EXCERPTS FROM THE INTERIM REPORT ON N.Y.C. EMPLOYEE HEALTH BENEFITS PROGRAM — September, 1973

by James Hester and Edward Salsberg

INTRODUCTION: EMPLOYEE HEALTH BENEFITS STUDY

Study Rationale

At the end of the summer of 1972, the Health Insurance Plan of Greater New York (HIP) negotiated a premium increase for its New York City employee and retiree subscribers of 15 percent instead of the 30 percent it had originally requested. This cut precipitated a major crisis at HIP, including the freezing of a series of internal reforms begun earlier that year and the resignation of HIP's two senior executives. At about the same time United Medical Service of New York (Blue Shield) negotiated a 10 percent premium rise for its New York City employee and retiree subscribers. But as with HIP, this increase was insufficient for their needs. During the year prior to this increase Blue Shield had incurred expenses on the city contract that were 24 percent, $3.8 million, above their premium income. This was the fourth straight year of losses--totaling about $17 million--and was a major factor in the State Insurance Department review of Blue Shield which led to the forced resignation of their president, and the possible dissolution of Blue Shield.

The 1972 HIP and Blue Shield crises were only the latest in a series of events indicating the need for the city to reconsider both the basic policy foundations and the day-to-day administration of its Employee Health Benefits Program. The HIP crisis was an especially poignant indication. With the city employees accounting for over 50 percent of HIP's 730,000 subscribers, the city policy decisions on its employee health benefits programs play a unique role in governing the evolution of HIP. HIP, the second largest prepaid group practice in the nation, has for the last two decades been one of the major research sites and examples of this modality of care. Their

262

crisis stimulated several independent reviews, including the
HSA analysis described in this report.

The HIP crisis raised the general issue of whether the
city can use the program to stimulate desirable changes in the
health insurance and medical care delivery system in the city.
Since the program covers over one million persons, the agreements reached by the city with insurance carriers can have a
substantial impact on the health care system, on general benefit
patterns and the cost of medical services for all residents of
New York. The purpose of the HSA analysis was first to understand the functioning of the program and its impact within the
city, and then to weigh the benefits and costs of potential options
for improving overall health care through the health insurance
program. The total health insurance premiums paid by the city
are equivalent to approximately one-sixth of the total expense
budget administered by HSA for health services. This resource,
a sum greater than the budgets of either the Department of Health
or the Department of Mental Health, has been completely ignored
as an explicit tool for shaping health care policy in the city.

In essence this study started with the pivotal issue of: How
can the city use the approximately $200 million which it devotes
to employee health benefits each year to improve the health care
available to both city employees and the city's population as a
whole? To date, negotiations with insurers have traditionally
focused on immediate short-term questions of costs and direct
benefits. An effort was made to step back from the recent
breath-taking growth in the employee health program, survey
the scene before the next round of negotiations, and make explicit the longer-term implications of the decisions now being
made.

Currently the Employee Health Benefits program cannot
be effectively used as a health policy tool. The program must
first deal with its own numerous problems. Thus this final
report concerns itself not so much with how the program can be
used to improve health insurance and health care city-wide as
with how the city program itself can operate more efficiently
and effectively. The recommendations, if followed, should
however, not only improve the operation of the city program but
should facilitate reaching the wider goals suggested above.

The problems of, and generated by, the city's Employee
Health Benefits Program are of considerable importance and
complexity. The major concerns include:

1. a phenomenal rate of growth of total cost;
2. the impact of the city's minimum cost attitude;
3. a fragmentation of benefit programs, including the
responsibilities for their development and administration;
4. an inability to monitor the performance of the carriers
other than total costs--or assess the quality of care given
under the program; and
5. the day-to-day administration by the city.

In 1965 New York City paid $16 million toward employee
health insurance. In 1974 the city will pay nearly $150 million
for basic health insurance, and an additional $75 million plus
for union health and welfare funds, of which a majority goes to
employee health benefits. Total costs of the basic program have
been growing at an annual rate of about 16 percent for the last
five years. If these trends continue, the cost to the city will
double within the next five years.

Currently city tax funds account for nearly two-thirds of
the cost of the basic benefits program, with the state and federal
governments paying the remainder. Thus if current trends continue, in five years the taxpayers of the city will be paying an
additional $100 million per year for employee and retiree basic
health insurance benefits.

Forced by the unions to pay 100 percent of the premiums,
the city's reaction to these rising costs has been to resist any
premium increases in the annual contract negotiations with the
insurance carriers. Unfortunately, this short-range perspective
of minimizing this year's cost, in the absence of cohesive policy
built around an understanding of the long-range implications of
policies, has often been counterproductive. Too often quality,
effectiveness, and long-run efficiency and cost control have been
sacrificed for short-run savings.

The impact of the city's minimum short-run cost attitude
on the health insurance carriers has been significant. The two
crises mentioned above were a consequence of this policy. In
general the effect of the city's policy upon the three medical
insurance plans available to city employees has varied by the
type of plan. The three options are a prepaid group practice
(HIP), a major medical plan (now GHI[1] type E, Blue Shield
until 10/72), and a mixed service-indemnity plan which covers
health expenditures by a fixed fee schedule.

The major medical option, which generally pays 80 percent of charges, is most affected by health care inflation. Under
the tight premium policy of the city, Blue Shield lost nearly $20
million over a five-year period. The deficits were generally
covered by reserves and higher premiums for other subscribers.
The State Insurance Department was extremely critical of this
practice and forced major shake-ups at Blue Shield. Another
consequence of the city's policy was a major decrease in Blue
Shield benefits in 1970. When Blue Shield asked for a major
premium increase in 1973, the city chose to change the major
medical carrier to GHI, who offered the city a lower premium.
It is likely that some of the cost problems of the major medical
type plan will continue, given the absence of major programmatic changes.

While the GHI Type C premiums have not risen substantially since 1966, and were decreased in each of the last two
years, this has only been possible due to the use of a constant

fee schedule. This isolates the carrier from inflationary increases, and means that their premium reflects only the level of utilization. The effective level of benefits has steadily eroded, with the GHI subscriber forced to pay an increasing share of his expenses out of his own pocket. In addition, in 1971, there was a major reduction in GHI benefits. While GHI Type C advertises itself as primarily a service plan (no charge to subscribers who use participating physicians), the number of participating physicians is likely to decline as the fee schedule becomes more and more out of date. It now appears that this has happened, especially for physician services for outpatient care. Thus the city's policy is helping transform GHI from a service plan to an inadequate indemnity plan since a realistic fee schedule will require increased premiums.

As a prepaid group practice HIP is supposed to have better controls over costs and utilization, but the dominant portion of this effect should appear in its hospitalization cost, which for all city employees is covered by Blue Cross. On the medical side, its cost increases should be roughly comparable to the other plans, if not higher: it uses the same medical supplies, must pay somewhat competitive salaries for its professional staff, etc. HIP has been heavily penalized by the severe limits placed on its premium income during the last nine years. Because the other two medical plans are indemnity plans with a much greater percentage of noncity contracts, they have been able to meet the increased costs during this period through a combination of mechanisms. Blue Shield dropped benefits and used their reserves. GHI dropped benefits and has made no adjustments in its fee schedule.

With virtually no internal reserves to draw upon and no fees charged to subscribers, HIP has been able to maintain its initial comprehensive benefit package under the city's financial constraints only by letting the average quality of the services available decline. The site visits by the Department of Health evaluation teams,[2] conversations with proponents and critics of HIP and reviews of the State Department of Insurance all lend to this conclusion. A convincing sign of this is HIP's inability to expand its enrollment at a time when other established prepaid group practices in the country are expanding rapidly. In terms of the city program, the number of contracts with HIP for enrollees under sixty-five is unchanged since 1968 despite a 25 percent growth for the total program. The 19 percent premium increase granted in 1973 should help reverse HIP's downward trend.

The city's single-minded focus on the total premium cost of each of the plans has resulted in:

1. $20 million dollars in losses by Blue Shield;
2. inadequate coverage and drastically increased out-of-pocket expenditures for enrollees of GHI; and
3. a decrease in the quality of care available under HIP.

Another effect has been that new benefits are rarely con-
sidered--regardless of their merit. Fear of additional costs
has prevented consideration of correcting inadequacies or
inefficiencies in benefit packages. An incentive contract with a
carrier is not seriously considered due to the belief that the
city should reap all benefits of lower hospitalization and efficient
delivery of services. HMO's (health maintenance organizations)
are not seriously considered due to the fear that the unions will
force the city to pay 100 percent of the much higher premiums.

At the same time that the basic city employee health benefits have been growing in cost so too have the union health and
welfare funds. Most union funds now receive $300 per employee
from the city, and most of these funds go to health care services.[3]
Each of the fifty to seventy union welfare funds decides on their
own how to spend this city contribution. There is no coordination among funds, and little coordination with the basic insurance program. In addition, each employee, through payroll
deduction, can purchase specified supplemental benefits related
to each basic plan. Benefits are fragmented because there are
three relatively uncoordinated purchasers of benefits--the city,
the unions, and the employees.

The seriousness of this fragmented program is compounded
by the decision-making process, the relationship between the
city and the unions, and the inadequate administration of the basic
benefits program. The city maintains its sovereignty over the
basic program and the unions resist intrusions by the city in
regard to their welfare funds. Some unions are uncooperative
to the point of being unwilling to inform the city what benefits
they offer. This environment of mutual distrust precludes
effective planning and meaningful discussions of responsibilities.

Despite the growth of the basic employee health benefits
program the city still seems to be operating under an administrative setup appropriate for a small, simple program. The archaic
procedures for processing the city's and the employees' premium
payments has resulted in an administrative nightmare. For
example, GHI has to maintain 108 separate premium codes to
keep track of all possible combinations of coverage, family size,
and form of payment. Finding out how much the city paid for
health insurance or how many enrollees there are in a plan is
no easy task. The city usually relies on the carriers for this
information. It is foolish to expect that the city will be able to
effectively monitor the carriers, the quality of services, the
efficiency of coverage, and the effectiveness of carrier programs
and administration when the city cannot handle its day-to-day
administration. An annual statistical report on the health
insurance program has been produced for only two of the last
nine years, despite the fact that the report contains only limited
data--such as enrollment by type of contract by carrier, premium
charges, and total costs.

Description of the Program

All city employees who work more than twenty hours per week and most retirees can participate in the city's health insurance program. The employee or retiree selects for himself and his family one of three different plans for the medical part of his coverage: Group Health Incorporated (GHI)--Type C; The Health Insurance Plan of Greater New York (HIP); and a major medical plan, GHI--Type E as of October 1973. These plans cover the expenses of doctors' fees and other medical services, while Associated Hospital Services (Blue Cross) provides coverage for hospital expenses for enrollees of all three medical plans.

The city pays 100 percent of the premiums, including for spouses and children for whichever plan the enrollee choses despite the fact that each medical plan offers different benefits, functions in radically different ways, and have different premium costs.

It is clear that none of the basic benefit packages--that is, the medical plan combined with Blue Cross--can rightly be considered comprehensive. This is not meant to imply that the coverage now available is poor or totally insufficient, but rather that there are some important gaps. For example, none of the basic packages cover expenses for extended care facilities, most home health care services, dental care, drugs and medicine, or outpatient psychiatric care.

The general types of services covered by each medical plan are similar. Thus all plans cover physician services both in the office and in the hospital, surgical care, diagnostic and laboratory services, etc. Each plan has its own gaps: for instance, HIP doesn't cover anesthesia; the major medical plan doesn't cover preventive care; and GHI Type C will cover only in-hospital surgical services or in-hospital medical services during a hospital stay, but not both. Some of the gaps in coverage are relatively unimportant, but others are significant weaknesses.

More important than the differences in the types of services covered is how services are covered. This can affect the adequacy of coverage, the utilization of services, the cost of the service (to the carrier and the subscriber), and the total cost of the program. HIP consists of a series of group practices which provide services directly to enrollees. GHI Type C is a mixed-service-indemnity plan and relies on a set fee schedule. The major medical plan is an indemnity plan which pays a percentage of charges after a general deductible has been paid by the enrollee.

As a prepaid group practice, HIP provides a wide scope of benefits at no cost to the enrollee and comes closest to offering comprehensive care. There is no charge for services if (and only if) HIP provides the care; there is no coverage for nonemergency out-of-plan utilization. Its major weaknesses are in the areas of limitations on free choice of providers and its limited coverage for care outside the metropolitan region. Its advantages include low out-of-pocket costs to consumers who use HIP facilities and personnel, the potential for coordinated, high-quality care, and the potential for consumer input. A distinctive feature of HIP is that as a provider of services, as opposed to being merely an insurer, it has the added responsibility to ensure high-quality care--especially since consumers are economically locked into HIP's providers. Unfortunately, HIP has not vigorously carried out this responsibility.

If a physician agrees to "participate" in the GHI Type C program, then he agrees to accept the GHI fee schedule as full payment. There is no additional charge to the patient, and the physician bills GHI directly and is paid directly. This is a service benefit. If a physician is not "participating," then the enrollee receives an indemnity benefit. That is, GHI will reimburse the subscriber a dollar amount for medical charges he incurs. GHI pays its service and indemnity benefits according to a fixed fee schedule. Thus for indemnity benefits the amount reimbursed by GHI is unrelated to the provider's total charge. The fee schedules have not kept pace with inflation. The effect of this is that:

1. fewer physicians are willing to "participate" and accept the schedule as full payment; and
2. the difference between the usual charges and the fee schedule increases.

Thus, the end result is that consumers are facing, with increasing frequency and size, out-of-pocket expenses, and GHI is becoming largely an indemnity plan. Currently it is estimated that there are only 600 participating family physicians for outpatient care. Basically GHI Type C offers shallow coverage for a large number of services.

The major medical plan, now GHI Type E, offers good in-depth coverage (with a deductible and coinsurance) for major expenses. A major weakness is its lack of coverage for preventive care. In general an indemnity benefit based on a high percentage of charges (in this case 80 percent) is likely to offer good protection to consumers against medical care inflation. In addition, the major medical plan covers certain services not covered by the other medical plans. This includes such charges as hospital days and emergency room care not covered by Blue Cross. On the other hand, the insurer and the payer of the premiums for a major medical plan are likely to incur the rising costs of inflation. This was especially true in the past when Blue Shield was the major medical carrier. It is too early to determine whether the escalation of expenditures will continue under GHI. It is quite clear that they intend to carefully use a contract provision that payments not exceed 80 percent of the usual, customary, and reasonable charge for a service. This is likely to control GHI's costs, but it is uncertain whether inflation will be slowed or whether the additional costs will merely be shifted to the consumer.

Blue Cross covers hospital charges for all city subscribers. Under the basic plan, the first 21 days of hospitalization are fully covered, and for each of the next 180 days, 50 percent of the charges are covered. The major exception to this benefit is for maternity care. Only $80 of hospital charges are covered for routine deliveries.

Administration of the City Programs

One of the reasons why the city health insurance program is able to have a major influence on health insurance carriers is because on the city side, all dealings are handled centrally through the Department of Personnel. This gives the city tremendous market power in its contract negotiations.

The day-to-day administration of city responsibilities, which falls with the Department of Personnel, includes the processing of enrollment forms, premium payments to carriers, assisting enrollees with insurance problems, etc. In general, all city communications with the insurance carriers goes through the department.

Policy-making is the responsibility of the City's Health Insurance Directorate, which is composed of the Director of the Department of Personnel, the comptroller, and the director of the Bureau of the Budget. The administrator of the Health Services Administration was also a member for most of 1973. Most unions have input through the Health Advisory Committee, under the Office of Collective Bargaining. The Health Subcommittee of this latter group conducts direct discussions with the health insurance carriers concerning new contracts, premiums, and common subscriber problems. The key person in the policy-making process is the director of personnel. This is due in part to his administrative responsibilities, in part to his being the main liaison with the carriers, and in part from his membership on the city's Health Insurance Directorate.

The unions, while having only an advisory role officially, actually exert great influence upon the program. The unions are committed to seeing that the city does not decrease benefits or decrease its 100 percent share of the premium payments. Union pressure is a major factor in the city's short-run minimum cost policies. Despite the tremendous growth in cost to the city of the health insurance program, the unions insist that all of the increased cost is the city's responsibility.

The pressure on the city is magnified by the fact that the costs of health insurance are not considered as part of the wage

packages negotiated with the unions through collective bargaining.
Thus the city's increased cost in fiscal year 1974 of approximately
$30 per employee health insurance contract was not considered
by the unions as an increase in their members' salaries or
fringe benefits.

Historical Development

Until 1965 the city offered only one health plan, HIP-Blue
Cross, and paid 50 percent of the premium for city employees
and their families. Beginning in 1965 the city's share of the
premium increased, additional employees and retirees became
eligible, and the city program offered a choice of three plans:
HIP/Blue Cross; GHI/Blue Cross, and a major medical option
(Metropolitan and Blue Shield/Blue Cross). When the city
expanded the program, it committed itself to assuming the full
cost of all three plans. However, the premiums of the two new
plans were "not to exceed 100 percent of the full cost of HIP-
Blue Cross plan."[4] The benefit packages offered in 1965 by
GHI and the major medical option reflected the benefits that the
carriers believed could be covered by the HIP-Blue Cross rate.

Prior to mid-1969 the city interpreted the "100 percent
HIP-Blue Cross" rate to mean that GHI and the major medical
option would each receive the same premium as HIP, and the
Blue Cross rate would be identical for all employees. The
medical carrier rates were all raised effective July 1968--but
again the rates were the same regardless of carrier. Table 1
shows the history of premium changes (for individual contracts).

Beginning in mid-1969 the city reinterpreted "100 percent
of the HIP-Blue Cross" rate. Blue Cross premiums were
experience-rated by carrier, and Blue Cross was allowed to
take out their share of the "100 percent HIP-Blue Cross" rate
and the medical carriers got the remainder. Thus for GHI and
Blue Shield these rates were each determined by subtracting
the hospitals premiums for their enrollees from the combined
HIP-Blue Cross rate.[5] The total combined premium paid per
employee for medical and hospital insurance increased for all
enrollees, and the amount was basically equal for all three combinations of medical and hospital insurance. But Blue Shield
enrollees used significantly more hospitals days than the enrollees
of the other two plans. The result was that for medical coverage
GHI and HIP received an increase of nearly 40 percent in premiums, while Blue Shield on the average received about a 10
percent increase (see Table 1). Most of the city's additional
expenditures for the Blue Shield-Blue Cross enrollee went to
Blue Cross.

There were major consequences of this change in policy.

Table 1

History of Premium Rates - Individual Contracts

		HIP	GHI	Major Medical
1/1/66 to	Medical	$ 54.00	$ 54.00	$ 54.00
6/30/68	Hospital	58.08	58.08	58.08
	Total	$112.08	$112.08	$112.08
'68-'69	Medical	$ 54.00	$ 54.00	$ 54.00
	Hospital	57.24	57.24	57.24
	Total	$111.24	$111.24	$111.24
'69-'70	Medical	$ 74.40	$ 76.16	$ 54.12
	Hospital	58.80	59.04	78.84
	Total	$133.20	$133.20	$132.96
'70-71	Medical	$ 74.40	$ 76.16	$ 54.12
	Hospital	65.04	63.48	90.84
	Total	$139.44	$140.64	$144.96
'71-'72	Medical	$ 74.40	$ 74.16	$ 74.16
	Hospital	64.56	71.40	106.80
	Total	$138.96	$145.56	$180.96
'72-'73	Medical	$ 85.56	$ 68.52	$ 81.60
	Hospital	77.28	90.60	123.24
	Total	$162.84	$159.12	$204.84
'73-'74	Medical	$100.92	$ 63.24	$ 93.84
	Hospital	88.56	88.68	130.08
	Total	$189.48	$151.92	$223.92

In FY '70 GHI used the additional income to make some significant increases in many of its fee schedules and add some benefits, including out-of-hospital psychotherapy. Blue Shield maintained the same benefits but suffered a loss of $5.5 million, or nearly 50 percent above their premium income. The next opportunity Blue Shield had to reduce its losses, FY '71 contract, it dropped two major benefits. Coverage for outpatient psychiatric care and prescription drugs was ended effective July 1970. These two benefits had accounted for about 22 percent of all Blue Shield expenditures for city program enrollees.

There was no increase in the rates received by the medical carriers in FY '71. There was, however, an increase in the experience-rated Blue Cross premiums. The 100 percent HIP-

Blue Cross rate principle was violated slightly since the Blue Shield premium was not reduced to reflect its members' more rapid Blue Cross premium rise. The principle was, however, basically upheld, since Blue Shield decreased its benefits rather than increase its premiums to deal with its losses.

Unfortunately, despite the decreases in benefits in FY '71, Blue Shield lost another $3.6 million. This was a slight improvement and was about 32 percent above their premium income.

By the end of FY '71 it was clear that a serious problem existed. Blue Shield had already reduced benefits but it still could not live with the combined 100 percent HIP-Blue Cross rate if Blue Cross took out their share first. The city faced three options:

1. it could let Blue Shield further reduce benefits;
2. it could continue to apply the formula and let the employees pay the additional premium for Blue Shield; or
3. the city could increase its premium payments to Blue Shield and ignore the 100 percent HIP-Blue Cross formula mandated by the Board of Estimate.

Union pressure was intense. The city took the last option. Effective October 1971 the city dropped the 100 percent HIP-Blue Cross formula and increased Blue Shield premiums nearly 25 percent.

The city's expenditures for health insurance had increased from $62 million in FY '68 to $97 million in FY '71. Despite this increase they were forced to assume 100 percent of medical carrier premiums, regardless of the HIP-Blue Cross formula. The upper limit was removed. The city reduced GHI benefits in an attempt to limit their total cost increases.

In FY '71 while Blue Shield had dropped benefits, GHI was still offering the improved benefits they had added in FY '70. In FY '71 they lost about $300,000 or less than 2 percent of their premium income. The response was to drop some benefits effective September 1970. The benefits that were dropped were of far greater value than GHI losses. Coverage for out-of-hospital psychotherapy, out-of-hospital specialist consultations, private duty nursing and appliances were all dropped from the basic program. The effect of this decrease in benefits was a dividend of unspent premiums to the city of $2.6 million from GHI for FY '72 and a decrease in premiums of 7.6 percent effective June 1972.

The city was obviously very concerned with the rising costs of the program and resistant to any additional premium increases. The unions were frustrated by major decreases in benefits in two of the three plans. In this environment, the Health Advisory Committee was set up under the Office of Collective Bargaining to bring together city and union officials to deal with some of the basic issues. Perhaps because both sides have a great deal at stake, serious discussions to work out basic responsibilities for the program and its costs have yet to commence. The committee discusses a variety of health insurance issues, but the basic questions tend to be avoided.

The result of this environment is twofold:

1. policy decisions continue to be made under severe pressures, usually in crisis situations, in the absence of meaningful planning and analysis; and
2. the unions remain silent while the city squeezes the carriers as long as benefits aren't reduced, and the city pays 100 percent of the premiums.

The 1972 HIP and Blue Shield crisis occurred after the formation of the Health Advisory Committee. The HIP crisis is demonstrative of the program's decision-making. In the six and a half years prior to summer 1972 HIP's premium had increased 38 percent, an annual rate of about 5 percent. The consumer price index for physician services had increased about 52 percent over the same period. Unlike the other carriers, benefits had not been reduced. HIP's city enrollment had not grown despite the growth of the city program. Half of the requested 30 percent rate increase was to institute major internal reforms to improve the quality of care. Increased premiums for improvements were rejected, and the HIP crisis developed. Pressure from the community and some city agencies encouraged an additional 19 percent premium increase for HIP for FY '74. Unfortunately, many of the key people in the movement for internal reforms are no longer with HIP, a result of the initial city rejection.

Despite the increasing inadequacy of the GHI Type C fee schedule, the city received premium reductions of 7.5 percent in both FY '73 and FY '74. In the latter year there was a slight increase in benefits (actually a restoration of some of the less expensive benefits removed in 1971), but major improvements were rejected. As in FY '72, in FY '73, GHI returned to the city a large amount of unspent premiums. In FY '73 it came to $2.9 million.

In 1973 Blue Shield requested a 37 percent rate increase. They had been directed by the State Insurance Department to prevent any additional losses on the city contract. The city rejected the request. As the contract expired on June 30, the city signed a three-month contract with Blue Shield. Before the expiration of this contract, GHI agreed to take over the major medical option at the FY '73 Blue Shield premium level plus $2.9 million (its surplus under Type C). This is approximately a 15 percent increase in premiums.

Despite the forced change in carrier, and despite the growing discrepancy between the premiums for GHI Type C and the major medical plan, at no time was there a meaningful discussion of basic responsibilities for the program and alternatives to the current system.

SUMMARY OF RECOMMENDATIONS

   The eleven draft recommendations presented below are all
variations of two themes which run throughout this report. First,
the single-minded focus on costs in negotiating benefits with the
three carriers has substantially retarded the development of HIP,
and has sacrified the quality of coverage supplied to city employees.
This approach has been very effective economically, with the
city holding the increases in its health insurance premiums below
the rate of inflation of medical prices. However, the concern
with costs needs to be tempered with a recognition of the impact
the city has on the competitive position of the three carriers, on
the evolution of important new alternative forms of delivering
health services, and on the protection being supplied to city
employees and their dependents. This is not to say that the city
can swing to the other extreme and let health considerations
dominate the realities of the costs of paying for them. However,
this report will identify a number of specific options open to the
city to significantly improve the health care available within the
city at little, or in some cases even no, marginal cost.
   The second theme is that the rapid expansion in the size
and complexity of the program has brought it to the point where
it is under only marginal control by either the city or the carriers. There is little opportunity or capability to monitor the
performance of the city's employee health benefit program,
either in its components or as a whole. The information available to the city on the services being provided to its employees
and the prices being paid for those services is completely
inadequate to monitor and exercise control over a program with
cash flows in excess of $100 million per year and covering more
than one million people. The crazy quilt of data available to the
carriers on subscribers and premiums is completely insufficient
for efficient day-to-day administration of the program. Correcting this situation will undoubtedly involve short-term increases
in management manpower and data-processing costs, but those
costs are mandatory if the city is to cope with the continued
expansion of the program to twice its current size within five
years.

   The preliminary recommendations are as follows:
   A. Development of Health Maintenance Organizations (HMO's)
       Development of viable HMO's for New York City as
an alternative to the existing fee-for-service system is one of
the highest priorities in the restructuring of health delivery
within the city.
       1. The city should use the health benefits program to
       actively encourage the development of HMO's. In
       addition to taking the actions detailed below to strengthen
       HIP, it should open the program to other providers, such
       as Connecticut General and Blue Cross, who will be open-

ing HMO's within the New York metropolitan area within the year.

For a direct marginal cost of approximately $2 million in the first year, increasing to approximately $5 million per year by the completion of the program, the city can transform HIP from a loose confederation of medical groups into a city-wide network of HMO's. If the city does not act this year, it will in all probability lose the opportunity to ever act. After twenty-five years of almost functioning as a group practice, after a decade of steadily more stringent financial constraints, after last year's abortive attempt by HIP management to establish control over the groups and obtain the funding they needed to supply medical care, HIP is at a crossroads.

The decisions being made both internally within HIP as it negotiates its new contract with the medical groups, and externally by the city as it develops its positions for the 1974 fiscal year contract, will determine what path HIP takes from here. If the exclusivity agreement with the medical groups is dropped or significantly modified, HIP will lose any prospect of ever achieving control over the medical groups and will be forced to convert into a modified GHI within a few years. If HIP does not receive a rate increase high enough to relieve the fiscal pressures on its better groups, those groups can and will leave the plan.

The importance of this round of negotiations and the stance the city takes on its own contract and on the contract between HIP and the medical groups cannot be overestimated. The recommendations below are presented as a first step in developing the city's position with a full awareness of the consequences of its actions for what could be, with some changes in structure, the second largest HMO in the country.

2. The city should support HIP's voluntary regionalization program,[6] but only subject to the following conditions, which are essential to strengthening the control of HIP over its medical groups and narrowing the current wide spread in quality of those groups:

   o HIP must retain the exclusivity clause in its contracts with the medical groups. The weakening or abolition of this clause now being demanded by some of HIP's groups represents the single greatest threat to the plan's future development.

   o The regionalization program must be modified to include mandatory pooling of outside income by full-time doctors within two years of regionalization of each group.

   o HIP's standards for its medical groups must be revised to make them more explicit, and the techniques for enforcing them strengthened by adding a set of graduated penalties and by reinstituting clinical audits.

HIP must take intelligible comparative evaluation of
the groups more readily available to subscribers,
particularly at time of enrollment. HIP's internal
audits of each group should be made available to the
consumer council for that group.

3. The city should reinstate an ex officio representative
involved in setting city benefit policy on the HIP Board.

4. The city should support the development of an integrated
hospitalization package for all HIP enrollees which would
finance both medical and hospital expenses through a
single prepaid premium. If HIP and the city cannot persuade Blue Cross to make such an option available, the
city should use its employees and the HIP Medicaid population as the base for HIP's own hospitalization insurance.

5. The city should encourage HIP's present efforts to
make its groups hospital-based. However, the emphasis
must be on developing formal ties to or acquiring existing
hospitals, rather than on constructing new facilities. The
city should particularly review the ways in which HIP
could be linked to the Health and Hospitals Corporation.
Possibilities for such links range from outright purchase
of some hospitals to expanding the right of HIP doctors to
admit and attend their patients, as is now done in Sydenham Hospital.

B. Return to parity in the city's treatment of its three
medical insurers.

When the city expanded its health benefits program to
include a choice of carriers in 1965, one of the basic principles
established in the Board of Estimate resolution approving the
expansion was that the city would maintain parity between the
premiums of the plans. The radically different nature of the
structure and management of the plans, together with pressures
from employee unions, resulted in the "temporary" suspension
of parity three years ago. This temporary policy must not
become permanent in resolving the crisis anticipated when Blue
Shield demands the major rate increase (on the order of 30 percent) expected this spring.[6]

6. The city must restructure its fiscal policy toward
the three medical carriers by returning to parity in the
premiums for basic health coverage and eliminating the
gross imbalance between the premium paid for major
medical compared to that paid to GHI and HIP. This will
require (a) freezing the city's contribution to the major
medical plan (Blue Shield) at its current level; (b) absorb-
ing future increases in costs of major medical coverage
through increased deductibles and coinsurance until
parity is achieved; and (c) selectively increasing the
premiums and the city's contribution to GHI and HIP until
all three plans are equalized.

7. The city must also reestablish parity in the benefits
included under the basic coverage and bring those benefits
packages up to minimum standards. As a first step in
achieving this, the following recommendations are made:
> Full coverage for presurgical specialist consulta-
> tions by panels of preselected highly qualified
> specialists should be made available as soon as
> possible.
> Reinstatement by GHI of coverage for out of hospital
> specialist consultations.
> Blue Shield should (a) add coverage for preventive
> care; (b) add some first dollar coverage; and (c)
> drop or decrease the benefits for private duty
> nursing.
> Blue Cross should improve its coverage for emer-
> gency care.

C. Control over total program costs and quality.

The fourfold increase in program size since 1965
has been more than matched by an increase in program complexity. The city must move to control the growth rate of the
program in the future, and to deal with the administrative problems already present. If these controls result in only a 2 percent decline in the recent growth rate of 16 percent per year,
savings in total program costs would be $12 million in three
years and $27 million in five years.

8. The city should develop better control of its total
costs for health benefits. Once parity among the plans
is achieved as outlined in Recommendation #6, the city's
contribution should be tied to a fixed fraction of average
wages, with cost increases beyond that coming from
either payroll deductions or from the $250 per year per
employee which the city contributes to the union health
and welfare funds.

9. The city should immediately incorporate increased
costs of health benefits, including the basic coverage,
explicitly into the wage packages negotiated with the
unions through collective bargaining.

10. The city must take additional measures to ensure
that the cost increases requested by the carriers
actually reflect an increase in needed services. The
city should be much more active in monitoring the performance of the carriers, with a first step being to
incorporate more specific utilization and cost reports
into all new contracts. In addition, the carriers must
be encouraged to incorporate more effective cost and
utilization reviews into their internal operations.

One of the recurrent complaints about the program as it
now operates has been the difficulty in assembling reliable
information on which employees are enrolled in the program,

what premiums have been paid to the carriers, etc. At present this basic data required for the day-to-day operation of the program must be patched together from a variety of sources which do not use standardized definitions and categories. GHI estimated that these problems added 1-1/2 percent or $300,000 to its costs in 1972. If these costs are typical, the administrative complexity unnecessarily introduced by the existing system will cost the city $1.3 million this year, and will cost it $2.2 million per year within five years.[7]

    11. An external management consultant should be retained to review in detail the procedures now used in the day-to-day administration of changes in enrollment, payment to carriers, and monitoring of utilization. This is beyond the scope of either the current HSA study, or the research sponsored by the Health Benefits Policy Committee.

NOTES

1. Group Health Insurance, Inc.
2. Editor's note: As part of this study, site visits of HIP programs by NYC Department of Health personnel were made in 1973.
3. Resolution of Board of Estimate, December 16, 1965 (Col. No. 292).
4. In FY '70 it worked as follows: The single-person HIP-BC rate was $133 with $74 for HIP and $59 for BC. The BS-BC rate was also $133, but since BC now got to take out their share first, which was $79, this left Blue Shield with a premium of only $54.
5. Editor's note: This is a program to provide incentives to individual HIP groups to hire full-time physicians and to offer services in one facility instead of separate physician offices.
6. Editor's note: Blue Shield is referred to because, at the time these preliminary recommendations were written, GHI had not yet replaced Blue Shield as the major medical provider.
7. Editor's note: The detailed cost calculations were deleted from this section.

V-4 PHASED REPLACEMENT OF MUNICIPAL HOSPITAL FACILITIES — February, 1972

by Irving Levenson and Julie Northup

The New York City Municipal Hospitals comprise a system which currently encompasses 15,000 beds in eighteen institutions. The size and makeup of that system have undergone many changes over the years. Providing for replacement of facilities which deteriorate and become obsolete cannot be approached through a special effort once every few decades as might be appropriate for a single hospital. Replacement is instead an ongoing activity requiring continuing efforts to initiate construction of replacement facilities and to develop funding mechanisms equal to the task.

There is no agreed-upon rule of thumb about the length of time a facility should remain in operation until it is replaced. The need for replacement depends on not only age, but also the amount of renovation which has taken place, the seriousness of operational problems, the permanence of construction materials, flexibility of design, and a host of other conditions indicative of present conditions and expected useful life. These factors must be weighed against the alternative of renovation, considering the relative costs, the extent of improvement which can be gained, and the resulting addition to useful life.

In the absence of such extensive information, or in advance of making costly efforts to obtain such information, it is useful to make some crude assumptions and examine their implications. In such a way, it is possible to obtain a broad-brush picture of the system using techniques which would be too inaccurate if applied to a single institution.

If we made the arbitrary assumption that the average facility lasted for 60 years, a system of 15,000 beds would require 250 new replacement beds each year if construction had taken place at a uniform rate in the past. At a cost per bed of $250,000, this would require an annual expenditure of $62.5 million without inflation. We will alternatively assume useful lives of 40, 50,

279

and 60 years. These assumptions would imply annual replacement construction of 375, 300, and 250 beds respectively in the case of uniform past construction. We make no presumption that use of an assumed average life is correct for particular facilities but only for the system as a whole.

It is not possible to assume that the number of beds requiring replacement each year does not change. Figure 1 charts the number of beds now in existence by date of construction. Completions run as high as 2,600 beds in a single year (1955). It is apparent that on the basis of scale of effort required, the major challenge ahead is the replacement of Kings County Hospital, for which 1,148 beds were completed in the single year 1932 while an additional 228 beds are even older.

A detailed listing of the dates at which component groups of beds now in existence were constructed is provided in Table 1. The dates refer to the dates on the plot plans, which generally indicate the year in which construction was completed and the facilities turned over to the Department of Hospitals. Dates at which the facilities were established are noted in Table 2. It is apparent that establishment dates often do not provide a good indication of ages of structures.

A large number of major health facilities projects are already in the pipeline. These efforts, listed in Table 3, range in status from Gouverneur Hospital, which will be completed in a few months, to the Fordham Hospital, on which design will begin in the spring. Included are the four newest ventures, which can be expected to be completed in a six-year cycle through the assistance of the state, and several projects that were initiated quite some time ago.

The fourth table indicates the current age distribution of municipal hospital beds in New York City and the way it will change as a result of a number of major initiatives already underway. At present, 21 percent of the beds are over 40 years old, 12 percent are over 50 years old and 6 percent are over 60 years old. If we allow for the opening of the new Gouverneur, North Central Bronx, the facilities being constructed at Bellevue, and the Metropolitan Psychiatric addition, the renovated beds at Harlem and Sea View (assuming 200 of the 300 new beds at Sea View are for expansion) plus the replacement of Greenpoint by Woodhull, and replacement of Lincoln by the new Lincoln, together with the aging of facilities, in 1978 the age distribution of beds would have changed to the figures indicated as assumption A in Table 4. The proportion of beds over 40 years old would have risen to 26 percent, the proportion over 50 years would have fallen to 6 percent, and the proportion over age 60 would have declined to 2 percent. Assumption B adds to this the replacement of Fordham by the New Fordham. While this would eliminate some very old beds, the main impact would be on the number of beds which had become 46 to 50 years old in 1978.

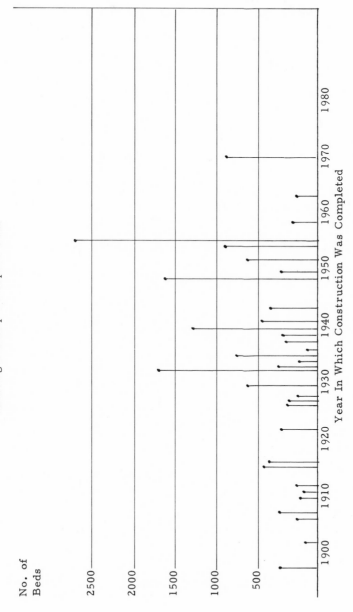

Figure 1

Distribution of Construction Dates
Existing Municipal Hospital Beds

Table 1

Existing Municipal Hospital Beds by Date of Construction
1-1-72

Hospital	No. Beds	Date Constructed
Bellevue	284	1908
	316	1915
	242	1916
	205	1926
	488	1932
	253	1938
	1,788	
Bronx Municipal	359	1954
	759	1955
	1,118	
City at Elmhurst	965	1955
Coney Island	99	1910
	476	1954
	575	
Cumberland	258	1922
	110	1962
	368	
Delafield	250	1949
Fordham	111	1907
	286	1929
	397	
Greenpoint	174	1912
Harlem*	100	1939
	127	1958
	801	1969
	1,028	
Kings County	68	1915
	160	1927
	1,148	1932
	81	1934
	308	1942
	532	1951
	2,297	

Hospital	No. Beds	Date Constructed
Lincoln	289	1896
	61	1902
	350	
Metropolitan	908	1955
Morrisania	308	1929
Queens	720	1935
	459	1940
	1,179	
Sydenham	209	1925
- - - - - - - - - - - - - - - - - - - -		
Coler	1,552	1948
Goldwater	1,112	1939
Sea View	78	1911
	100	1916
	298	1933
	34	1936
	200	1937
	710	

*120 beds constructed in 1934 are being renovated as of 1-1-72.

Source: Data made available to Health Services Administration as of 1-1-72 from Health and Hospitals Corporation, Hospital Statistics Service; Health and Hospitals Corporation, Bureau of Engineering and Maintenance; and selected individual hospital staffs.

Table 2

Dates of Establishment of Existing N.Y.C. Municipal Hospitals

Hospital	Date Established
Bellevue	1736
Bronx Municipal	1954
City at Elmhurst	1832
Coney Island	1910
Cumberland	1922
Delafield	1951
Fordham	1892
Greenpoint	1915
Harlem	1887
Kings County	1831
Lincoln	1839
Metropolitan	1875
Morrisania	1929
Queens	1935
Sydenham	1927
Coler	1952
Goldwater	1939
Sea View	1913

Source: American Hospital Association, Hospitals, Guide Issue, August 1, 1964.

While the North Central Bronx Medical Center was originally intended as a replacement for Morrisania, current policy is not clear on that matter. In assumptions A and B, it was assumed to remain open. In assumption C, in addition to the new Fordham, we assume the closing of Morrisania. This also has its impact in reducing the number of beds which will have become 46 to 50 years old in 1978. In assumption D, we additionally allow for the closing of Sydenham Hospital as it is replaced by the proposed Manhattanville Health Park, which would be a voluntary institution. This reduces the number of beds age 51 to 55. By that time nearly one-fourth of the beds are still over age 40, but the portion over age 50 has fallen to 4 percent.

Assumption E allows for moving forward with the 500-general-care-bed East New York Hospital, which the Health Services Administration has given a high priority as a partial replacement for facilities at Kings County. We assume that the oldest 500 beds at Kings County are replaced. The proportion

Table 3

Planned Municipal Hospital Openings
1972-1978

Hospital	Date Projected	Number of Beds
Gouverneur	1972	210
Bellevue	1972	1,274
Sea View wing	1972	312
Metropolitan Psychiatric wing	1972	250
Harlem (renovated wing)*	1972	120
North Central Bronx	1973	432
Lincoln	1974	899
Woodhull	1974	610
Fordham	1978	590-640

*Not in use in 1971 while being renovated.

Source: Health and Hospitals Corporation, November 1971.

of beds over age 40 then falls to 19 percent, the proportion over age 50 to 2.5 percent, and the proportion over age 60 to 1 percent. At that point, the remaining beds over 50 years old would include 99 beds at Coney Island built in 1910, 78 long-term care beds at Sea View built in 1911, and 258 beds at Cumberland built in 1922.

The proportion of old beds in 1978 under assumption D is shown by borough in Table 5. With the completion of construction now planned, if Morrisania were to close, all of the remaining general care beds over age 40 would be located in Brooklyn.

Next, we assume that the steps through assumption D have already been completed, and we examine the number of beds which will have to be built in order to achieve a particular average life of facilities. From the age distribution of beds, we can derive the number of replacement beds which must be constructed

Table 4

Percentage Distribution of Municipal Hospital Beds by Age,
1972 & 1978

% of Existing Beds:	1-1-72	1978 -- Assumptions				
		A	B	C	D	E
35 years & under	60.7%	61.1%	63.8%	64.9%	65.7%	68.5%
36-40	18.1	12.6	12.4	12.7	12.8	12.8
41-45	4.9	8.2	8.1	8.2	8.3	8.3
46-50	4.4	12.6	10.8	9.3	9.4	7.8
51-55	-	2.1	2.1	2.1	0.9	-
56-60	5.9	1.5	1.4	1.5	1.5	1.5
61-65	3.7	0.4	0.4	0.4	0.4	-
66-70	0.4	1.0	1.0	1.0	1.0	1.0
71-75	-	0.6	-	-	-	-
76-80	1.0	-	-	-	-	-

Assumptions: General - New Lincoln, Woodhull total replacements for Lincoln and Greenpoint; new Gouverneur;
new Bellevue and Sea View partial replacements;
addition of 120 renovated beds at Harlem and 250
new beds at Metropolitan; addition of new North
Central Bronx

A. Keep old Fordham, Morrisania, Sydenham

B. New Fordham as total replacement; keep old
Sydenham and Morrisania

C. New Fordham as total replacement; keep old
Sydenham and close Morrisania

D. New Fordham as total replacement; close
Sydenham and Morrisania

E. New Fordham as total replacement; close
Sydenham and Morrisania; open East New York as
partial replacement for 500 oldest beds in Kings
County

Table 5

Hypothetical Age Distribution of Municipal Hospital
Beds by Borough, 1978
(Assumption D)

Borough	Percent Over 60	Percent Over 50	Percent Over 40
Bronx	-	-	-
Brooklyn	2.6	4.3	15.2
Manhattan	-	-	-
Queens	-	-	-
Staten Island	8.5	8.5	8.5

each year, assuming alternative values of the average useful
life. In doing so, it is not assumed that all beds which opened
on the same day will be closed on the same day. Rather, we
assume that retirement will be spread out over a 15-year period
in the following way: For 100 beds built in year zero with an
average life to 50 years, we assume that half the beds will be
replaced between the ages of 48 and 52 at an even rate of 10
beds per year. The remaining beds are assumed to be replaced
in years 43 to 47 and 53 to 57 at an even rate of 5 beds per year.
As a result, even with a 50-year average life, some replacement
beds must be ready as soon as the 43rd year.

Secondly, we determine the number of beds on which construction must be initiated by shifting the date of construction
forward to reflect the length of the construction period. The
number of replacement beds on which construction must be
newly initiated is calculated on the assumption that construction
takes 6 years. Thus, with a 50-year life, construction of the
average replacement bed must begin in the 44th year and some
construction must be initiated as early as the 37th year.

Before a calculation is made of the extent of replacement
construction which must be initiated, one further assumption is
needed. Some beds exceeding the age at which they should have
been replaced will still be in existence at the present time. We
assume that initiation of replacement for this backlog will be
divided equally among the years 1972 and 1973.

Utilizing these assumptions, the number of replacement
beds on which construction must be initiated in each year from
1972 to 1985 is shown in Table 6 for alternative average lives of
40, 50, and 60 years. The calculations correspond to assumption D of Table 4, in which Fordham is complete but East New

Table 6

Number of Beds on which Construction Must Be Initiated
for Phased Replacement with Alternative Average Lives
of 40, 50 & 60 Years, by Year
1972 through 1985
(Based on assumption D)

Year of	Useful Life		
Initiation	40 Years	50 Years	60 Years
1972*	2,334	599	151
1973*	2,334	598	150
1974	299	244	36
1975	347	270	37
1976	287	342	37
1977	229	400	34
1978	252	401	33
1979	226	336	111
1980	290	336	126
1981	285	388	136
1982	396	377	172
1983	424	377	174
1984	407	299	244
1985	338	347	270

*Assumes backlog will be made up in 1972 and 1973.

York is not yet started. Under the assumption of a 60-year life,
we see that it will be necessary to initiate construction on 300
replacement beds in addition to Fordham over the next two years.
The 50-year assumption yields a total of 1,200 additional replacement beds, while a 40-year life implies 4,700.

Table 7

Hypothetical Number of Municipal Hospital Beds
Over Time If No Replacements Occur
(Assumption D)

Number of beds, Assuming	1/1/71	1/1/79	1/1/86
40-year life	15, 286	11, 670	9, 304
50-year life	15, 286	14, 844	12, 438
60-year life	15, 286	17, 154	15, 951

The difference between the 60-year and the 50-year assumption is large. The 40-year assumption differs from the 50-year assumption primarily in the size of the backlog it implies, with both series indicating the need to initiate further construction of about 300 beds per year.

Table 7 indicates the assumption D estimates of the number of beds remaining in existence if the oldest beds were to be closed rather than replaced.

The financial requirements of a phased replacement policy can be ascertained by applying the cost experience of recent municipal hospital construction to the replacement load. The estimated cost of the four most recent projects is reported in Table 8. In no case is the cost per bed excluding interest below $200, 000. Fordham is the most recent and therefore makes the most up-to-date allowance for cost inflation. The cost in that case is $337, 000 per bed.

In Table 10, we have calculated the cost of a replacement policy based on 40-, 50-, and 60-year lives with construction costs of $300, 000 per bed in 1970 excluding interest and alternative assumptions of construction cost inflation of 5 percent and 10 percent per year thereafter. (The cost-per-bed figures used are given in Table 9.) On these bases, the funds required for the next two years plus the $207 million for Fordham would range from $310 million to $2 billion, and for the remainder of the period through 1985 would range from $763 million to $2.2 billion.

It is apparent that the level of funding required is strongly dependent on the kind of replacement policy we want to have. Yet availability of funds will not permit a wide range of choices. New beds at Bellevue will be replacing beds which are 56 years old, those at Lincoln 78, Greenpoint 62. A 60-year life was acceptable by historical standards since it allowed for deteriora-

Table 8

Construction Costs of New Municipal Hospitals

Hospital	Date Design Initiated	Cost/Bed
New Fordham	1972	$337,000
New Lincoln	1968	266,000
North Central Bronx	1969	222,000
Woodhull	1969	264,000

Note: Based on all beds including long-term care and mental
health.

Source: New York City Health and Hospitals Corporation, 1972-
1973 Capital Budget CB-3 forms; Capital Project Summary,
November 1971.

tion of physical facilities, and it may be appropriate for long-
term care beds today since these are less touched by new
technology, but that is all.

A major problem of obsolescence of facilities exists. [1]
It has been created by a combination of growth in incomes and
insurance coverage, technological advances in medicine, technological advances in construction, and changing medical care
organization. The newest facilities are best able to accommodate the latest technology and amenities by provision of adequate
space, flexibility, and support systems. Most of these changes
have occurred during the last 30 years, yet to achieve initiation
by 1985 of projects leading to a 40-year average life would
require new annual commitments averaging approximately $300
million per year. Under our assumptions, replacement implies
not only replacement of current activities, but the simultaneous
provision of additional space, new equipment, and the like.

The lack of funds to finance replacement on such a scale
makes it possible to do little more than deal with circumstances
in which deterioration and obsolescence occur together. For
such a policy, a look at the implications of "oldest first" replacement is useful. The outlines of a replacement strategy on the
basis of age might be as follows:

1. It is expected that the beds at Sydenham and perhaps
Delafield will be replaced by the proposed Manhattanville

Table 9

Assumed Construction Cost per Bed by Date
of Initiation, Based on 1970 Cost of $300,000,
with 5 & 10 Percent Inflation, 1972 to 1985

Year	5% Inflation Cost per Bed	10% Inflation Cost per Bed
1972	$330,750	$ 363,000
1973	347,286	399,300
1974	364,650	439,230
1975	382,884	483,153
1976	402,027	531,468
1977	422,127	584,613
1978	443,235	643,074
1979	465,396	707,382
1980	488,667	778,122
1981	513,099	855,933
1982	538,755	941,526
1983	565,692	1,035,678
1984	593,976	1,139,247
1985	623,676	1,253,172

Health Park. Some closings of obsolete beds may also
be advisable in view of the size of the planned expansion
of the voluntary sector.
2. It is imperative that the city continue to finance major
renovation projects such as Kings County, preventive
maintenance and renovation and related activities in the
Capital Budget at an annual rate of $40 to $60 million for
the foreseeable future.
3. The New York State Housing Finance Agency allocated
$700 million of its initial $1.2 billion authorization for
Chapter 359 loans to New York City. This allocation

Table 10

Construction Cost by Date of Initiation for Phased
Replacement of Municipal Hospitals with Useful Lives
of 40, 50 & 60 Years, Assuming 5% & 10% Inflation
and 1970 Average Cost of $300,000/Bed, 1972-1985

| | TOTAL COST ($ MILLIONS) | | | | | |
| | 40-Year Life | | 50-Year Life | | 60-Year Life | |
Year	5% Infl.	10% Infl.	5% Infl.	10% Infl.	5% Infl.	10% Infl.
Fordham	207	207	207	207	207	207
1972	773	848	198	218	50	56
1973	810	932	207	239	53	60
1974	110	132	89	107	14	17
1975	134	168	104	131	14	18
1976	116	153	138	182	15	20
1977	96	134	170	234	15	20
1978	111	162	177	258	15	21
1979	105	161	156	237	51	78
1980	141	225	164	261	62	98
1981	146	245	200	332	71	117
1982	213	374	203	356	93	162
1983	240	440	213	390	99	180
1984	242	464	177	341	146	278
1985	212	423	216	435	168	339
TOTAL	$3,656	$5,068	$2,619	$3,928	$1,073	$1,671

Source: Tables 6 & 9.

includes all projects up to but not including Fordham. If
a comparable share of the additional authorization of $600
million were allocated to New York City, this would provide about $350 million which would be available over a
period of about three years. These funds would enable
the city to both construct the replacement facility for
Fordham and build the East New York Hospital to partially replace Kings County only if the total project costs
can be scaled down. Early efforts to obtain commitments
for these efforts from city and state agencies are required.
Additional efforts at the present time, such as the construction of 500 replacement beds at Kings County,
require an immediate increase in HFA authorizations and
an accelerated rate of new bond financing.
4. After three years, funding for new construction would
come from:

   (a) A further increase in HFA authority.
   (b) Financing by the Health and Hospitals Corporation floating its own bonds.

Efforts would primarily involve initiation of replacement
of appropriate portions of the remainder of Kings County,
Queens General, and possibly Coler, Goldwater, and
Morrisania.
5. The principal and interest on bonds floated for hospital construction, whether through the state mechanism or
directly by the Health and Hospital Corporation, are normal costs of providing service and should be financed by
inclusion in hospital reimbursement rates. It is essential
the agreement be reached with the State Health Department
at the time they issue approval for new construction, in
order for appropriate increases in reimbursement rates
of all third-party payers under their control to be assured
when the facilities open for business.

Once a shift to construction using architectural techniques
which permit ready adaptation of existing structures has been
completed, it should become possible to replace facilities after
a 60- or 70-year life once more. This would result in a greatly
reduced rate of new construction and require more extensive
renovation for regular renewal of facilities in the future.

FOOTNOTES

1. New York City Health Services Administration, Office of
Program Analysis, "A New Health Facility Construction Program for New York City," November 1970. Also see the
Metropolitan Hospital Master Plan for an interesting discussion
of the problem.

V-5 EXCERPTS FROM THE 1974-75 CAPITAL BUDGET MESSAGE OF THE HEALTH SERVICES ADMINISTRATION OF THE CITY OF NEW YORK*

A decade ago, the municipal hospitals faced a crisis. Over the years circumstances developed which threatened to adversely affect the quality of medical care. A major component of the strategy which evolved to raise quality was the modernization of physical facilities. Modernization would make it possible not only to eliminate physical barriers to the provision of decent levels of care, but to take advantage of new technology and to attract the kind of talent necessary to achieve those ends. Efforts at modernization have been a huge success, and as a result of these and other measures the quality of care in municipal hospitals is generally comparable to voluntary hospitals.

We cannot become complacent and let another crisis develop in the future. Instead of a crash program of new construction, we must continuously commit resources for a systematic program of phased replacement of antiquated facilities. We can no longer be content with a one-time crash program for renovation, but instead must invest in an adequate level of renovation on a regular basis.

The rise in costs of hospital construction cannot be ignored. A generous commitment of funds to preventive maintenance and renovation can defer the need for costly new construction. Replacement of facilities can be staged so that high technology services can be kept up-to-date while structurally sound components provide less demanding services for their full useful lives. Full replacement can be carried out on a more selective

*Remarks by Gerald Frug, Health Services Administration, Chairman of the Board of the Comprehensive Health Planning Agency and Chairman of the Board of the New York City Health and Hospitals Corporation, at the City Planning Commission Departmental Hearings on the 1974-75 Capital Budget, October 12, 1973.

basis in order to conserve scarce resources. But we cannot deny the expensive solutions without a concurrent commitment to alternatives which demand immediate action.

In seeking funds for a continuing modernization program, our objective has been to provide decent facilities for those patients who currently use the municipal hospitals and are expected to continue to use the facilities for a long period of time. The decline which has taken place in the general care census of municipal hospitals has allowed some antiquated units to be retired, resulting in an even more rapid improvement in the average condition of facilities than was possible through the program of replacement construction alone.

Future changes in census will depend on a number of factors. These include the growth of demands for services such as alcoholism, rehabilitation and prison health; the ability to use alternative sources of care such as clinics, nursing homes, health-related facilities, and home care for patients now being unnecessarily hospitalized; opportunities to organize hospital services to improve utilization of existing facilities; and the ability to attract the staff necessary for high occupancy and patient turnover.

In spite of a normal range of uncertainty regarding fluctuations in census, at any given time we can identify a list of projects which will continue to have strong merit and whose financial implications far exceed our current capabilities to provide funds. I do not see a time in the near future where such opportunities will be exhausted so that we can safely say the job is done. Even after current replacement construction is completed, there will be many facilities which are still or will become obsolete unless substantial action is taken. The list of facilities which will be more than 50 years old in 1985 includes 807 beds at Kings County, 720 at Queens, and 1,100 beds in five other institutions. While some of these may be closed because they have been chronically unused or because other facilities are available, a substantial need to rebuild remains. . . .

The current wave of new construction reflects a series of commitments that were made many years ago. The North Central Bronx Hospital first appeared in the 1963-64 Capital Budget. Fordham, Lincoln, and Woodhull all entered the budget initially for 1965-66. The gestation period for planning, design, and construction has been quite long even with the use of turnkey methods. In recognition of the lead time necessary for systematic replacement in the future, the 1974-75 Capital Budget requests design funds to advance the three-stage construction of a new 650-bed tower at Kings County committed last year.

Three years ago, the Health Services Administration began to seek the construction of an East New York hospital as a further step in the modernization of facilities to serve patients using Kings County. The proposal was also intended to reduce Kings County to a more manageable size and to bring services closer to the people while keeping within guidelines which do not permit the expansion in the number of beds. Since that time there have been changes in state reimbursement formulas effective January 1, 1974, which mean that many currently empty beds cannot be replaced. There has also been a reduction in the census at Kings County Hospital. When these factors are taken together with the committed reductions in bed census at Kings County when Wood-hull opens, it is no longer possible to separate all of the beds proposed for an East New York Hospital at Kings County and retain Kings County at a viable size. Smaller replacement efforts could be more economically handled by the construction of further bed towers at Kings County rather than construction of a separate hospital.

At the same time there has been a reduction in the availability of inpatient resources in voluntary hospitals in the Brownsville-East New York area and other voluntary hospital expansions have been little used to serve that community. Existing voluntary hospitals are in great need of replacement and face serious financial difficulties. A combined effort to replace municipal and voluntary hospitals is one approach which could keep services in the community without an increase in bed count and provide the basis of a replacement construction program....

Another set of difficult planning questions includes the areas of Manhattan served by Knickerbocker, a voluntary, and the municipal hospitals Delafield and Sydenham. All three facilities are small and poorly utilized and require major renovations or replacement. Yet services could be provided more efficiently in a single new 500-bed hospital. Knickerbocker hospital has proposed a 500-bed Manhattanville Health Park and the Delafield community has proposed addition of a 240-bed wing. Both must come to grips with the need to offset additional beds with a reduction somewhere else and difficult issues of financing and staffing....

The need for mental health beds is currently being reexamined. Substantial new construction has taken place at Bellevue and Metropolitan Hospitals and planning and construction of additional short-term mental health beds has been an integral part of the replacement of new facilities. The number of outpatient psychiatric visits to municipal hospitals has been greatly expanded, and the occupancy rates at inpatient facilities have declined. At the same time there have been substantial reductions in the availability of operating funds and in the ease of approval of new inpatient programs. There continue to be serious maldistributions in the availability of mental health services, manifested not only geographically, but in the availability of services to children and other population groups, and in the allocation of existing facilities and resources among programs, and modes of treatment. Historical plans will be modified as specific methods of dealing with these problems are developed.

V-6 TRANSITION ISSUES IN HEALTH SERVICES —
January, 1974

by James Hester and Irving Leveson

INTRODUCTION: WHAT IS A TRANSITION ISSUE?

The transition issues presented here are the consensus of
the HSA planning staff on the major issues facing the new administration. The reason for including any particular one of them
varies. The one common criterion is that all of the issues
represent continuing problems which are unlikely to be resolved
by any single action or decision. Beyond that, some represent
best guesses on major problems whose timing will be forced by
external pressures--from the state, from the many new community boards, or from problems which simply will not stay
submerged any longer. Others are key opportunities for the
administration to take initiative on its own.

The eight issues below could each have easily been the
subject of a separate major paper, and some of them have been.
Only the barest description has been presented here in order to
keep this document to a manageable length. Back-up documentation in the form of special papers, completed staff reports, or
internal memos and letters is available on each issue.

THE TRANSITION ISSUES

The eight transition issues are divided into two groups:
those focused primarily within a single department and those
involving multiple agency problems. The issues have also been
roughly grouped by function to indicate their similarities. The
first four issues deal with the monitoring and control of services
secured by the city involving annual expenditures of more than
1-1/4 billion dollars by contracts either from the Health and
Hospital Corporation (HHC) or from outside providers. The
next two issues center about changes in the health delivery sys-

tem itself: the bed supply in the municipal system, the city-run
ambulatory services, and health maintenance organizations.
The seventh issue looks at changes in the regulatory function of
the Health Department. The last focuses on issues regarding
the organization and functions of health planning and the role of
the comprehensive health planning agency. [1]

Single Agency Issues
1. Structure and Financing of the Health and Hospitals
Corporation.
2. Staffing the Municipal Hospitals and Related Issues.
3. Management of Performance and Treatment in
Addiction Services Agency Contracts.
4. Response to Unified Services Act: Planning and
Contract Monitoring in the Department of Mental Health
and Mental Retardation Services.
5. Expansion, Contraction and Renewal of Municipal
Hospital Facilities.
Multiple Agency Issues
6. Ambulatory Care: Alternatives to Hospital Services.
7. Monitoring in the Medicaid Program: Quality of
Care Standards and Inpatient Utilization Review.
8. Issues in the Development of Comprehensive Health
Planning and Review Functions.

1. STRUCTURE AND FINANCING OF THE HEALTH AND HOSPITALS CORPORATION

The New York City Health and Hospitals Corporation was
established by state legislation at the request of the city effective
July 1, 1970. The main purpose was to free the municipal hospitals from the bureaucracy and constraints of the city's systems
of purchasing, personnel, etc. There was strong pressure for
greater authority and flexibility to be given to hospital administrators and communities.

In spite of three and a half years of operating experience,
the Health and Hospitals Corporation has serious management
problems. The problems are large and pervasive, affecting
such matters as the ability to collect bills, the effectiveness of
internal budgeting and purchasing systems, the ability to assure
performance from affiliates, the implementation of new programs
and services in new facilities, the ability to deal with inefficient
utilization patterns, and the provision of effective organizational
mechanisms for reaching and carrying out decisions. Some
aspects of these are elaborated in the discussions of other issues.

The legislation creating the corporation committed the city
to provide an annual operating subsidy (which totaled $364 million
in 1972-73) to cover the costs of services not reimbursed by
either third-party payers or patients and the city's share of

Medicaid. In order to minimize its financial commitments, the city has exerted great pressure on the corporation to increase its collections from patients and insurers. This area has received the greatest attention from HHC management and yet success has been very limited. Issues as to the size of the legally required financial commitment and the way that commitment is changed as health insurance coverage of the population expands will require resolution.

The city's current method of paying HHC involves a lump-sum transfer of funds. There is no specification of the numbers and kinds of services provided, and no explicit overall policy as to eligibility of patients for subsidies for inpatient care. The patients and services subsidized are determined by the vagaries of a haphazard collection process.

Payments to the Health and Hospitals Corporation are provided without performance incentives. Incentive contracting approaches are becoming a feasible method of providing financial pressures to induce hospitals to increase the intensity of use of physical plant and to reduce unnecessary hospitalization by raising occupancy rates and reducing length of stay. The method could readily be extended to provide incentives to restructure outpatient departments, shift resources toward primary care, or increase productivity by in effect providing financial bonuses for discretionary uses to responsive institutions.

Effective January 1, 1974, the New York State Department of Health is instituting a strong penalty for low occupancy rates in the Medicaid reimbursement regulations. At the same time the revised federal regulations for the Economic Stabilization Program contain powerful incentives for hospitals wishing to expand to reduce length of stay. A carefully designed payment formula for municipal hospitals could eventually reinforce such provisions. As an interim step, however, it is critical that the payment conditions be modified so that city subsidies do not become a method of escape from externally imposed incentives and a force which make it easier for inefficiencies to remain.

The municipal hospital system is by far the largest non-federal network of general hospital services under one management. Reimbursement is based on a single system-wide rate for a given type of care. This creates particular opportunities to change the allocation of resources among hospitals within the system and to provide incentives for individual hospitals. At present, hospital budgets are determined largely based on past experience with little relation to level of service provided and the desired intensity of service.

The central office of the Health and Hospitals Corporation has taken over many of the functions previously handled by city agencies in the areas such as personnel and purchasing. There are a number of substantial issues concerning the relationship of the central office to the individual hospitals. A key question is the degree of autonomy to be given to local hospital executive directors, the organizational relationships for combining central and local considerations, and the methods of bringing together the diverse interests wishing to be represented in discussions over major decisions.

Beyond these issues is a set of questions dealing with the role of the municipal hospitals in relation to the voluntaries. Shifts of demand toward the voluntary sector occurred since the advent of Medicare and Medicaid. The municipal hospitals continue to function as a provider of last resort, with a disproportionate number of emergency and charity cases. There are a variety of possible courses of action, including improving the municipal system, shifting some efforts to voluntaries, and developing integrated forms between the two sectors.

2. STAFFING THE MUNICIPAL HOSPITALS AND RELATED ISSUES

In the 1950's there was an increasing deficiency in the number and quality of physicians in municipal hospitals. The shortage was created by a number of factors, including low physician salaries, the unattractiveness of the administrative systems, and the absence of sufficient opportunities for interaction with teaching and research. The city's response was to rely upon affiliation contracts under which voluntary hospitals and medical schools would provide professional services. The affiliation contracts were initially intended for the selective purchase of managerial services and were shown to be successful on that basis. The decision to rely upon this mechanism for the extensive purchase of professional services led to expansion of the program to today's $160 million payments.

This expansion of the scope and size of the affiliation program led to a number of problems. While some arrangements may be working out well, others seem to be costly and ineffective. The principal difficulty is that in their present form the affiliation agreements are virtually impossible to monitor in any effective way. The number and kinds of doctors provided by voluntary hospitals under the contracts vary greatly and show little relationship to the funds received. The contracts do not require systematic reporting of either services or man-hours provided, and contain no real performance standards.

Over the years the contracts have been expanded to include nonphysician personnel, since they could be recruited more easily than under the city's salary restrictions. The use of affiliation contracts led to the "rollback issue" in which District Council 37 of the State, County and Municipal Employees Union insisted that nonphysician jobs paid for under the affiliation contracts and under the jurisdiction of Local 1199 of the

Drug and Hospital Employees Union be transferred to city hospital payrolls.

The affiliation contracts are under review (as they have been almost continuously in recent years) by a special HHC Affiliation Review Committee. The recommendations of this group must include some means of specifying what services will be delivered under each affiliation contract and the provisions for monitoring and enforcing that performance. The city has a further responsibility to review other options for improving the quality of the professional services in the municipal hospitals. The city could initiate selective attempts (perhaps at Coney Island and Kings County) to increase its recruitment of physicians through two measures. First, the salary policy could be modified, as has already been done successfully in the case of nurses. At one time the city followed a deliberate policy of keeping nurse salaries 10 percent below the levels of voluntary hospitals. In 1969 the Hospital Department initiated a policy of wage parity and alleviated its shortage of registered nurses.

The incentives for physician recruitment are more complex than salary level alone. If suitable arrangements for patient care services could be worked out, the municipal hospitals probably have enough resources to negotiate many tie-ins for teaching and research needed to enhance their attraction to physicians.

The admission of private patients has also been proposed as a technique for improving the level of care in municipal hospitals. However, this approach raises three questions serious enough to limit it to a trial basis only. Would city resources continue to be used to the same extent for the needs of the medically indigent? How would preferential treatment for private paying patients be avoided? Would the morale of the salaried doctors be impaired by having to work alongside others receiving substantially higher salaries?

5. EXPANSION, CONTRACTION AND RENEWAL OF MUNICIPAL HOSPITAL FACILITIES

Pressures to build new hospital beds have been an important cause of high medical care costs. The total cost of construction, equipment, interim financing, and administration until a new municipal hospital opens is about $400,000 per bed. With mortgage interest added, the cost of construction accounts for more than $100 per day in the cost of hospital care in a newly constructed municipal facility.

There are substantial numbers of patients in hospital beds who would be more properly served in doctors' offices and clinics, on home care, in nursing homes, health-related facilities, old age homes and housing for the elderly. Many could be hospitalized less frequently or for shorter duration. Expansion of alternative sources of care will not by itself reduce the use of inpatient services since freed-up beds will be used for other patients as long as they are staffed and the services financed. A shift in emphasis from inpatient to noninstitutional care requires controlling bed supply at the same time as the financing and availability of alternative treatment modes is expanded.

With the opening of three major facilities imminent, and the patient census of municipal hospitals on the decline, one issue now is where will the city cut back on its acute care bed supply? At the same time eleven different hospital expansion and replacement programs of substantial size are being proposed by community planning boards, elected officials and others.

Capital improvements will continue to be important because a regular program of physical renewal is a major component of a strategy to maintain and improve the quality of care. However, cost restrictions dictate that such a policy must be carried out by replacing entire hospitals only selectively, rebuilding existing facilities in stages where possible and providing a high level of maintenance and renovation for the system on a continuing basis.

The hospitals already under construction, being upgraded, in planning, or with substantial unused capacity form one of the major sets of issues facing the city. The issues surrounding four facilities are sketched below. The list omits situations which are certain to generate pressures in 1974, such as the question of long-term financing for Fordham Hospital, community pressures to expand the new Gouverneur Hospital, the future of municipal long-term care institutions and the questions of replacement of Cumberland and Queens.

(1) North Central Bronx Hospital and Morrisania Hospital

North Central Bronx (NCB) is a new municipal facility which was intended as a replacement for Morrisania Hospital. The extent of adjustment at Morrisania was left vague because of community opposition to closing it. NCB is being constructed adjacent to and connected with Montefiore, the affiliate of Morrisania, and is expected to be physically ready to initiate service in April 1974.

Health activists in the borough are antagonistic to Montefiore and are afraid of a give-away of the hospital. They are concerned that services in it will not be available to the indigent. A Comprehensive Health Planning Agency (CHPA) task force has prepared a set of general guidelines for governance and operations.

Since the facility is new, the city retains title. As a result it can potentially exercise substantial control over the financial arrangements and conditions of service in negotiations over transfer of the facility.   These negotiations are one of the first major issues facing the new city administration.

The recommendations for adjustments in Morrisania Hospital are a longer-term issue.   A special Comprehensive Health Planning Agency report on hospital needs in the Bronx is planned for 1974.   The Health and Hospitals Corporation is engaged in a planning and architectural study of Morrisania which is expected to be completed by the summer.   The Morrisania community has been pressing for a new hospital in their area.

(2) Lincoln Hospital

This facility, a replacement and expansion of the existing Lincoln Hospital, will be physically ready to be opened in the spring of 1975.   But there is a potentially very serious problem over how soon and how fully the hospital can provide services, especially since Lincoln Hospital was always particularly difficult to staff.   While a new hospital was seen as a way of making staffing easier, the greatly expanded size, the history of community militance, and the unsettled leadership situation in Einstein, the affiliate, may make staffing very difficult.   Extensive delays have already occurred in the development of functional programs, staffing patterns, and the required training programs.   A loss of years can be expected before the new facility can utilize most of its capacity.   Mounting pressures as delays continue will add to the complexities which already exist.   Early action is critical in order to establish programs and services which are effective and to have any real chance of an orderly process.

(3) Kings County Hospital and the Proposed East New York Hospital

There has been community interest in the East New York Hospital for about ten years.   In 1970, as a result of an analysis of the city-wide obsolescence problem, the Health Services Administration began to press for extensive physical renewal of Kings County, including East New York Hospital as a partial replacement for Kings County Hospital.   Approval was granted in the 1973-74 Capital Budget for the construction of a new 650-bed tower at Kings County to be built in three 200-bed vertical units over several years.   This would allow selective replacement of obsolete patient facilities without destroying recently renovated infra-structure components and permit spreading out the funding so that city Capital Budget funds could be used.

As a result of plans to close beds due to declines in census and due to the opening of the new Woodhull Hospital, Kings County Hospital already faces a major reduction in size.   If beds were separated from Kings County beyond that number, it would become too small to be viable as a regional and teaching center. The East New York Hospital could be developed without an expansion of beds, if the reduction in beds at Kings County for Woodhull did not take place or if a joint effort with voluntary hospitals could be developed. In lieu of committing the $220 million proposal, the 1973-74 Capital Budget included $50,000 for an East New York Hospital study. HSA committed itself to performing this work as part of a regional study of Brooklyn. Strong pressure for the commitment of an East New York Hospital can be expected during 1974.

(4) Knickerbocker-Sydenham-Delafield

These three north Manhattan hospitals have 700 beds and are underutilized and obsolete. The same number of patients could be admitted more efficiently in a single 500-bed general hospital.

Knickerbocker is a voluntary hospital which is in extremely poor physical and financial condition and has persistently sought the aid of the city in dealing with its problems. For the last ten years Knickerbocker has sought a Manhattanville Health Park, a proposed 500-bed facility to replace both Knickerbocker and Sydenham, a municipal. Funding is partially committed by the New York State Housing Finance Agency, and the State Health Department claims this is their highest priority. However, sufficient funds have not been allocated, and there is no plan which would enable them to pass the financial feasibility test. The new facility has also been delayed by awaiting a site which requires relocation of a bus garage. The city now appears ready to provide parking space that will be acceptable to the Metropolitan Transit Authority. There is no city commitment of financial support for the project. Sydenham Hospital has not often been included in the planning and plans for use of the present structure have not been developed.

Delafield, a municipal, is a former cancer hospital staffed by Columbia. It has an occupancy rate of 50 to 60 percent and a high length of stay. It is small, has no emergency room, and admits patients only through Vanderbilt Clinic. At various times, thought has been given to closing or selling the facility. The community has exerted strong pressure to convert the facility to a full community hospital and is now pressing for a 240-bed expansion.

The viability of such an expansion depends on the ability to get an acceptable agreement for staffing with the affiliate. In view of the controls on bed expansion, it will be necessary to close other beds such as by combination with Sydenham to get state approval. This makes the Delafield expansion an alternative to the Manhattanville Health Park.

The 1973-74 Capital Budget contains $65,000 for a Delafield study. In October 1973, it was decided that CHPA would conduct the study in-house, focusing on the region as well as the hospital.

6. AMBULATORY CARE: ALTERNATIVES TO HOSPITAL SERVICE

The City provides direct subsidies for ambulatory care through a limited number of programs:
- --The city's contribution to Medicaid.
- --Subsidies to patients attending municipal hospital out-patient departments and emergency rooms, and Health Department clinics.
- --Operating subsidies to neighborhood family care centers (NFCC's).
- --Contributions to the Ghetto Medicine Program for voluntary hospital outpatient departments.

There is no general funding mechanism to cover ambulatory care by the non-Medicaid indigent because of the high cost of comprehensive coverage and the high tax levy requirement. The restriction on the number of NFCC's constructed has resulted from a deliberate intention of limiting the city's financial commitment to ambulatory care subsidies.

Negotiations over the construction and size of previously committed NFCC's and over new ambulatory care proposals are attempts to redefine the boundaries of that limit. The ease with which funds flow for institutional forms of care which cost from $30 to $200 per day and require 10 to 365 days of care is in marked contrast to the availability of funds for ambulatory centers which can maintain large populations on 5 visits per year at $20 to $30 per visit including laboratory, pharmacy, and public health services. The approach of piecemeal negotiation for ambulatory care and home care under tight restrictions on funds is totally inappropriate to the scale of misallocations of resources by intensity of service which exist. Problems remain in the efficiency and implementation of ambulatory care programs which must be worked out. Yet what is needed is an environment which gives priority to intensive experimentation with forms of delivery which are less costly and better tailored to needs of different populations. Two programs providing opportunity for such experimentation are the neighborhood family care centers now under construction, and the development of health maintenance organizations in New York City.

Implementation of Neighborhood Family Care Centers

The Neighborhood Family Care Center Program was a substantial effort by the city to commit funds for the provision of ambulatory care, not only to fill gaps in service where the number of private physicians was low or declining, but also to restructure the delivery of services into a comprehensive care model. The essence of the approach is that a team of physicians is assigned to the patient, members of the same family are assigned to the same team, there is a uniform medical records system, and services now provided in a fragmented and over-specialized manner are consolidated with an emphasis on the needs of the patient as a whole.

Initial plans for a network of forty NFCC's each providing services to 55,000 patients were drawn up hurriedly based on very imperfect information. The city ultimately adopted a reduced program of fifteen NFCC's but only four of the centers reached the construction stage by 1973. The major reason was that the cutbacks in income eligibility limits for Medicaid sub-stantially increased the operating costs to the city for the cen-ters. In the renegotiation of the program HSA used more recent data and methodology to reassess priorities among the fifteen centers and in some cases tailor the size of facilities more closely to community needs.

A principal issue now is what is going to happen to the NFCC's already completed or under construction. Who will run them, exactly what services will they provide, what will be the responsibility of their community boards, and what will be the backup hospitals? These and other basic questions remained unanswered even though two ceners are now completed.

The Morrisania NFCC, a conversion of an existing out-patient department, was able to begin limited operations in September 1973, drawing on staff and patients from the hospital. Although a draft performance contract was prepared for discus-sion by Morrisania Hospital, the Health and Hospital Corporation, and HSA, no agreement has been signed even though Morrisania is now providing services. The Mott Haven NFCC, a free-standing center, has been physically ready to receive patients since July 1973, but will remain empty until the problems are resolved.

Major problems include disputes between the HHC and the city on the basic contract for services, e.g., the city's ability to fix operating responsibility, to choose backup hospitals, etc. A related problem has been the lack of continuity in the HHC planning due to multiple shifts in the people responsible for the NFCC program. The corporation has refused to discuss the Morrisania contract since December 1972, and communications have been completely cut off. However, the responsibility for making the decisions on the contract, management and backup facilities is the city's. Seeing that these issues are resolved will be a major task for the new administration.

One of the issues underlying these problems has been the dispute with HHC over the interpretation of the corporation's

charter. The corporation has taken the position that the legislation which created it committed the city to eventually transfer all
direct health services to the corporation. This provision was
intended to transfer services which were produced by the city
at the time HHC began operation so that the city would no longer
provide services itself. It was not intended to limit the city's
ability to contract with the most appropriate and efficient provider. The issue of restriction on the city's choice of provider
was raised most explicitly in the discussions over backup hospitals for child health stations being converted to comprehensive
pediatric centers, but it has also been raised with respect to
questions such as governance of the Lower Washington Heights
and Riverside NFCC's and the choice of backup hospital for the
Brownsville and East New York NFCC's. It has far-reaching
implications for many other programs as well, including mental
health services contracts to both voluntary and municipal institutions, contracts for addiction services, and performance contracts
to voluntary hospitals under the Ghetto Medicine Program. Union
pressure has been a major factor in the restrictive interpretation.

An interagency committee on this issue was established by
the Mayor's office to be convened by the Bureau of the Budget.
The Corporation Council has been studying the interpretation of
the current legislation and new legislation may be necessary to
preserve flexibility in contracting. An additional factor to be
weighed in deciding on the relative value of the corporation versus voluntary hospitals as the NFCC backups is the potential for
state financing. If a voluntary hospital is used, the NFCC would
be eligible for state subsidy of 50 percent of the NFCC's operating
deficit caused by services provided to non-Medicaid eligibles.
It is important that these issues be resolved quickly and decisively to allow a wide range of negotiations to proceed.

Health Maintenance Organizations

Health maintenance organizations (HMO's) have been proposed as a means of restructuring the current system for delivering medical care in order to revise the existing economic and
medical incentives. By offering prepaid comprehensive benefits
to an enrolled population, the HMO would emphasize preventive
ambulatory care instead of hospital care, with demonstrated
savings of the order of 20 percent in the costs of providing hospital care. Federal legislation providing both financial and legal
aids to developing HMO's has just been signed. In the meantime,
New York City has two financial levers which could be used to
encourage the development of HMO's:

(1) The Medicaid program, which spent $1.3 billion in
1972 for medical services to the poor, could be partially

converted to prepayment, using existing facilities such
as HIP Medical Groups, the OEO neighborhood health
centers, or the corporation's neighborhood family care
centers to deliver services. The prototype contract for
such a program was recently signed with the Martin
Luther King, Jr., Neighborhood Health Center in the
South Bronx.
(2) The employee health benefits program of the City of
New York now covers over one million city employees
and their dependents and costs the city $150 million each
year for basic coverage. This program could be used to
finance and encourage the development of new HMO's in
two ways: supporting the two insurance-company-sponsored
HMO's beginning operations in New York City early in
1974; and adding a fiscal incentive for reduced hospital
use to the HIP contract to convert HIP into a full HMO.

8. ISSUES IN THE DEVELOPMENT OF COMPREHENSIVE HEALTH PLANNING AND REVIEW FUNCTIONS

Over the years a number of organizational structures have
been created to deal with health planning and review. The Health
and Hospital Planning Council of Southern New York (HHPC) was
originally established by the federal government in order to
review plans for facilities financed under the Hill-Burton program,
but was later asked by the state to review applications for establishment or construction regardless of source of funds as the
first step in licensing and certification of need. The Johnson
administration's heart, cancer and stroke program set up local
regional medical program agencies charged with encouraging
regionalization of facilities to reduce duplication and lower costs
while better matching patients with services. The Partnership
for Health Act called for the creation of state and local comprehensive health planning agencies to bring together consumers
and providers and permit planning to take place in a coordinated
way. The considerable overlap between these agencies is leading
administrative and legislative bodies in both New York and
Washington to seriously consider how to integrate their functions.
At the same time the growth of new mechanisms for utilization
review and cost control raise further questions about the scope
and structure of planning and review agencies. These two themes
set the issues in comprehensive health planning: first, a continuing debate over the appropriate form of the planning agency,
especially its relation to existing institutions and consumers;
and second, a steady expansion in the formal powers and responsibilities of the planning and review function.
The former is illustrated by tracing the development of
the Comprehensive Health Planning Agency (CHPA). When initial

efforts were made to define a CHPA for New York City, the
Health and Hospital Planning Council argued that it would be
best able to gain cooperation of the voluntary hospitals, while
the Health Services Administration took the position that it could
best insure public accountability. As a compromise CHPA was
created as a separate agency within the Health Services Administration with the Health Services administrator serving ex officio
as chairman of the board. No decision was made on how to
incorporate the Health and Hospital Planning Council effort.

CHPA was planned by the Mayor's Organizational Task
Force for Comprehensive Health Planning (MOTF) over a two-
year period and was officially established in October 1971. The
MOTF had as a primary concern the problem of overlapping
boundaries for different functional areas, yet the decision was
made to establish an entirely new district, the comprehensive
health planning district (CHPD). The CHPD's were aggregates
of whole community planning districts, the geographic unit used
by community planning boards charged with local planning via
the borough presidents and City Planning Commission. The
imperfect cooperation between community planning boards within
the same district, the difficulties of deciding which community
planning districts to combine, and problems in developing CHPA
district boards from scratch for the new geographic units set
back the process of formation of CHP district boards for years
(see below).

After four and a half years of planning and operation, New
York City's CHPA is just starting to formally charter its thirty-
three local boards. Completion of the full process of initiating
the boards is still a full year away, and the development of
experience in staff and board members will take further time.
Since the only limitation is that local boards cannot be larger
than the central board of 83 members, there is every indication
that the boards will be unwieldy. The logistical problems of
communication with and coordination of 1,000 to 2,000 members
of the boards are enormous. The sheer volume of individual
initiatives which could be made by a decentralized planning
system of this size, together with the uncertain ability of the
central CHPA staff to effectively screen those actions, will be
a major issue in itself.

A second theme has been the erratic expansion of responsibilities for the planning function, beginning even before the
CHPA was created. Several months before CHPA was officially
established the federal government asked the new agency to review
and comment on all grant applications. This area of work was
not even anticipated by the MOTF, but it quickly dominated the
agency. The decision not to defer any part of the review until
systematic criteria and analyses could be developed contributed
to the development of the agency from the top down rather than
from the neighborhoods up.

The state is still digesting the impact of federal legislation requiring local planning agency review of all major capital improvements in facilities receiving Medicaid or Medicare funding, but CHPA should end up with major new responsibilities. Several bills in Congress propose restructuring of health planning by combining the CHPA's Regional Medical Program and Hill-Burton agencies, possibly including rate-setting authority as well.

CHPA has made little progress in developing the effective capacity to meet its responsibilities at either the central or district level. Mere existence of the district boards by no means implies effective procedures or staff support for their individual operation, nor the capacity of the central agency to synthesize and coordinate the output of the local boards into a coherent policy. CHP's past performance and the prospects for a further major delay in meeting its growing responsibilities have attracted increasingly sharp criticism of the agency from the City Council, the state CHPA, and the City Planning Commission. In an unprecedented move, three of seven members of the City Planning Commission filed a dissenting opinion to the December 1973 Capital Budget Message, calling for a thorough reexamination of the organization and functions of CHPA.

A reexamination of the planning and review functions within the city is needed, focusing first on CHPA and later on a broader group of agencies. Some of the immediate issues include:

--Can the district boards be made smaller to allow appropriate local input without creating a process so cumbersome and unwieldly that it fails to operate?

--How can the community input be used to restructure services with existing resources rather than generating unrealistic demands for new funds?

--How can the numerous new demands and proposals from the local boards be effectively reviewed and shaped into a coherent city-wide policy?

--How should regulatory functions be related to review and planning functions?

--How can an effective environment for analysis of basic issues and long-range research be developed?

As these issues are resolved through the development of a variety of structures it will become possible to more exactly determine in which mechanisms specific powers can best be lodged.

FOOTNOTES

1. Editor's note: Issues 3, 4, and 7 have been omitted here.

V-7 PERSPECTIVES ON LONG-TERM CARE —
August, 1972*

by Byron Bruce Zellner

      The collection of multiservice programs grouped under the
heading of long-term care has attracted growing attention as the
total amount of public funds expended on such programs has risen.
By cloaking general public assistance services under the more
respectable gowns of the medical nomenclature of long-term care
a more rapid growth in both public funds and confusion has been
generated than might otherwise have been the case.

      It is difficult to isolate individual issues when examining
long-term care programs. Issues areas or problem definitions
which are analytically manageable seem to leave out too much
to be useful, given the policy alternatives available. On the
other hand, policy relevant problem definitions turn out to be too
broad in scope to be treated within an explicit analytic framework.
I believe this is because many of the administrative and allocative
problems in the long-term care area derive from this society's
rapidly changing and sometimes conflicting set of values concerning who should get how much of what kind of public assistance--
including medical care.

      There has always been an allocative problem in the public
provision of medical care between the medical services per se
and the more general type of support services that are an inevitable part of the medical care service package. The very origins
of the modern-day hospital and nursing home are found in the
poorhouses of the nineteenth century. The problem then was
defined by the recognition and acceptance of responsibility by the
public that many of the institutionalized poor were also sick.
Today we must face the problem that many of the institutionalized
sick are also poor; and though today's medical programs were

*Editor's note: This paper was part of the 1972 Annual Report
of the Office of Health Systems Planning.

not intended to serve as general public assistance programs,
they do in fact, at least for the aged, alleviate the sufferings
of poverty as well as illness.

The term "long-term care" is commonly used to denote a
wide range of services (associated in most people's minds with
a medical service) utilized mostly by elderly people. The range
extends from long stays in an intensive care hospital environment
to the once-or-twice-weekly services of a housekeeper delivered
to the "patient" in his or her home.

The organizations and public agencies that administer medical care programs including long-term care programs have been
reluctant to withhold the general support services from elderly
clients who may not want or need the specifically medical services which are part of the program service package. The
legislative development of the federal reimbursement system in
the health care area over the past twenty years reflects a set of
responses to this situation.

Up to 1951 the municipal hospitals were the only source of
care available to specific categories of indigent patients. The
Department of Welfare at that time had a strict policy of avoiding
putting indigent patients in nursing homes. In 1950 there were
2,200 proprietary nursing home beds that had a total of 38 indigent patients in them. There were only 894 voluntary nursing
home beds, and the Department of Welfare did rely on them to
some extent--although the number of indigent patients in them
is not readily available. The municipal general care hospitals
were packed with patients who were described, by numerous
investigative reports, as not needing the medical services of a
general care hospital. The occupancy rate for municipal general
care hospitals was 93 percent in 1950, compared to an average
occupancy rate for voluntary hospitals of 75 percent. The
average length of stay was 16.3 days in the municipal general
care hospitals, compared to 9.8 days in voluntaries.

Federal legislation in 1950 and amendments to the New
York State Social Welfare Law in 1951 establishing a new reimbursable welfare category--"aid to the disabled"--made federal
and state reimbursement for nursing home care delivered to
indigents clearly available to the city. In response to this opportunity the Department of Hospitals and the Department of Welfare
began to move indigent patients out of the municipal hospitals
and into nursing homes. The supply of nursing home beds grew
rapidly--due mostly to the growth of proprietary nursing home
beds from 2,200 in 1950 to 9,489 in 1958 and to 12,512 in 1970.
Voluntary nursing home beds remained almost constant over
this period; in 1970 there were only 1,049 beds. By 1966, 73
percent of proprietary nursing home patients were receiving
public assistance (40.2 percent partial and 32.8 percent full).

The effect of these changes on the municipal general care
hospitals was to lower the average length of stay from 16.3 days

in 1950 to 13.5 days by 1962. This direct relation between the
change in policy of the Department of Welfare and the increased
efficiency of the municipal hospitals was apparently due to the
close administrative coordination between the Department of
Hospitals and the Department of Welfare. As we shall expand
upon below, there is no assurance that without such coordination
further expansion in the use of nursing home care or lower levels
of care will increase the efficient utilization of health facilities.

By 1970, with Medicaid and Medicare available for four
years, 90 percent of proprietary nursing patients were receiving
public assistance. (3 percent of patients are being paid for by
Medicare--the reasons for this small number will be discussed
below.) However, the same problem which plagued the municipal
hospitals (and still does to some extent), of patients not requiring
the level of medical services offered, now exists in the proprietary nursing homes. A study of New York City Medicaid patients
in proprietary nursing homes conducted in 1971 by the office of
the state comptroller, concluded that between 53 and 61 percent
of such patients did not require skilled nursing care. The solution suggested in that report (but also anticipated by the federal
government), and currently being implemented, was to employ
federal reimbursement available under Title XI of the Social
Security Act (enacted in 1969) for care in "intermediate care"
facilities. These facilities would be lower in cost than skilled
nursing homes and offer fewer medical services. The reimbursement formula would be the same as for Medicaid.

There were 4,297 beds in facilities classified as intermediate care facilities in January 1971 and at least 12,000 currently in planning or construction.

Home care programs, which could provide selected general
support services so as to be a lower-cost program than any of
the existing institutional care programs, are not reimbursable
under the Medicaid Program and are available only for posthospital skilled nursing care under Medicare.

In retrospect, the development of state and federal reimbursement for health care has fostered a great deal of inefficiency
from the point of view of providing the amount and levels of medical and general support services which came to be demanded.
The historical pattern has been to offer to reimburse local
administrative agencies for the medically intensive types of
care first. The legislative intent was to direct concern toward
the more seriously ill. Less intensive types of care are reimbursed at lower rates or not at all. The administrative agencies
have found themselves in the situation where the more expensive,
medically intensive types of care represent a less expensive form
of care in terms of their own budgets than cheaper, more general
support intensive types of care. This type of perverse incentive
has fostered a state of affairs where the real cost of a day's
stay in a hospital or nursing home has often been above the value

of that day's stay to the indigent patient. If all types of care were at least equally priced (per day) to the agencies administering delivery of care to the indigent, both the patient and the agencies would have, in at least some cases, chosen the cheaper type of care.

Ideally, the cost to agencies and patients for various types of care should be reflective of their real costs. As a practical strategy for implementation of medical-general support services it would be more efficient to reimburse the city for less expensive types of care first to allow city agencies to find how far these could substitute for more costly types of care. This more efficient route may well mean larger initial expenditures, but if coverage becomes broad enough over time, in the end it might result in less total real resources and funds being expended than under the past pattern of growth of the reimbursement system. It must be emphasized that efficiency here is defined as providing-- at minimum cost--the amounts and levels of medical-general support services which come to be demanded after the system has fully evolved.

The development of the reimbursement system being from top down, so to speak, can be ascribed to two reasons:

1. legislators have felt that the public was sympathetic to the welfare of the sick and more willing to give aid to the more acutely ill.

2. the broadening of the definition of the type of care eligible for public support was a legislative response to the inefficient utilization of the more medical service intensive types of care.

Thus, nursing home care became reimbursable to allow hospitals to deliver acute care, and intermediate care facilities care became reimbursable to allow nursing homes to deliver skilled nursing care, and, one may conjecture, it is only a matter of time until it is discovered that many clients of health-related facilities could get along with the less medical intensive and cheaper care of a home care program.

The extent to which broadening the coverage of federal and state reimbursement allows the more medical service intensive programs to operate more efficiently (i.e., closer to the point where real costs equal real benefits) has, given the pattern of development of the reimbursement system, depended on administrative responsiveness to this objective rather than any economic incentive.

During the 1950's the then newly established machinery for reimbursing the city from state and federal funds for the delivery of nursing home care to indigents did serve to lower the average length of stay in municipal hospitals. The extent to which the currently planned expansion in nursing home and intermediate care facility beds will further increase the efficiency of the health care system will depend in part on the way in which the Depart-

ment of Social Services, which is responsible for the administration of Medicaid and Title XI funds and for placement of eligibles
into nursing homes and intermediate care facilities, exercises
its mandate. There are two very different choices. The department could conceivably give first priority to clients not receiving
any type of care. In this way, the greatest possible number of
clients could be assured some kind of care and some future
pressures for costly institutional facilities might be reduced as
a result. There is some indication that such a situation may be
developing.

Of the total number of persons placed in nursing homes in
1955, 95 percent were referrals from a hospital. Data for three
months in 1971 shows that of total Department of Social Services
nursing home placements 66 percent were referrals from a hospital. Furthermore, the 1971 data shows that placements as a
percentage of referrals was 73 percent for nonhospital referrals
and 64 percent for hospital referrals. (This latter percentage
was the same for both voluntary and municipal hospitals.) Is
this the distribution of placements which assures maximum
efficiency of the health care system? Reports as late as 1971
indicated a substantial number of elderly patients in municipal
hospitals who no longer needed the medical services of the
hospitals but were not transferred to nursing homes. However,
we cannot be sure that this situation is necessarily inefficient.
The municipal hospitals have had excess capacity and the marginal cost of keeping an additional long-stay patient in a hospital
may not be very different than it would be in a nursing home. It
is only that there is no guarantee that the utilization of nursing
home beds is efficient from the point of view of the health care
system. Some improvement in efficiency would result if the
occupancy rates of hospitals were taken into account in developing a set of placement priorities.

At present the Department of Social Services has no
explicit criteria for setting priorities other than consideration
of individual emergencies. Hospitals, nursing homes and
intermediate facilities may all willingly provide care to those
who do not need the intensity of medical services, or even
general support services, offered in each type facility; not
because they are sympathetic to the claims of elderly indigent
patients, but because of our average cost reimbursement system,
it may be profitable to do so. An incentive to overuse more
sophisticated levels of care arises when the marginal cost of an
additional day's stay for such patients were less than the charge-
able rate.

The experience with Medicare reimbursement for nursing
home care illustrates what may happen if it is insisted upon that
long-term care be provided only to those requiring the medical
service component of the medical-general support services
offered by a nursing home. By the end of 1967, six months after

the extended care portion of the Medicare act went into effect,
15 percent of proprietary nursing home patients were paid for
by Medicare. Given the distribution of length of stays, this was
near the maximum number of patients who were Medicare-eligible.
(Medicare covers only the first hundred days of care). Due to a
policy of strict enforcement of the intent of the Medicare Act
by the federal government to provide posthospital care to patients
who might otherwise have had a longer stay in the hospital, the
proportion of Medicare patients in proprietary nursing homes
fell to 2.5 percent by the end of 1970.[1] Furthermore, the
average length of stay in nursing homes fell slightly, so the
proportion of Medicare eligibles, presumably, increased.

As far as I know, there has been no pressure brought to
bear on nursing homes to increase the number of Medicare
patients--all of whose costs are paid by federal funds.

It is because most long-term care programs deliver a
service package which contains a strong general support service
component that the "need" for long-term care appears to some
observers to be almost infinite. Dr. Jack Haldeman, president
of the Health and Hospital Planning Council of Southern New York,
Inc., has recently proposed that the measure of need for long-
term care be defined as that amount of long-term care we are
willing to support with public funds. One may take it as axio-
matic that the more general the properties of a good, the more
of it that will be demanded at any given price; at a zero price
to the patient the amount demanded would indeed head out toward
infinity.

Rather than aim at simply increasing the amount of public
funds going into long-term care, we should seek a broadening of
the scope of long-term care services eligible for federal and
state reimbursement to include less medically intensive, cheaper
forms of care.

FOOTNOTES

1. The initiation of the strict enforcement policy took the form
of retroactive disallowances. This harsh measure had been
credited with initially a general reluctance on the part of nursing
home administrators to accept Medicare patients. It is possible
that this attitude still exists to some extent and is partly responsible for the low proportion of Medicare patients in nursing
homes. Medicare lags in payments have also been mentioned
as a factor contributing to this phenomenon.

VI

Program Development

and

Implementation Planning

ALCOHOLISM

     "New York City Alcoholism Study: A Program Analysis" was one of the first program development and implementation studies undertaken by the program analysis staff of HSA. The decision to do this study was made in the summer of 1970. HSA had many potential topics to study and relatively few analysts on board, since the program analysis staff was just being formed. In the absence of external pressures to undertake specific studies at that time, John Guerin was offered a choice of several topics for analysis, and he chose alcoholism.

     Alcoholism was on the list of topics offered to John Guerin because it was known that there were few public or private programs designed to deal with the problem of alcoholism. Alcoholism was known to be a major health problem in New York City. An HSA Advisory Council on Alcoholism, established by Chase's predecessor and the mayor, had communicated with Chase and indicated its concern over the lack of any new activities by HSA in this area. Also, the N.Y.C.-RAND Institute had previously done a "think-piece" which attempted to outline the extent of the alcoholism problem in New York.

     Jack Guerin was instructed to develop and emphasize whatever facts were available on the magnitude and effects of alcoholism in New York City. In addition, he was asked to develop program alternatives and their associated costs. The analysis had to be completed by January 1971 so that it could be presented to the city's Bureau of the Budget with HSA's formal budget request to support any budgetary proposals on the subject.

     The study helped to convince Chase of the specifics of the program and convince the Bureau of the Budget of the general need for city funding of alcoholism programs. The

analysis recommended the establishment of a particular model
for a comprehensive treatment program, including emergency
care, an alcoholism recovery unit, residential care, partial
hospitalization, and outpatient treatment. Alternative models
were not presented because there appeared to be a reasonable
consensus among professionals involved in treating the problem
as to the preferred type of program.

In April 1971 Chase launched a new city alcoholism program by forming a new Bureau of Alcoholism Services in HSA's
Department of Mental Health. In addition to assuming the
administrative responsibilities for the fragmented city-funded
alcoholism programs then operating, this new bureau was given
enough funding to start six alcoholism centers similar in structure to the model recommended in the analysis.

Guerin was involved in the program development work
necessary to detail to the city's Bureau of the Budget exactly
how HSA intended to spend money on alcoholism programs.
This experience led to Guerin leaving HSA's program analysis
staff to assume the position of assistant director of HSA's new
alcoholism program. He subsequently became director of the
city's Bureau of Alcoholism Services, which had grown from a
$2.8 million program in April 1971 to a $17 million program
three years later, with eleven comprehensive alcoholism
treatment programs in operation throughout the city.

The original study included sections which are not
included here describing and recommending outreach, education, and prevention programs. Sections detailing estimated
program costs and possible sources of funding were deleted.
Also, an analysis of the geographic incidence of alcoholism
in New York City was included in the original study. This
geographic analysis was helpful in locating the new alcoholism
treatment centers.

THE NFCC ANALYSIS

Shortly after the federal Medicaid Law was enacted in
1966, the State of New York developed its counterpart Medicaid
Law. The New York State Medicaid Law took unusual advantage
of the definition of "medically indigent." The original federal
Medicaid Law said that medical indigency was whatever the
individual states defined it to be, and the federal government
was to share with the states a major portion of the costs of
financing health services for the medically indigent. New
York's Medicaid Law defined the medically indigent in a manner which included more than half of the citizens of the state.
The federal law was modified in 1967 to limit federal cost-
sharing to families with incomes below one and a third times
the public assistance benefit level, a modification which

affected only New York State. [1] In the interim the city established a major neighborhood family care center (NFCC) program, which was predicated on about two-thirds state and
federal financing under Medicaid for ambulatory health care
expenditures of about 40 percent of New York City's population.

The decision, in 1966, to launch a city NFCC program
was initiated by the city Bureau of the Budget and supported
by HSA. There was only limited consideration given to the
details of the program, including the question as to how physicians could be recruited to provide services in NFCC's. [2] The
NFCC program proposed by Howard Brown, the first Health
Services administrator, was to include forty NFCC's, and it
was planned that each NFCC would serve 55,000 people with
275,000 visits per year. Formal New York City capital budget commitments were made to construct the first increment
of fifteen NFCC's.

By the time the HSA program analysis staff was formed
in May 1970, the NFCC construction program was well underway with sites being cleared, and several NFCC's were actually
ready for construction. While community expectations had
risen during the previous three years of this program, there
had been no serious planning by HSA with respect to a series
of important questions concerning this program. What were
HSA's funding priorities for each NFCC? In view of the federal
cutback in Medicaid eligibility requirements, how were these
NFCC's to be financed? Who would manage each NFCC? What
hospitals would "back up" each NFCC? What specific types of
programs should be in each NFCC? How could the city attract
and hold the physicians and other skilled personnel necessary
to operate the NFCC's?

Since the NFCC construction program was rolling along
without any serious consideration being given to answering
any of these questions, it was quite obvious to new HSA staff
that the city was heading for a major programmatic debacle
unless a large number of decisions were made and implemented.

Thus, in the fall of 1970, James Posner, a sociologist,
and Arthur Levin, M.D., were asked by the then deputy administrator for program analysis, planning, and budgeting (Robert
Harris) to do a comprehensive analysis of the NFCC Program.
This analysis was to be completed by the end of 1970 so that
decisions concerning the HSA's Capital Budget could be made
in conjunction with the city's capital budget cycle.

The initial Posner-Levin study described the history of
the NFCC program, it analyzed construction costs and operating
costs under various assumptions, it examined manpower requirements, it detailed proposed manpower training programs, and
it examined the need for future program planning and coordination for the program.

An important facet of this study was a catchment area

analysis which presented criteria for deciding priorities among the various NFCC's which were to be constructed. A major portion of this catchment area analysis is presented in this book because we view this as the most interesting portion of the NFCC study. With one important exception, the decision criteria developed in this analysis were relied upon to make decisions about which NFCC's to construct and which to cancel. One NFCC was fifteenth on the final priority list of fifteen NFCC's, but it was ultimately included in the list of seven NFCC's which were to be completed because it was within the district of an important state legislator who supported the mayor's requests to Albany. But the planned size of this facility was reduced by two-thirds, since other sources of care were available in the community.

The Posner-Levin NFCC analysis led to the establishment of an NFCC planning unit in HSA. This planning unit was originally headed by Posner, and a number of other studies were undertaken on NFCC and other ambulatory care issues. A follow-up study was made to deal with specific implementation issues concerning the seven NFCC's which were to be constructed. A study on the priorities for additional ambulatory care units was also completed.

This ambulatory care planning unit was transferred to the Office of Health Systems Planning when that office was established in the fall of 1971. Since there was no other administrative mechanism for coordinating and implementing administrative decisions regarding the NFCC's, the ambulatory care planning unit eventually became involved in such matters as developing and coordinating a city-funded physician assistants program and negotiating with the HHC over the specifications of a "model" contract to run the first two NFCC's, which were completed in 1973-1974. Other activities of the unit included review of staffing and budgets, development of requirements for information and evaluation systems and preparation of an extensive transition paper by Steve Raleigh on ambulatory care issues and administrative problems.

During the last year of Mayor Lindsay's term, the city decided to avoid making decisions regarding which organization would administer each NFCC and which hospital would back up each NFCC. This was an important factor which hampered efforts to rationally plan the detailed implementation of the NFCC program. Since jurisdictional disputes between the HHC and various voluntary hospitals and community groups plagued the program, City Hall sought to avoid suffering politically by deferring decisions until the next mayor came into office.

GONORRHEA CONTROL

The gonorrhea control study by Lynda Brodsky was selected for inclusion in this book because it is representative of situations in which an analysis is undertaken over the initial strong objections of program personnel; but in this instance key personnel in the City Health Department eventually changed their views and supported the main recommendations contained in the analysis.

In late 1970 the Health Department formally asked HSA to support and forward an "emergency" request to the Bureau of the Budget for the purpose of strengthening the Health Department's VD Control Program. This program was largely funded by the federal government, and it has been operated by federal personnel. The Health Department requested funds for a major strengthening of its traditional syphilis case-finding program because there was a "VD epidemic in New York City." However, an examination of the data on disease trends indicated that the number of syphilis cases had not increased substantially in New York City, while the number of gonorrhea cases had been increasing at a very rapid rate. When the Health Department personnel were questioned by HSA analysts and by the HSA administrator about their rationale for requesting additional funds for syphilis control, the answer was essentially that: (1) "we know how to find enough syphilis cases to prevent an epidemic but we do not know how to find enough gonorrhea cases to control the spread of the disease; and (2) the probability of serious consequences from untreated gonorrhea cases is too low to justify a mass screening program."

In response, Chase decided to support a modest increase in expenditures to strengthen the syphilis case-finding program. He also decided to support an HSA study of the possible alternatives for dealing with the increasing number of reported cases of gonorrhea in New York City. Chase was impressed with the HSA staff argument that a decision to find and treat gonorrhea was dependent not only upon the probability of serious consequences from the disease, but also the total number of cases of gonorrhea, and the costs of finding and treating the disease. At that time, there were about ten times as many reported gonorrhea cases as syphilis cases in New York City.

Ms. Brodsky, then an economist on the program analysis staff of HSA, proceeded to undertake an analysis of the gonorrhea control problem. In view of the strong initial opposition of the Health Department to this study, she attempted to work closely with the then director of the Health Department's

Bureau of Venereal Disease Control, Mr. Norman Scherzer,
and his staff. At times she functioned as if she were working
for the Bureau of VD Control. The resulting analysis recommended a low-cost detection and treatment program to learn
more about the nature of the disease.

As a direct consequence of Brodsky's willingness to listen
to the views of the program personnel, the Bureau of VD Control
willingly implemented the major conclusions of the gonorrhea
control study. Most of the conclusions were jointly developed
by Brodsky and Scherzer. Two years after the analysis was
undertaken, a mass screening program aimed at high-risk
populations was detecting and treating more than 20,000 cases
of asymptomatic gonorrhea per year.

PRISON HEALTH

In the summer of 1970, the Health Services Administration began to focus on ways to improve prison services. This
concern was motivated by the high number of suicides among
municipal prisoners, and the abysmal state of health care in
the city jails. The mayor's office focused on the issue after
prison riots that fall, with the hope that preventive measures
such as improving prison health services would defuse the
potential for violence in the New York City correctional system.
An initial assessment of the problems and the city's role was
undertaken by Richard Nathan. This study was used by Chase
to generate interest in the problem.

In the fall of 1970 prison riots in New York City brought
the issue to the point of action. Subsequently, the Health
Services Administration was given administrative responsibility
for implementing improved health and mental health services
in the city's correctional institutions. This decision by Mayor
Lindsay was necessary in order to create the potential for
improvements in prison health and mental health services.
The N.Y.C. Department of Corrections was naturally mainly
concerned with security, and thus services to the prisoners
received a low priority. The different priorities of the Health
Services Administration and the Department of Corrections
would prove to be a source of administrative conflict, and an
obstacle to change, throughout the period 1970-74. However,
Chase did largely succeed in upgrading existing operational
prison health services, and providing the physical basis for
future improvements in the health and mental health services
offered to inmates of the New York City corrections systems.

The piece by Anita Altman on "Upgrading Prison Health
Facilities in New York City" was part of the 1972 Annual Report
of HSA's Office of Health Systems Planning. This paper outlines some of HSA's efforts to develop the physical facilities
required to create a coordinated system of outpatient and

inpatient facilities for prison health services. Other efforts were also made with respect to mental health facilities.

For three years, Anita Altman was HSA's coordinator of planning and implementation of capital projects for prison health and mental health services, acting largely as an extension of the staff of Alan Gibbs, first deputy health commissioner, who had overall implementation and operating responsibility for prison health programs. A number of positive changes were made during this period, including developing a twenty-million-dollar major construction program at Riker's Island Infirmary and Health Center which provided health services for all sub-acute prison cases requiring more than ambulatory services, but less than acute hospital care. A contractual arrangement was made for the provision of services by Montefiore Hospital in order to bring quality care to prisoners. (Sixty percent of all city prisoners were detained on Rikers Island.)[3] New inpatient and outpatient medical and psychiatric facilities were also developed at Bellevue Hospital, a new prison inpatient medical and surgical unit is in the process of being created at the North Central Bronx Hospital, and Kings County Hospital's medical and surgical and psychiatric units for prisoners are in the process of being renovated.

HOME CARE

The paper on home care by Regina Reibstein was initiated by the HSA Office of Health Systems Planning. One reason for developing the paper was to stimulate discussion among city officials who had various fragmented responsibilities for home health services. In New York City, HSA, HHC, the Human Resources Administration (HRA), and the Office of the Aging all had some responsibilities for home care. Another reason for HSA staff interest in this subject was the stated interest of incoming Mayor Beame in the aged during his campaign. One of his campaign promises was that he would establish a N.Y.C. Department of Aging.

While several previous HSA studies, including the "Study of Long Stay Patients Unnecessarily Hospitalized," (Chapter II) had noted the potential importance of home care services, it was thought that a paper which proposed a specific home care program would be helpful in getting various key city decision-makers interested in doing something about the problem.

Thus the Reibstein paper recommends the establishment of a central city office for home care services, and it outlines various other administrative steps necessary to coordinate and implement an expanded home care program. This paper also outlines and presents cost estimates of two alternative home care programs.

One key omission of this paper is its lack of a detailed

discussion on how an expanded home care program might be
financed; and the specific actions New York City government
might consider taking to change third-party payers' policies
toward the financing of home care services. Also, this paper
does not focus on the problem of the virtually unlimited demand
by the elderly and disabled for home care services, although
this issue is discussed briefly in an appendix that could not be
included due to space limitations. These were the subject of
further staff work after the initial attempt to generate interest.

The Office of Health Systems Planning in early 1974 circulated this paper among key policy people in the new Beame
administration, and follow-up discussions were held with
interested officials. However, there was no administrative
leadership on this issue, and possible implementation steps or
further studies were not seriously considered.

FOOTNOTES

1. A history of eligibility levels is included in "The Recent
Growth of Hospital-Based Ambulatory Care" in Chapter II.

2. A study of the decision-making history of the New York
City NFCC Program was made in 1970 by a summer intern
with the HSA program analysis staff. See Carol Paul Marshall,
"The Planning of the New York City NFCC's: A Case Analysis,"
unpublished Master's essay, Yale University, 1971.

3. The city jails held 12,000 prisoners in 1972, of which
7,000 were in pretrial detention and 5,000 sentenced for less
than one year.

VI-1   EXCERPTS FROM THE NEW YORK CITY ALCOHOLISM STUDY: A PROGRAM ANALYSIS — January, 1971

by Jack Guerin

ALCOHOLISM IN NEW YORK CITY

The high incidence of alcohol addiction in New York City has an enormous impact on the health and social functioning of the city's population. Of all the legalized drugs, alcohol is probably the most debilitating to the human organism. Its excessive use has been implicated in carcinoma of the esophagus. It causes an inflammation of the stomach which can lead to a severe pernicious anemia and is associated with gastric cancer. Even in the occasional heavy drinker, alcohol causes an increase in the gastric hormones gastrin and histamine, which in turn increase the secretion of stomach acid and precipitate peptic ulcers and further bleeding. Alcohol stimulates pancreatic excretion and causes pancreatitis, which in the long-term drinker becomes chronic and relapsing and leads to diabetes.

In approximately 10 percent of alcoholics, the drug results in the replacement of normal functioning liver cells by useless fat cells and the process of cirrhosis begins. The cirrhotic requires repeated hospitalization for fluid removal, blood transfusions, and attempts to stop bleeding. Operations to alleviate cirrhosis require long hospital stays and usually result in little definitive improvement.

In the final stages of the disease, chronic alcoholics often suffer nerve damage. The chronic ingestion of alcohol, combined with the nutritional deprivation that attends it, results in the destruction of nerves to the arms and legs. As the nerves are gradually destroyed, the muscles waste away. At this stage alcohol can also attack the brain. It can lead to the loss of ability to walk without swaying, impairment of eye movements, and tremens. The alcoholic suffering from brain damage experiences impairment of memory and learning ability.

Alcoholism is a major killer in New York City. In 1968,

445 people died of acute and chronic alcoholism. Another 3, 004
died of cirrhosis of the liver. Because 98 percent of cirrhosis
deaths in New York City are caused by alcoholism, the total
number of deaths directly attributed to alcoholism is 3, 389.[1]
Alcoholism ranks fifth as a cause of death in New York City.

Alcoholism deaths are not evenly distributed throughout
the city. In three health districts, Central Harlem, East Harlem,
and the Lower West Side, alcoholism is the third greatest killer.
In eight others, it ranks fourth.

Because cirrhosis of the liver accounts for the largest
portion of alcoholism deaths, it is important to note that the
cirrhosis mortality rate has been rising rapidly for several
years. Graph A shows that the number of deaths from cirrhosis
of the liver more than doubled between 1955 and 1969. In New
York City, for the 1965-1967 period, the median age at death
from cirrhosis of the liver was 53.7 years, compared with a
median age at death from all causes of 68.4 years.[2] By 1967, it
ranked third as a cause of death in the age groups 25 to 44 and 45
to 64. The 1967 death rate for cirrhosis in New York City was
2.5 times the national average.

A significant percentage of violent deaths must also be
attributed to alcoholism. In one-half of the deaths caused by
motor vehicles, a significant amount of alcohol has been found
in the driver or the victim.[3] Although popular belief maintains
that most drunken drivers are only social drinkers, the high
levels of blood alcohol concentration present in fatally injured
drivers and pedestrians has stimulated researchers to explore
this question. Two studies done in Michigan reached identical
conclusions: 75 percent of alcohol-related fatalities involved
problem or pathological drinkers.[4] Applied to 1968 statistics
for New York City, these percentages produce a total of 370
motor vehicle deaths attributable to alcoholism.

Another category of violent death which is related to alcoholism is suicide. A number of studies have explored this question producing the conclusion that about one-quarter of all
successful suicides are alcoholics.[5] This accounts for 213 New
York City suicides in 1968. Adding these two categories of
violent death to the previous total produces a new total of 3, 972
deaths attributable to alcoholism.

There are other categories of violent death which are
related to the misuse of alcohol. A study of 588 homicides in
Philadelphia demonstrated that alcohol was a factor in 64 percent
of the cases.[6] If this ratio holds for New York City, then 681
homicides are related to alcohol misuse. An additional 124
motor vehicle deaths can be added to this, i.e., the 12.5 percent
which are attributable to alcohol misuse but not to alcoholism.
Another study has examined deaths due to nonindustrial, nontraffic accidents. In 24 percent of these deaths alcohol was
present.[7] This percentage produces a figure of 492 for New York

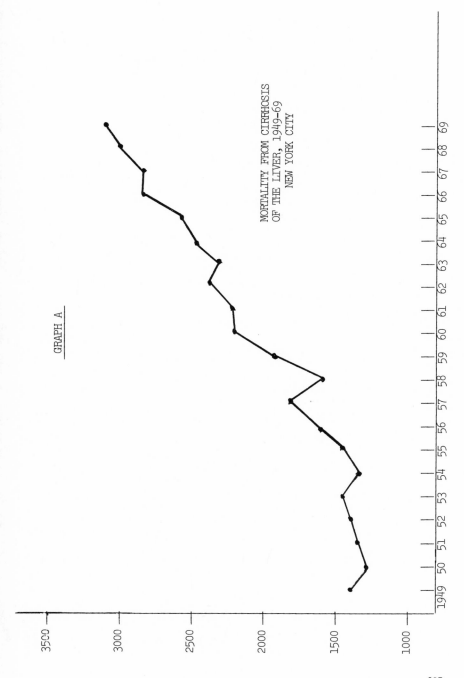

GRAPH A

MORTALITY FROM CIRRHOSIS
OF THE LIVER, 1949-69
NEW YORK CITY

City. These three estimates add up to a total of another 1,297 deaths attributable to misuse of alcohol but not necessarily to alcoholism. Adding this to the previous total for alcoholism deaths produces an estimate of more than 5,000 alcohol-related deaths in 1968. This estimate is based on academic studies done in other areas of the country. The office of New York City's Medical Examiner estimates that the relative percentages are higher in New York City. The Medical Examiner's office places the total for alcoholism-related deaths at more than 6,000.[8]

Alcoholism also has a significant economic impact upon the City of New York. Alcoholics are accident-prone and suffer from a wide variety of medical problems which are complications of alcoholism. As a result, large numbers of them are frequently hospitalized. A survey of the medical and surgical wards of Harlem Hospital during the summer of 1969 revealed that 47 percent of the patients were alcoholics.[9] A similar survey on the medical ward at Kings County Hospital produced a prevalence rate of 27%.[10] Another recent survey by the Health and Hospitals Corporation solicited estimates of alcoholism prevalence from the chiefs of service in the municipal hospitals. If the prevalence rates for ten of the hospitals which responded to the survey are extrapolated to the other hospitals in the municipal system, the cost to the city in 1969 was $96 million for inpatient services and almost $11 million for emergency services. This amounts to more than 20 percent of the hospitals budget. The prevalence rate in the voluntary hospitals is probably lower because they serve populations with higher socioeconomic status and lower rates of alcoholism. Nevertheless, there is evidence that the voluntary sector also expends huge sums treating patients who are hospitalized as a result of alcoholism. If the prevalence of alcoholism is only half as great in the voluntary hospitals, the cost would be approximately $90 million.

Because three out of every four alcoholics are between the ages of 35 and 55--the most productive years--another major loss to the city's economy is the lowered productivity of employed alcoholics.[11] The National Council on Alcoholism (NCA) has estimated that alcoholism costs United States industry about $4 billion annually. This estimate takes into account such factors as absenteeism, tardiness, sick leave, other fringe benefits, wasted time, accidents, wasted material, and the loss of trained manpower. The New York City Advisory Council on Alcoholism has applied the NCA formula to New York City and estimated the loss in productivity to business in the city at $260 million annually. Loss of productivity due to early death of persons afflicted with alcoholism amounts to another $210 million.

Another way in which alcoholism affects the city's economy is through the welfare system. The Advisory Council on Alcoholism has estimated that 15 percent of the families on public assistance are plagued with alcohol problems, and the cost to the city in welfare payments to these families amounts to $165 million annually.

Traffic accidents must be considered another major cost to the city. The Advisory Council on Alcoholism estimated the cost to New York City of traffic fatalities related to alcoholism to be $50 million annually. Injuries due to traffic accidents result in an additional cost of more than $200 million which includes loss of productivity, hospitalization, and property damage.

It is extremely difficult to assess the cost of alcoholism to the legal system. New York City's police force spends a much smaller portion of its resources dealing with drunkenness offenses than do other municipalities. Nevertheless, 12.5 percent of all nontraffic arrests are for public drunkenness and disorderly conduct, usually associated with drunkenness. Applied against a police budget for patrol of $432 million this percentage produces a cost of more than $50 million.

The total of all these costs is $1.132 billion. This total must be considered only the most visible economic cost to the City of New York.

Alcoholism also creates an enormous amount of social dislocation in New York City. The image of the skid row alcoholic without family ties applies to only a small percentage (perhaps 5 percent) of the alcoholic population. It is estimated that the average alcoholic has a significant impact upon the social functioning of four other individuals.[12] Applying this ratio to New York City results in an estimate of 1.5 million people affected by this disease. A large number of these people are children who are denied a stable home life because of an alcoholic parent.

Moreover, 20 percent of all divorces can be attributed to alcoholism. In New York City this statistic represents more than 1,400 divorces a year. The functioning of those families which do remain intact is seriously threatened by alcoholism. More than half of alcoholic husbands have lost at least one job because of drinking. Two-thirds of all alcoholic husbands have been physically abusive to their wives and one-third have been abusive to their children.

Statistics presented in the next section of this report will demonstrate that alcoholism is a major problem in ghetto areas. Alcoholism must be considered comparable to narcotics addiction as an impediment to economic development in ghetto communities. Narcotics afflict a younger population than alcohol, the addiction is more severe, and the impact on the individual is more immediately destructive. But alcoholism.is a much broader problem, with an incidence rate of two to three times that of narcotics and a death rate almost four times as high.

It is incorrect to consider alcoholism as a problem of the past in ghetto neighborhoods, or as a problem which is being replaced by a growing drug culture. The two problems exist

side by side in these areas and cannot be neatly separated. In
many ways these problems are related. A very high percentage,
perhaps a majority, of young narcotics addicts are the products
of alcoholic homes. Ninety-five percent of the young addicts in
Odyssey House experimented with alcohol before using other
drugs. Many heroin addicts are cross-addicted to alcohol. Five
percent of the applicants for the methadone program are rejected
because of alcoholism. Another 6 percent of those admitted to
the methadone program are eventually discharged because of
alcoholism. Alcohol abuse is one of the major causes of failure
in the second and third year of the program.[13] Another way in
which alcoholism disrupts the social life of the community is
through criminal activity. The use of alcohol plays the greatest
role in crimes of violence, where it acts as a depressant of
inhibition control leading to release of impulses. Alcoholism is
also related to criminal activity in other ways. An alcoholic who
is unable to hold a job or maintain his social position because of
chronic drinking may resort to criminal behavior.

In conclusion, alcoholism has a substantial effect upon the
health, economy, and social life of this city. Alcoholism is
responsible for the loss of an estimated five thousand lives and
$1.132 billion in productive resources each year. By every
reasonable index--i.e., incidence, deaths, occupational disability, and social disruption--alcoholism ranks as a major
health problem in New York City.

THE COMPONENTS OF AN EFFECTIVE ALCOHOLISM PROGRAM

Different types of alcoholic patients have different treatment needs. A multifaceted program is necessary if public policy
is going to have a significant impact on this problem. There are
three essential components which must be coordinated to form an
effective alcoholism program. The development of a specialized
network of treatment services is basic to any comprehensive effort
in this field. The treatment system must be supported by an outreach program to identify persons suffering from alcoholism
and motivate them to enter treatment. The outreach program
should be oriented toward early case-finding. Education programs are the third essential element required to combat alcoholism. Education programs in this area have two major
purposes. The first is to alter the climate of opinion surrounding
alcoholism and to reduce the stigma associated with this disease.
The second objective is to educate and train professional and
paraprofessional personnel in the treatment of alcoholism.

I. A Specialized Treatment Network

There is controversy over the development of specialized
facilities. Many people concerned about the problem of alcoholism

believe that adequate services for New York City's 300,000 alcoholics will only be achieved when alcoholism is properly treated in all health facilities. This is probably true. Involving the treating professions as extensively as possible must be the ultimate goal of the alcoholism program. Nevertheless, the present lack of understanding of the alcohol problem by the medical profession is so widespread that effective treatment in all generalized facilities must realistically be considered a distant objective.

Specialized facilities must be developed for two reasons. First, many alcoholics are in need of help at the present time. Huge numbers of people will continue to live wasted and disrupted lives if specialized services are not developed. Secondly, specialized programs will serve as a mechanism to involve the medical and paramedical professions in alcoholism treatment. The specialized network of services must not be separate from other elements of the health care system. Linkages must be built which will stimulate general health care institutions to undertake greater responsibilities in the field of alcoholism.

A.   Detoxification Services

The first stage in the treatment of alcoholism is detoxification. To be detoxified, the alcoholic must stop drinking long enough for his body to eliminate all traces of alcohol and to restore itself to a reasonably normal functional level. This usually requires five days. Most professionals involved in the treatment of alcoholics consider the lack of adequate detoxification services to be New York City's greatest need in this area.

The need for detoxification beds in general hospitals is not clearly understood by either the general public or the treating professions. Detoxification should be done on an inpatient basis for two reasons:

(1) Delirium tremens or other medical emergencies may develop during withdrawal. The national average of deaths from delirium tremens is 15 percent. It is extremely difficult to predict who will have convulsions or when they will occur during the detoxification process.

(2) The majority of alcoholics do not suffer from convulsions during the withdrawal from alcohol but all patients experience extreme discomfort. Only in a structured inpatient situation can most alcoholics cease drinking successfully.

In demanding that general hospitals provide detoxification services, proponents have usually maintained that beds were needed to treat acutely ill alcoholics. This need has been stressed because at present hospital treatment for alcoholics is extremely inadequate. There is a reluctance on the part of general hospitals to admit patients whose primary diagnosis is alcoholism and who are suffering from the symptoms of withdrawal, which are extremely dangerous. Also, alcoholic patients are often discharged prematurely.

Another major problem is that alcoholics seldom receive a primary diagnosis of alcoholism. While a recent survey indicates that approximately one-third of the patients on the medical and surgical wards of the municipal hospitals are alcoholics, only a small percentage of these patients had a primary diagnosis of alcoholism. Because these patients are treated under other diagnoses, they do not receive treatment for their alcoholism. Many patients are not properly detoxified. Often, they do not receive the medication necessary to ease withdrawal symptoms. Because of lack of proper treatment, alcoholics sometimes create a disturbance on the ward. This occurrence only increases the reluctance of the hospital staff to admit alcoholics. Another reason that patients are not properly detoxified is that the ward of a general hospital is not an alcohol-free environment. The overworked staff places a low priority on policing the use of alcoholic beverages. Finally, when alcoholic patients leave the hospital, no provision is made for after-care treatment.

New York City is establishing five-bed detoxification wards at three city hospitals. This policy is a response to the general reluctance of the municipal hospitals to admit acutely ill alcoholics. The ultimate goal of this policy is to eliminate the prejudice against alcoholics in need of acute medical care.

Only about 5 to 10 percent of alcoholic patients, however, develop any form of medical emergency during detoxification. There is a much larger number of alcoholics who are not acutely ill, but do need a structured inpatient environment in order to free themselves from alcohol as a first stage in the treatment process. New York City badly needs beds for this purpose. At present, the general hospitals are the only facilities which can serve this purpose, but this group of patients does not require the intensive medical care available in the hospital setting. Alternative facilities should be created to perform this function at much lower cost, reserving hospital beds for acute medical care.

Baltimore is the only city in the United States which has developed this system. The alternative facilities, referred to as alcoholism recovery units or quarterway houses, are located near general hospitals and operate in conjunction with the hospitals' acute care programs. The alcoholism recovery units are staffed only by paraprofessional alcoholism counselors who have received a six-month training program. The counselors work under the direction of the hospital's nurse coordinator. Patients are given a thorough medical examination before admission to the unit. If delirium tremens or another medical emergency develops, the patient is transferred to the hospital. This has proven to be a safe and reasonable procedure.

This type of facility would receive patients from many different sources. Patients who were motivated to contact Alcoholics Anonymous, an outpatient clinic, or another agency could be referred to the hospital for the first stage of treatment. For other patients the hospital staff itself can be a motivating factor in seeking further treatment. It is very difficult to counsel the alcoholic while he is drinking. A detoxification ward can provide a contact point where staff providing after-care treatment and members of Alcoholics Anonymous can meet with the patient. Hospitalization is a traumatic experience for the alcoholic patient. If properly approached during this crucial period of recovery, he may be persuaded to admit that he has a drinking problem and to accept an after-care program.

There are two types of patients for whom the quarterway house could serve as a bridge into an after-care program. One is the alcoholic emergency room patient. A recent survey of emergency room supervisors in the municipal hospitals indicates that a high percentage of the patients are acute alcoholics. Most of these patients are not hospitalized and most of them are sent home safely. However, these patients receive no long-term benefit from this treatment. The emergency room serves as a revolving door for these people until they are seriously injured or develop an acute illness.

Johns Hopkins and Massachusetts General Hospitals both have an Alcoholism Overnight Area in the emergency room. At Johns Hopkins this area is a well-lighted room with six low cots. The emergency room is staffed by an alcoholism counselor. In the AOA the patient receives a physical examination and vital signs are frequently checked. The twelve-hour stay in the AOA provides an opportunity to evaluate whether the patient should be admitted to the general hospital or the alcoholism recovery unit or be sent home. Through the AOA and the alcoholism recovery unit, the health care system can retain emergency room patients until they are detoxified. Only then can alcoholism be treated in any meaningful way.

The alcoholism recovery unit might also receive patients who were recovering from an inpatient stay on a medical or surgical ward. The hospital staff should be trained to refer an alcoholic patient to an alcoholism counselor. The counselor first meets with the patient on the acute care ward. If the alcoholic sees a connection between his hospitalization and his drinking and is willing to seek treatment, he is transferred to the alcoholism recovery unit for the final stage of his convalescence. This transfer serves several purposes. It insures that the patient is able to remain in the hospital until he is completely detoxified. In the alcoholism recovery unit the patient meets volunteers from Alcoholics Anonymous and recovered alcoholics employed by the hospital. He receives education about alcoholism and explores the options for further treatment. Together with the counselors, the patient decides whether Alcoholics Anonymous, the hospital's outpatient program, a halfway house, or the state hospital is best suited for his needs.

The need for this type of facility in New York City cannot be overemphasized. The private sector provides detoxification services to very few people in New York City and has developed no specialized facilities for this purpose. For the unemployed alcoholic with little money, detoxification services are almost nonexistent.

B. After-Care Treatment

"After-care treatment" is a term applied to all treatment programs which <u>follow</u> the detoxification process and adopt a long-range goal of partial or full rehabilitation. Success rates for after-care treatment programs vary widely from 10 percent in some Skid Row programs to 70 percent in the most successful industrial programs. A successful after-care treatment program for alcoholics requires a number of different types of facilities. Patients who enter alcoholism treatment programs represent a wide range of social and/or psychiatric problems from mild to extremely severe. For analytical purposes it is useful to divide alcoholics into three general types:

(1) <u>The Socially Intact Alcoholic</u>. The two most important qualities of the socially intact alcoholic are occupational and family stability. In addition, he is better-educated than the other types of alcoholics and is seldom arrested because of his alcoholism.

(2) <u>The Socially Disadvantaged Alcoholic</u>. This category includes those alcoholics who demonstrate a pattern of occupational and family instability. In New York City the large majority of socially disadvantaged alcoholics live in ghetto areas, as evidenced by the high rates of unemployment and broken homes in these neighborhoods.

(3) <u>The Deteriorated or Skid Row Alcoholic</u>. The disease state of alcoholism is usually accompanied by a decline in socioeconomic status. The Skid Row alcoholic represents the final stage of this development. These men have no ties to family, permanent jobs, or any social organization. They have little or no money or property. The culture which surrounds them blights a large area of the city and serves as a reservoir for tuberculosis and other health problems. There is another syndrome of deteriorated alcoholic who occupies the single room occupancy hotels in Greenwich Village and on the Upper West Side of Manhattan. The SRO occupants are slightly better off than the Bowery men. They demonstrate some stability in their place of residence and more consistency in daily living patterns.

It is difficult to estimate with any precision how many alcoholics fall into each of these categories. However, almost all students of the alcohol problem agree that:

(1) The socially intact alcoholic represents a majority of the afflicted population.

(2) The socially disadvantaged suffer a higher rate of alcohol addiction than do lower-, middle-, and upper-class people. If 25 percent of the population is defined as socially disadvantaged, this group will represent a significantly higher percentage of the alcohol problem.

(3) The deteriorated or Skid Row alcoholic is a small part--perhaps 3 to 5 percent--of the alcoholic population.

Different types of treatment programs are required to serve the needs of these three groups:

(1) <u>Treatment for the Socially Intact Alcoholic.</u> For the socially intact person alcoholism is easier to cure than many other types of physical and mental illness. It is rational to treat alcoholism as an isolated problem for these patients. Successful cure requires only that the patients cease using a substance which has become toxic to them. A well-structured program should be able to achieve substantial benefits from investment in treatment sources for this population.

The large majority of socially intact alcoholics will not accept an inpatient stay longer than two to three weeks. For them a longer inpatient stay represents too great a disruption of work and family life. Considering the fact that these patients will have no other inpatient or residential care, the initial hospital stay should be extended beyond the five-day period necessary for detoxification to approximately two weeks. An alcoholism recovery unit operating in conjunction with a general hospital is the appropriate facility to provide this service. Any patient who will be treated on an outpatient basis upon leaving the hospital should be encouraged to extend the stay in the alcoholism recovery unit beyond the five-day detoxification period. This facility would serve a dual service for these patients, initiating long-term treatment in addition to detoxification.

During this extended stay patients should receive education about alcoholism from paraprofessional alcoholism counselors, from Alcoholics Anonymous volunteers, from the medical staff of the alcoholism unit, and from professionals in the community. The socially intact alcoholic is often receptive to both group and individual psychotherapy. The alcoholism program should be able to utilize the professional resources of the hospital to provide these services as they are deemed necessary by the director of the alcoholism program. Professional counseling on both social and vocational problems should also be made available to these patients.

An alternative to the extension of the inpatient stay in the alcoholism recovery unit is transfer to an inpatient rehabilitation unit after five days of detoxification. The recommended length of stay for this type of patient is two to three weeks.

After a relatively short inpatient stay, two after-care treatment programs are appropriate for the socially intact alcoholic: outpatient treatment or Alcoholics Anonymous. Professional outpatient treatment is well suited to the needs of this

type of patient. Outpatient programs for this population should
be able to attain good recovery rates judged by a high standard
of success. Alcoholics Anonymous can be considered an alternative to outpatient care for patients who do not require professional treatment. For other patients, AA sometimes provides
a follow-up to outpatient care.

(2) <u>Treatment for the Socially Disadvantaged Alcoholic</u>.
The Kings County Alcoholism Clinic has had extensive experience in treating socially disadvantaged alcoholics. Studies have
revealed that approximately 60 percent of the clinic population
belong to this category. The results of outpatient treatment for
this group have been discouraging. The director of the clinic
has concluded that outpatient treatment is largely ineffective for
this type of patient. For many of these people, a life style of
drinking fills most of their waking hours. Outpatient treatment
provides an alternative to this life style for only one hour a
week. More intensive services are required to help these
people.

Inpatient rehabilitation provides one alternative for members of this group. Many socially disadvantaged alcoholics,
however, are not receptive to a program which is highly oriented
toward psychotherapy. This type of program has been most
successful with patients who are socially disoriented but have a
fairly high level of education. The transition from this short-
term (five or six weeks) hospital-based program back to the
community is difficult for many alcoholics. With outpatient
care the transition is easier, but in the present system there is
seldom continuity of care between inpatient rehabilitation and
outpatient treatment. During the inpatient rehabilitation program the patient develops strong personal ties with the treatment staff. As an outpatient he must adapt to a new set of
relationships. For the alcoholic patient this is extremely difficult.

The Harlem Hospital Center Alcoholism Unit has developed
a day center program for the socially disadvantaged alcoholic.
The purpose of the day center program is to provide a therapeutic alcohol-free environment from 9 A.M. to 5 P.M. five days
a week. Day center activities include group therapy, occupational therapy, vocational and nutritional counseling, educational groups, remedial reading, individual counseling, and
family casework. Antabuse[14] is also found to be effective in
helping patients control their drinking.

The program has achieved a considerable degree of success with a severely disadvantaged population. One-third of
the patients have been able to leave the day center program and
to maintain their sobriety while continuing to attend an evening
group therapy session once a week.

The experience at Kings County has demonstrated that
outpatient treatment is ineffectual for the socially disadvantaged
alcoholic. The program in Harlem indicates that better results

can be achieved by offering more intensive service. For many
alcoholics in ghetto areas the problem of alcoholism is inextri-
cably linked with other social and economic problems. A program which attempts to cure the patient's alcoholism in isolation
from other problems will certainly fail. Massive intervention
is required to assist the patient in developing a constructive
and satisfying life style in which sobriety is one element. The
halfway house is the most appropriate facility to provide the
required level of services.

New York City should develop a system of halfway houses.
Each facility would offer residential programs, partial hospitalization, and outpatient treatment. In the early stages of treatment patients would live in the halfway house. Day and evening
programs would assist both residents and patients in the community. The day center program would be designed for the
unemployed alcoholic. Primary emphasis would be upon vocational rehabilitation, including work in a sheltered workshop.
The evening center program would be oriented more toward
therapeutic socialization and recreation. The purpose of these
programs is to place the patient in a treatment sequence including residential care, partial hospitalization, outpatient treatment, and finally complete independence. Centering these
stages of treatment in a single facility insures maximum continuity of care.

(3) Treatment for the Deteriorated or Skid Row Alcoholic.
The Manhattan Bowery Project is designed to provide short-term
intervention when the Skid Row alcoholic is in a crisis state. The
greatest need is for facilities to follow up this acute phase of
treatment. The project treats patients--older men suffering
from severe brain damage and psychiatric illnesses and younger
men free of brain damage.

It is extremely doubtful that the older, brain-damaged
men will ever be rehabilitated and reenter society. These men
require semicustodial care for the rest of their lives. The proposed enlargement of Camp La Guardia will make available more
facilities for these people. The second group of men should be
offered a chance for rehabilitation in the therapeutic halfway
house program described above.

The single room occupancy hotels also contain a large
population for whom any form of complete rehabilitation is an
impossible goal. A movement has been developing in many
agencies to bring social and health services into these hotels.
To date, this is a largely voluntary effort with very little funding. The goals of this program must be modest. The objectives
are to improve the lives of the hotel residents somewhat, to
reestablish contact between them and the larger community, and
to control the public health aspects of the SRO problem. One
aspect of an enlarged SRO program would involve finding those
individuals who could profit from the therapeutic halfway house
program.

C. The Alcoholic in Treatment

Success for the alcoholic in treatment depends heavily on continuity of care. Low self-esteem, extreme difficulty in relating to others, and low tolerance for frustration are characteristic of this type of disorder. These personality traits render the alcoholic incapable of achieving recovery unless a smooth transition is provided between treatment components.

The alcoholic lives in a social climate in which his affliction is generally regarded as a moral failing. Because of the stigma attached to this disease, most alcoholics deny the existence of a drinking problem for years before seeking help. When the alcoholic is finally motivated to ask for help, the initial contact with the treatment system represents a crisis in his life. Based on his experience, the chances of meeting anyone who understands his problem and offers assistance are not very great. It is the responsibility of the treatment system to make this initial contact a success. If the patient is forced to travel independently to obtain detoxification, inpatient rehabilitation, outpatient, or residential care, and to develop new relationships with an entirely different set of treating professionals, his motivation may be insufficient for him to progress through the disorganized maze of treatment resources.

The tremendous importance of continuity of care in the treatment of alcoholics was documented by a research study at Massachusetts General Hospital in 1959. The purpose of this study was to determine whether more patients would enter outpatient treatment if the staff of the alcoholism clinic made initial contact with patients in the emergency room. With the new approach, the percentage of emergency room patients later appearing at the alcohol clinic rose from 5 to 65 percent. The proportion remaining for at least five visits increased from 1 to 42 percent. [15] In addition to providing a comprehensive range of services, it is necessary that the treatment system be carefully planned and organized with linkages between facilities which permit continuity of treatment relationships.

EXISTING ALCOHOLISM SERVICES

The present services available in New York City do not constitute an effective program. The most common criticism of the present alcoholism program is that it is underfinanced and extremely limited in scope. This criticism is profoundly justified. The alcoholism budget is presented in Table II. [16] This accounting includes present funding plus money allocated or earmarked for 1970-71. Present funding is $2.8 million. About 28 percent of this money goes to finance services on the Bowery. The budget includes more than half a million in federal

funding which is devoted to research and training. The greatest
gap between allocation and need is in services for the non-Bowery
alcoholic. This group represents at least 95 percent of the
afflicted population of 300,000. The present allocation for these
people is $1.4 million.

   This extremely low level of expenditure bears little relationship to that problem itself. The alcoholism problem is
probably equal in magnitude to the mental illness problem. The
National Council on Alcoholism estimates that 50 percent of the
patients admitted to state mental hospitals nationwide are alcoholics. But in New York City, the mental health budget is more
than forty times as great as the alcoholism budget. The Health
and Hospitals Corporation spends more than $100 million each
year treating people who are hospitalized as a result of their
alcoholism, but it spends less than $1 million to treat alcoholism
itself. Alcoholism is a major problem which is receiving only
minor attention.

   Another measure of the inadequacy of the present program
is the limited capacity of the existing treatment system which is
outlined in Table III.[16] The summary totals cannot be combined
because the different types of facilities represent stages of treatment. If the system works as it should, the patients are double
or triple counted in the tabulation. The public sector in New
York City is currently treating less than 2 percent of the afflicted
population. It is impossible to calculate exactly how many people
receive detoxification services in private hospitals in New York
City, but the total is certainly very low--a few hundred at most.

   Another resource which must be mentioned is Alcoholics
Anonymous, which is a significant part of the treatment system.
Alcoholics Anonymous has about 6,500 members in the five
boroughs and adds about 850 to 900 new members each year.
AA depends primarily on private hospitals and rest farms outside New York City for inpatient treatment. Including the private sector and Alcoholics Anonymous, the total treatment
network cannot provide services to more than 2 to 3 percent of
New York City's alcoholic population.

   Not only does the present system treat a very small percentage of the afflicted population; it offers these patients only
a narrow range of services. After-care treatment appropriate
for the socially disadvantaged alcoholic is almost totally lacking.
Specialized emergency services and vocational rehabilitation
for alcoholics do not exist at all. Most treatment resources are
directed at one aspect of the patient's needs: hospitalization,
outpatient treatment, inpatient rehabilitation, shelter, food,
counseling, family casework, employment, etc. The present
treatment system places primary responsibility upon the alcoholic patient to negotiate his way through a complex and fragmented maze of services.

   Not only are present alcoholism treatment services

limited in capacity and ineffectively organized; they are also
poorly located. No analysis of alcohol problems has been used
in program planning. Only the Manhattan Bowery Project and
the Shelter Care Treatment Center have been located to meet
the special needs of one area of the city. Other treatment facilities have been located at random. Most of the facilities in
Manhattan are located toward the southern end of the island.
There are no facilities in the Riverside Health district or in
East Harlem, although both of these districts are areas of
extremely high incidence. There are three facilities in the
Bronx, but none of them are located in the areas of greatest
need. The two hospitals in Queens serve catchment areas which
have relatively low rates of alcoholism. The two Brooklyn facilities are located on the periphery of a high-incidence area.
Unfortunately, however, neither of these facilities is supported
by halfway house or partial hospitalization programs. Their
limited assistance is not adequate for the large numbers of
socially disadvantaged alcoholics in the ghetto area.

One reason for the present state of New York City's alcoholism program is that the city government has provided very
little leadership in this field. Publicly funded alcoholism treatment activities are initiated and operated by a variety of local
agencies. The budget is never considered as a unified program.
The limited treatment system which exists has evolved with
almost no initiative, control, or evaluation by the city government. Four city agencies are involved in the alcoholism program. For each of them alcoholism is a very small segment
of their total activity.

(1) The Department of Mental Health. The Department of
Mental Health is the contracting agency for several treatment
programs. It assists local agencies in application for state
funds and undertakes some minimal evaluation. No single administrator is responsible for alcohol programs as such.

(2) The Department of Social Services. Alcoholism services in the Department of Social Services are handled by the
relatively small Bureau of Shelter Services. This Bureau's
responsibility is to provide food, lodging, and medical services
to homeless persons who cannot maintain themselves on public
assistance. About one-third to one-half of this population is
alcoholic. Only one of the bureau's programs, Bridge House,
is specifically designed to treat alcoholics. An outpatient clinic,
the Shelter Care Treatment, also treats a large number of
alcoholics. Approximately 5 to 10 percent of the bureau's budget is devoted to the treatment of alcoholism.

(3) The Health and Hospitals Corporation. The Health and
Hospitals Corporation has no administrative personnel assigned
to deal with alcoholism programs. Such programs amount to a
very insignificant portion of the corporation's activity, although
the hospitals treat large numbers of people for the complications
of this disease.

(4) <u>The Health Department</u>. The Health Department is
the only organization in New York City government which assigns
alcoholism a place on the organization chart. A one-man bureau
in the Health Department is the only capability which New York
City has to initiate activity and exert leadership in this field.

The need for more effective organization in this field is
illustrated by the Harlem halfway house project. This project
was initiated more than two years ago. The capital budget contains funds for the project, and Columbia University has agreed
to staff it under the affiliation agreement with Harlem Hospital.
Prospects for obtaining funds from either the state or federal
government are excellent. However, to date, the chief of the
Bureau of Alcoholism Services has been unable to make an
application. Before application can be made, a city agency has
to be responsible for using the available funds to acquire and
maintain a facility. The one-man Bureau of Alcoholism Services
has been unable to exert sufficient influence upon the large
operating agencies to persuade one of them to undertake this
small but necessary function.

What results are being achieved by the present alcoholism
programs? A realistic alcoholism program is based upon a
hierarchy of goals. Even if patients fail to achieve successful
rehabilitation, treatment can improve both health and social
functioning. The primary goal of most programs, however, is
recovery. Professionals in this field aim for "recovery" rather
than "cure" because alcoholism technically cannot be cured.
Alcohol remains a toxic substance for the recovered alcoholic.
For this reason, alcoholism must be considered a chronic disease
with acute manifestations.

Very little evaluation of New York City alcoholism programs
has been done. This failing, although typical of alcoholism programs, must be considered another major weakness of the program. Two follow-up studies do exist. A study at Kings County
Alcoholism Center discovered a success rate of 23.6 percent. [17]
Follow-up was carried out approximately one year after registra-
tion. The criterion of success was either total or near abstinence
associated with significant improvement in the patient's social
and vocational adjustment over a period of at least six months
prior to the time of evaluation. Unfortunately, it was only possible to interview about 50 percent of the original patients, i.e.,
225 of the original 458. The patients who were not followed up
were considered as failures, so that the overall improvement
rate is probably somewhat higher than the figure quoted above.
This study also used a control group who received no treatment.
4.9 percent of this group were considered significantly improved.

The second study is an evaluation of 79 patients in the partial hospitalization program at Harlem Hospital. This study was
rigorous in its admission requirements, including 21 patients
who came for only one visit, while Kings County excluded people
who did not complete the intake procedure. However, the criterion

of success at Harlem was less clearly defined. Recovery was defined as relative sobriety for a period of indeterminant length and involved some achievement of success in the patients' employment or training situation. Judged by this criterion, 33 percent of the original 79 patients achieved recovery.[18] If patients who dropped out after a single visit are excluded, the recovery rate is boosted to 44 percent.

Considering the inadequacy of the treatment system in general, these results achieved by isolated treatment components must be considered surprisingly good. Neither of the programs was supported by detoxification facilities, residential care, or vocational rehabilitation. Both of the patient groups studied included a majority of socially disadvantaged people. The Harlem program involved a particularly difficult patient population. According to the Hollingshead classification of social class, 93 percent of the patients were in the lowest two classes. These studies provide evidence that treatment programs for alcoholism can achieve significant results. They also indicate that more intensive services, i.e., partial hospitalization versus outpatient care, produce higher success rates for socially disadvantaged alcoholics. An adequately funded and well-organized treatment system based on the above model should achieve greater success.

A PROGRAM FOR NEW YORK CITY

The essential elements of an effective alcoholism program have been analyzed. There are two prerequisites which are required for the development of an effective program. First, there must be increased funding for alcoholism programs. New York City should allocate substantially greater resources to alcoholism programs and lobby vigorously for increased state and federal assistance in this area. Secondly, and equally important, the city must designate and staff an agency within the Health Services Administration which would have the capability to initiate, plan, implement, and evaluate alcoholism programs. This agency should have responsibility for the alcoholism program in its entirety and should process all requests for federal and state funds. The designated agency should receive a mandate to develop and coordinate all the necessary components of an effective program.

Treatment

A rational organizational structure is equally important at the local level. Based on the preceding analysis it is possible to design a local program structure which will deliver the comprehensiveness and continuity of care which this patient population

requires. Two principles should be followed in the organization
of this system:

(1) Each treatment facility in the system provides a broad
spectrum of services appropriate to the community which it
serves.

(2) Continuity of treatment relationships is maintained
between all program elements in the system.

New York City's alcoholism program should be organized
around the general hospitals. Other cities such as Chicago and
Washington, D.C., have created large centralized institutions
devoted solely to the treatment of alcoholism. This approach
should not be adopted in New York. Alcoholism treatment can
be more effectively developed as an integrated part of the health
care system. A hospital-based program has several advantages:

(1) A hospital-based system is more efficient. The
general hospital is already equipped to provide acute medical
care. Because of this capability, the hospital can support the
less intensive detoxification services required by the majority
of alcoholics.

(2) A hospital-based program is ideally situated to involve
the medical and paramedical profession in the treatment of alcoholism.

(3) The emergency services and acute wards of the general
hospitals are excellent case-finding resources. Hospital-based
systems promise high cost-benefit ratios. By supplying preventive care for alcoholic patients, treatment programs can provide
relief for the overburdened health care system.

(4) A decentralized system organized around New York
City's general hospitals would provide more community-oriented
services. This is important both for case-finding activity and
for transition back to the community.

The potential role of the general hospital in the treatment
of alcoholism has been described in detail. The well-organized
general hospital provides the full range of services required by
the socially intact alcoholic. The therapeutic halfway house
offers an after-care treatment program designed for socially
disadvantaged alcoholics and for those Skid Row alcoholics suitable for a rehabilitation program. A fully developed hospital
program affiliated with a therapeutic halfway house constitutes
a complete alcoholism treatment subsystem which offers the
comprehensive network of services outlined in Diagram I.

Patients enter the subsystem at the top of the diagram.
The patient cannot be admitted directly to the alcoholism recovery unit, which is staffed only by paraprofessionals. He must
receive a physical examination either from a doctor in the
emergency room or from the professional staff of the alcoholism
program. The medical director of the alcohol program admini-
sters the entire inpatient service. A certain number of beds
in the hospital are reserved for acutely ill alcoholics and three

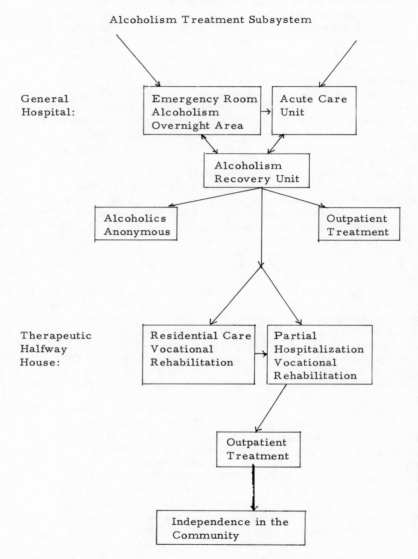

Diagram I

Alcoholism Treatment Subsystem

General
Hospital:

Emergency Room
Alcoholism
Overnight Area

Acute Care
Unit

Alcoholism
Recovery Unit

Alcoholics
Anonymous

Outpatient
Treatment

Therapeutic
Halfway
House:

Residential Care
Vocational
Rehabilitation

Partial
Hospitalization
Vocational
Rehabilitation

Outpatient
Treatment

Independence in the
Community

or four times as many additional beds in the alcoholism recovery unit, which may or may not be located in the hospital proper, are designed to provide less intensive care administered by paraprofessionals. The medical director and his staff are responsible for deciding which patients should begin their hospital stay in the acute care unit and which should be placed in the alcoholism recovery unit. In the diagram the arrows between these two units point in both directions. Patients who no longer require acute care are transferred to the alcoholism recovery unit. Patients in the recovery unit can be transferred back to an acute care bed if a medical emergency develops. The stay in the alcoholism recovery unit prepares the patient for after-care treatment.

Three after-care treatment options are available within the subsystem. Either professional outpatient treatment or Alcoholics Anonymous is appropriate for the socially intact alcoholic. The socially disadvantaged alcoholic discovers additional choices within the therapeutic halfway house program. He can either live in the halfway house during the initial period of his rehabilitation, or he can participate in the day or evening center partial hospitalization program. He can work, using the halfway house only to provide a therapeutic living environment, or he can take advantage of the vocational rehabilitation-sheltered workshop program. The natural progression is to move from the residential care program through partial hospitalization and outpatient treatment to complete independence in the community.

The alcoholism treatment subsystem, consisting of two affiliated facilities offering a complete range of services, has been designed to provide a highly unified organizational structure. Organizational unity is necessary to maintain continuity of therapeutic attachments throughout the entire treatment sequence. Continuity of care is provided by the paraprofessional alcoholism counselor. The counselor is not employed by one element of the treatment system but rotates between assignments in the emergency room, the acute ward, the recovery unit, the halfway house, and the outpatient clinic. One counselor is always free to accompany a patient from one service to another. Staffing patterns are extremely flexible. For example, if a paraprofessional wished to assist a patient whom he had counseled in the alcoholism overnight area in transferring to the recovery unit, the at-large counselor would replace him on the emergency service. The patient would develop and maintain treatment relationships with several counselors during his progress through the system. This type of continuity of treatment relationships has a dramatic effect upon success rates as demonstrated by a research study at Massachusetts General Hospital.

An alcoholism treatment subsystem which combines a general hospital having five acute care beds and twenty recovery unit beds with a fifty-bed therapeutic halfway house would have the following capacity:

General Hospital:

Inpatient	Ten-day average inpatient stay, detoxification, and initiation of long-term care, assuming 90 percent occupancy	810
Outpatient		300

Therapeutic Halfway House:

Residential Program	Four-month average stay	150
Partial Hospitalization	Four-month average stay	225
Outpatient		200

The subsystem does not provide after-care for all inpatients. More than half the people in the partial hospitalization program will probably be graduates of the residential program. If this relationship holds, the therapeutic halfway house will accept about 250 different patients each year. Another 300 will receive outpatient treatment. These are rough estimates based on averages. The system exists to serve individual needs. People will not flow through the system with mathematical precision, even with the effective linkages built into it. The after-care facilities will accept patients who are detoxified in other facilities or on an ambulatory basis. Some patients will receive after-care in state hospitals or private rest farms. Generally, however, the subsystem will accept about 800 new patients each year and serve their treatment needs.

New York City's alcoholism treatment program should consist of a series of subsystems. [19] The prototype described above can be adapted to community needs. The capacity of supporting halfway house programs should vary with the proportion of socially disadvantaged patients treated in the hospital program. Hospitals which serve a predominantly socially intact population may not affiliate with a halfway house at all. Other hospitals treating a relatively small percentage of socially disadvantaged alcoholics might operate a halfway house in conjunction with another hospital. Those hospitals located in communities having a high proportion of socially disadvantaged people should be supported by a complete therapeutic halfway house program.

FOOTNOTES

1. Michael M. Baden, M.D., Office of the Medical Examiner, New York, personal communication, September 7, 1970.
2. "Mortality from Cirrhosis of the Liver, New York City, 1949-1967," City of New York, Department of Health, Bureau of Records and Statistics Division, February 1969.
3. Selden D. Bacon, "Traffic Accidents Involving Alcohol in the U.S.A.," Quarterly Studies on Alcohol, May 1968, Supplement #4, p. 11.

4. Task Force Report: "Drunkenness," p. 29.

5. Ibid., p. 36.

6. Ibid., p. 40.

7. Ibid., p. 39.

8. Michael M. Baden, M.D., Deputy Chief Medical Examiner, City of New York, "Fatalities Due to Alcoholism," presented to the Eastern Psychiatric Research Association, November 7, 1970.

9. Jane McCusker, M.D., Charles E. Cherubin, M.D., and Sheldon Zimberg, M.D., "The Prevalence of Alcoholism in a General Municipal Hospital Population," New York State Journal of Medicine, 71 (April 1971), pp. 751-754.

10. Renee Wachtel, "The Incidence of Alcohol Abuse among General Admissions to Medical and Surgical Wards of Kings County Hospital," unpublished manuscript, p. 8.

11. New York City Alcoholism Study, The National Council on Alcoholism, 1962, p. 6.

12. Ibid., p. 6.

13. Frances Row Gearing, M.D., "Methadone Maintenance Treatment Program: Progress Report of Evaluation," unpublished manuscript, March 31, 1970.

14. Antabuse is a drug which produces an extremely unpleasant reaction in conjunction with alcohol. It is used to inhibit drinking.

15. Milton Terris, M.D., F.A.P.H.A., "Epidemiology of Cirrhosis of the Liver: National Mortality Data," American Journal of Public Health, Vol. 57, No. 12.

16. Editor's note: Tables II and III were deleted.

17. Benjamin Kissin, Arthur Platz, and Wen Huey Su, "Selective Factors in Treatment Choice and Outcome in Alcoholics," in N.H. Mellow and H.J. Mendelson, editors, Recent Advances in Studies of Alcoholism: An Interdisciplinary Symposium, NIMH, NIAA, Washington, D.C.: 1970, pp. 781-804.

18. Sheldon Zimberg, Henry Lipscomb, and Elizabeth B. Davis, Sociopsychiatric Treatment of Alcoholism in an Urban Ghetto, American Journal of Psychiatry, (June 1971), pp. 1670-1674.

19. Editor's note: Various cost analyses were deleted.

VI-2 EXCERPTS FROM THE NFCC ANALYSIS — January, 1971*

by James Posner and Arthur Levin, M.D.

CATCHMENT AREAS AND ALTERNATIVE HEALTH
RESOURCES

Table 4 lists the NFCC's and gives their location, construction status, target population and other data.[1] The catchment areas of the fifteen proposed NFCC's are drawn on the
enclosed maps of Brooklyn, Manhattan and the Bronx. Shading
indicates that the plans for the project have been completed and
the project is more or less ready to begin construction (perhaps
pending relocation of present occupants). St. Francis is presently underway and Morrisania will begin almost immediately.
Areas marked by hatching are those where the plans have not
been drawn and/or site has not been acquired. As our first
decision rule, we give higher priority to projects where plans
are complete and where the program is ready to proceed.
One of the striking features of the catchment areas of the
NFCC's is their close proximity to each other. If a catchment
area does not enroll the estimated 55,000 individuals, the possibilities to expand are seriously constrained in many areas,
such as Bedford-Stuyvesant, Fort Greene, Bushwick, and Long-
wood. The rule of thumb suggested to estimate the likely enrollment is that 100,000 population would generate an enrollment
of 55,000 individuals in the NFCC. As shown in column E of
Table 4 many of the catchment areas are far below this figure,
and may have been drawn to generate an enrollment of only
30,000. In the light of this possible difficulty of recruitment,
and as a second decision rule, we give lower priority to areas
where the catchment area could not be expanded.
Furthermore, the population eligible for Medicaid and/or
Medicare (as of 1968) as a percentage of 55,000 (column H of

*NFCC - Neighborhood Family Care Center.

Table 4) varies from a low of 37.8 percent in South Bedford and 40.5 percent in Soundview to 116.5 percent in Williamsburg-Greenpoint. It is unfortunate that 1969 Medicaid data are not available to revise these estimates. Nevertheless, given the fact that Titles 18 and 19 are still the major sources of reimbursement for medical care, our third decision rule is to give higher priority to those areas with a higher proportion of the population eligible for Medicaid or Medicare.

One indirect indicator of health status in the catchment areas is the infant mortality rate. Tom O'Flaherty has ranked ambulatory care catchment areas for the City as a whole into deciles. In column I, we see that nine of the fifteen NFCC's are located in the highest infant mortality areas (deciles 8, 9, 10), whereas the Morrisania NFCC is in the middle rank of infant mortality (decile 5), and Soundview is in the third decile. We did not try to incorporate the infant mortality rate per se into our decision rules, but it is included here for the reader's benefit.

Another element in our assessment of the placement of NFCC's was to gather information about the alternative sources of care in each area. Table 6 lists the hospitals, child health stations, and district health center located near each proposed NFCC. The distance to each facility is given; and the total OPD and ER visits for 1969 at each hospital are also given. Our fourth decision rule was to consider those areas with more access to alternative health resources to have lower priority for an NFCC.

For example, East New York, Brownsville, Bushwick and Bedford-Stuyvesant have limited access to OPD's and ER's whereas Fort Greene and Riverside are very adequately served by hospital outpatient departments. We included the district health centers and child health stations because in many cases these facilities could be renovated and expanded to deliver a wider range of services. For example, the Bedford-Stuyvesant NFCC is basically the addition of a 39,000-square-foot wing to the existing district health center.

In order to take into account the physicians, dentists, and other "private vendors" who serve the populations covered by the proposed NFCC's, a special analysis was made of the 1969 Medicaid participation tape, to estimate the magnitude of services delivered by these sources of care. It is unfortunate that we have no comparable source of data on individuals in the second quarter of the income distribution, who are not eligible for Medicaid but who are still "medically needy."

Our procedure was to add up the number of physicians or other providers in each zip code who had submitted invoices to Medicaid, and the amount of those invoices. We then (arbitrarily) divided the total physician dollars by $7 (for general practitioners) or $10 (for specialists) to get a rough estimate of the volume of physician visits delivered to Medicaid eligible individuals. By mapping zip codes into NFCC catchment areas and by dividing the total number of visits estimated above by the estimated Medicaid population in the catchment area, we made an estimate of the total number of physician visits per person in each NFCC catchment area. (For dentists, we estimated the per capita expenditure but did not attempt to calculate a number of per capita visits.) From the table on physician and dentist services, we note that the number of physician visits per capita varies from 0.8 in the St. Francis area to 8.1 in the Morrisania area (See Table 5).

In general, we would give higher priority to those NFCC's with the fewest physician visits. However, there is a difficult statistical problem of interaction between the access to hospital outpatient departments and the access to physicians. For example, both the Riverside and the East New York NFCC's show between five and six visits per person, and yet we feel that the access to care in East New York section of Brooklyn is less than in the mid-West Side of Manhattan. A potential explanation might be that in East New York, the access to hospitals is so constrained that the Medicaid individuals must fall back on the available physicians. In the mid-West Side, on the other hand, there is ready access to large outpatient departments at Roosevelt, St. Clare's and St. Luke's Hospitals via the subway. Therefore, we might argue that the total volume of care available through both the hospitals and the private practitioners leaves the Riverside area in a very good position compared with East New York. In nine NFCC catchment areas, however, we note that the volume of physician visits for Medicaid enrollees falls below the average number of physician visits in the city as a whole for Medicaid enrollees, as estimated above.

Rather than rely only on our calculation of physician visits per Medicaid enrollee, it seems appropriate also to use the total supply of physicians to the Medicaid population in each catchment area. In Table 6 we calculate the number of physicians who bill the Medicaid program, per 10,000 Medicaid enrollees in the area. As a fifth decision rule, we give lower priority to NFCC's where there is a high number of physicians available for the size of the Medicaid population.

The last criterion used in the analysis of the NFCC's by geographical area is the relationship between the NFCC and back-up hospital. With perhaps two exceptions there are no firm commitments from hospitals to provide backup services for the NFCC's. Given the magnitude of the NFCC program, it is clearly advantageous to start out with close working relations with a hospital. Furthermore, in those areas where the NFCC will take the place of a hospital OPD, we can consider the operating expenses to substitute for rather than add to the level of expenditure (and deficit) anticipated for the hospital in question. As a sixth decision rule, then, NFCC's were given higher priority if they are to serve as the outpatient department of a hospital. Five NFCC's are affected by this criterion: Williamsburg-Greenpoint, Morrisania, East Tremont-Crotona, East New York, and Soundview.

The Williamsburg-Greenpoint NFCC will be constructed on the grounds of the existing Greenpoint Hospital and will serve as the OPD there. Greenpoint Hospital will subsequently be closed as soon as its replacement, Woodhull Hospital, is completed. The Woodhull Hospital is located further south than Greenpoint Hospital, and it will have its own outpatient department, which draws partly from the Williamsburg section and partly from Fort Greene and Bedford-Stuyvesant areas. We assume that the existence of an NFCC in the Greenpoint area will ease the transition for the community of a hospital closing up and moving.

Morrisania NFCC is being constructed on the grounds of the Morrisania Hospital, and when the NFCC is complete it will take over as the outpatient department of the hospital. Although there are no immediate plans to close up Morrisania Hospital, it is certainly one of the facilities that will be considered most expendable as the bed capacity expands in the Bronx. Probably by 1980, there will be pressure to close Morrisania, and the existence of an NFCC on the grounds may make this decision more palatable to the community.

East Tremont-Crotona NFCC is sited on the same grounds as the new Fordham Hospital, and reportedly it will serve as the outpatient department there. At present, it appears likely that the NFCC could be completed well ahead of the new Fordham Hospital and could begin to serve a population which has only limited access to care at present.

The East New York NFCC is expected to fill a gap in a section of Brooklyn with seriously constrained access to any hospital. Tentatively, a municipal hospital is planned for the East New York area, and presumably it could be designed to complement the NFCC already well underway.

Finally, the NFCC proposed for Soundview fits a similar situation as East New York. There is no hospital in the immediate area. The NFCC's proposed for both these areas offer the prospect of bringing ambulatory care to the area sooner than would otherwise be possible if we had to wait for construction of a hospital outpatient department. On the other hand, the construction of an NFCC in each of these areas must be reconciled with the plans for hospital construction. If a hospital with an outpatient department is built either in Soundview or in East New York, it would be redundant with the present plans for an NFCC. The choice in both locations boils down to one of three options:

(a) Build an NFCC but no hospital.
(b) Build a hospital with an OPD but no NFCC, or
(c) Build a hospital without an OPD and also build an NFCC.

If the interest is to preserve the NFCC program, then the first or third alternatives are obviously the most attractive. If the objective is to pare back the NFCC's, then three of the proposed NFCC's (East New York, Soundview, and East Tremont-Crotona) can be replaced by the proposed hospitals in those locations. It should be pointed out that we have not attempted to compare the "program" at an outpatient department with that of an NFCC to decide between options (b) and (c). What seems more to the point, given the interminable construction delays in the city, is the prospective advantage of completing an NFCC within three years and putting it into service while its backup hospital is still being built. Therefore, we have given higher priority to those NFCC's which can operate as the outpatient department of a hospital.

Summary of proposed NFCC's on basis of decision rules related to characteristics of project and geographical area.[2]

NFCC SUMMARY

Brooklyn

1. Williamsburg-Greenpoint
   a. Plans complete
   b. Large catchment area and population
   c. Large proportion of enrollees eligible for reimbursement by Medicaid or Medicare
   d. Limited alternative resources
   e. Relatively large number of physicians; average number of visits
   f. Will be OPD at existing hospital

2. East New York
   a. Plans complete
   b. Large catchment area and population
   c. High proportion reimbursable
   d. Seriously limited alternative resources
   e. Relatively large number of physicians and visits per person
   f. Could be OPD at proposed hospital

3. Brownsville
   a. Plans complete
   b. Relatively small catchment area and population

      c. Relatively low proportion reimbursable
      d. Limited alternative resources
      e. Relatively low number of physicians and visits
      f. Will not be OPD

4. N. Bedford-Stuyvesant

      a. Plans incomplete. Anticipate addition to District Health Center
      b. Large catchment population. Area constrained on all sides
      c. High proportion reimbursable
      d. Limited access to alternative resources at present; new Woodhull Hospital will serve the area
      e. Low number physicians and visits
      f. Will not be OPD

5. Fort Greene

      a. Plans incomplete
      b. Relatively small and impractical catchment area
      c. Relatively low proportion reimbursable
      d. Access at present to Brooklyn and Cumberland Hospitals, and in future, to Woodhull
      e. Low number physicians and visits
      f. Will not be OPD

6. Bushwick

      a. Plans incomplete
      b. Moderate catchment population. Area constrained on one side.
      c. Relatively high proportion reimbursable
      d. Alternative resources seriously limited
      e. Low number of physicians and visits
      f. Will not be OPD

7. South Bedford

      a. No site. Plans incomplete
      b. Small catchment population. Area constrained on one side
      c. Low proportion reimbursable
      d. Limited alternative facilities
      e. Relatively high number of physicians and visits
      f. Will not be OPD

RECOMMENDATIONS BASED ON GEOGRAPHICAL ANALYSIS OF NFCC'S

Based on the discussion and summary above, we arrive at the following recommendations:

(1) Proceed to build the seven NFCC's which are presently under construction or at the stage where construction can begin.

(2) Proceed with either the North Bedford-Stuyvesant or the Bushwick NFCC, but not both. Both are in areas of high priority, but each is at an early stage in development. We recommend the Bedford-Stuyvesant NFCC because the construction of a new wing to an existing district health center there can probably proceed faster than the construction of a new facility in the Bushwick area. On the other hand, a well-organized community group reportedly has already formed in the Bushwick area, which would favor proceeding in that area.

(3) Proceed with NFCC's proposed for East Tremont-Crotona and Soundview only upon satisfactory resolution of the decision to build the proposed hospitals in those two areas.

(4) Do not proceed with the NFCC's proposed for Fort Greene, Riverside, Mount Morris or South Bedford.

FOOTNOTES

1. Editor's note: Tables 4, 5, and 6 were deleted.
2. Editor's note: Comments on the other eight NFCC's were deleted.

VI-3 AN ANALYSIS OF ALTERNATIVE GONORRHEA CONTROL PROGRAMS IN NEW YORK CITY — March, 1971

by Lynda Brodsky and Norman Scherzer

In 1969 there were over 36,000 cases of gonorrhea reported in New York City. The number of unreported cases is estimated to be ten times as great. Having picked up this fact, the press has labeled the current situation as having reached epidemic proportions.

In the past, there has been no gonorrhea control program per se in New York City. But there has been an intensive syphilis control program despite the fact that the number of reported cases of gonorrhea is ten times higher than the number of reported cases of primary and secondary syphilis. There are a number of reasons why this has been the case. First, the city has historically followed the lead of the Public Health Service, which has not until recently been concerned with gonorrhea. Also, the short incubation period of the disease (as short as two days) made it nearly impossible to treat gonorrhea as a public health problem. That is, infected individuals could have been treated, but too late to prevent the disease from spreading. Finally, the probability of a serious complication resulting from gonorrhea was believed to be small, and treatment with penicillin was simple and effective.

While these reasons were sufficient for inaction in the past, they may no longer possess that validity. For, even if we cannot tackle gonorrhea as a public health problem, we are interested in treating it from a community health perspective. Furthermore, we are reassessing the consequences of the disease and there is an increasing feeling among physicians that gonorrhea has been the cause of many chronic pelvic disorders. In addition, in many cases gonorrhea has become resistant to penicillin, thereby making treatment more difficult.

The purpose of this paper is not to give another lengthy description of the historical growth of the problem but rather

to determine whether or not a control program is feasible in
New York City.[1]

There are several control programs in which the city
could invest in an attempt to reduce the incidence of gonorrhea.
We could institute a detection program and screen for otherwise undetected cases. Or we could beef up the diagnostic
procedure so that we minimize false negatives. Another area
for investment would be in treatment so that once a case is
detected it is cured. We could also begin a preventive program
which could consist of public information and prophylactic measures. Another form of gonorrhea control program would be an
extensive full-time epidemiological research program. This
would differ from other programs in which research is inciden-
tal to another objective.

Ideally, the optimal level of investment in each program
should be derived before the optimal mix of programs is considered. For the first analysis, however, we are assuming
that the results of each program will increase in proportion to
the program size (although some investments are indivisible).
While this assumption is not justifiable since treatment and prevention presumably have an additive effect in their impact on
"collapsing" the disease, we do not have an estimate of this
effect. That is, at some point, curing a case of gonorrhea will
have the additional purpose of collapsing the gonorrhea reservoir--
but we don't know which case will take on this effect.

On the other hand, the product of the combined programs
may be less than the sum of the separate programs. If the two
programs draw on the same population, the yield of the second
will be diminished by the first. We should bear this in mind
when choosing the target populations for the control program.

For each control program, we want to have a measure of
the benefit and the cost. The benefit is dependent upon the number of infections and complications prevented. These are a
function of the number of persons reached by the program and
the nature of that population. If we make the simplifying assumption that detection programs, laboratory programs, and treatment programs deal with populations of like sexual behavior,
we may may further assume that a case treated in one program
will prevent the same number of new infections as a case
treated in another program.

In order to judge the merits of a program on its own, a
refined concept of negative impact of the disease is necessary.
Early gonorrhea in the male is characterized by urethral discharge and severe dysuria. In the female, there may be discharge, dysuria, abdominal pain, or no symptoms at all.
Untreated cases result in pelvic inflammatory disease of sufficient severity to merit emergency hospital attention. Although
gonorrhea is commonly confined to the genitourinary system,
there may be complications resulting from blood stream dis-

semination. Gonococcal arthritis and endocarditis may occur.
Sterility in both male and female is another possible result.
In addition, if a newborn passes through the birth canal of an
infected mother, he may be blinded. In New York, all hospital
births are treated prophylactically with silver nitrate or penicillin. Home births, of course, are still vulnerable to the
small probability of this catastrophic consequence. Treating
infectees would not only prevent these complications from
occurring but would also prevent the complications in a chain
of sexual contacts.

Estimates of the number of people affected by these conditions and the costs associated with these effects would be desirable.[2] Even without a quantifiable measure of the harm of
untreated infection, programs can be evaluated once a rough
estimate of benefit is made. In such a case, the <u>relative</u> benefits of the programs are still visible. Here, "positive cases"
indicate cases treated and that is the benefit we are after.
Throughout most of this analysis, "cost per positive test" is the
unit of comparison. In the final program recommendation, "cost
per person treated" is the benefit measure used.

I. DETECTION PROGRAMS

While gonorrhea is easily identified by most male infectees,[3]
it is reported to be between 28 percent and 80 percent asymptomatic in females.[4] Even when symptoms are present, they are
usually of a nonspecific nature (abdominal pain, vaginal discharge),
not allowing the infected female to identify her problem. Because
of the unlikelihood of self-discovery, a mass screening program
seems appropriate.

A. Mass Screening

For women, the gram stained smear is considered to be
too insensitive and the serologic test is still experimental.
Currently the most widely recognized diagnostic procedure is the
GC pelvic culture with 82 to 86 percent sensitivity (sensitivity
is the percentage of infections detected).[5] Multiple site testing
(cervix, vagina, uretha, rectum) has been shown to increase
positive yield to 90 percent, an increase of 10 percent over the
yield for one site.[6] Repeated cultures on separate visits are
reported to have doubled positive findings.[7]

<u>Municipal Hospitals</u>. One plan for an immediate program
would be to utilize existing facilities. Screening women who are
receiving pelvic examinations anyway would minimize inconvenience to them and cost to the city. Municipal hospitals provide an obvious program base because we have more control

over programs in these facilities and because they are reported
to service high-yield populations. Tables I and II[8] show estimates
of the number of admissions to municipal gynecological inpatient
services and visits to gynecologic outpatient clinics each month.
The inpatient admission figure was estimated by multiplying the
actual hospital census (for August 1970) by a low and high
admissions/census ratio derived from sample data for that month.
The number of outpatient visits per month was estimated from
the 1969 totals for that clinic.[9] No allowance is made for patients
referred from the OPD to the inpatient service. They are counted
twice. No deduction is made for patients already routinely
tested.

There is some question as to whether the gynecologic service is the population we desire for a GC culture program. The
first difficulty is that they are not unduplicated visits. But
because the incubation period for gonorrhea is so short, it seems
appropriate that each time any sexually active woman is admitted
to the service, she be considered a new patient with a new chance
of having contracted the disease. Another question is whether
the obstetrical service should be included as well as the gynecologic service since it, too, eliminates the fixed cost of providing for a pelvic examination. While this would obviously
increase the number of gonorrhea cases apprehended, it is
excluded here for several reasons. Admission and visit data
is less complete for the OB service. Transfers from GYN outpatient to OB outpatient would have to be considered. Research
literature reveals OB patients to have a lower incidence of
gonorrhea.[10] Finally, the reduction of sexual activity during
pregnancy further reduces the desirability of using this patient
population. If outpatient visits were excluded from the test
population most of these difficulties would be overcome, but the
inpatient population that gives birth presents comparable difficulties.

Predicting the percentage yield of gonorrhea in the various
health facilities presented a tremendous problem. Recent Center
for Disease Control data verify "gut feelings" about the relative
yield in various types of health facilities. These do not, however,
help us determine the high priority clinics of a given facility
nor do they reveal the expected yield of the facility type. One
method of prediction is to assume the gonorrhea incidence of a
given area to be a positive function of the reported gonorrhea
in that area. This implies that gonorrhea reporting is accurate
when we, in fact, believe it is understated in higher income
neighborhoods. If this problem is overlooked, we must determine which "given area" to use. High and low intraborough
extremes wash-out interborough differences and lessen the usefulness of the analysis for planning screening programs. So we
decided to use the health district as the incidence unit. The
percentage yield figure is, then, based on reported gonorrhea

incidence among females in the health district of the health facility indicated. This leaves us with two questionable assumptions but no acceptable alternatives. The assumptions are that the reported incidence of gonorrhea of health districts is monotonically related to the true incidence of gonorrhea in those districts and that the users of the given health facilities are representative of the health districts in which the facilities are located. Relaxation of these assumptions would not probably increase the yield of cases in middle-income areas and tend to discount recommendations to concentrate programs in areas revealed to be high yield.

A yield of 531 outpatient cases and 215 to 335 inpatient cases per month is estimated for the entire municipal hospital system. Apprehension of these cases would reduce gonorrhea by 6,500-10,400 cases a year. (This is not to say that the number of reported cases of gonorrhea would be reduced by this amount. The procedures might uncover previously undetected, and therefore unreported cases.) No allowance is made for an increase in the incidence of gonorrhea. A breakdown of yield by municipal hospital is shown on Tables I and II.

Costs consist of physicians and laboratory costs. Since screenees are already undergoing pelvic examinations in this program, the cost of physician services is figured to be just the incremental demand upon his time. If the culture is taken by a session physician it would cost about one dollar (for a little over four minutes of his time). The laboratory cost for initial handling is estimated to be $2.00 per culture. The additional cost for confirmation of those cultures which test positive is $1.15.[11] If the test is a true positive, a treatment cost of $.85 penicillin (or another drug) should be included.[12] Finally, a test of cure should be performed. In such a case, all laboratory costs are repeated but the pelvic examination is no longer a fixed cost.

The costs then are $1.00 plus $2.00 times the number of tests plus $1.15 plus $.85 plus $6.00 plus $2.00 times the number of positives. These cost calculations refer only to single-site, single-visit testing. Detailed costs per positive test by hospital are shown in Tables I and II. Table III presents additional costs and yields of multiple site and repeated visit testing. A second site, by doubling the laboratory costs, increases the total cost to $5.00 times number of tests plus $12.00 times number of positives. Two additional visits are assumed to triple laboratory costs and add twelve dollars to the physician cost. Thus the total cost for a three-visit series would be $19.00 times the number of tests plus $10.00 times the number of positives. The cost per positive figures in Table III reflect the increase in yield that may be expected with the improved procedure. In this draft, figures are not supplied for municipal obstetrical visits, but it is conceivable that repeated visits testing on such a population would not incur the same dramatic

cost increase attributable to the cost of physician services. In
such a case, only the additional cost of the doctor's time would
be relevant (as is the case of the first visit for other populations
considered).

Planned Parenthood. Planned Parenthood of New York City
provides another potential screening population. A comparison of
demographic characteristics of the parents of the two plans leads
to an across-the-board reduction in expected percentage yield
from PPNYC of 25 percent. The proportion of new to first visits
was assumed to be equal to that of the MIC-FP project.[13] The
method of costing was also like that of the MIC-FP project.

Pap Smears. The city laboratory does 110,000 Pap smears
for cervical cancer per year. Each represents a pelvic examination being done at some "existing facility." Fifty thousand of
these lab specimens are done at Harlem and Metropolitan
Hospitals, and probably come from "public" facilities. If we
assume that all 50,000 of these women and half of the remaining
have already been counted, there is a residual of 30,000 pelvic
exams per year--probably by private physicians--for which the
city is doing free lab work. If we coax these physicians into
doing a GC culture as well as the Pap smear, we will reach an
additional 30,000 women. The difficulty here is that if these
Pap smears are being done by private physicians, the percentage
yield is probably low. Here it is estimated to be 3 percent.
This makes the cost per positive quite high (Table VI).

We could carry the idea of linking GC cultures to Pap
smears one step farther and consider all of the Pap smears being
done in NYC by private laboratories. If we offered the same
laboratory subsidy for such a population the volume of GC cultures would increase tremendously. The difficulty again is the
low yield. Besides, this type of program amounts to education
of physicians to do the screening procedure. This matter is
discussed later in connection with public education.

B. Serologic Testing

A blood test for gonorrhea has been developed and is currently being tested at the National Communicable Disease Center
in Atlanta.[14] Although it has been over a year since the test
was developed and its sensitivity (86 percent for females) established, CDC is not releasing the procedure for general use.
If we were to initiate a serologic test program at this time, it
would be necessary to couple each blood test with a GC pelvic
culture. This would, of course, simply increase costs above
the culture alone. Once the test is released, however, it will
offer several advantages. It will be less expensive and probably be bait for autoanalyzing equipment. In addition, it will
enable us to reach greater numbers of women with less incon-

Table VI

Summary of Annual Yields and Costs of GC Culture Screening

	Tests	% Yield	#Yield	Cost per Positive
Municipal Hospital				
GYN In	25,584-40,164	10.0%	2,580-4,032	$40.
GYN Out	73,548	8.6%	6,372	45.
OB		5.0%		70.
OB		4.3%		80.
Planned Parenthood				
New Visits	9,105	6.5%	591	34.
Estimated Revisits	22,993	6.5%	1,494	34.
Residual Pap Smears Done by Lab	30,000	3.0%	900	70.

361

venience to them because a pelvic exam will not be necessary.
Because this greatly advantageous test will be available soon,
some analytical effort should be devoted to determining how it
will be integrated with other programs.

C. Epidemiologic Case-Finding

Each positive culture could be followed up with a public
health adviser search for contacts. Each adviser can conduct
900 syphilis interviews per year. [15] At a starting salary of
$7,600 plus 27 percent fringe and $444 for use of a car half-
time (variable costs), the cost per interview follow-up is
roughly $11. The Bureau of VD Control feels, however, that
gonorrhea interviews can be conducted more easily and cheaply
than syphilis interviews. The pursuit of the first sexual contact, which is the cheapest (easiest) to find, would only cost $5.
The cost of lab tests and physician time are extra. Research
literature reveals the transmission rate to be from 22 percent
to 60 percent. [16] This makes the cost for follow-up per positive
from $18 to $50 exclusive of regular test costs. Since women's
sexual contacts are men, their symptoms will bring them in
for medical care without an interview. The disease is not
generally transmitted between female homosexuals. Inter-
viewing females may be useful, however, to plot the course of
the disease, determine the duration of infectious state, etc.
The cost of investigator and culture for female contacts
of male infectees is $42 to $96 per positive. If the rate of transmission is 60 percent, the gonorrhea interviewer need be only
10 percent more productive than the syphilis interviewer in order
to make the case finding approach less costly than the municipal
hospital screening program. The prudent inclusion of a case-
finding program is dependent upon stopping the interview effort
when the marginal productivity of the interviewer is still high.
If the program is strictly for screening, rather than for traditional epidemiologic research, we may further reduce costs by
eliminating the initial laboratory culture and pelvic examination
and treat the contact prophylactically. A test of cure would
still be performed.

VI. CONCLUSIONS [17]

When this analysis was undertaken, the conclusion was
expected to be a radical departure from conventional thinking on
gonorrhea control. The arguments against such a conclusion,
however, are overwhelming. First, we are at a brink of several
important breakthroughs (such as serological testing for gonorrhea and an effective prophylactic for women) which would make
a major investment in a radical program risky.

That is, we are interested in maintaining a position of maximum flexibility to be able to accommodate the change that is expected, but we desire to do "something" in the meantime. Second, it is difficult to imagine an area in which we know less about the epidemiology of a disease. We do not desire to plunge forward without greater certainty about the output of our efforts. Finally, we are now in a state such that we can predict a relatively dramatic effect from even a "routine" program of GC culture screening in existing facilities.

In view of the preceding analysis, the following general recommendations are made:

Go ahead with a limited GC culture screening program but... only in existing facilities with a minimum of new hiring to provide for easy exit from the program in the event of the release of a more efficient, serologic screening test.

... implement the program in the "low yield" areas last and drop them from the program to reduce cost if they do in fact prove to be low yield.

... design the program carefully so that we can evaluate the results to illuminate such issues as the relative incidence of gonorrhea in first and subsequent clinic visits, the relative incidence in GYN and OB clinics, and the extent of recidivism.

Initiate epidemiological program.

... interview all male infectees for sexual contacts and pursue the contacts.

... interview female infectees as part of the attempt to determine the course of gonorrhea in females.

... structure this program carefully to illuminate such issues as the transmission rate of gonorrhea from male to female, the duration of the infectious stage, etc.

Review the present public education program and augment it to...

... provide propaganda directed toward physicians to encourage GC pelvic culture testing among private patients.

... provide a well-controlled experiment to determine the effects of a public information program.

Review possible sources of funds aside from a budget allocation including...

... Medicaid reimbursement for laboratory work.

... Health Research Council.

... Federal government and private research grants.

Above all, absolutely all programs undertaken must be designed to provide answers to some unanswered aspect of the gonorrhea problem. This is particularly important because we are not certain of the impact of

the program on the incidence of gonorrhea. If the
impact is not great, at least we will have purchased
information for our investment.

FOOTNOTES

1. For background see "The Venereal Disease Issue in New
York City," Department of Health, December 15, 1969, and
"An Emergency Request for Funds to Attack the Venereal
Disease Epidemic," Department of Health, June 5, 1970.
2. RAND is working on a measure of the badness of a disease
based on inability to continue one's regular activity. We may
also want to estimate loss of productive activity. Santa Clara
County is now assessing medical complications of acute gonorrhea resulting in hospitalization. The study is based on medical
records coded according to a national system. A similar study
could be undertaken here, or we could try to use the results
of the California study when it is completed.
3. R.W. Thatcher et al.: "Asymptomatic Gonorrhea." JAMA
210: 315-317 (1969). They report .2 percent of asymptomatic
males to have gonorrhea. However, Dr. Harry Pariser reported
later (Med. Trib. 5/19/71) that as many as 12 percent of males
may be asymptomatic during incubation.
4. V.G. Cave et al.: "Gonorrhea in the Obstetrical and Gynecologic Clinic," JAMA 210: 309-11 (1969), and Bacti-Lab Vag-
Plate^{TM} literature respectively.
5. A.L. Schroeter and G.J. Pazin: "Gonorrhea Diagnosis
and Treatment," Ann. Int. Med. 72:553-559 (1970). Cave, op.
cit.
6. Cave, op. cit.; Schroeter, op. cit.; J.D. Schmale et al.:
"Observations on the Culture Diagnosis of Gonorrhea in Women,"
JAMA 210:312-314 (1969).
7. Cave op. cit.; Schroeter, op. cit.; D.W. Johnson et al.:
"An Evaluation of Gonorrhea Case Findings in Chronically
Infected Females." Am. J. Ep. 90:438-448 (1969).
8. Editor's note: Space considerations necessitated the deletion of Tables I, II, III, IV, V, and VII.
9. Hospital Statistics Service.
10. Cave, op. cit.; G.W. Kraus and S.S.C. Yen: "Gonorrhea
during Pregnancy." Obstet. Gynec. 31:258-259 (1968).
11. This is based on a cost analysis of the city's Bureau of Labs.
12. The costs of drugs used for treatment of females are:

1.	PAM	procain penicillin G in oil	$ .34/treatment
2.	APPG	procain penicillin G in aqueous suspension	1.88/ "
3.		tetracycline hydro chloride	.65/ "
4.		E-mycin	2.48/ "
5.		Sulfa	.31/ "

13. Editor's note: Space considerations necessitated deletion of the section analyzing the costs of detection in Maternal and Infant Care-Family Planning (MIC-FP) Projects.

14. L. Lee and J.D. Schmale: "Identification of a Gonococcal Antigen Important in the Human Immune Response," Infection and Immunity 1:207-208 (1970). J.D. Schmale: "Serologic Detection of Gonorrhea," Ann. Int. Med. 72:593-595 (1970).

15. "An Emergency Request," op. cit., p. 14.

16. K.K. Holmes, et al.: "An Estimate of the Risk of Men Acquiring Gonorrhea by Sexual Contact with Infected Females," Am. J. Ep. 91:170-174 (1970).

17. Editor's note: Sections on prevention, treatment, and sources of funds were deleted.

VI-4 HOME CARE — AN AGENDA FOR ACTION — December, 1973

by Regina Reibstein

Home care is ideally suited for the elderly and chronically ill. It is far less expensive than institutionalization, and in most cases, patients fare better at home than in a hospital or nursing home. Home care as used in this report refers to an organized program of care given to homebound patients as part of a comprehensive medical service. Multiple professional services are provided through a centralized coordinating unit, and the needs of each patient are served in the context of his home, [1] thus forestalling, curtailing, or preventing hospitalization or nursing home placement.

Articles have been written in professional journals reporting successful home care programs and recommending their widespread adoption. Several studies dealing with health care in the city issued in the past few years have urged the expansion of home care services. It was generally believed that with the inception of Medicare, home care programs would be used extensively to avoid institutionalization and to help the aged remain in their homes as long and as comfortably as possible.

However, neither nationally nor locally have home care programs expanded. Less than 1 percent of the national Medicare expenditures are being used to provide the "home health" form of noninstitutional care to Medicare recipients. [2] Few new programs have been introduced, and for the aged there has been a negligible difference in the numbers served. This experience contrasts with trends in services provided to the aged in European countries. Home care services are used extensively in Western European countries, particularly for older chronically ill patients. Governments have encouraged the growth of this

*Editor's note: Various introductory sections and an appendix reviewing the literature were deleted.

366

service, providing considerable financial support, offering
many ancillary services to assure successful operation, and
utilizing contributions in service from voluntary community
groups.

If home care, on the face of it, is so sensible and desirable
a program, why is it not burgeoning? If so many people need it,
if it is less costly than alternative kinds of care, why is it consistently being ignored? In 1954, the average daily census in
home care in municipal hospitals was 2,013. In 1971, the total
was 2,328.

OBSTACLES TO HOME CARE

Some of the obstacles to expansion of home care are not
unreasonably difficult to overcome. Other problems are less
tractable and the possibility of changing approaches or instituting
new systems is dubious. Among the reasons home care has been
at a standstill for many years are the following:
   --Reimbursement policies by third-party payers encourage
   hospitalization.
   --Medicare and Medicaid pay only a part of home care
   costs and restrict the service to those who need skilled
   nursing.
   --Blue Cross payments are made to assist the acutely ill,
   those who require a substantial amount of medical attention during an illness with an expected termination.
   --Third-party payers view home care as a rehabilitation
   program, and implicit in the treatment is the expectation
   that the patient will improve.
Physicians and hospitals are not usually enthusiastic about
home care programs. Physicians prefer the relative efficiency
with which patients can be treated in hospitals, focusing on their
own activities rather than efficiency in the larger sense.

There is a general trend away from home service and a
tendency to treat patients at a central facility or in a physician's
office. Physicians in recent years are making fewer house calls
than in previous years. Hospitals and clinics have equipment,
specialists, and auxiliary personnel which permit more extensive examinations at a more efficient pace.

Home care patients are not "interesting" or challenging.
In general, the medical input required is of a routine nature and
few physicians and nurses are intrigued by the program.

Inpatients requiring little medical care are profitable
customers, and hospitals operating at less than full capacity are
reluctant to part with such low cost for care patients. Transferring these patients to home care results in loss of revenue
and an increase in expenses, since reimbursement rarely covers
costs.

Home care units within hospitals usually have directors with lower status and less authority than directors of other units in the hospital. The home care program is therefore given a low priority position in planning and in allocating resources.

The supply of physicians, nurses, and auxiliary personnel willing to provide home care service is not sufficient to permit a sizable increase in patients to be served.[3] On the other hand, recent findings suggest that the supply of housekeepers and homemakers may be adequate.

The incidence of crime in many of the areas where patients live and inconvenience in traveling and parking have, in general, reduced staff willingness to participate in outreach and home visit care projects and added to cost.

Home care programs throughout the city are diffuse and fragmented. Services are not centralized and responsibilities are not focused into one agency. The population in need of home care is dispersed and relatively impotent. Demands for service, therefore, become muffled by more insistent voices more strategically placed. Without a vigorous concerted demand for service by an organized constituency or by a securely entrenched agency of government, support is difficult to mobilize and sustain.

RECOMMENDATIONS

I. Expansion of Home Care Programs

We propose that the city encourage municipal and voluntary hospitals to adopt or expand home care programs so that thousands of aged, infirm, and chronically ill people can maintain themselves comfortably in their homes and thus avoid or postpone institutionalization or rehospitalization.

The most urgent need among most of the aged and chronically ill is homemaking and housekeeping services. Therapeutic services are generally of little avail; the health conditions of these people are not likely to improve, and only periodic medical monitoring and attention are required. But by providing housekeeping and daily necessities, the patient's condition can be stablized. Although the service is mainly housekeeping, the reason for furnishing that service is health. Because of feebleness or infirmity, the individual is unable to take care of himself adequately in the home. As a result of neglect, he is likely to suffer malnutrition and physical deterioration and eventually will require institutionalization. The objective of the proposal is to enable these people to remain at home by providing home care services.

Even a rough estimate of the number of people needing home care, who are not now served, is difficult to obtain. It has been estimated that from 70,000 to 80,000 persons over fifty-five in the city need home care, deriving this figure from a nation-wide percentage reported in the National Health Interview Survey. The estimate, however, is very high, since the percentage refers to all kinds of home care, including as its principal component unpaid care provided by the patient's family.

An estimate of home care needs made by Comprehensive Health Planning notes that more than 45,000 persons age sixty-five or over are confined to their homes because of chronic conditions affecting mobility.[4] This estimate was also obtained from a national percentage and refers to that category of persons who are "confined to the bed all or most of the time and those persons who must stay in the house more or all of the time."

In 1971, four visiting nurse associations provided services to 61,824 patients, of whom 27,000 were over sixty-five. The kind of care--whether it is skilled nursing or homemaking, short-term or prolonged--is not indicated by the report. If we assume that about one-half of the 27,000 were not chronically ill and received short-term care after discharge from a hospital, then at least 31,500 housebound people over sixty-five did not receive home care (13,500 subtracted from 45,000) and are in need of a sustained home care service. Not all of this number, it should be pointed out, are in need of financial support and will be able to purchase services if they are available and appropriate referrals are made.

Many of the 10,000 persons over sixty-five living in single rooms need some medical attention and personal care on a regular basis. The health condition of most of these people is precarious, and the risk is great that without proper dietary attention and health precautionary measures, a large majority will be institutionalized at public expense.

It was estimated from 1971 data that on any given day at least 500 people were unnecessarily hospitalized in municipal hospitals.[5] The 1971 report determined that even after prolonged hospitalization, 141 patients of 552 (25 percent) unnecessarily hospitalized patients studied in general hospitals could have been placed on home care. The savings then estimated for substituting home care for hospitalization amounted to $2.5 million.

The health needs of the aged population will be better known, and a more reliable estimate of the home care potential population will be ascertainable, upon completion of a health survey now being conducted by the Office of the Aging.

In a survey conducted by Comprehensive Health Planning of 265 persons over sixty-five, noninstitutional arrangements were preferred by most respondents. The percentage rose with the age of the respondent, indicating perhaps that institutionalization becomes less attractive as the prospect nears reality.

In the noninstitutional category, most respondents preferred to
live in their own homes. Here, too, the percentage rose with
age, demonstrating psychological needs of the aged, an
increasing reluctance to leave familiar surroundings and to make
a major rupture with the past.

II. Administrative Structure

A. Establishment of A Central Office on Home Care

In all earlier studies on home care, the consensus has
been that a central agency is needed to provide direction,
coordination, and impetus to the program. It was also agreed
that each home care program should be developed and administered by the hospital in charge of the program. The central
agency's purpose is to advise individual home care directors,
to assist and to promote home care programs. The agency might
also allocate funds for demonstration projects, develop long-
range plans, and work with other city agencies to coordinate
activities affecting health care for the patients. The duties and
responsibilities of the home care bureau should be:
    --Promulgation of standards.
    --Negotiation with appropriate city, state, and federal
    agencies' insurance carriers for reimbursement.
    --Negotiation with private groups and other municipal
    and other government agencies for services or review
    of contracts made by individual hospital for services.
    --Development of central referral and routing system for
    assignment of potential clients.
    --Maintenance of a clearing house of information.
    --Development of a model management system, including
    recommendations for internal record-keeping, billing,
    and cost accounting.
    --Evaluation of programs, recommending reforms and
    changes, if indicated.
    --Promotion of cooperative programs.
    --Encouragement of innovative programs and demonstra-
    tion projects.
    --Recruitment of personnel and development of training
    programs for new careers in home health care.
    --Serving as advocate for home care in the budget and
    legislative process.
    The location of this central office has been a matter on
which there is not total agreement. Some favor the Health and
Hospitals Corporation, although HHC has not indicated a desire
to take over this responsibility. Other suggestions have been to
set up a special division on home care in the Health Department
or to place responsiblity for all home care services in the

Department of Social Services, which at present provides home
care to needy patients.

It is our conviction that centralization of home care programs would be achieved if responsibility for overall supervision
and development of home care programs were embodied in a
separate agency of HSA. In this way, a city-fostered home care
program would permit as broad coverage as possible to all persons in the city needing such services. The agency would concern itself with the interests of all residents, regardless of
ability to pay, extent of insurance protection, sponsorship of
medical care received, private or public.

Even though the service for most patients will be essentially maintenance or custodial care, the reason for providing
housekeeping is ill health. The purpose is to preserve, maintain, or restore moderately good health. That posture is more
plausible if the home care program is operated by an agency
primarily engaged in health services, and reimbursement from
third-party payers may be easier to arrange.

B. Establishment of A Special Unit in the Department of Social Services (DOSS) to Coordinate Services Pertaining to Home Care

One of the principal functions of this unit will be to channel
patients to the appropriate health service, heading off hospitalization, if possible, by arranging for home care. Although the
program envisioned in this report is intended to accommodate
persons of all income levels in the city, it is recognized that a
large proportion of those needing home care will be derived from
the group receiving or eligible for public assistance.

The home care bureau in the Health Services Administration and the home care bureau in DOSS should work closely together on matters regarding reimbursement, selection of patients,
recruitment of personnel, and provision of social services to
improve the environment so that the patient can remain at home
in relative comfort.

It is further suggested that DOSS refer candidates for homemaker or home health aide positions to HSA and channel applicants to them for enrollment in a training program.

C. Appointment of A Full-Time Director of Home Care within Each Municipal Hospital

The director would have responsibility for coordinating
medical, social, therapeutic, transportation, maintenance and
other services needed by patients. He would furnish statistical
reports to the central office in the Health Service Administration and would maintain liaison for assistance in placement of

personnel, training, and exchange of information for developing and improving the program.

III. Program Content

A. Traditional Home Care Programs

In addition to the director of home care in each hospital, there should be one physician for every fifty patients carried by a home care program and one social worker for every thirty to thirty-five patients. The social worker is considered by some to be essential to a good home care program. Although the doctors decide whether the patient needs home care, it is the social worker who investigates the patient's environment, interviews the patient, and recommends whether he would do well under home care. Particularly if the physicians in the hospital are indifferent to home care capabilities, the social worker can sensitize their awareness, seek out candidates for home care, and activate a program. It is recommended that each patient receive a social service visit at least once every two weeks.

A full-time nursing coordinator with experience in public health nursing should be employed to integrate nursing care with other professional services. The hospital may contract for nursing and aide services or it may choose to employ its own nurses and home health aides. Assignments should be scheduled so that patients are visited by the same personnel each time and traveling time is minimized.

Each of the hospitals would be responsible for placement of patients in home care after discharge from inpatient care or through outpatient and emergency room referrals. Frequent interprofessional conferences should be scheduled to assure thorough review at regular intervals of every patient's care. Prior to acceptance for home care, a complete evaluation by the team should be completed. No patient should be accepted whose home situation may prove detrimental to his care at home. Neither should any patient be rejected without consideration of ways in which his social situation might be rendered favorable to home care.

B. After-Care Programs

Recognizing the reluctance of physicians and other professional staff to visit patients in their homes and acknowledging the economies which can be effected by treating and serving patients as a group at a central facility, some modifications of the traditional home care program are suggested.

Montefiore Hospital has introduced an after-care program which serves as an alternative to home care for those patients with a modicum of locomotion (some are wheelchair patients). Started in January 1972, the project functions five days a week, serves thirty patients a week, six each afternoon. The patients are transported from their homes to the hospital, where they are examined, given laboratory tests, therapy and consultation services. Physical and occupational therapy is given in group sessions; appointments are scheduled so that specialists can treat patients in quick succession. The afternoon also includes a social hour, which patients apparently appreciate. Twenty-six of the first twenty-seven patients polled who had experienced both home care and after-care, preferred after-care, and the reasons generally cited were leaving the house and socializing.[6]

We suggest that each hospital design a home care program which incorporates group hospital services and use of the out-patient department as much as possible. The logistics have to be carefully worked out with regard to transportation and scheduling of services; special equipment such as a minibus might have to be acquired and hospital space allocated to the program.

After-care has many advantages. It overcomes staff resistance to house calls. It permits utilization of the hospital's diagnostic resources. It increases physician and specialist efficiency. And it reduces isolation and provides social diversion and variety in what is for many a boring, uneventful existence.

C. Auxiliary Services and Cooperative Programs

The hospital should investigate the possibility of using its facilities for providing housekeeping services to patients on home care. Instead of a visiting homemaker for cooking meals, it may prove more economical to deliver meals from the hospital kitchen to home care patients. Food purchases might be handled through the hospital's food purchasing department. Laundry services might also be provided through the hospital laundry.

Liaison with voluntary agencies should be established to provide social and recreational services. A system of daily contacts through reassurance calls (daily telephone calls) or visits by community workers might be set up. Transportation to community centers and to special social programs can be arranged through contacts with voluntary and city agencies in charge of such activities.

IV. Demonstration Projects

Demonstration projects should be encouraged to test new approaches and to determine the feasibility of some of the recommendations in this report. For example, the practicability could be determined of providing meals to patients on home care through the facilities of hospital kitchens. Most important would be a test of the hypothesis that housekeeping services and assistance in maintaining an individual in his home can keep a sizable number of chronically ill and aged people out of institutions. The project might be useful in determining the amount and type of housekeeping service necessary and the logistics in deploying personnel and equipment to patients on home care.

The Human Resources Administration's Services Planning Unit, working with three community voluntary groups (Union Settlement House, Self-Help, and the Jewish Association for Services to the Aging) has set up pilot projects providing home care to three hundred persons about to be admitted to nursing homes. The project is scheduled to be operational by September 1973.

V. Utilization of Neighborhood Family Care Centers (NFCC's) for Assigning Patients to Home Care

The family health worker in each NFCC should screen eligibles for home care. An arrangement should be made with the backup hospital to refer candidates for home care to the hospital. NFCC's, it is expected, will be able to identify potential candidates and direct them to home care programs, making it possible for them to function longer on their own and forestalling hospitalization. Without a screening program, the demand for home care and its potential total cost would be virtually unlimited.

COSTS

Estimates of costs of home care programs range from less than $10 to more than $40 per day. Data on costs are difficult to obtain, since hospitals have made little effort to isolate all costs which are properly attributable to home care services. It should be noted that one of the obstacles to receiving Medicare and Medicaid reimbursement is the absence of appropriate billing and cost accounting.

The cost per patient day for a patient in the home care program at Montefiore Hospital is approximately $10.[7] If a patient were on home care for an entire year, the cost would be $3,650, but this estimate does not include housekeeping services or costs of maintaining the home. It does, however, include a large component of skilled nursing services and special therapy.

In municipal hospital home care programs, the cost is estimated at about $2,500 per patient per year for an average length of stay of 320 days. The estimated cost for 365 days is $2,800. This figure also does not cover maintenance costs, but

it does include homemaking for many patients.[8] Another study
estimates the cost of municipal home care at a higher figure--
$3,325 per year.[9]

A home care program which includes income maintenance,
one visit per month from a social worker or nurse, one clinic
visit and 30 hours of housekeeping assistance per week would
cost about $7,500 per year, assuming a patient stayed on home
care the entire year. Currently, the average length of stay on
hospital home care is 105 days.[10] Since many patients are
receiving care after an acute illness and discharge from hospitals, the program is not comparable to that recommended, and
the average length of stay will undoubtedly be longer in the program for the chronically ill. The population to be served in the
prospective program is more like that reached by the municipal
hospitals' home care services. Average length of stay in municipal hospital home care is 320 days. It is also worth noting
that in domiciliary institutions, the average length of stay is
two to three years.

Monthly Cost

Social worker or nurse visit	$ 25
Clinic visit	35
Housekeeper--30 hours per week	
@ $3.50 per hour	420
Medicine and transportation	40
Public Assistance	110
	$630 a month

For persons needing more care and attention, the cost of
services which comprise a home health aide in attendance 15
hours per week, a housekeeper 30 hours a week, one visit from
a social worker or nurse, and two clinic visits plus income maintenance payments, the total reaches $14,000 a year.

Montly Cost

Social worker or nurse visit	$ 25
Clinic visit	70
Housekeeper--30 hours per week	
@ $3.50 per hour	420
Home health aide--15 hours per week	
@ $8.00 per hour	480
Medicine and transportation	40
Public assistance	110
	$1,145

The estimates, therefore, range from $2,800 to $14,000
for a standard type of program for 365 days of care, depending
on amount of services rendered and the financial needs of the
patient.

The population which is currently not being served, those
people who are likely to end up in institutions if they are not
given adequate attention, and for whom this proposal is mainly
designed, will be best served by the program which comprises

30 hours of housekeeping, one clinic visit and one social worker visit. This program would cost about $7,500 a year, excluding additional administrative expenses which would be incurred by introducing the new home care unit in the Health Services Administration. This cost compares with $12,000 a year, the average cost of maintaining a person in a nursing home, and $25,000 for maintaining a patient in an extended care unit in a city hospital.

Experimentation with institutional focus will significantly reduce the cost estimate. This could not be adequately determined unless part of a serious effort to attract resources and talent to this area.

Not all patients to be served by the program will be medically indigent. Eliminating public assistance and the cost of the clinic visit which is partially covered by Medicare (and possibly the social worker visit), the cost to the patient is a little more than $450 a month. New nursing homes are being reimbursed at the rate of $1,500 a month, and it is reasonable to surmise that the more affluent elderly would choose such a nursing home. The comparison of costs between home care and nursing home care is $450 to $1,500 or $1,050 a month.

For those elderly and chronically ill patients covered by Medicare the cost to the city will be a great deal less than $7,500 a year. Administration and a major part of the cost ($1,300 a year) of public assistance payments to the aged will be assumed by the federal government in January 1974. Changes in Medicaid regulations and reimbursement rates have not been definitely established, and it is not clear as yet how much of the program suggested would be reimbursed by Medicaid.

FOOD DELIVERY PROGRAM--A LOWER COST ALTERNATIVE

The housekeeper's major contribution is in preparing meals so that the patient receives an adequate diet. Cleaning the house, changing bed linen, and attending to personal needs of the patient comprise a small fraction of the time required. If meals can be brought in, the housekeeper's function can be considerably reduced, and substitute arrangements can be made for daily phone calls and visits to the clinic or a day-care center. A home health aide, a specially trained paraprofessional, could visit the patient once a week to minister to the patient's personal needs. This proposal is based on a plan which involves meals prepared and delivered by the hospital providing home care.

Several groups in the city operate Meals on Wheels programs. The Stanley M. Isaacs Neighborhood Center delivered a two-day supply of meals every other day (four meals each delivery) to 30 to 40 housebound people. The meals are prepared in the center's kitchen, which also provides meals for

150 to 180 people in its cafeteria. The cost of the raw food alone is estimated at $1.50 for two meals per day. Knickerbocker Hospital has a contract with Central Harlem Meals on Wheels, for which it provides 25 to 40 meals each day. The hospital charges the Meals on Wheels program $1.10 for each meal, basing the cost on cafeteria prices.

If meals were provided by the hospital, only minimal housekeeper assistance would be needed. The estimate and comparison of costs rendered below refer to Medicaid eligible patients only. For those who are financially able to pay for the service (Stanley M. Isaacs Neighborhood Center reports that almost all their clients pay for their meals themselves), the city would not have to shoulder the financial burden of the program. The cost of meals estimated here includes transportation and is, therefore, considerably higher than the costs reported by local Meals on Wheels programs.

Meals seven days a week, two meals a day	$20 per week
Health-homemaker, 3 hours per week @ $5.50	16.50
Housekeeper, 3 hours per week @ $3.50	10.50
	$47.00/week

Meals, housekeeper, etc.	$168/month
Social worker or nurse	25
Clinic visit	35
Medicines	40
Total cost	$268/month

NOTES

1. U.S. Public Health Service Report on Roanoke Conference on Organized Home Care, June 1958.
2. "Home Health Services and Health Insurance," by Brahna Trager, Medical Care, February 1971.
3. White House Conference on the Aging, 1971, recommends a tenfold expansion in the supply of home health aides--a ratio of 1 per 100 elderly, or 9,500 home health aides for New York City.
4. N.Y.C. Comprehensive Health Planning Agency, Long Term Care in New York City, November 1972, Table 18.
5. "Study of Long-Stay Patients Unnecessarily Hospitalized," See Chapter II.
6. "The After Care Project: A Viable Alternative to Home Care," Isadore Rossman, 1972, to be published in Medical Care.
7. Rossman, Ibid.
8. Robert Soliz and Bruce McClenahan, The Home Care Programs of the New York City Health and Hospitals Corp., unpublished manuscript, New York City Health and Hospitals Corporation, 1973.
9. Long Stay Patients Unnecessarily Hospitalized, See Chapter II.
10. N.Y.C. Comprehensive Health Planning Agency, op. cit.

VI-5 UPGRADING PRISON HEALTH FACILITIES IN NEW YORK CITY — August, 1972*

by Anita Altman

The correction system consists of nine institutions. There are five houses of detention for pretrial inmates located in each borough but Staten Island. Rikers Island contains the Women's House of Detention, which houses both detention and sentenced inmates; the Adolescent Remand Shelter, which houses adolescent detainees; the Reformatory, which houses sentenced adolescents; and the Men's Correctional Institution, which houses sentenced adult males with terms of less than one year and those prisoners awaiting housing in a state prison. A new Adolescent Remand Shelter is scheduled to open this year on Rikers. Extensive renovations are planned for the existing building, which will continue in use. The Rikers Island complex also contains an infirmary which serves as the main subacute inpatient facility for the entire male prison system. The Women's House has its own infirmary unit.

The prison health program was developed to both serve the needs of the correctional system and to care for the acute and subacute health care needs of the detention and sentenced population.

The first level of health care is provided in all of the houses of detention and the sentenced facilities. This includes basically two components--reception and sick call. The balance of services are provided at Rikers or the hospitals; this requires extensive transportation between these units.

Reception: Every inmate coming into the system requires an entrance physical and the collection of some base-line data. This requires several exam/consultation rooms.

Sick Call: In each of the institutions facilities are avail-

*From the 1972 Annual Report of the Office of Health Systems Planning

able for dispensing of drugs, examination and treatment of minor complaints, and some dental chairs for emergency dental work. These areas consist of exam/treatment cubicles. There are some minimal specialty services provided at some of the facilities, but usually any problem of more than a simple nature is referred to an outpatient department or to Rikers infirmary. The Women's House also contains specialty services and an infirmary.

Hospital OPD's: Currently, Bellevue Hospital OPD is used by inmates coming from the Bronx and Manhattan Houses of Detention and also those inmates from those two boroughs who are located on Rikers Island. Kings County is used by the inmates from the Queens Houses and Brooklyn House of Detention. The same is true for inmates located on Rikers who come from those boroughs. Elmhurst provides OPD services for the Women's House of Detention. Emergency services have been further decentralized so that Bronx House of Detention emergencies go to Morrisania, The Tombs to Bellevue, Brooklyn to Kings County, and Queens to Queens Hospital Center.

Rikers Island Infirmary: All subacute care cases requiring more than ambulatory services, but less than hospital care are located at the infirmary. These cases range from influenza to noncontagious TB, diabetes, broken legs and hospital convalescence. A few of the houses also contain very small infirmary units.

Hospital Prison Wards: Those patients requiring acute medical and surgical care are transferred to the prison wards at either Bellevue or Kings County, depending on their borough of origin. All women prisoners are cared for on open wards at Elmhurst.

PROPOSED CHANGES

The Health Services Administration has proposed several programmatic changes which will affect the type of facilities which will be required in the future. Concurrently several proposals are pending which do not relate to any specific programmatic change but which result from the recognition that the present state of these facilities is abysmal and that renovation is imperative for the delivery of adequate and humane medical care.

1. Rikers Island

The Rikers Island proposal results from a combination of program improvement and current inadequacies of the facilities. At this time, the proposal has been scaled down to focus on our priority need for major renovation of the infirmary and the development of the health center. The infirmary, which serves the whole correctional system, plays a crucial role in providing an environment in which subacute care can most efficiently be delivered in a security setting. Because of the very poor physical state of this facility, physicians in the hospitals are reluctant to transfer convalescing inmates, which results in excessively long lengths of stay in the prison wards. Frequently these wards are used to 100 percent of capacity, and additional patients must be placed on regular wards with around-the-clock guard coverage. This is very costly. Renovations and improved staffing will result in a substantial upgrading of the quality of medical care delivered, and will help us to most efficiently utilize both the infirmary and prison ward beds.

The health center is a crucial component of our proposed health program. Although we have tried to resolve the problems of coordinating outpatient care for the inmates with Kings County and Bellevue, we are convinced that the problem is not resolvable. Many inmates never receive treatment or require many visits before being seen by a physician in the OPD. The costs to the Corrections Department for guards used in this process have already been developed by the BOB staff. The intangible costs of poor health care delivery to the inmates is very real. HSA has decided that the only real solution to this problem is the development of a specialty center on Rikers Island which will provide the most efficient and effective delivery of specialty care and diagnostic work. Montefiore Hospital, which will be affiliating with us for the provision of professional services on the island, will not enter into an agreement unless this facility is provided. Quality health care cannot be provided in the existing system. The Corrections Department is most anxious to see this facility developed because it will provide them with tremendous cost savings in correctional officer time.

2. Bellevue Prison Ward

Bellevue currently has a male medical prison ward of 30 beds. The building in which this ward is located is slated for demolition. The new prison ward at Bellevue is a straight replacement for the existing facility.

3. North Central Bronx

The prison wards are currently overutilized. For many years there have been discussions concerning the placement of a ward in a Bronx municipal hospital. This has been most diffi-cult because of the high occupancy rate, and/or severe deterio-ration and political opposition. With a new hospital set to open in the next two years and with the same proposed affiliate for Rikers and North Central Bronx Hospital, it is eminently reasonable to project the inclusion of a 30 to 50 bed prison ward in that hospital.

4. Woodhull Hospital

It may be possible to develop a 28 bed prison ward in this hospital which is the replacement for Greenpoint. This new ward would replace Kings County as the prison ward which has usually served Brooklyn. This would result in a net addition of 10 secure beds in the borough. Development of this unit depends upon agreement of the Budget Bureau, the Hospital Administrator and the Health and Hospitals Corporation.

5. Queens Hospital Center

Queens Hospital Center has a number of beds which are currently unutilized. The current need for additional security beds to serve the Corrections Department could be alleviated in the short run by the development of a prison ward at this hospital. If beds are available, it may be possible to assist the Police Department, which currently is responsible for guarding prisoners who are in need of hospitalization at the time of their arrest. Because of the shortage of security beds the Department must provide policemen around the clock to guard these prisoners on open wards. There are about 25 to 30 of these prisoners at any time who are guarded by the police. This results in a severe drain on Police Department manpower.

Because of the availability of these beds now, the Health Services Administration is negotiating with the hospital administration and the Health and Hospitals Corporation for the allocation of an area in the hospital for this use. The successful development of this ward will depend on funds being available for the renovation of a unit into a secure facility and the provision of sufficient operating funds to the hospital. These beds would be used on a temporary basis until the other units are developed, unless the combined demands of both Corrections and the Police Department required that it continue in operation.

6. The Tombs

Health Services Administration has proposed some alterations of the first, tenth and twelfth floors of this facility. These proposals have been developed because we recognized that the areas were inefficiently laid out and in deteriorated condition:

a. First Floor: The current exam/consultation area for
reception is being renovated as a chest X-ray room. We
have proposed that an area currently laid out for showers,
but which goes unused, be renovated into two exam/con-
sultation rooms.

b. Tenth Floor: This floor currently houses the inmates
with observed psychiatric disturbances. An existing room
is to be subdivided and will be used for psychiatric offices.

c. Twelfth Floor: This floor currently houses the sick
call area and contains an 18 bed infirmary (12 beds medical, 6 beds psychiatric). This area is very poorly laid
out and is in a deteriorated state. We have recommended
that a currently unused sunporch be built out to and the
major renovations be undertaken. The space limitations
in this facility are a severe problem. We have developed
a program which will, without displacing any program,
result in a far superior medical installation. This program includes the retention of the infirmary, the development of adequate exam/treatment rooms, and the inclusion
of several psychiatric offices.

A

Abstinence programs, 110, 140
Addiction
    addict-related crime, 139
    and criminal behavior, 117
    and Health and Hospitals
        Corporation, 173
    characteristics of heroin
        addiction
        as a contagious disease, 133
        manufacture and distribu-
            tion system, 119-121
        physiological aspects, 116,
            132
        skin popping, 119
        sniffing, 119
    employment programs, 152-
        153
    evaluating and improving pro-
        grams, 142-145
    Mayor's Narcotic Control
        Council, 130
    methadone diversion, 145-146
    methadone maintenance, 109,
        110, 122, 124, 134-136,
        145-146
    overdose deaths, 139
    outreach and referral, 148-
        150
    prevention and treatment pro-
        grams, 118
    research on studies, 144-145
    school drug prevention pro-
        grams, 146-148
    six-month status report, 6, 27,
        138-153
    soft drug problem, 150-152
    study, 9, 112-137

    treatment programs, 140-142
Addiction Services Agency (ASA),
    15, 109-110, 117, 130, 153
Admissions, see utilization
Affiliation contracts, see staffing
Alcoholism, 7, 9, 24, 25, 113,
    317-318, 325-347
    Alcoholics Anonymous, 325,
        333, 339
    Bureau of Alcoholism Services,
        318
    Camp La Guardia, 331
    Harlem Hospital Alcohol Unit,
        330
    Kings County Alcoholism Cli-
        nic, 330
    Manhattan Bowery Project,
        331, 340
    Shelter Care Treatment Cen-
        ter, 340
Altman, Anita, 60, 322-323
Ambulances, 172
Ambulatory care,
    and City Health Insurance
        Plan, 256
    and program guidance letter,
        167
    average physician time, 99
    background to studies, 42-43
    changes in number of visits,
        76, 78
    ghetto medicine program, 160,
        305-307
    Martin Luther King, Jr. Neigh-
        borhood Health Center, 308
    Medicaid experience, 78-80
    Neighborhood Family Care
        Centers, 6, 8, 25, 27, 305-
        307, 318-320, 348-354

Employment programs for ex-
addicts, 152-153
Empty beds, see utilization
English, Joseph, 16
closing hospitals, 164
need for management support,
165
reaction to physician staffing
study, 44
resignation, 20

F

Facilities, see capital planning
Federal Bureau of Narcotics and
Dangerous Drugs, 151
Feeley, Rick, 19
Financial information, control
and procedures, 171-172
Financing, see health insurance
Fiscal audits, 143
Fiscal drop, see Health and
Hospitals Corporation
Fordham Hospital, 100, 302
Foster care, 54
Frug, Gerald, 237

G

Gibbs, Alan 323
Ghetto medicine, see ambulatory
care
Gonorrhea, 321-322
Gonorrhea control programs, 7,
24, 25
decision to undertake, 26
Gouveneur Hospital, 302
Greenpoint Hospital, 142
Group Health Insurance (GHI),
15, 264-278
Guerin, John, 317-318

H

Haldeman, Jack, 316
Hamilton, Edward, 22, 33
Harlem Hospital, 140
Harris, Robert, 21, 107, 108,
319

Hayes, Fred, 33
Health and Hospitals Corporation
(HHC),
affiliation contracts, 162, 168
and alcoholism, 339-40
and Health Services Administration, 20, 164-165
and Health Services Administration Analysis Staff, 27
and Neighborhood Family Care
Centers, 15, 306-307, 320
and prison health, 323, 381
as a fiscal drop, 160
board of directors, 17, 28, 44,
162, 165
budget submission, 169-170
capital planning, 173, 293, 303
capital construction, 173
collections, 16, 161, 163, 167
description of, 15-17
financing of, 160, 169-170,
171, 232-234, 254-260, 297-
300
historical background, 159-
161
incentive budgeting, 173
management, 17, 107, 108,
163, 165, 168, 172
Office of Program Analysis,
40
physician overstaffing, 96
planning staff, 35
problems with, 108, 159-167
program guidance letter to,
167-173
results, 161-163
staffing, 168, 172
the future, 164
Health and Hospitals Planning
Council of Southern New York,
see planning
Health insurance, 175-176, 196,
208-209, 231-232, 240-253
American Medical Association
Plan, 247
catastrophic health insurance,
243-245
health insurance experiment,
175-178, 182-192